Tanzania

Africa: Policies For Prosperity Series

Series Editors

Christopher S. Adam and Paul Collier

For the first time in more than a generation, sustained economic growth has been achieved across Africa—despite the downturn in global economic fortunes since 2008—and in many countries these gains have been realized through policy reforms driven by the decisive leadership of a new generation of economic policy makers. The process of reform is continuous, however, and the challenge currently facing this new generation is how to harness these favourable gains in macroeconomic stability and turn them into a coherent strategy for sustainable growth and poverty reduction over the coming decades. These challenges are substantial and encompass the broad remit of economic policy. Each volume in this series brings leading scholars into the policy arena to examine, in a rigorous but accessible manner, the key economic challenges and policy options facing policy makers on the continent.

BOOKS PUBLISHED IN THIS SERIES

Kenya: Policies for Prosperity
Edited by Christopher S. Adam, Paul Collier, and Njuguna Ndung'u

Zambia: Building Prosperity from Resource Wealth
Edited by Christopher S. Adam, Paul Collier, and Michael Gondwe

Tanzania: The Path to Prosperity
Edited by Christopher S. Adam, Paul Collier, and Benno Ndulu

Tanzania

The Path to Prosperity

Edited by Christopher S. Adam, Paul Collier,
and Benno Ndulu

OXFORD
UNIVERSITY PRESS

OXFORD

UNIVERSITY PRESS

Great Clarendon Street, Oxford, OX2 6DP,
United Kingdom

Oxford University Press is a department of the University of Oxford.
It furthers the University's objective of excellence in research, scholarship,
and education by publishing worldwide. Oxford is a registered trade mark of
Oxford University Press in the UK and in certain other countries

First Edition published in 2017
Impression: 1

Published in the United States of America by Oxford University Press
198 Madison Avenue, New York, NY 10016, United States of America

British Library Cataloguing in Publication Data
Data available

Library of Congress Control Number: 2016941486

ISBN 978–0–19–870481–2

Printed in Great Britain by
Clays Ltd, St Ives plc

Series Preface

Policies for Prosperity

Since the mid-1990s the economic prospects for Africa have been transformed. The change has been uneven: some countries remain mired in conflict and economic stagnation. But for many macroeconomic stability has been achieved—even through the global financial crisis and its aftermath– and far-reaching policy reforms have been put in place. For these countries, growth prospects in the first quarter of the twenty-first century are much brighter than at any time during the final quarter of the last century. But converting good prospects into sustained growth and decisive poverty reduction requires a degree of good luck, good policy formulation, resources, and a lot of good economic management. For policy improvements to be sustained they must be underpinned by more fundamental shifts in political power; sectional interests ruling through patronage must be defeated by the public interest. And for the shift in power to be decisive, the achievements of individual reformers must be locked in through the development of effective institutions in both the public and private sectors. The challenges are formidable: they range beyond the conventional agenda of macroeconomic management, infrastructure provision and the improvement of the investment climate. For example, land policy, which has usually been left dormant, will need to be rethought in the face of high population growth rates and rapid urbanization; trade and industrial policies will need to be rethought so as to engage more effectively with changing global opportunities; and the continent will need to develop adaptive policies in the face of rapid climate change.

Many of the successes of recent decades have been wrought by the progressive leadership of a new generation of policy makers. To build on these successes, this same generation needs both the support of, and restraint by, an informed and engaged society. This is the fundamental philosophy of this series: informed societies are strong societies. If citizens are to hold governments to account they require information, debate and dispassionate analysis on the challenges and choices confronting countries and their people. This is especially relevant in the realm of economic policy where path-dependency is powerful and the consequences of choices are far-reaching and long-lasting.

In many industrialized economies there is a long tradition of informed debate and analysis sustained in large measure by high-quality financial journalism. In Africa, by contrast, while a dynamic and often fearless free press is now quite widely established, it still lacks a tradition of solid, durable, and independent writing on economic policy. As a result local debate is too often ill-informed or is perceived to be driven by the agendas, and chequebooks, of sectional interests and international organizations.

There is now considerable academic research on the issues that matter for Africa and it could potentially inform Africa's debates. But to date it has been disconnected from them. Increasingly, academics write only for other academics rather than to inform the public. With this series of books we seek to build bridges between the evidence from solid research and contemporary policy debates. Each book aims to bring together the best international and domestic scholars with policy makers working on economic policy issues across the continent. Throughout, our contributors are required to write with clarity, avoiding academic jargon, but equally avoiding advocacy. Focusing on the key issues that matter for a society, each chapter aims to leave readers better able to draw their own conclusions about important choices.

Acknowledgements

This book is the outcome of an active collaboration amongst a wide range of scholars, officials and policy makers working on the economics of Tanzania. Its origins lie in the close relationship forged over the last eight years between the Governor and staff of the Bank of Tanzania and the International Growth Centre (IGC). The IGC, of which two of us are members, is an international research network partnership hosted by the London School of Economics and the University of Oxford, and funded by the UK Department for International Development. The IGC's core objective is to promote sustainable growth in developing countries by providing demand-led policy advice based on frontier research. The Bank of Tanzania's commitment to promoting research-informed policy, both within its own domain and also across the whole of the economic policy spectrum in Tanzania, has made it a natural partner for the IGC and, indeed, many of the chapters in this book emerge directly from work done under the aegis of the IGC and in close collaboration with the Bank. We are particularly grateful to the Bank for hosting a highly productive authors' writing workshop in Stone Town, Zanzibar, in June 2015. We thank the IGC in London for its financial support to the project and the current and former staff of the IGC-Tanzania office in Dar es Salaam—Pantaleo Kessy, Anne Laski, Joshua Chipman, Claire Lwehabura, Benjamin Langford, Angela Ambroz, Ambassador Charles Mutalemwa, and our non-resident Country Director, John Page—for their support and assistance as this project has evolved.

As the Series Editors stress in their preface to this volume, the fundamental idea underpinning the *Policies for Prosperity* series is that an informed society is a strong society. This principle is central to the new dynamism in Tanzania and it has been our privilege to have been able to draw so deeply on the talent and insights from a wonderful set of authors based in the universities, research groups, institutes, think-tanks, and official institutions in Tanzania. We thank all these institutions for their commitment to the book. We also extend a special note of thanks to the Honourable Minister for Finance and Planning, Dr Philip Mpango, who was an important supporter of this project during his time as Executive Secretary of the President's Office Planning Commission.

Our final thanks go to our colleague, Rose Page, for her superb work behind the scenes in managing the process of turning our often chaotic contributions into a volume of which we can all be proud. Rose has been our managing editor since the inception of this series. It has been a great pleasure working with her and, as with the previous volumes, her guidance, support, and unfailing good humour has made our jobs as editors immeasurably easier.

Contents

Contents

List of Figures

List of Figures

List of Tables

List of Tables

List of Boxes

List of Abbreviations

AICD	Africa Infrastructure Country Diagnostic
ASDP	Agricultural Sector Development Programme
ASIP	Annual Survey of Industrial Production
BAFIA	Banking and Financial Institutions Act
BIS	Basic Industrial Strategy
boe	barrels of oil equivalent
BoT	Bank of Tanzania
BRN	Big Results Now
BRT	Bus Rapid Transit
CAADP	Comprehensive Africa Agriculture Development Programme
CBD	central business district
CCBG	Committee of Central Bank Governors
CCTTFA	Central Corridor Transit Transport Facilitation Agency
CGE	computable general equilibrium
CGIAR	Consultative Group for International Agricultural Research
CIT	corporate income tax
CMSA	Capital Markets and Securities Authority
CNG	Compressed Natural Gas
COMESA	Common Market in East and Southern Africa
CPI	consumer price index
CRDB	Cooperative and Rural Development Bank
CSD	Central Depository System
DAC	Development Assistance Committee
DHS	Demographic and Health Surveys
DMO	Domestic Market Obligations
EAC	East African Community
EACB	East African Currency Board
EACSCO	East African Common Services Organization

List of Abbreviations

EAMU	East African Monetary Union
EFT	Electronic Fund Transfer
EPIC	Energy Policy Institute of Chicago
EPZA	Export Processing Zones Authority
ERP	Economic Recovery Plan
ESAAMLG	Eastern and South Africa Anti-Money Laundering Group
EWURA	Energy and Water Utility Regulatory Authority
FAOSTAT	Food and Agriculture Organization of the United Nations Statistics Division
FBS	Food Balance Sheets
FDI	foreign direct investment
FEED	Front-End Engineering and Design
FID	Final Investment Decision
FOD	first order dominance
FSAP	Financial Sector Assessment Program
FYDP	Five-year Development Plan
GDP	gross domestic product
GIIP	gas initially in place
GIZ	Deutsche Gesellschaft für Internationale Zusammenarbeit
GSS	Government Securities System
HBS	Household Budget Survey
HDI	human development index
HGA	Host Government Agreement
HFP	Housing Finance Project
HIPC	Heavily Indebted Poor Countries
HIV	Human Immunodeficiency Virus
ICDs	inland container depots
ICT	Information and communications technology
IGC	International Growth Centre
IIDS	Integrated Industrial Development Strategy
IIR	institutional investor ratings
ILFS	Integrated Labor Force Survey
ILO	International Labour Organization
IT	inflation-targeting
IMF	International Monetary Fund
KK	Kilimo Kwanza

LMIC	lower middle income country
LNG	Liquified Natural Gas
LPG	Liquefied Petroleum Gas
LPI	Logistics Performance Index
LSCI	Liner Shipping Connectivity Index
LTPP	Long-Term Perspective Plan
MAC	Monetary Affairs Committee
MCF	marginal costs of funds
MDGs	Millennium Development Goals
MDRI	Multilaterial Debt Relief Initiative
MEM	Ministry of Energy and Minerals
MKUKUTA	National Strategy for Growth and Poverty
MLSC	Measuring Living Standards within Cities Survey
mmbtu	million British thermal units
MMT	millions of tonnes
MOF	Ministry of Finance
MSME	Micro, Small, and Medium Enterprise
MTEF	Medium-Term Expenditure Framework
MSC	Mediterranean Shipping Company
mscuf/d	millions of standard cubic feet per day
NACTE	National Council for Technical Education
NBC	National Bank of Commerce
NDC	National Development Corporation
NEDF	National Entrepreneurs Development Fund
NEMC	National Environment Management Council
NEPAD	New Partnership for Africa's Development
NGOs	non-governmental organizations
NHC	National Housing Corporation
NMB	National Microfinance Bank
NOC	National Oil Company
NSSF	National Social Security Fund
NTB	non-tariff barrier
ODA	Official Development Assistance
ODCYs	off-dock container yards
OECD	Organisation for Economic Co-operation and Development
O&M	operations and maintenance

List of Abbreviations

PAYE	pay-as-you-earn
PEPA	Petroleum (Exploration and Production) Act
PMAESA	Port Management Association of Eastern and Southern Africa
POPC	President's Office Planning Commission
PPP	purchasing power parity
PRSPs	poverty reduction strategy papers
PSA	production sharing agreement
PURA	Petroleum Upstream Regulatory Authority
RECs	Regional Economic Communities
RTG	rubber tyre gantry cranes
SACCOS	Savings and Credit Cooperative Societies
SADC	Southern Africa Development Community
SAGCOT	Southern Agricultural Growth Corridor of Tanzania
SAP	Structural Adjustment Programme
SELF	Small Entrepreneurs Loan Facility
SEZs	special economic zones
SIDO	Small Industries Development Organisation
SIDP	Sustainable Industrial Development Policy for Tanzania
SIRESS	Southern African Development Community Integrated Regional Settlement System
SME	small–medium enterprise
SMEDP	Small and Medium Enterprise Development Policy
SSA	sub-Saharan Africa
SSRA	Social Security Regulator Authority
STS	ship-to-shore
SWIFT	Society for Worldwide Interbank Financial Telecommunication
TAFSIP	Tanzania Agriculture and Food Security Investment Plan
TASAF	Tanzania Social Action Fund
TCF	trillion cubic feet
TDHS	Tanzania Demographic and Health Surveys
TEUs	twenty-foot equivalent units
TFP	total factor productivity
TICTS	Tanzania International Container Terminal Services
TIRA	Tanzania Insurance Regulatory Authority
TISS	Tanzania Interbank Settlement System
TMRC	Tanzania Mortgage Refinancing Company

TNBC	Tanzania National Business Council
TPA	Tanzania Ports Authority
TPDC	Tanzania Petroleum Development Corporation
TRA	Tanzania Revenue Authority
UN COMTRADE	United Nations Commodity Trade Statistics Database
UNU-WIDER	United Nations University World Institute for Development Economics Research
USAID	United States Agency for International Development
VETA	Vocational Education and Training Authority
VICOBA	Village Community Banks
VPO	Vice President's Office
VSLA	Village Savings and Loans Association
VSO	Voluntary Service Overseas
WAY	weighted average yield
WDI	World Development Indicators
WHC	Watumishi Housing Company

List of Contributors

Editors

Christopher S. Adam is Professor of Development Economics at the University of Oxford and Research Associate of the Centre for the Study of African Economies.

Paul Collier is Professor of Economics and Public Policy at the Blavatnik School of Government, University of Oxford, and founding Director of the Centre for the Study of African Economies.

Benno Ndulu is Governor of the Bank of Tanzania.

Contributors

Jehovaness Aikaeli is Head of the Department of Economics at the University of Dar es Salaam.

Channing Arndt is a senior research fellow at the United Nations University World Institute for Development Economics Research (UNU-WIDER).

Douglas Gollin is Professor of Development Economics at the University of Oxford and Research Associate at the Centre for the Study of African Economies.

Radhika Goyal is a predoctoral fellow at the Energy Policy Institute of Chicago (EPIC), University of Chicago.

Mahjabeen Haji is an Economist with the World Bank Group, currently based in Tanzania.

Olivier Hartmann is Senior Trade Facilitation Specialist at The World Bank.

Mark Henstridge is Chief Economist at Oxford Policy Management.

Patricia Jones is Project Manager and Researcher for a joint LSE and Oxford research project on Urbanization in Developing Countries in the Department of Economics, University of Oxford.

Pantaleo J. Kessy is Principal Economist, East African Community (on secondment from the Bank of Tanzania) and Senior Country Research and Policy Fellow at IGC Tanzania.

Kennedy Komba is Head of Strategy, Governance and Member Relations at Alliance for Financial Inclusion (on secondment from Bank of Tanzania).

List of Contributors

Charles Kunaka is Senior Trade Specialist in the World Bank Group Trade and Competitiveness Global Practice.

Anne Laski is Country Economist for Tanzania, International Growth Centre.

Vincent Leyaro is Senior Lecturer in Economics at the University of Dar es Salaam's Department of Economics.

Margaret McMillan is Professor of Economics, Tufts University and Senior Research Fellow at IFPRI.

Kristin Mahrt is an independent consultant.

Nangi Massawe is Assistant Manager, Real Sector and Financial Inclusion at the Bank of Tanzania.

Jacques Morisset is Lead Economist and Program Leader at the World Bank.

Natu Mwamba is Deputy Governor of Economic and Financial Policies (EFP) at the Bank of Tanzania.

Nkunde Mwase is Senior Economist at the IMF.

Johnson Nyella is Director of Economic Research and Policy at the Bank of Tanzania and Accredited Fellow of the Macroeconomic and Financial Management Institute of Eastern and Southern Africa.

Stephen A. O'Connell is Gil and Frank Mustin Professor of Economics at Swarthmore College and former Chief Economist of the United States Agency for International Development (USAID).

John Page is Senior Fellow in the Global Economy and Development Program at the Brookings Institution and non-resident Senior Fellow at the World Institute for Development Economics Research (UNU-WIDER).

Gaël Raballand is Senior Public Sector Specialist at the World Bank.

Dennis Rweyemamu is Research and Policy Specialist at the UONGOZI Institute, and heads the Research and Policy Department.

Rukia Shamte is the Executive Secretary, Central Corridor Transit Transport Facilitation Agency (CCTTFA), Dar es Salaam, Tanzania.

Finn Tarp is Director UNU-WIDER and Professor of Development Economics at the University of Copenhagen.

Samuel Wangwe is Associate Principal Researcher, REPOA, Tanzania.

1

Introduction

Productivity, Organizations, and Connectivity

Christopher S. Adam, Paul Collier, and Benno Ndulu

This book is about Tanzania and the challenges it faces in realizing its enormous economic potential over the coming decades. This potential is rooted in a spectacular natural endowment—the same that made East Africa the cradle of humanity—a young population, and a political legacy forged in the transition to independence in the early 1960s.[1] The central theme of the book is the role of effective organizations—both public and private—in harnessing this potential for the economic benefit of the people of the region. This has not been a straightforward endeavour, however. Tanzania's natural resources—a climate that is for the most part favourable to a wide range of agricultural activity, and in some parts of the country very much so; a strategic location that for centuries has been nodal to regional and global trading systems, connecting a large African hinterland to the large fast-growing economies of India, China, and the Middle East; and abundant natural resources from deposits of gold, precious minerals, and offshore natural gas to spectacular mountains, national parks, and sun-soaked beaches—have for centuries been a magnet to traders. For most of this time, outsiders, whether fifteenth century Portuguese adventurers, the slave-traders of the Sultanate of Oman from the seventeenth century, or the German and British imperialists from the mid-nineteenth to the mid-twentieth century, extracted significant benefit from the region, leaving little value in the country and even less under the direct control of the people of Tanzania.

The half-century since the creation of the United Republic of Tanzania has been shaped by efforts designed to overturn this legacy. As discussed by Ndulu and Mwase (this volume, Chapter 2) and others, the radical economic regime described in President Nyerere's 1967 *Arusha Declaration* sought to place a powerful and far-reaching State at the centre of the system with the aim both of forging a specific national political identity and controlling the allocation of resources. As has been widely discussed elsewhere, a strong national identity did indeed flourish during this period and contributed to Tanzania being one of the most peaceful countries on the African continent at a time when internal peace and security was far from common. This success was accompanied by extremely poor economic outcomes, which saw the country's early post-independence economic progress stutter and reverse.[2] Traditional exports stagnated, the already small industrial sector contracted, and widespread shortages of basic goods and services became the norm while the limited supply of public (and private) goods was only sustained by very substantial aid flows. Over the quarter-century from 1964, gross domestic product (GDP) growth measured in purchasing power parity (PPP) terms averaged only about 1.7 per cent per annum so that with the population growing at close to 3.0 per cent per annum over the same period, per capita incomes fell sharply: by 1989 per capita incomes were only 70 per cent of their levels at independence.[3]

By the mid-1980s, Tanzania had reached a crossroads. The prospect of continued economic deterioration risked eroding the highly-valued social and political achievements that were beginning to define the nation, and so with the support of President Nyerere, the country embarked on a radical economic transformation. Nyerere relinquished the presidency to Ali Hassan Mwinyi, whose government, through a sequence of knock-down battles with the International Monetary Fund (IMF) and World Bank, laid the foundations for a new, more market-oriented economic framework that began to emerge in the early 1990s. The exchange rate was allowed to float; external trade was liberalized, and domestic prices and interest rates deregulated; and the state began to progressively disengage from many sectors of the economy, including agriculture, industry, and finance.

A quarter of a century on, the long-run effects of these reforms are still working through the system. Headline economic growth has been impressive, averaging 6 per cent per annum between 1995 and 2015, which raised average per capita incomes by more than 75 per cent over the same period and began to make inroads into the high levels of poverty,[4] especially in rural areas, that burdened the country in the early 1990s. Between 1991 and 2011 (the period spanned between first and most recent estimates of poverty in Tanzania) the proportion of the population living below the basic needs poverty line fell from 38.6 per cent of the population to 28.2 per cent. Measures of food poverty show a similar decline, from 21.6 per cent of the population living in food poverty threshold in 1991 to 9.7 per cent two decades later.[5]

This is a remarkable performance but, in some important respects, these impressive numbers flatter to deceive. Part of Tanzania's improved growth performance, especially in the early years, is attributable to the decompression of the previously heavily constrained economy, while the generally favourable economic tailwinds that have blown across the continent since the early 2000s have meant that reforms have enjoyed the support of strong global demand and, thanks to China adding huge volumes to global aggregate supply, low and falling prices for key imported inputs.

But as tailwinds weaken and decompression is completed, sustaining high growth becomes much more challenging. Growth must emerge for improvements in labour productivity, which in turn requires a mixture of increased organizational efficiency (making labour more efficient at doing what it does) and structural change (the movement of people from low- to high productivity sectors activities). It is this set of deep-set challenges that define contemporary economic policy objectives and that provide the unifying theme of this book.

1.1 Effective Organizations, Productivity, and Prosperity

Along the path to prosperity ordinary people become radically more productive. Although it has made substantial gains in the last quarter century Tanzania remains relatively poor because its people, despite working hard, produce much less than ordinary people in most other societies. What accounts for this low productivity? Initially, economists thought that it was due to a shortage of capital: people would be more productive if they had more capital to work with. We now know that this is a substantially incomplete answer. The amount of capital people have to work with is a consequence, not a prime cause. Then it was thought that low productivity was due to a lack of education—'human capital'. But while it is certainly true that the path to higher productivity involves more complex production processes, education is merely the first lowly rung on the ladder of mastering such knowledge.

The productive knowledge that a society possesses is *quantized*. The smallest package of knowledge is the individual human *brain*: education indeed expands the capacity of the brain to acquire knowledge. But all complex production processes require far more knowledge than can be stored within an individual brain. They need groups of people with different specialist skills organized so as to be interdependent. The entity that manages such teams of people is the *organization*: globally such organizations are largely an invention of the twentieth century. When functioning in market conditions, the pertinent form of an organization is the *firm*; when functioning within government, the pertinent form is a *bureaucracy*.

All organizations that are effective at making ordinary people productive need scale: without scale it is not possible for people to specialize in different skills. As we show in this book, in the market sector of the economy Tanzania remains chronically short of firms with sufficient scale to permit meaningful specialization: indeed, the most common size of a Tanzanian firm is to have a workforce of only a single person. Such tiny firms doom their workforces to low productivity. Building a large team of specialized people who are interdependent and jointly productive is a demanding task. Very few small firms grow organically into productive large firms. Most large firms start off large, as the offshoots of existing large firms. To date, Tanzania has not been able to attract enough large firms to provide sufficient productive work opportunities for its population.

But even scale and specialization are not enough to achieve productivity. Within the non-market sector of the Tanzanian economy, there are many bureaucracies that are large and specialized. But most of them are nevertheless quite unproductive. For example, the typical Tanzanian school is about the same size as its counterparts elsewhere in the world, but the attainment of its students is markedly lower. An important reason for this is that many teachers are insufficiently motivated to show up for classes and to learn their subject thoroughly. This is ultimately not just a failure of individual teachers, but a failure of the bureaucratic organizations in which they work. All large, specialist organizations face potential challenges of worker motivation: employees may prefer to free-ride on the efforts of others, or be unwilling to cooperate with others. A successful organization overcomes these problems, reconciling scale and specialization with high motivation. Good management achieves this by a judicious combination of persuading the worker to internalize the objectives of the organization, and providing incentives for good performance. Evidently, the managements of many Tanzanian bureaucracies have not created environments which induce high motivation in their workforce.

Thus, Tanzania has a severe shortage of effective organizations. Those working in the market sector are employed in firms that are far too small to enable them to be productive; those working in the non-market sector are employed in bureaucracies which, though large enough, have not reconciled scale with motivation.

But even effective organizations are not sufficient in themselves to store the knowledge necessary for many of the complex operations required for high productivity. Just as people need to be combined into organizations to make the whole more than the sum of its parts, so organizations need to be combined. A group of firms each with a different specialism needs to be organized so as to be interdependent by means of a *network* or 'value chain'.

For a network to function effectively, the connections between its constituent organizations need to as easy as possible. These connections take three principal forms: spatial, information and communications technology (ICT), and legal. All three require government action. In a production network many of the connections are evidently spatial: the inputs to a product need to be moved to a point of assembly, the completed product needs to be moved to distributors. A vital role of government is to provide good transport connections both between firms within a city, and between cities and global markets. Many of the connections in modern production networks are for the exchange of information: production must be highly responsive to changes in market conditions. Over the past two decades, the dominant means for such flows of information has become ICT. Around the world, governments are now in a race to provide state-of-the-art ICT infrastructure for firms. But one aspect of inter-firm and firm–government relationships has remained constant for centuries: transactions require the support of a legally enforceable contract. In turn, this requires the rule of law: both an appropriate framework of laws, and their speedy, predictable, and honest application through decisions of courts.

In summary, rising prosperity depends upon rising productivity and this in turn depends upon accumulating the capacity to manage ever more complex production processes. The knowledge necessary for complexity is quantized in three types of package. At the lowest level there is the individual human brain: education enlarges the capacity of the brain to retain knowledge. Tanzania has greatly expanded its education system, but this alone does not get a society far on the path to managing complexity. At an intermediate level, effective organizations reconcile scale with motivation. Tanzania is chronically short of such organizations, both large firms and motivated bureaucracies. At the highest level, knowledge is stored in networks of interconnected organizations. This depends critically upon the technologies of connectivity: transport, ICT, and the rule of law.

Superficially, it might appear that this hierarchy of quantized knowledge can be done as a sequence: education, then organizations, and finally networks. But this may be wrong. Education may not be very productive until there are sufficient effective organizations to create the opportunities for educated people. As we show, the returns to education in small firms and peasant farms are not high. And effective organizations may not be forthcoming until the infrastructure of good connectivity enables them to prosper.

1.2 Outline

The chapters in the rest of this volume span a wide range of issues but can be clustered into three main groups. Chapter 2, by Governor Benno Ndulu and Nkunde Mwase, sets the stage by describing Tanzania's economic history from independence in terms of the interplay between the changing external environment and the evolution of economic thinking on growth and development across the country's first four presidencies. Drawing these threads together the chapter concludes by setting out the key economic challenges facing the country over the coming decades. These challenges provide a background for the next set of chapters concerned with the deep structural determinants of growth and prosperity. Mark Henstridge and Dennis Rweyemamu (Chapter 3) consider how the discovery of large offshore natural gas reserves present opportunities for structural change in Tanzania; Paul Collier and Patricia Jones (Chapter 4) discuss how processes of urbanization can alter the fundamental organization of production and consumption in ways that, if handled correctly, can radically increase economic productivity and well-being; while Charles Kunaka, Olivier Hartmann, Gaël Raballand, and Rukia Shamte (Chapter 5) focus on the role of infrastructure and logistics in supporting an increasingly modernizing and urbanizing economy. The final chapter in this group, by Douglas Gollin and Radhika Goyal (Chapter 6), focuses on Tanzania's large agricultural sector and explores how the development of effective rural–urban links is essential to supporting the rapid expansion of an increasingly affluent urban population.

The second main cluster of chapters is fundamentally concerned with employment, incomes, and poverty. The starting point in Margaret McMillan, John Page, and Samuel Wangwe's chapter (Chapter 7) is the 'manufacturing deficit' in Tanzania, the idea that the manufacturing sector has generated a small share of economic output and hence fewer quality jobs than is the case in comparable low- and lower-middle income countries. They argue, however, that a 'new industrial dynamism' is beginning to emerge, in part from large firms but particularly amongst the so-called 'in-between' sector, but this trend will require an activist industrial development strategy if this growth potential is to be nurtured. As discussed by Mahjabeen Haji and Jacques Morisset (Chapter 8), a central element in this strategy is equipping the labour force, and particularly the large number of youth entering the labour force, with the education and skills required to thrive in the increasingly skill-intensive economy anticipated by the new industrial dynamism. The final chapter in this section, by Channing Arndt, Vincent Leyaro, Kristin Mahrt, and Finn Tarp (Chapter 9), steps back from the detailed discussion of policy options to consider the impact of economic policy and performance over the last decade on poverty and well-being. The core conclusion from this chapter is that the combination of underlying growth and the expansion in social expenditures—in health, education, and water and sanitation—have generated substantial improvements in both narrow and broad-based measures of poverty reduction, although the ability to sustain these gains remains a challenge.

The final three chapters in the volume switch the focus to the core concerns of the macroeconomic agencies. These are areas of intense and regular discussion and debate; the chapters in this section are, therefore, selective and concentrate on a narrow range of policy issues. In their chapter on fiscal issues, Christopher Adam, Jehovaness Aikaeli, and Anne Laski (Chapter 10) return to the question of the provision of public infrastructure inputs to support the structural changes discussed in earlier chapters. The central theme of their chapter is how fiscal institutions can manage the twin challenge of efficient domestic revenue mobilization—which has, historically, been low by comparative standards—with investing in public infrastructure in a fiscally sustainable manner. In Chapter 11 Pantaleo Kessy, Stephen O'Connell, and Johnson Nyella are concerned with a similar set of issues in the monetary policy domain. They provide a detailed discussion of how radical reforms to the monetary (and fiscal) framework in the mid-1990s laid the foundation for almost two decades of impressive macroeconomic stabilization policy. The key question in this chapter is how this framework can best serve the emerging interests of the central bank and financial authorities, as new external and domestic policy challenges emerge, including those posed by the discovery of natural resources and the increased integration of Tanzania in the global economy. One of their key concerns, however, is how best the monetary framework can support the process of financial development in Tanzania. This issue is taken up by the final chapter in the volume, by Deputy Governor Natu Mwamba, Nangi Massawe, and Kennedy Komba (Chapter 12), which charts the evolution of the financial system in Tanzania from a wholly bank-centric system to one whose architecture is increasingly better able to provide financial access at the small-scale level—including through innovations such as mobile money services—and to provide financial intermediation at the scale required to support the structural change anticipated over the coming decades.

We close by reiterating the central message of this Introduction, that prosperity builds on productivity and productivity depends on the emergence of effective organizations capable of both managing increasingly complex processes of production, trade, and distribution and, through effective bureaucracies and public policy, coordinating the public sector inputs into these processes. It is exactly this challenge, of creating the effective organizations that will underpin the future prosperity of Tanzania, that ties the collection together.

Notes

1. Archaeological excavations in the second half of the twentieth century at Laetoli and Olduvai Gorge near to modern-day Arusha played a critical role in dating the emergence of modern humanity. The *Laetoli Footprints* left in volcanic ash trace the

predecessors of the earliest hominids back 3.7 million years, while the excavations at the Gorge date the emergence *Homo habilis,* probably the first early human species, to approximately 1.9 million years ago. *Homo sapiens* occupied the site at least 17,000 years ago.

2. Bevan et al. (1991); Ndulu (2007); Coulson (2013); Edwards (2014); Gray (2016).
3. Data from Penn World Tables (version 8.0).
4. Source: World Bank, World Development Indicators. Real GDP growth measured as average annual percentage growth rate of GDP at market prices based on constant local currency; per capita GDP measured in constant 2011 US$ at PPP rates.
5. The national poverty headcount ratio is the percentage of the population living below the national poverty lines estimated from the National Bureau of Statistics Household Budget Surveys.

References

Bevan, D., Collier, P., and Gunning, J. W. (1991). *Controlled Open Economies: A Neo-Classical Critique of Structuralism.* Oxford: Oxford University Press.

Coulson, A. (2013). *Tanzania: A Political Economy.* Oxford: Oxford University Press.

Edwards, S. (2014). *Toxic Aid.* Oxford: Oxford University Press.

Gray, H. S. (2016). *Turbulence and Order in Economic Development: The Political Settlement and Economic Transformation in Tanzania and Vietnam.* Oxford: Oxford University Press.

Ndulu, B. J. (2007). 'The Evolution of Global Development Paradigms and Their Influence on African Economic Growth.' In: B. J. Ndulu, S. A. O'Connell, R. H. Bates, P. Collier, and C. C. Soludo (eds), *The Political Economy of Economic Growth in Africa, 1960–2000,* vol. 1. Cambridge: Cambridge University Press: 315–47.

2

The Building Blocks towards Tanzania's Prosperity

Lessons from Looking Back, and the Way Forward

Benno Ndulu and Nkunde Mwase

2.1 Introduction

Tanzania's quest for prosperity since independence and the trajectory of the economy have been shaped by endowments, by the state of the global economy, and by the evolution of political and economic ideas under its first four presidents (Mwalimu Nyerere, Mwinyi, Mkapa, and Kikwete). Where Tanzania stands today—at the outset of its fifth presidency—and the choices it faces for the future reflect the complex interaction of these factors over the last half-century. A powerful element determining this trajectory has been the role of ideas and how the shifting sands of development theory, both globally and as it has been interpreted and re-interpreted in Tanzania, have affected the policy space and influenced policy choices and ultimately the economic path.

Over Tanzania's first half-century, development thinking has gradually shifted from a preoccupation with government intervention in addressing market failure and supporting infant industries in the 1960s to concerns about government failure and the consequent push for liberalization of the economy in the mid-1980s (Ndulu, 2007; Edwards, 2014). Over the same period, the focus of macroeconomic stabilization policies shifted from a focus on the trade-off between inflation and unemployment, which was still prevalent in the late 1960s to the early 1970s, to a much narrower focus on delivering price stability in the case of monetary policy, a shift that was accompanied in the late 1990s with a move towards greater central-bank independence. Throughout this period, the economic fortunes of Tanzania, as a small open economy, were closely tied to global economic cycles (e.g., the recessionary 1970s and early 1980s compared with the booming 1990s and mid-2000s). Abundant global liquidity and new creditors in recent years have contributed to increasing Tanzania's access to external financing.

Indeed, the current state of Tanzania's economy and its prospects also reflect her initial endowments and her policy efforts to bolster these further. For example, the strong policy focus on promoting religious and ethnic harmony has contributed to the country's background of a period of peace and political stability that is almost unparalleled across the continent and is a valuable endowment in the current period—notwithstanding Tanzania's high ethnic diversity even compared with other countries (see Green, 2011; Ndulu and Mbowe, 2013). Tanzania's geographic location makes it an important coastal gateway to the landlocked countries, and, in particular, to six landlocked countries for which Dar es Salaam Port currently is their shortest direct conduit to the outside world. Other endowments include Tanzania's large population and its strong comparative advantage in natural resources, including arable land and water for irrigation; forest reserves and wildlife; a wide range of ornamental (e.g., gold, diamonds and tanzanite) and industrial minerals (including iron, nickel, uranium, phosphates, and soda ash); and large potential for energy (e.g., coal and natural gas).

This chapter begins by 'looking back' at the four presidencies, describing first the initial economic conditions, the objectives and policies of each political regime, the prevailing development thinking and external environment, and their different economic performance. In Section 2.3, we 'look forward' by outlining a plausible growth strategy for Tanzania. This starts with a baseline assessment of the current growth performance and the constraints and challenges that emerged from development models pursued by the different presidencies, while also highlighting current major risks, including that of a collapse of commodity prices and the rising cost of capital. It identifies challenges that need to be addressed by the new presidency to unlock the country's growth potential and place Tanzania firmly on the road to becoming a middle-income economy.

2.2 Looking Back

2.2.1 *First Regime: Mwalimu Julius K. Nyerere, 1961–85*

We distinguish between two periods of Mwalimu Nyerere's rule. The first covers the immediate post-independence period, 1961–6, during which the focus was on the indigenization of administration while retaining the core of pre-independence economic policies. The second period covers 1966–85, during which Nyerere instituted a substantive paradigm shift in Tanzania's development strategy.

2.2.1.1 THE STATE OF TANZANIA'S ECONOMY AT INDEPENDENCE
AND DEVELOPMENTS, 1961–6

Tanzania, at independence in 1961, was an underdeveloped country with little physical and human capital, even compared with neighbouring countries such as Kenya, but was rich in natural resources.[1] The country, while benefiting from its large size (947,303 km^2), was encumbered by a dispersed population (11.7 people per km^2). The production processes were very basic, focusing on extracting raw materials for exports and subsistence farming. The country had vast resources, including large agricultural landholdings (estimated at 260,000 km^2 in 1961), abundant water sources,[2] a long coastline, mineral reserves (both discovered and prospective), and great potential for tourism due to its geography and wildlife.[3] These resources were largely under-utilized; for example, only 0.9 per cent of the land area was used as permanent cropland.

Tanzania's national institutions were embryonic. It was part of the East African Community (EAC) together with Kenya and Uganda, with which it shared various institutions. This included a single common currency, which was issued and managed by the East African Currency Board (EACB), and an East African Common Services Organization (EACSCO), which administered on behalf of the three governments' common services such as income taxes, customs and excise taxes, airports, railways, and ports.[4] While the various institutions were spread across the three countries, key policymaking centres—including the EAC, the customs and excise departments, treasury, railways, and ports—were headquartered in Kenya. The countries were part of a 'common market' within which capital and goods could circulate freely.

The government's stated aim was nation-building, which included heavy investment in physical infrastructure, human capital stock and institutions (including a central bank in 1965 and the creation of other government agencies following the dissolution of the EACB in 1966), and forging national identity and social cohesion, with, for example, the promotion of Swahili as the national language, as well as an education policy that emphasized ethnic and religious tolerance. The government sought to improve education in all parts of the country and to actively enrol students in regions that were foreign to them in order to build and foster openness. Similar, broadly inclusive employment policies were also adopted to support social cohesion.

The sectoral allocation of economic activity was similar to that of many African economies. Agriculture was the economic mainstay in the early 1960s accounting for more than half of GDP, about 80 per cent of exports, and employing about 80 per cent of the population. Approximately half of the agricultural exports were produced on large estates, owned and managed by foreigners. The industrial sector accounted for about 6 per cent of GDP but grew quickly, reaching about 16 per cent of GDP by 1965.

Overall, while output growth was quite strong during the first years of independence, the economy remained agrarian and sensitive to exogenous shocks. Specifically, real growth was averaging at 6.9 per cent in 1961–4 but nearly halved to about 3.6 per cent in 1965 on account of a fall in the price of major export crops and adverse weather shocks before picking up again in 1966, albeit at a slower pace than in 1964. Despite strong activity in the manufacturing, mining, and construction sectors, the economy remained centred on the production and export of raw agricultural products. The government attributed the limited transformation of the economy during this period to a serious shortage of skilled manpower, paucity of foreign and domestic funds, the adverse weather conditions of 1965, and the collapse in the country's major exports.

The external environment turned less benign for Tanzania from about 1965, with a decline in world prices of Tanzania's export crops, including a 35 per cent and 12 per cent decline in the price of sisal and coffee prices, respectively. The macroeconomic effects were large—sisal was the most important export crop accounting for about 20 per cent of total export earnings in 1965. Though interest rates in advanced economies were fairly low in 1960, Tanzania, like many newly independent economies at the time, had limited access to capital markets and faced large outflows of capital.

2.2.1.2 PRESIDENT NYERERE'S PARADIGM SHIFT OF DEVELOPMENT, 1966–85

The development model implemented by the Nyerere regime moved from a market-based approach (1961–6) to a state interventionist approach, albeit with some easing of controls towards the end of the regime. The founding father of the nation, Mwalimu Julius Nyerere, characterized this phase of Tanzania's journey to prosperity as a war to rid the Tanzanian society of three 'enemies'—ignorance, disease, and poverty. This war was to be fought in three ways:

- Increasing the pace of industrial growth in order to narrow the rapidly widening development gap with the developed world by exploiting Tanzania's position as a late starter to borrow technology and build an industrial base at a lower cost than developed economies (avoiding research and development costs). Nyerere famously stated that 'we must run while they walk'.

- Ensuring that prosperity was achieved without undermining interpersonal, inter-regional, and rural–urban equity. The government sought to implement a development strategy that was egalitarian, and, in particular, one that did not alienate the peasant majority. Achieving growth while reducing inequality was a key objective of government policy.

- Reducing Tanzania's external dependence, which had remained high in the post-independence era. While noting that economic development would require large amounts of resources, including grants, loans, and foreign direct investment (FDI), that were at that time limited, Nyerere—fearing conditionality would constrain independence of policy choice and recognizing the pivotal role of domestic resource mobilization—de-emphasized the perception that financing would be key to development. He stated that 'money is not the foundation for Tanzania's development' and instead emphasized 'self-reliance'.

These objectives were articulated in the Arusha Declaration in 1967, in which Mwalimu Nyerere laid out the policies that would make Tanzania a socialist and self-reliant nation. The cornerstone of the Arusha Declaration was *ujamaa* ('familyhood'). Drawing on the extended family system in traditional Africa, Nyerere posited a new development theory that was based on 'the recognition that society is an extension of the basic family unit' (Nyerere, 1962).[5] It underscored that a strong state was needed that could mobilize Tanzania's resources (both labour and land) on behalf of the people to achieve development.

This commitment was implemented through a range of policy measures, including the nationalization of all banks; the acquisition of controlling stakes in existing industries and services; and the moving of all productive and distributive sectors of the economy into state control. State ownership in the financial and industrial sectors was accompanied by a radical programme of intervention in agriculture built around heavy subsidization of fertilizer, training, and support for irrigation to ensure food self-sufficiency, and an extensive 'villagization' programme in order to improve peasants' welfare and provide inputs for the manufacturing sector.[6] The final leg of this programme was the imposition of income limits in order to reduce the gap between the highest paid civil servant and the farmer, and discouraging non-labour income in order to reduce inequality and urban bias.

Nyerere adjusted the policy message slightly towards the end of the regime, relaxing some of the hard controls. The initial process of liberalization of trade and prices in 1984 and 1985, including the partial import liberalization via the Own Funded Import Scheme, occurred primarily as a home-grown reform and partly in response to pressure from the donor community to reform.[7,8]

2.2.1.3 THE EXTERNAL ENVIRONMENT

Tanzania was exposed to a number of adverse external shocks, particularly in the 1970s (Figures 2.1–2.3). The global economy, after strong growth in the 1960s, experienced recession throughout most of the 1970s to the mid-1980s (Figure 2.2). The oil price hikes in the 1970s and the collapse in global

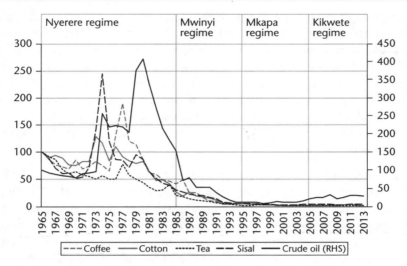

Figure 2.1. Trends in commodity prices, 1960–2013

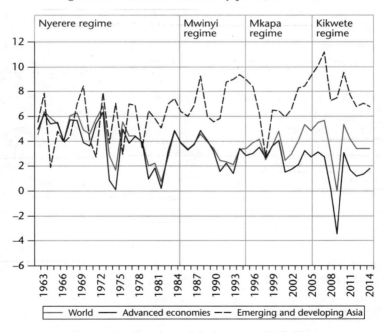

Figure 2.2. Trends in global output, 1963–2014

agricultural commodity prices in real terms contributed to a decline in Tanzania's terms of trade (in both real and current terms, Figure 2.3). The collapse of the EAC in 1977 (which could be partially considered an external shock) adversely affected Tanzania, for example the Tanzanian tourism sector had relied on Kenya-based tour operators for the bulk of its clientele (Barkan, 1994).

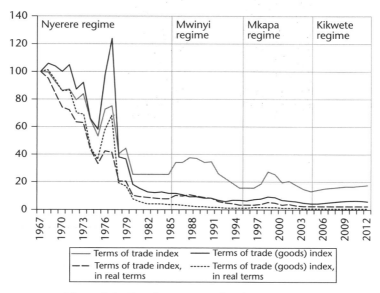

Figure 2.3. Trends in terms of trade, 1967–2013

Tanzania benefited from large aid flows throughout this period, albeit with some decline towards the end of the regime. At first glance, it may seem striking that a country with a socialist ideology, that had fully nationalized all major forms of production, was able to interact with both communist/socialist and capitalist states. Indeed, Tanzania was one of the largest recipients of Chinese aid and was also a major recipient of Western aid (including from Canada and the Nordic states).[9,10] This broad base of donor support was partly prompted by the remarkable achievement by the regime in forging national cohesion in contrast to several other countries in the region where ethnicity became divisive and could lead to conflict. However, by the 1980s, with the increasing focus on aid effectiveness and governance issues, some donors withheld financial support to encourage the Nyerere regime to adjust its hard controls, in part due to mounting evidence that the policy regime had been unsuccessful in achieving its goals (Edwards, 2014 and Adam et al., 1994).[11]

Development thinking evolved sharply during this period. Prior to the early 1980s, development theory put the emphasis on industrialization, supporting industries in their infancy, and heavy state intervention as critical steps towards development. The basic-needs approach was embraced as a strategy to achieve poverty reduction and equity, and this, in line with the government's concerns about inequality and poverty, received broad donor support, including from the World Bank. However, by the late 1970s and early 1980s, a neoclassical counter-revolution in development thinking was underway and concerns about the inefficiency of government policy rather than market failures began to dominate the debate on public policy.

2.2.1.4 THE OUTCOME

Tanzania's economic performance during the Nyerere regime was at best stagnant, but not constantly so, with fast growth in the pre-*ujamaa* period; a rapid slowdown during the early years of *ujamaa*; and virtual collapse from about 1979/80 to 1983 (Figure 2.4). Real GDP growth declined from 6.6 per cent in 1961–6 to 4 per cent in 1967–79 and was subsequently stagnant at 0.2 per cent in 1980–83. Income per capita, which had generally been rising until 1976, reversed this pattern and declined steadily until about 1982/3.

Tanzania's economy during the Nyerere regime was also characterized by severe macroeconomic instability. The weakening output performance was reflected in widening external and fiscal deficits. In addition, policy misman-agement in response to these developments—including expansionary monetary and fiscal policy, and exchange rate and import controls—contributed to soaring inflation and a sharply increasing parallel exchange-rate premium. Unable to cover its current account bill and debt obligations and with a collapse in reserves (reaching 0.05 months of reserves in 1982), the economy was eventually faced with a balance of payments and debt crisis. This period was characterized by extensive shortages, including basic consumer goods.

Analysis of the impact of government policy on equality and other social indicators suggests a reduction in inequality but a mixed impact on other welfare indicators.[12] Income inequality increased between 1969 and 1976/7 as reflected by the rise in the Gini coefficient from 0.39 to 0.44 but this fact masks

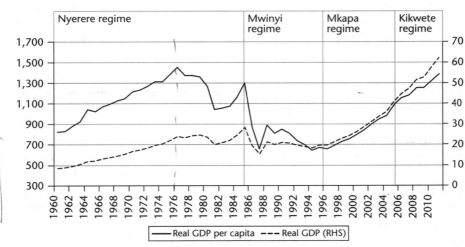

Figure 2.4. Trends in key output and production, 1960–2014

different trends within the country. Wangwe (1996) finds an increase in rural inequality but a decrease in urban inequality with the rise in the former more than offsetting the latter. As a result, the urban–rural ratio declined from 11.3:1 in 1969 to 3.5:1 in 1976/7. There was a sharp increase in school enrolment rates from 33 per cent of the total to over 97 per cent by 1981 but this declined steadily thereafter, reaching 76 per cent by 1985. Health-care indicators point to rising infant mortality rates.

The regime bequeathed an important 'endowment'—social cohesion and political stability. The resulting sustained national cohesion is evidenced by several surveys (e.g., Afrobarometer, see Section 3.2) and this can be attributed directly to the strong foundation laid by the Nyerere regime.

Overall, the first regime government demonstrated the challenges of focusing on multiple objectives, undertaking too rapid a pace of industrialization policy in areas where the country has limited comparative advantage, and also highlighted the deficiencies of an economic model that does not emphasize incentives for production and efficiency (Rydenfelt, 1984). While the focus on human and social welfare was important, the drive for more inclusive growth could have been undertaken with a different economic ideology that prioritized economic growth supported by structural policies to stimulate human capital (Aghion, 2012; Aghion et al., 2015). Distortions and government interventions led to economic malaise and eventually contributed to the erosion of social welfare.

2.2.2 Second Regime: Ali Hassan Mwinyi, 1985–95

2.2.2.1 INITIAL CONDITIONS: THE STATE OF TANZANIA'S ECONOMY AND DEVELOPMENT

The Mwinyi regime inherited an economy that was in a dire state with large macroeconomic imbalances—medium- and long-term external debt at the end of 1984 was over 50 per cent of GDP and 700 per cent of exports of goods and services—and low total factor productivity. In addition, the evidence suggests that the high investment by the Nyerere regime had been desperately inefficient: the stock of capital relative to GDP was broadly the same level as at independence and, of this, the stock of agricultural machinery tractors was lower than at independence, and the general quality of the country's physical infrastructure severely debilitated.

However, Mwinyi also inherited a country with a relatively skilled workforce to run government agencies, reflecting an accumulation of human capital since independence and a high degree of social cohesion and political stability. Tanzania had avoided the pitfalls of ethnic conflict that have affected many other African countries.

The development discourse, both domestically and externally, increasingly questioned the concept of *ujamaa*. The population, which was fully conscious of the abundance of goods in neighbouring countries, was weary of controls and rampant bribery involved in day-to-day activities, arising in part from the large shortages of goods, and controls on imports and foreign exchange. The shift in the development paradigm towards emphasis on 'government failure and leaving the market to flourish' (Ndulu, 2007) which was set in the early 1980s, also galvanized support for change from both donors and Tanzanian academics. Ndulu (2007) notes that criticisms by donors levelled against dirigisme, and more specifically against the once-beloved socialist vision of the country, helped to propagate a process of what could best be described as the dismantling of controls rather than the creation of a new market-oriented management system.

2.2.2.2 MWINYI ERA

The entrance of a new political actor, President Ali Hassan Mwinyi, in 1985 enabled the government to carry forward the shift towards a market-based economy much more decisively and quickly (Mwase and Ndulu, 2008) than seen in the previous regimes. The new regime was most famously known for its 'liberalization' policy and in a marked shift away from the previous heavy-control regime was epitomized by the simple slogan 'ruksa' (loosely translated as 'permission granted'), reflecting the regime's open approach to loosening controls.[13] However, this downplays the overall objective of the regime, which was far broader and entailed intense adjustment to restore macroeconomic stability in the short term, with a view to moving to deeper structural reforms in the medium to long term in order to improve resource allocation and enhance production incentives.

The government embarked on an intensified adjustment programme in the period 1985–90, focusing on the following five key areas:[14]

- Devaluing the shilling in order to improve external competitiveness. The misalignment of the exchange rate had been a key factor underlying the decline. While there was sharp disagreement on the pace of devaluation, there was broad consensus that the currency was overvalued and had contributed to the surge in the import bill and collapse in export sector.

- Tightening fiscal and monetary policies to help reduce the large fiscal and external imbalances and also reduce inflation. For example, the 1986/7 budget announced a 50 per cent increase in interest rates in June 1986, with ensuing additional increases in order to achieve positive real interest rates in mid-1988.

- Removing controls on domestic prices and gradually increasing nominal producer prices for agricultural exports to increase incentives for production and contain losses of state enterprises.

- Trade liberalization to support private sector-led growth, particularly, broadening the spectrum of imported goods that were permitted, in order to enhance capacity utilization and operational efficiency, and liberalization of the export retention scheme.

- Rehabilitation of the physical infrastructure in order to support productive activity.

The second-generation reforms, from 1990 to 1995, were supposed to focus on deeper structural reforms to move institutions towards a market-based economy by improving the incentive structure. A four-pronged strategy entailed the following:

- Reorganizing public enterprises, parastatals, and other statutory bodies in order to increase the role of the private sector in the economy, improve the efficiency of agricultural, industrial, and transport sectors, and contain fiscal losses (e.g., repayment of credit).

- Moving to a more market-based policy framework, for example by setting up foreign exchange markets and mobilizing domestic revenues to help to restore debt and fiscal sustainability.

- Progressing with additional price and trade reforms and further improving the transportation capacity, including rehabilitating the railways and major roads.

- Reforming the civil service in order to reduce the wage bill and enhance efficiency.

Institutional weaknesses over time emerged, as key economic actors sought to obtain the 'rents' arising from the increased aid inflows and to prevent deeper liberalization of the foreign exchange market and import controls. Similarly, despite the reforms, expenditure remained high, in part reflecting governance issues. The relaxation of the policy stance and reform efforts in the 1990s was reflected in the increase in tax exemptions and laxity in public finance management, and was symptomatic of corruption and governance issues.

However, there were some corrections towards the end of the regime, including the passing of key laws and reforms that were later operationalized by the ensuing regime. This included the law granting the Central Bank autonomy, to focus primarily on ensuring price stability and prudent exchange management, and the establishment of the Tanzania Revenue Authority (TRA), a semi-autonomous authority that was designed to limit the direct political interference in revenue collection and administration. The introduction of cash budgets towards the end of the regime provided important grounding for the discipline of 'spending what you have', which was used also by subsequent regimes.

2.2.2.3 THE EXTERNAL ENVIRONMENT

The external trade environment remained broadly unfavourable for Tanzania, with the terms of trade in real terms continuing to decline, albeit at a slower pace, and although global economic growth picked up, it remained far lower than the 1960s (see Figure 2.2). In addition, the advanced economies experienced an economic recession in the early 1990s.

The neoclassical development paradigm gained policy traction during this period as did a change in aid priorities towards effectiveness and efficiency. There was a shift in attitude towards 'international conditionality' with a greater push to use aid as a tool to improve institutions and governance. Tanzania experienced its second aid boom in the mid-1980s as the international community welcomed the change in government policy, but the heightened focus on aid efficiency and effectiveness in the 1990s contributed to a slowdown in aid.

The aid boom essentially substituted for monetary financing of the deficits pursued in the early 1980s reducing pressure in inflation. However, institutional weaknesses affected donor relations leading to the suspension of assistance in 1995. The work by the independent reviewers contained in the Helleiner report provided the bridge, as it helped to identify the key weaknesses in the fiscal and governance system (the main bones of contention with donors), as well as those in the aid relationship operative in the country.

2.2.2.4 THE OUTCOME

Tanzania's economic growth picked up sharply during the Mwinyi regime, reflecting the positive impact of liberalization, but policy slippages and delays in critical reforms contributed to a slowdown in the second half of the regime (Figure 2.4). Output grew by an average of 4 per cent during 1985–95, with a sharp increase in 1986–90 averaging at 5.7 per cent and slowing to about 1.8 per cent from 1991 to 1995. There was a sharp (6 per cent) decline in per capita income in PPP during 1986–95 suggesting that output growth rate was not able to keep up with population growth and/or improvements in other countries.

The regime was unsuccessful in restoring other dimensions of macroeconomic instability. Overall, inflation remained high during the period, averaging 29 per cent in 1986–95; it declined from 36 per cent in 1985 to 32 per cent in 1987, but thereafter was very volatile with some surges (e.g., 48 per cent in 1988 and 37 per cent in 1994). In addition, the fiscal position worsened and debt surged. External debt increased from 52.5 per cent of GDP in 1985 to a peak of 118.7 per cent in 1993 before declining to 94.4 per cent by 1995.

The current account deficit improved in the short run from 3.9 per cent of GDP in 1985 to a dip of 1.1 per cent in 1988, before rising and reaching a peak of 10.3 per cent in 1994. The widening of the current account deficit was mainly driven by the increasing trade deficit, which more than overshot other inflows. At its peak, in 1993, the trade deficit stood at 16.6 per cent of GDP.[15,16] The weak performance of the current account was mainly a result of a sharp increase in the import price deflator (in US$ terms) and lacklustre export volume growth.

Overall, despite the economic turnaround, Tanzania's growth fundamentals remained weak. While investment, particularly from the private sector, increased sharply during this period—albeit with a slowdown in the 1990s—the economy's capital stock continued to decline as a share of GDP. In addition, total factor productivity also continued to decline while human capital stock remained unchanged. Data suggest a continued decline in manufacturing and other industry as a share of output; agriculture remained the largest sector, accounting for nearly half of GDP. Data further suggests that output growth was mostly associated with an expansion in household consumption.

There was a decline in the pace of improvement of social indicators but it is unclear the extent to which this was driven by the reforms. The introduction of user charges for basic services coupled with retrenchments contributed to gaps in income between the winners and losers. Primary school enrolments collapsed but those for secondary school picked up. The health indicators continued to improve, albeit at a slower pace.

Overall, this period reflects the challenge of moving an economy facing high debt and stagnant growth towards a path to prosperity while within a less benign external economic environment. This policy challenge was exacerbated by the absence of market-based institutions to provide warning signals, and by pervasive market distortions and the large informal/underground economy. In addition, it exposed the political challenges of implementing economic reforms. While reforms may have been too fast and implemented rather chaotically, as the term 'ruksa' ('permission granted') associated with this regime connotes, in their absence, Tanzania would still be suffering from the inertia of the deeply embedded vested interests for controls and associated rents in the public sector that defined the control era.

2.2.3 Third Regime: Benjamin William Mkapa, 1995–2005

2.2.3.1 INITIAL CONDITIONS: THE STATE OF TANZANIA'S
ECONOMY AND DEVELOPMENT

The Mkapa regime inherited an economy faced with large macroeconomic imbalances—high public debt stock, large current account imbalances, and excessive inflation—and competitiveness issues. The stock of skilled labour had continued to accumulate but there were concerns about its quality, in part reflecting the impact of the introduction of user fees for services. In addition, continued deterioration in terms of trade, particularly for agricultural products, had contributed to heightened concerns about poverty.

2.2.3.2 MKAPA, 1995–2005

The entrance of Mkapa provided a fresh platform to consolidate the economic reforms undertaken in the previous decade and move the country to a well-functioning market-based economy. The objectives of the regime were to achieve macroeconomic stability, economic growth, and poverty reduction. A three-pronged strategy was undertaken:

- Macroeconomic stability: Mkapa underscored the need to rein in spending in order to achieve debt sustainability—he famously coined the phrase 'Fungeni mikanda' ('tighten your belts') to emphasize the need for austere fiscal policies. To achieve this, he implemented a number of fundamental institutional and legal changes, most notably the Central Bank's autonomy and the Tanzania Revenue Authority (TRA) which became operational in 1996. Mkapa also engaged closely with donors in order to secure debt relief for Tanzania.

- Structural reforms: The government intensified the pace of reforms with a focus on reducing the size of government and providing a conducive environment for private sector investment. Reforms included divesting or privatizing government assets; providing leases to the private sector to commercially manage key public utilities; liberalizing the banking services and offering fiscal incentives to investors—in particular for the mining sector—that included generous depreciation allowances; indefinite loss carryforward; exemptions from import duties and the value-added tax; and implementing some income tax holidays.

- Poverty eradication: The regime underscored the importance of increasing the efficiency and effectiveness of projects and providing basic social services targeted to the poor and most vulnerable. In this regard, significant resources were dedicated to identifying and building road networks in Tanzania, with a focus on high-density communities where the poorest typically reside. The government emphasized poverty eradication in its development strategy—National Vision 2025—and also developed a separate poverty strategy.

2.2.3.3 THE EXTERNAL ENVIRONMENT

The external environment improved moving from donor fatigue to a resurgence of interest in aid, particularly with rising acceptance of the need for debt relief and forgiveness to heavily indebted poor countries (Baker, 1972). The

1990s, which began with an analysis of external aid including concerns about efficiency and effectiveness of aid, were characterized also by a resurgence in aid flows by the mid-1990s, with a growing acceptance of the need to provide debt relief to poor countries. The human development index (HDI) was launched in 1990 to measure a country's overall achievement in its social and economic indicators. The Heavily Indebted Poor Countries (HIPC) Initiative was an important initiative in this regard and was closely followed by the Multilaterial Debt Relief Initiative (MDRI), from both of which Tanzania stood to benefit.

In addition, there was renewed interest in poverty alleviation. There was a concerted effort by the international community to eradicate extreme poverty by 2015 as part of the Millennium Development Goals (MDGs). This period was also characterized by a proliferation of donors, including non-governmental organizations and private philanthropy. From Tanzania's perspective, this also raised concern about the harmonization of various donor programmes and policies as well as concerns about policy ownership.

Development thinking continued to be dominated by theories which underpinned adjustment programmes to reduce the size of the government, liberalize the economy to react to market forces, and rely on market signals instead of state intervention for policymaking. However, towards the mid-2000s the pendulum in development thinking swung towards the middle path of governments working with the markets to more efficiently provide public goods.

Global economic conditions were broadly benign with rising growth (Figures 2.1–2.2). Commodity prices, particularly oil prices, also picked up, albeit from a low base. In real terms, Tanzania's terms of trade improved during the period. In addition, global interest rates continued their steady decline in long-term yields, which contributed somewhat to investor interest in African countries (e.g., a surge in the number and size of sovereign bonds issuances).

2.2.3.4 THE OUTCOME

The results from these changes to growth and inflation were phenomenal. Per capita income growth in the current US$ (and in current US$ PPP terms) increased from a paltry $181 ($998) in 1995 to $449 ($1,645) in 2005, an increase of 148 (65) per cent, based on data from the World Bank World Development Indicators (WDI). Inflation was brought down from about 24 per cent in 1995 to an average of 4.4 per cent in 2005 and foreign reserves were built up to the equivalent of nine months' worth of imports of goods and services, though this declined to about 5.8 by 2005. The debt-to-GDP ratio declined to 40.7 per cent, in part reflecting Tanzania's success in receiving HIPC and MDRI debt relief. Owing to the strong track record of policy implementation, the country experienced a resumption of, and a sharp increase in, aid. Debt forgiveness under HIPC and subsequently under MDRI played an important role in improving the country's creditworthiness.

Data available suggest that there was an improvement in investor perception of the business environment, albeit with some levelling-off towards the end of the regime, a sharp pick-up in investment, and some change in the structure of real output. The institutional investor ratings (IIR) point to an increase in confidence from 1995 to 1999 and this period was associated with a pick-up in investment and FDI, albeit with some large swings. Private–public partnerships increased from a low base of 0.07 per cent of GDP in 1995 to 0.71 per cent of GDP by 2005. Some major developments also occurred, including the entrance of a large number of banks and a surge in tourism and mining activity.

The share of agriculture in the economy declined from an average of about 47–48 per cent of GDP in 1995–97 to 33 per cent in 1998–2004. This was broadly mirrored by an increase in services.[17] In addition, the share of manufacturing increased during this period, in part reflecting the opening of new mines. For example the Bulyanhulu Mine opened near the northern town of Mwanza in 2001, making Tanzania Africa's third-largest producer of gold. There was a steady pick-up in credit to the private sector provided by banks as a share of GDP during the Mkapa regime, from 3 per cent in 1996 to 8 per cent, but the increase was small.

However, after a steady decline in the current account deficit from 9.2 per cent of GDP to 1.1 per cent by 2002, this trend was reversed, reaching 5.5 per cent by 2005 mainly due to a surge in the price of imports (Figure 2.5). The volume and price (deflator) of exports of goods increased only marginally by an average of 0.8 per cent and 0.7 per cent, respectively, during the period, despite the mining sector activity. However, the surge in volume of exports of goods and services was much higher at 17.9 per cent and suggests a higher impact from the tourism industry.

These developments raise a number of questions on the underpinnings of growth, including vulnerability to the external environment and policy slippages. However, a number of challenges also occurred during this period, with the public raising questions about governance, including the country's mining policy, and some high-profile cases of corruption and mismanagement. These may have contributed to the later levelling in the IIR.

Despite the strong growth performance, the data suggest that this had not translated to a marked reduction in poverty, and that inequality had changed only marginally.[18] Nevertheless, there was a turnaround in agricultural productivity from previous episodes, and this likely had a positive, albeit small, trickledown effect on the poor, given that agriculture was the economic mainstay of the population. In addition, the pace of increase in value-added-per-worker

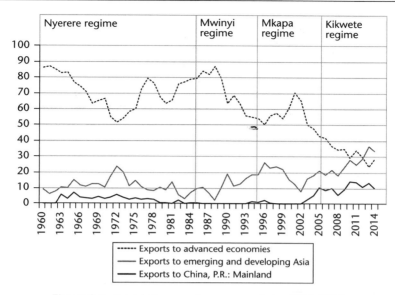

Figure 2.5. Trends in export source markets, 1960–2014

strengthened in agriculture, and the country was able to narrow the gap with the sub-Saharan Africa (SSA) average (excluding South Africa). In addition, ownership of agricultural machinery surged during this period. Low global agricultural prices (in real terms), however, continue to negatively affect farmers' incomes (see Figure 2.1).

2.2.4 Fourth Regime, Jakaya K. Kikwete, 2005–15

2.2.4.1 INITIAL CONDITIONS

This was the first regime to inherit an economy that did not face major macro-economic imbalances, as inflation had been brought under control and the debt was at sustainable levels. In addition, the economy was transforming into a resource-rich exporter, with large discoveries of minerals.

However, Tanzania was faced with a number of major challenges—a large infrastructure gap, income poverty concerns, and a low quality of health, education, and agricultural productivity, particularly compared to regional countries. The collapse of power, water, and rail concessions further empha-sized the need for action. Also, while investor confidence had improved from the lower levels when Mkapa took power it had levelled off (e.g., IIR rating). There were concerns about continued challenges in the business environment, particularly with regard to the incentive regime offered to investors under this phase, and the tough problem of corruption. Some key legal reforms in property and financial rights, and the adjudication of some commercial disputes, were pending.

2.2.4.2 KIKWETE ERA

President Jakaya Mrisho Kikwete's strategy focused on consolidating gains in macroeconomic stability and growth, in particular continuing structural and institutional reforms, addressing the infrastructure gap, and also aggressively attracting foreign financing and investment to Tanzania.

The regime initially focused on achieving the objectives laid out in the 2005 National Strategy for Growth and Poverty Reduction (MKUKUTA), in particular, implementing the infrastructure projects to support rapid growth and provision of socials services to the poor and vulnerable. In 2009, it launched the 'Kilimo Kwanza' ('farming first') initiative which prioritized the agricultural sector, and in 2010 it launched MKUKUTA II. Government policy emphasized social inclusion. In 2013/14, recognizing the need for clear operational steps to achieve its objectives, the government adopted the Big Results Now (BRN) initiative which drew from the Malaysian model of development. This initiative emphasized prioritization, a focus on achieving big results in the chosen areas, and public commitment and accountability for cost-effective high-quality results.

Various policies were implemented targeting four key areas: addressing the infrastructure gap; the institutional and policy environment; poverty and inclusion; and financial market development. The policy actions included:

- Investment: Investment in the gas pipeline and gas processing is particularly noteworthy and could help lower the cost of power generation by switching from expensive (and imported) oil to (locally sourced) gas-based power generation. In addition, under BRN, access to water was also prioritized. The central railway line is being upgraded and impediments to transit traffic removed to improve the gateway services to neighbouring landlocked countries.

- Institutional and policy environment: Instead of depending primarily on incentives to attract investors, the regime focused on improving the business climate, including enacting legislation to remove uncertainties in the enforcement of property rights.

- Financial services: Enhancing access to financial services and deepening the market by legislating to enable a wider range of financial products (for example, mortgages and leasing) and using technology-based cost-effective mobile money services. In addition, the government undertook policies aimed at widening the reach of Tanzanian financial markets, especially the stock exchange, and addressing the demand for insurance products, both of which have grown phenomenally.

2.2.4.3 THE EXTERNAL ENVIRONMENT

The external environment between 2005 and 2015 was mixed. On the one hand, a more benign environment emerged, mainly reflecting Asia's rising demand for Africa's exports and interest in investing in frontier markets, including Tanzania.

- There was an expansion in export markets, with the rising share of exports to Asia (Figure 2.5), which may have helped Tanzania adjust to the decline in advanced economies' aggregate demand following the global financial crisis. Indeed, despite the surge in oil prices in real terms (while agricultural prices remained flat) throughout most of the period— with a sharp drop in 2008/9, the global financial crisis in 2007/8, and the Eurozone debt crisis in 2011—Tanzania's terms of trade remained flat. This suggests that demand from developing counties (notably Asia) helped the Tanzanian economy somewhat withstand these shocks.

- The global liquidity conditions also softened, with interest rates declining, reaching low levels particularly after the global crisis. This, coupled with the emergence of new major actors in the development architecture (e.g., China), contributed to an increase in financing options and a reduction in the cost of accessing finance. Tanzania, as one of the countries perceived to be a frontier economy, experienced substantial investor interest.

On the other hand, the global financial crisis of 2008/9, which was followed by the Euro crisis of 2011/12, seriously tested the resilience of the country's macroeconomic stability and sustainability of growth, particularly after the fiscal and external reserves buffers built up in the preceding years were depleted. Oil prices declined sharply in real terms in 2008/9 and despite the pick-up thereafter, they remained at a lower trajectory, and since mid-2014 have declined. The fall in oil prices in real terms has partly helped to cushion Tanzania from the impact of the global financial crisis, as the country is a net importer of oil.

Development paradigms have continued to evolve. The development dialogue in the aftermath of the Arab Spring and global financial crisis and recession, has emphasized the importance of social inclusion, in particular the inclusion of women and young people. In addition, there have been new development theories and models put forward, including 'new structuralism' (see for example, Lin and Wang, 2014) which emphasizes the importance of governments picking winners and highlights the success of China and other East Asian economies in that regard. There has also been greater discussion and focus on sustainable development and climate-change issues.

2.2.4.4 THE OUTCOME

On the macroeconomic front the results on growth from these changes are phenomenal. Per capita income growth in current US$ (and current US$ PPP) terms increased from a low $449 ($1,649) in 2005 to $998 ($2,591) in 2014, an increase of 122 (57) per cent (WDI). GDP grew at an average rate of 6.5 per cent during this regime.

However, other macroeconomic indicators suggest mixed results.

- External debt remains low at about 28 per cent of GDP as of 2014, down from 41 per cent in 2005 when Kikwete took over (Figure 2.4). Nevertheless, after a steady decline through 2007, both external debt and total public debt-to-GDP ratios have increased.

- Average inflation increased steadily from 4.4 per cent in 2005 reaching a peak of 16 per cent in 2012 but has declined since then, reaching 6 per cent in 2014 (Figure 2.4). Inflation declined to 4.2 per cent in early 2015 before picking up to 5.4 per cent by the end of the fiscal year 2014/15. Core inflation has declined and remained steady at 2 per cent. The increase in headline inflation compared to the level at the end of the last regime could be attributed in part to the fuel and food price shocks that occurred during the period. Analyses of central bank short-term deposit rates and monetary aggregates suggest a tightening in policy.

- The current account deficit has been increasing steadily and has averaged at over 10 per cent of GDP since 2010, even though the price deflator of goods exports has increased at a faster pace than that for imports between 2006 and 2014. This mainly reflects the effect of continued lacklustre increase in volume of exports (1.8 per cent) relative to imports of goods (3 per cent increase) (Figures 2.6 and 2.7). By June 2015 the account deficit declined to 8 per cent of GDP, partly helped along by the sharp fall in global oil prices.

The underpinnings of growth have continued to improve. Data suggest that Tanzania's productivity has increased relative to other countries. In addition, the country's capital stock has increased sharply with the growing importance of private investment. Public–private partnerships have continued to increase, from 0.7 per cent of GDP in 2005 to 1.1 per cent of GDP in 2013, and public–private capital stock was estimated at 7.7 per cent of GDP in 2013, up from 3.7 per cent in 2005.

Overall the structure of the economy has become more diversified. In real terms, services has the largest share having increased to 50.5 per cent by 2013; followed by industry which has seen a sharp increase to 22 per cent; closely followed by agriculture which accounts for 21 per cent of real GDP. What is perhaps more striking is the fact that the contribution of agriculture to real

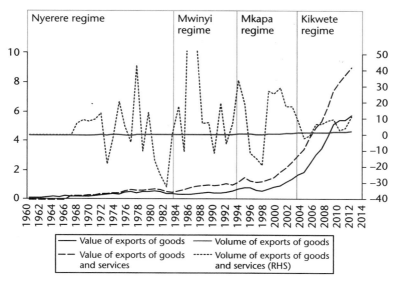

Figure 2.6. Trends in exports, 1960–2014

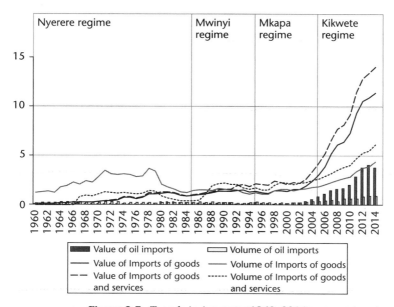

Figure 2.7. Trends in imports, 1960–2014

GDP growth has sharply declined to 13.3 per cent with the other two sectors rising more sharply. In terms of the exports of goods and services, there has been a major shift in structure with non-traditional exports (other than the six traditional export crops dominant in the past) increasing their share to 90 per cent. These items include tourism (25 per cent), gold (15 per cent), manufactures (14 per cent), and services in trade (predominantly transit trade at 10.5 per cent).

Analysis of GDP from the expenditure side indicates that household consumption continues to dominate but that gross fixed investment has continued to pick up. Private investment to GDP increased from about 14 per cent of GDP in 2005 to 19 per cent by 2013 while public investment has remained at about 5 per cent of GDP, albeit with a slight surge to about 7 per cent in 2009. The rise in investment has been driven mainly by a sharp rise in FDI into mining and prospecting for gas. The other destination sectors have been communications, banking, manufacturing, and tourism. Growth in public investment was mainly in infrastructure.

Analysis of poverty and other social indicators points to mixed performance. The recent household budget survey and the World Bank's Poverty Assessment completed in 2015 suggest a positive turn in the impact of growth on poverty reduction. Based on the 2012 Household Budget Survey, the World Bank (2015a) notes that poverty has declined for the first time in twenty years. The poverty gap has narrowed and the income share of the lowest 20 per cent of the economy has increased. In addition, life expectancy and other health indicators have improved. Energy per capita usage has increased, suggesting a positive impact of the infrastructure projects. However, primary school enrolment rates have declined during the regime. (See Arndt, Leyaro, Mahrt, and Tarp, Chapter 9, this volume, for a detailed discussion on poverty measurement and inequality in Tanzania.)

During this period, paved roads increased by 17,700 km. There was a major investment of 11,000 km in the fibre-optic network, which also connects six landlocked neighbouring countries to the undersea global cable network. Data suggest that the number of Internet users has increased steadily from about 1.1 user per 100 people to 4.9 per 100 between 2005 and 2014, while mobile cellular subscriptions have increased from 7.6 subscribers per 100 people to 62.8 per 100 people over the same period.

What is perhaps most striking is that supporting the use of the mobile money platform has helped reduce financial exclusion by more than half within four years. It has also made Tanzania a clear leader in the competitive operation of this platform and interoperability among the multiple providers, helping to reduce cost substantially. By the end of 2014 nearly 60 per cent of all adult Tanzanians were active users of mobile money services for payments, savings, and accessing credit, up from less than 4 per cent in 2009.

The adoption of BRN has helped to speed up the achievement of phenomenal results during the three-year period, 2013–15. These achievements have actually largely been brought about via improvement in organizational efficiency supplemented by well-targeted investments to address identified critical performance constraints. Most noteworthy to point out in infrastructural terms are (i) the transport sector with a reduced shipping turnaround time at port from 7 to 2.5 days; the average time for trucks from gate-in to gate-out at port reduced from 8 hours to 2.4 hours; increased average availability of rail wagons from 48 per cent to 80 per cent; and reduced transit traffic days from 14 to 2 days; (ii) increased rural access to water from an annual average of 300,000–500,000 rural dwellers to 2,360,000 dwellers; and (iii) increased rural access to electricity is estimated to have risen from 14.55 per cent to 46 per cent in 2015. (See also Kunaka et al., Chapter 5, this volume, for a more in-depth discussion.)

However, despite the progress, the infrastructure gap remains a major challenge. A survey by Afrobarometer (2015) of the five most pertinent problems facing Africans suggests that the top two most common issues that Tanzanian respondents highlighted were health and education (Table 2.1). In many SSA countries, the most cited problem is unemployment.

2.2.5 *Drawing Key Lessons from Looking Back*

Three features stand out with regard to Tanzania's development experience. Successive regimes are associated with (i) greater stability of the institutional and policy framework; (ii) higher economic growth and human capital indicators; and (iii) a more benign external environment. These features are derived partly from the fact that the nation has been on a learning curve, with successive regimes drawing lessons from the previous regime and thus able to address the challenges experienced earlier. This political stance of continuity with change provides substantial lessons for Tanzania as it develops its growth model, specifically: (i) the need to ensure local policy ownership and stability of the institutional framework; (ii) the importance of market forces; (iii) the importance of investment in infrastructure and human capital in stimulating economic growth; and (iv) the need to increase resilience to external shocks. In Sections 2.2.5.1–3 are three key lessons gained from the growth periods in Tanzania's history.

2.2.5.1 LESSON 1: GREATER STABILITY OF THE INSTITUTIONAL FRAMEWORK IN RECENT REGIME CHANGES

Tanzania's sitting head of state has tended to play a decisive role in the country's development objectives and there have been large swings in policy and institutional framework, particularly between the Nyerere and Mwinyi regimes (with the break from 'hard control' to 'laissez-faire' policies). Indeed, despite Nyerere's 'self-correction speech', the moves from hard control were minute and were only able to progress further with a change in leadership. Subsequent moves, particularly from the Mkapa to the Kikwete regime, have been marked with greater continuity in government policies. This could suggest reduced sensitivity to the political regime but could also be a mirror of external discourse on development, which has been broadly stable throughout the period.

While policy makers should be open to changes particularly where the development paradigm has been unsuccessful (either from the country's own experience or from cross-country experience) it is important to ensure that the changes are not constrained by the leadership or overly influenced by external discourse. Indeed, with the resurgence of interest in development theories, in part reflecting the global financial crisis and China's economic rise), this challenge is even more pressing. One could argue that the downward rigidity in Africa's risk premium, despite improvement in macroeconomic performance in many countries, could be linked to investor concerns about changes in attitudes towards the underlying development paradigm (for example with the election of new political leadership). More explicit ownership of policies at the Tanzanian institutional level, combined with improved transparency in the policy setting, could help instil greater confidence in the stability of the institutional framework and political autonomy.

2.2.5.2 LESSON 2: BROADLY BETTER ECONOMIC GROWTH AND SOCIAL INDICATORS IN MORE REGIMES

Tanzania's economic performance has improved with each subsequent political regime, with the more recent actors achieving the highest growth rate. Real GDP growth has increased from an average of about 3.6 per cent during the Nyerere era to about 6.5 per cent during the Kikwete period (Figure 2.4). This is broadly consistent with the production data which suggests that the Kikwete regime was characterized by the highest overall GDP growth as well as the fastest increase in both food and non-food production indicators.[19] Similarly, real per capita income growth has increased steadily from a mere 0.5 per cent during the Nyerere era to nearly 4 per cent under Kikwete. In contrast with the end of the Nyerere and Mwinyi eras, at the end of Mkapa's regime, Tanzania's GDP per capita exceeded the average for low-income countries.[20] This progress has been maintained during the Kikwete regime. However, despite these improvements, Tanzania's GDP per capita remains far lower than the average in SSA, suggesting the need to raise growth at a faster pace.

Social indicators point to more mixed evidence but suggest sharp improvements in recent regimes. Indicators of primary education suggest that the Mkapa era had sharp improvements in both health and education sectors, and at a much faster pace than previous surges. For example, the under-five mortality rate declined by about 44 per cent between 1995 and 2005 compared to 30 per cent and 10 per cent in the Nyerere and Mwinyi era, respectively. Energy use per capita also declined sharply in the earlier regimes, particularly during the Nyerere era, and this trend was reversed during the Mkapa regime and increased very substantially under Kikwete.

Analysis of inequality is constrained by a lack of reliable data, in part due to limited surveys, but points to a worsening in inequality during the Nyerere era and a broadly unchanged performance since the 1990s. Estimates by the World Bank of the Gini coefficient for Tanzania suggest that it has remained unchanged according to recent surveys, rising from 34 per cent in 1992 to 35 per cent in 2000 and stabilizing at about 38 per cent since then. The income share of the bottom 20 per cent has also remained broadly unchanged, hovering between 6.8 and 7.4 per cent between 1990 and 2012. Though Nyerere alluded to a decline in income inequality, analyses by Bevan et al. (1988), in which they compared household budget surveys from 1969, 1976/7, 1978–80, and 1982/3, find a sharp decline in rural living standards, which they attribute to a decline in cash income from farm sources. Specifically, the authors find that real per capita rural incomes fell by 5 per cent between 1976/7 and 1982/3 with subsistence farming taking the place of cash production and non-farm earned income replacing wage earnings.

2.2.5.3 LESSON 3: OUTTURNS ARE GREATLY INFLUENCED BY EXTERNAL DEVELOPMENTS

The external trade environment that Tanzania has faced has worsened with each subsequent regime but the growth outturns during the Mkapa and Kikwete regimes have been more resilient to these developments. While the commodity price index (in current terms) indicates that Tanzania has experienced an improvement in its agricultural commodity prices since the Mkapa regime, suggesting a somewhat more benign environment in recent years, this is not the case once one accounts for cost of living. In real terms, agricultural commodity prices have declined steadily since their peak in the 1970s (Figure 2.1). Moreover, the increase in oil prices (in both real and current terms) has been at a much faster pace, suggesting that Tanzania was paying more for imports than what it was receiving for exports. This is confirmed by an analysis of the terms of trade which points to a sharp reduction in terms of trade in real terms in each subsequent regime, and that the trade environment facing the Mkapa and Kikwete regimes was far less benign than earlier regimes.

Similarly, an analysis of global economic growth suggests that the Tanzanian economy has been heavily influenced by the global economy, with the country's downturns generally coinciding with periods of global shocks. While domestic factors were important, there is strong co-movement between global economic growth and the country's economic performance, for example the global downturn in the 1970s coincided with that in Tanzania (Figures 2.1 and 2.3). Nonetheless, the previous regime has been successful in maintaining growth despite the global financial crisis and ensuing recession, although more recently the slowdown in and rebalancing of the Chinese economy is also affecting commodity prices and the appetite for Tanzanian (and other African countries') raw materials.

However, it is also important to note the major changes that have occurred in the global economic landscape that may have reduced Tanzania's vulnerability to external shocks and increased access to finance. First is the increasing importance of emerging markets in the global economy and trade particularly from the early 2000s. Figure 2.3 shows a decline in the co-movement between global and advanced economies' output growth and an increase in the share of Tanzania's exports to emerging and developing Asia. In addition, there is excess liquidity in the global markets which has contributed to a surge for yields and increased investor appetite for new frontiers, and also a surge in financing from emerging market creditors (including China). This has contributed to a surge in access to international capital markets and a reduction in the cost of borrowing. Domestic factors have also played a role (for example, the low debt has reduced the risk of debt distress). However, the data suggest that poorer countries face higher vulnerability to an increase in the cost of financing and their ability to issue bonds during a period of market tension.

Aid flows have declined substantially in real terms. Net bilateral flows of aid from the Organisation for Economic Co-operation and Development Development Assistance Committee (OECD-DAC) to Tanzania have increased sharply since the 1960s but this finding is reversed once control for increase in the global cost of living is applied. The net bilateral aid flows that Tanzania has received have increased over time both as a share of that provided to SSA countries (excluding developing countries) and also of total global aid flows, but there is some volatility with big increases (particularly relative to other SSA countries) in the late 1970s and also in the late 1990s. In addition, the OECD country programmable aid (CPA) surveys suggest that the aid flows into Tanzania will remain far lower than in 2005, notwithstanding a slight increase in 2018.

From a policy perspective, the role that Tanzania's improved policy buffers play (including reserves and low debt) has helped the economy respond to these shocks, and points to the need to maintain macroeconomic stability. Tanzania will need to bolster its reserves to ensure that it can withstand big shocks without requiring a sharp contraction in domestic consumption and investment. In addition, it will need to manage its ongoing investment scale-up well to ensure the debt pick-up does not adversely affect debt sustainability, thereby hindering the country's ability to access international capital markets in the face of a shock or increasing vulnerability to capital flight during shock episodes. Continued efforts to diversify the economy (both source markets and products) as well as to enhance the resilience to weather changes (including the improvement of irrigation techniques) would also help.

2.3 Looking Forward

This section first presents the factors underpinning Tanzania's growth, providing, in particular, an assessment of opportunities and the growth drivers, the relative strength in Tanzania's factors of production, and the gaps that Tanzania needs to address in order to move to a new steady state. It then lays out a roadmap for moving Tanzania to a middle-high-income economy.

2.3.1 Opportunities for Prosperity

2.3.1.1 SUSTAINED PEACE

Tanzania stands out amongst many African countries, including its neighbours, for its sustained peace since independence. In contrast, most of its neighbours have experienced episodes of civil war and/or ethnic tension. Tanzania has a heterogeneous population with over 126 tribes and two dominant religious beliefs (Christian and Muslim), and is ethnically very diverse. The ethnic fractionalization index, which measures the likelihood that two people chosen at random will be from different ethnic groups, tends to support this view. Various studies suggest values for Tanzania far above 0.15, signifying high ethnic diversity. The index value ranges from that of 0.53 estimated by Posner (2004) to 0.95 proposed by Fearon (2003). This implies that Tanzania is home to many ethnic groups, each comprising a small percentage of the population (Green, 2011; Ndulu and Mbowe, 2013).

Notwithstanding this diversity, the country has, for the most part, had a fairly stable history with strong social cohesion founded on a common national language and tolerance. The socio-political stability could be an important driver of growth, particularly in fostering the growth of Tanzania's nascent tourism sector which is very sensitive to any signs of civil unrest and insecurity. In addition, there is scope for Tanzania to highlight this endowment and encourage capital inflows by reducing perceptions about the political risk of investing and operating business in Tanzania. Moreover, evidence from developing countries point to a large decline in per capita income during episodes of war (e.g., Bosnia Herzegovina, Côte d'Ivoire, and Mozambique), suggesting that the opportunity costs in terms of 'lost decades of growth' in the face of prolonged instability could be substantial.

2.3.1.2 GEOGRAPHIC LOCATION

Tanzania's geographic location makes it a coastal gateway to the landlocked countries of the Great Lakes Region. Tanzania shares boundaries with six landlocked countries which use it as an important conduit, generating external trade for the country with foreign exchange from transport and logistical services and through re-exports. Dar es Salaam's port currently presents the shortest distance to these countries without crossing into another country. It also presents an opportunity for attracting investors to relocate from Asia and establish hubs for producing and supplying goods to the region. With appropriate investment and policies, Tanzania can take advantage of these growth opportunities in transit and logistical services. To the extent to which Tanzania can position itself to attract labour-intensive industries to relocate from Asia to serve the regional market, or to serve as a location for major warehouses for trade from Asia in the coastal areas, it can promote industrialization and growth of services in trade. Indeed the country's rich agricultural potential and large labour and natural resources provide useful inputs which, when coupled with its coastal location, could be important drivers for attracting companies to relocate to Tanzania.

2.3.1.3 NATURAL RESOURCE ENDOWMENT, INCLUDING LAND, MINERALS, AND WILDLIFE

Tanzania has a strong comparative advantage in natural resources, including arable land and water for irrigation; forest reserves and wildlife; a wide range of ornamental and industrial minerals; and a large potential for energy production. Some of the discoveries are at an early stage but the potential is huge. What these endowments offer for economic transformation is resource-based industrialization, that is, food manufacture and agroprocessing, and services linked to tourism to take advantage of its natural attractions.

The tourism sector has flourished in Tanzania, with an average growth rate of 12 per cent between 2000 and 2012 (World Bank, 2015b). A World Bank (2015b) report cites key industry players projecting Tanzania's potential at as many as 8 million tourist arrivals (eight times the current level) by 2025 with estimated annual foreign exchange earnings of $16 billion. The report identifies two key strategies to realize this potential: (i) encouraging an increase in the number of visitors and earnings, and (ii) the expansion of tourism activities towards the south of the country. The achievement of both would require innovative marketing; new investment in infrastructure to improve accessibility and reduce the cost of access; and the reliable provision of power, key to providing improved services to the tourists.

Besides ornamental minerals such as gold, diamonds, tanzanite, and a wide range of other gemstones which currently contribute the largest portion of earnings from Tanzania's mineral wealth, Tanzania is home to a number of industrial minerals. These include iron and coal, nickel, uranium, phosphates, soda ash, and natural gas deposits. This mineral wealth not only provides a strong base for future export expansion but will also support natural resource-based industrialization. We will focus here on three minerals that have the greatest potential for supporting the country's economic transformation.

- Coal and iron: The Liganga area is rich in iron, vanadium, and titanium minerals, with reserves estimated to be between 200 and 1200 million metric tons. Some 45 million metric tons have already been mined. Coal reserves in Mchuchuma are estimated to be more than 480 million tons. Discussions are at an advanced stage to exploit this reserve to produce steel and for use in power generation.

- Soda ash: The Engaruka basin, located 190 km northwest of Arusha, is endowed with huge underground deposits of soda ash, raising Tanzania's profile as one of the most sodium carbonate rich countries in the world. The Engaruka basin has an estimated 4.68 billion cubic metres of brine, with an annual replenishment rate of 1.9 million cubic metres. As a result, Tanzania has mandated the National Development Corporation (NDC) to fast-track the use of this resource in order to create a base for the development of chemical industries in the country. Engaruka basin soda ash is estimated to have the potential to bring nearly $300 million in revenue per year in to Tanzania's economy. Soda ash is an essential ingredient used in the manufacturing of all kinds of glass, the production of detergents and industrial chemicals for water treatment, and in the paper industries and petroleum refining.

- Natural gas: Although Tanzania has been producing small quantities of gas from onshore and near-shore locations mainly for power generation, large quantities have been found more recently offshore. Offshore natural gas explorations were undertaken in Tanzania with very positive results—8 out of 13 wells drilled were successful. The current proven reserves amount to about 55.8 trillion cubic feet (TCF). Although actual gas reserves are still uncertain as exploration and appraisal is ongoing; usually, recoverable reserves do not exceed 70 per cent of the gas initially in place (GIIP) which would lead to an estimate of about 39 trillion cubic feet. Investment for exploitation is expected to begin by 2017 and gas exports by 2023. Given the uncertainty about the likely path of gas prices in global markets, there is considerable uncertainty about the potential macroeconomic consequences of these offshore gas discoveries. What is certain, however, is that both during the construction phase and for the duration of the resource, economic output, private incomes, and, importantly, government revenues will be significantly increased. Henstridge and Rweyemamu (Chapter 3, this volume) provide a detailed discussion of these numbers. What is clear from their analysis is that while the development of offshore Indian Ocean natural gas is unlikely to be transformative for the Tanzanian economy, realizing these resources offers the country a unique opportunity to pursue its broader economic policy agenda.

2.3.1.4 DEMOGRAPHICS

Abundant and youthful labour is another opportunity the country can exploit when put against the background of an ageing population in developed and a number of emerging economies. Labour costs in Asia have been increasing, providing an opportunity which Tanzania could exploit with appropriate policies to enhance the business environment.

2.3.2 *Underpinnings of Growth: Strengths and Key Challenges*

Tanzania's growth process has been driven by an increase in capital stock and also a more recent surge in productivity but anecdotal evidence suggests that innovation has been low, contributing to the low value added. This next section examines the drivers of Tanzania's growth and the challenges.

2.3.2.1 HUMAN CAPITAL STOCK

The health-care and primary education levels of the average Tanzanian are far higher than for the populations of many other African countries, but it has a far lower rank in higher education and training than most countries (with the exception mostly of fragile and-post conflict states).[21]

- On the positive side, this, coupled with the large and cohesive labour force, suggests some strength in moving to labour-intensive low-skill production (including by importing technologies to support a quick catch-up). This could include moving to simple agroprocessing and low-value construction and intensifying tourism services. Indeed, the strong cohesive society suggests scope to expand the tourism sector. Surveys from Afrobarometer provide strong evidence of social inclusion in Tanzania, notably respondents reported very low concerns about ethnic discrimination and had the highest percentage of people who viewed themselves as having a national identity first, before identifying with their ethnic group.[22]

- However, despite rapid growth, unemployment remains high and there are skills mismatches that contribute to difficulties in moving up the value chain, including to relatively low-skill processing. Both the international and local business community cite the scarcity of skilled labour as a primary concern. An important challenge is the shortage in the labour force of those who speak an international language (notably, English) which hinders communication (for example, in the tourism sector). This also raises questions about the inclusiveness of the growth process.

- The skills shortage is a big challenge if the economy is to transition to higher value-added production, including applying imported technologies.

Tanzania's universities produce fewer graduates than those in neighbouring countries, suggesting that an increase in both quality and quantity of education is needed. The very rapid recent growth of both secondary and tertiary education points to a catch-up at both education levels (see also Haji and Morisset, Chapter 8, this volume).

2.3.2.2 PHYSICAL CAPITAL STOCK

Tanzania's competitiveness ranking for its infrastructure is also far lower than that of many other African countries, despite the surge in capital stock, but recent investments in targeted areas such as roads and information technology have yielded positive results. Tanzania scores somewhat unfavourably in its infrastructure competitiveness according to 2011 data from the Global Competitiveness Index, which may not reflect the effect of recent investment (due to the lack of more recent data), and 2011 data on electricity consumption per capita would support this.[23] The cost of transportation is high and the country on average has scoring that points to much difficulty in trading across borders than is the case in Kenya or South Africa (based on data from the 2015 World Bank Doing Business Report). Again, as pointed out in section 2.2.4.2, recent initiatives under BRN are showing very rapid results in these areas and also in port efficiency. Indeed, the World Bank's Doing Business Report (2015) notes that 'Tanzania invested in port infrastructure. New cranes, a conveyor belt and anchorage tankers at the port of Dar es Salaam helped reduce berthing and unloading time as well as congestion. The reduction in the time required for port and terminal handling activities benefits not only traders in Tanzania but also those in the landlocked economies of Burundi and Rwanda that use the port.'

Moving to higher value-added production will entail the use of basic infrastructure (most importantly, electricity and transportation). Indeed, low-knowledge intensive sectors (such as milk processing and storage and the flower/horticulture industry) have been constrained by frequent power outage and poor transportation network. The discovery of natural gas provides scope to improve and help to launch new energy-intensive sectors.

The increase in gross capital formation has been largely financed through aid flows, raising questions about how to finance Tanzania's growth process going forward. An important challenge will be how to sustainably finance the investment programme and how to choose infrastructure projects. Aid has been an important source of financing and has some times been equivalent to nearly two-thirds of the gross capital formation. With Tanzania's improved debt-sustainability position and low-interest environment, the scope to borrow from international capital markets has increased. It will be important for the country to choose carefully projects that have sufficient return and that enhance the supply side, without adversely affecting the debt position over the long run. A focus on providing basic infrastructure coupled with private–public partnerships would be helpful.

2.3.2.3 PRODUCTIVITY

Tanzania's total factor productivity (TFP) in constant national prices remained broadly flat during the first regime but increased particularly during the Mwinyi and Mkapa regimes. However, trends during the Nyerere era can be separated into two main strands: there was a sharp increase from 1961 until about 1970, but thereafter it declined steadily with a dip around 1983. A turnaround occurred during the Mwinyi regime and TFP growth picked up sharply during the Mkapa regime—by about 27 per cent in 2005 compared to 1985, broadly similar to China's pickup during the same period. However, the first two regimes were lost years: while TFP grew by about 5 and 8 per cent, respectively, between 1961 and 1985 and 1985 and 1995, that for China grew by about 45 and 54 per cent, respectively. Though Tanzania is among the African countries that experienced the largest increase in TFP growth in constant national prices, this was much lower than the typical Asian economy.

Overall, this suggests that for Tanzania to move to a baseline scenario that would take it to a middle-high-income economy, it needs to take measures to increase its productivity substantially. The data suggest that the collapse in economic activity in the Nyerere era may have had large lingering effects on the ensuing regime. There was a large collapse in economic activity during the *ujamaa* period, which was also characterized by a large decline in investment and capital stock, particularly from the 1980s onwards. Disinvestment in areas such as agricultural machinery likely contributed to a reversal in some of the gains in agricultural productivity and the more limited growth rebound in the Mwinyi era. Beginning in the Mkapa era, there has been a strong and sustained pick-up in investment, mainly in the private sector.

2.3.2.4 INCLUSIVE GROWTH

One important challenge that remains is how to facilitate a growth process that is inclusive against the challenge of a relatively sparsely distributed population and a still very high proportion of the population dependent on the low value-added sector, that is, agriculture.

Though Tanzania's population density has increased (reaching 52.2 people per km^2 in 2011) and is much higher than the SSA average (36.6 people per km^2), it is much lower than that in neighbouring Kenya and Uganda at 73.1 and 172.7 people per km^2, respectively. This increases the cost of provision of various services and available avenues to recuperate costs from infrastructure investments.

Though the value added from agriculture has declined over time as new sectors have emerged, including communications and mining, the share of the population engaged in agriculture has remained relatively high. Tanzania remains largely dependent on agriculture, which currently accounts for only about 25 per cent of real GDP but is the main source of livelihood for about 70 per cent of the population. To shift Tanzania to a higher income level, the economy would need to generate much higher value added by moving up the value chain in agriculture (for example, to agroprocessing) and/or diversifying to other sectors (including manufacturing and mining).

2.4 Managing Challenges from Natural Resource Exploitation and Sustainable Financing of Development

Tanzania's recently found natural-resource wealth could create additional benefits but also challenges as has been seen in many countries. Indeed, the push for productivity-based growth may weaken due to large potential rents from commodity exports. In addition, the government may find it easy to 'pay off' its population with transfers instead of focusing on employment. Indeed, though unemployment in Tanzania has remained high, survey analysis from the 2014/15 Afrobarometer Survey suggests that it is not the most important problem. Many resource-rich countries are faced with the challenge of Dutch disease—the increase in the economic development of a specific sector (for example natural resources) and a decline in other sectors (like the manufacturing sector or agriculture).

The availability of financing coupled with the ambitious investment plans could lead to issues pertaining to how to maintain the investment and avoid the recurrent cost problem, which dogged Tanzania in the 1980s, leading to a rapid and deep deterioration of the infrastructure that had been built in the 1970s. Also, there are questions about a possible problem of a currency mismatch arising from the fact that the ambitious infrastructure investment funded through foreign loans generates local currency revenue streams, while servicing of this debt will have to be in foreign currency. Roads, power, and communications services—all largely non-tradable services—generate local currency revenue streams. Liquidity rather than solvency constraints in servicing such debt will be more binding unless export growth significantly exceeds GDP growth. This is particularly important given the risks of the rising cost of capital and a further decline in commodity prices.

Two policy recommendations emerge. First, the importance of ensuring that not only is investment used in a productivity-enhancing manner by expanding the supply capacity of the economy, but also enables the growth of foreign exchange (e.g., exports) and generates a current-account surplus in order to service the interest, repay the maturing foreign debt, and maintain the infrastructure. Second, the nature of the financing (both the maturity and the currency) is also important. If higher investment stimulates a consumption (or broad-based domestic-driven) demand process, it would be important to ensure that the financing is in the local currency, as the country would not be able to generate sufficient foreign exchange to finance foreign sources and would face a currency mismatch. Similarly, if the investments are expected to have a long gestation period and the benefits would accrue over a longer period of time, it is important to ensure that the financing is longer term such that the repayments could be made when the country has reaped some of the benefits from the investment.

There are various approaches that could be taken to achieve this, including a bottom-up approach or a top-down approach. The latter has gained some traction recently including in the new structuralism work (e.g., Lin and Wang, 2014 and Stiglitz et al., 2013) which underscores the role of the government in identifying sectors and creating winners. This approach is a more focused approach of the policies implemented in the first political regime, albeit with a more targeted approach in picking a few select sectors (preferably existing sectors) and expanding through backward and forward linkages to other sectors over time. However, given the limited human capital, lower development, and the potential for rent-seeking, we would advise against the state picking winners. Instead we would encourage a bottom-up approach that relies heavily on the market in picking winners, with the state providing institutions to support technology transfer and to correct for externalities and market failures. At the same time the government should pursue in earnest an investment strategy to build capacity for prudent public investment, an unavoidable large component in infrastructure investment.

2.5 Moving to a Middle-High-Income Economy

This section describes strategy focused on moving Tanzania to a middle-high-income economy through an inclusive growth process. It proposes a framework for achieving Tanzania's growth objectives, highlights the challenges to be overcome, and lays out key strategic elements.

Tanzania will require significant structural transformation in order to sustain the current levels of economic growth and address the problems of mass unemployment and concerns about the inclusiveness of growth. This will entail a shift in current economic activity to a new structure and will require a clear roadmap of optimal policy choices. Given the productivity differentials between Tanzania and its trading partners such as China, India, and Malaysia, it is unlikely that Tanzania will succeed in pursuing the economic transformation agenda through an 'East Asian mass manufacturing for export' model alone. Rather, Tanzania must seek to build a broader range of high value-added-per-worker activities to complement the recovering manufac-. turing sector and to utilize its natural resource base. Strategy should focus on three key areas.

First, increase value added from agriculture. Focusing on this sector is important since it is the economic mainstay of the population. With nearly 70 per cent of the labour force identifying itself as employed in the agricultural sector, this suggests that the potential impact on poverty would be high. Policy intervention in agriculture and agroprocessing should focus on improving factor productivity; capital accumulation, particularly in transportation and irrigation infrastructure to enhance growth; resilience to climatic shocks; and increasing access to markets. Specifically:

- Disseminate new agricultural techniques and invest in research and development to support a move to more modern and efficient production and storage techniques.

- Improve incentives for increased production including improving rural infrastructure to increase physical access to domestic, regional, and international markets. This will entail an aggregative strategy to develop an efficient transportation network, linking rail, air, and port network systems, as well as the logistical capacity for linking the various components of the value chain.

- Establish a viable agroprocessing industry in order to bolster the returns from agriculture and support entrance to regional and global value chains. This will entail an education policy that bolsters human capital, and also an agricultural policy initiative that supports a move up the value chain, including through enhancing linkages with the domestic economy (e.g., the tourism sector).

- Improve Tanzania's access to global markets, particularly moving up the value chain. Continued engagement at the government level to these food markets is key.

Second, utilize natural resources to stimulate heavy industrialization and labour-intensive manufacturing to transform the economic structure of Tanzania from lower to higher productivity and value added. While many developing countries have been plagued by resource curse issues, where natural resources are associated with a surge in rent-seeking, a collapse in other sectoral activities, and at worst civil instability, several countries have been able to use natural resources to provide a base to kick-start their industrialization. Having a clear strategy for the use of the natural resource 'windfalls', ensuring that relative wages and cost of business remain competitive, and that governance and the business environment remains supportive (including fostering an efficient business registration process and reducing red tape involved in business operations) is central to economic transformation.

43

Third, where geography and other endowments provide a comparative advantage, efforts should also be directed towards promoting industries without smokestacks and services in order to maximize potential economic growth. Bolstering the services sector would help ensure that the economy remains diversified and would maximize linkages in the economy. In this regard, additional efforts must be made to increase the value added from tourism and foster ICT-based services. Central to the development of an ICT-based sector is having sound infrastructure, particularly knowledge-based capital. In addition, access to finance to support this sector will remain important. Given the risks involved (high-risk high-potential return) greater attention could be provided to deepen financial instruments in order to support financing this sector. Given the lower capital cost of start-up, this sector will likely be dominated by small–medium enterprises (SMEs). In countries such as Germany whose industrial base is made up largely of SMEs, asset securitization provides a funding alternative to the traditional channels of external finance captive to a bank-based financial system. Improvements in the legal and regulatory environment to support property rights could also help to enhance development of this sector. Given that Tanzania also has a growing tourism sector whose potential has yet to be maximized, it is important to ensure careful coordination and planning so that any shift to heavy industry does not adversely affect this sector. Brazil and Australia could provide useful lessons on how to transition and move up the value chain without hampering the tourism sector.

Finally, infrastructure and human capital investment feature heavily in the growth strategy. To maximize the growth impact, infrastructure development could be supported by a comprehensive policy mix to reinforce the backward and forward linkages of infrastructure investments in the economy. However, the financial costs entailed would be large and would exceed current official development assistance, which would require a strategy to unlock additional sources of financing. Domestic revenue mobilization coupled with innovative sources of external financing to leverage potential funds that Tanzania could obtain from official sources, and borrowing from capital markets, could help. A careful strategy that balances the benefits from increased liabilities (and the associated debt-sustainability implications) with expected returns is important. In this regard, greater use of debt-sustainability analysis to manage macroeconomic risks is absolutely necessary.

Authors' Notes

The views expressed herein are those of the authors and should not be attributed to the IMF, its Executive Directors, or its management.

Notes

1. The United Republic of Tanganyika gained independence in 1961 and, in 1964, it united with Zanzibar to become the United Republic of Tanzania. The analysis focuses on the United Republic of Tanzania.
2. This includes Africa's deepest lake (Lake Tanganyika) and largest lake (Lake Victoria), both of which have very diverse fish environments. It is also home to part of Lake Nyasa—third largest and second deepest lake in Africa. Lakes Victoria and Nyasa are also the world's third and ninth largest lakes, respectively.
3. The highest mountain in Africa (Mount Kilimanjaro) and various islands are located off the coast of Tanzania.
4. In anticipation of the independence of Tanganyika, Kenya, and Uganda, the British Government convened a conference of political leaders and officials of the three countries as well as the EAHC in 1961 in London and agreement was reached to continue to provide common services on an East African basis. The EACSO was thus created to replace the High Commission. In addition, the EAC was reconstituted and its headquarters was moved from London to Kenya.
5. ' "Ujamaa" ... describes our Socialism. It is opposed to Capitalism, which seeks to build a happy society on the basis of the Exploitation of Man by Man; and it is equally opposed to doctrinaire Socialism which seeks to build its happy society on a philosophy of Inevitable Conflict between Man and Man' Nyerere (1962).
6. This involved creating development villages ('vijiji vya maendeleo') to support collective production 'villagization'. See Edwards (2012), Jerven (2014), Mwase and Hyden (1976) and Nyerere (1977).
7. In his landmark 1981 speech, dubbed 'Tujisahihishe' ('self-correction'), Nyerere set the stage for this review. A number of home-grown programmes were launched such as the National Economic Survival Programme (1980–1) and Tanzania's own Structural Adjustment Programme (SAP) (1982–5).
8. See Kaufmann and O'Connell (1999) for a discussion.
9. The Tanzania–Zambia railway (TAZARA) is one of China's largest foreign-aid projects. It was financed through an interest-free loan of US$ 500 million and was built between 1970 and 1976.
10. Armstrong (1977) notes that one of the key tendencies that China sought to encourage was the pursuit of self-reliance. Tanzania was the second largest non-communist recipient of Chinese economic aid. The main recipients of Chinese aid [up to] 1970 were: Pakistan ($309 million), Tanzania ($256 million), Zambia ($217 million), Indonesia ($122 million), and Cambodia ($92 million). Armstrong cites the source of his data as 'China's Aid to the Third World' (British Foreign Office, May 1972).
11. Two of the staunchest Nordic supporters of the government decided to withhold their financial support in 1984–5 partly due to voters' concerns about aid wastage and that their altruistic goals were not being attained. Sweden and the Netherlands too reduced their support from 1981 to 1982 (Adam et al., 1994; Edwards, 2014).
12. Detailed analysis is constrained by the lack of data, as very few household surveys were conducted during the period 1961–85. Wangwe (1996) notes that 'the first large scale household budget survey (HBS) was carried out by the Bureau of

Statistics in 1969 followed by another in 1976/7. The smaller surveys were conducted in 1980 (ILO (Collier et al., 1986)) and in 1983 (see Bevan et al., 1988).

13. Socially, this period was characterized by a shift from 'collectivism' to new phrases such as 'bongo' and 'kujitegemea' ('self-reliance'), and a shift to a self-reliance centred on survival without state support (Perullo, 2011).

14. The reforms have been extensively discussed, including in Mwase and Ndulu (2008), Nord et al. (2009), and Robinson et al. (2011).

15. Median data are reported mainly due to the large outliers. Similarly for export analysis.

16. During the period 1986–95, the volume of imports of goods and services grew by an average (median) of 1.7 per cent while the price deflator increased by 2.6 per cent. As a result, the value of imports of goods and services increased by about 1.6 per cent. The volume of exports of goods and services increased by an average of 7.7 per cent in 1986–95 while the price deflator declined by 4.3 per cent in the same period. As a result, the value of exports of goods and services increased by about 1 per cent.

17. There was a turnaround in this pattern in 2005 with agriculture rising to 37 per cent and services declining to 37 per cent.

18. See Arndt, Leyaro, Mahrt, and Tarp, Chapter 9 in this volume, for a discussion on poverty measurement and inequality.

19. The agricultural sector accounted for a much larger share of GDP particularly in the earlier regime.

20. Based on the US$1.25 per day poverty line that was used by the World Bank.

21. This analysis is based on the Global Competitiveness Report (ranking in 'Health and Primary education' (4th pillar)) and 'Higher Education and Training' (ranking in 5th pillar) 2011 data; the latest available.

22. This is based on the 2014/15 Afrobarometer survey asking 'Most important problems?'

23. All data are obtained from the World Bank database; the latest year availability is 2011.

References

Adam, C., Bigsten, A., Collier, P., Julin, E., and Connell, S. O. (1994). *Evaluation of Swedish Development Cooperation with Tanzania*. A report to the Secretariat for Analysis of Sweden Development Assistance. Stockholm: SIDA.

Afrobarometer (2015). Available at: <http://www.afrobarometer.org/> (accessed 16 August 2016).

Aghion, P. (2012). 'From Growth Theory to Growth Policy Design', LSE Growth Commission and Institute for Government.

Aghion, P., Akcigit, U., Bergeaud, A., Blundell, R., and Hémous, D. (2015). 'Innovation and Top Income Inequality', NBER Working Paper no. 21247.

Armstrong, J. D. (1977). *Revolutionary Diplomacy: Chinese Foreign Policy and the United Front Doctrine*. Berkeley, CA and London: University of California Press.

Baker, A. (1972). *Shaping the Developing World: The West, the South, and the Natural World*. Boulder, CO: University of Colorado at Boulder.

Barkan, J. (1994). *Beyond Capitalism vs Socialism in Kenya and Tanzania*. Boulder, CO and London: Lynne Rienner Publishers.

Bevan, D., Collier, P., and Gunning, J. W. (1988). 'Incomes in the United Republic of Tanzania during the Tanzania Experience'. In: van Ginneken, W. (ed.), *Trends in Employment and Income: Case Studies on Developing Countries*. Geneva: International Labor Organization.

Collier, P., Radwan, S., and Wangwe, S. (1986). *Labor and Poverty in Rural Tanzania: Ujamaa and Rural Development in the United Republic of Tanzania*. Oxford: Clarendon Press.

Edwards, S. (2012). 'Is Tanzania a Success Story? A Long Term Analysis'. Cambridge, MA: NBER Working Paper 17764.

Edwards, S. (2014). *Toxic Aid: Economic Collapse and Recovery in Tanzania*. Oxford: Oxford University Press.

Fearon, J. D. (2003). 'Ethnic Structure and Cultural Diversity by Country', *Journal of Economic Growth* 8 (June): 195–222.

Green, E. (2011). 'The Political Economy of Nation Formation in Modern Tanzania Explaining Stability in the Face of Diversity', *Commonwealth and Comparative Politics* 49(2): 223–44.

Jerven, M. (2014). *Economic Growth and Measurement Reconsidered in Botswana, Kenya, Tanzania, 1965–1995*. Oxford: Oxford University Press.

Kaufmann, D. and O'Connell, S. A. (1999). 'The Macroeconomics of Delayed Exchange-Rate Unification: Theory and Evidence from Tanzania'. Washington, DC: Policy Research Working Paper Series 2060, World Bank.

Lin, J. F. and Wang, Y. (2014). 'China-Africa Co-operation in Structural Transformation: Ideas, Opportunities, and Finance', WIDER Working Paper, 2014/046. United Nations University, World Institute for Development Economics Research, Helsinki.

Muganda, A. (2004). 'Tanzania's Economic Reforms'. A case study from 'Reducing Growth: What Works, What Doesn't, and Why a Global Exchange for Scaling Up Success', prepared for 'Scaling Up Poverty Reduction: A Global Learning Process and Conference' Shanghai, 25–27 May. UNU-WIDER Helsinki, Finland.

Mwase, N. and Hyden, G. (1976). *Co-operatives in Tanzania: Problems of Organisation*. Dar-es-Salaam: Tanzania Publishing House.

Mwase, N. and Ndulu, B. (2008). 'Tanzania: Explaining Four Decades of Episodic Growth'. In: Ndulu, B., O'Connell, S., Azam, J. P., Bates, R., Fosu, A., Gunning, J. W., and Njinkeu, D. (eds), *The Political Economy of Economic Growth in Africa, 1960–2000*. Cambridge: Cambridge University Press: 426–70.

Ndulu, B. J. (2007). 'The Evolution of Global Development Paradigms and their Influence on African Economic Growth'. In: Ndulu, B. J., O'Connell, S. A., Bates, R. H., Collier, P., and Soludo, C. C. (eds), *The Political Economy of Economic Growth in Africa, 1960–2000*, vol. 1. Cambridge: Cambridge University Press: 315–47.

Ndulu, B. J. and Mbowe, W. E. (2013). 'Ethnic Diversity, National Building and Economic Performance: A Case of Tanzania', Contribution to the JICA Research Project on 'Ethnic Diversity and Economic Instability: Policies for Harmonious Development'. JICA-Research Institute, Japan.

Nord, R., Sobolev, Y., Dunn, D., Hijdenberg, A., Maziad, S., and Roudet, S. (2009). *Tanzania: The Story of African Transition*. Washington, D. C.: International Monetary Fund.

Nyerere, J. K. (1962). *Ujamaa: The Basis of African Socialism*. Dar es Salaam: Tanganyika Standard.

Nyerere, J. K. (1977). *The Arusha Declaration, Ten Years After*. Dar es Salaam: Government Printer.

Perullo, A. (2011). *Live from Dar es Salaam: Popular Music and Tanzania's Music Economy*. Bloomington: Indiana University Press.

Posner, D. N. (2004). 'Measuring Ethnic Fractionalization in Africa', *American Journal of Political Science* 48(3): 849–63.

Robinson, D., Gaertner, M., and Papageorgiou, C. (2011). 'Tanzania: Growth Acceleration and Increased Public Spending with Macroeconomic Stability'. In: *Yes Africa Can: Success Stories from a Dynamic Continent*. Washington, D.C.: World Bank: 21–50.

Rydenfelt, S. (1984). *A Pattern for Failure: Socialist Economies in Crisis*. New York: Harcourt Brace Jovanovich.

Stiglitz, J., Lin, J., Monga, C., and Patel, E. (2013). 'Industrial Policy in the African Context'. Washington, D.C.: Policy Research Working Paper 6633, World Bank.

Wangwe, S. (1996). 'Economic reforms and poverty alleviation in Tanzania'. Geneva: International Labor Organization.

World Bank (2015a). *Tanzania Mainland Poverty Assessment*. Washington, D.C.: World Bank Group.

World Bank (2015b). *Tanzania's Strong Economic Growth Shows Signs of Trickling Down*. Washington, D.C.: World Bank Group.

3

Managing Hydrocarbon Resources

Mark Henstridge and Dennis Rweyemamu

3.1 Introduction

Tanzania's natural wealth has increased with the discovery of large deposits of deep-water off-shore natural gas by two consortia led by private multinational companies.[1] Making something of that opportunity depends on how the investment in hydrocarbon projects takes place and on the macroeconomic management of a potential boom. The opportunity for faster growth and development also critically depends on the quality of public policy focused on the competitiveness and growth of the *non*-hydrocarbon economy ahead of investment in the production of gas. This chapter presents the scale of the gas finds in terms of the economic impact, outlines some of the factors that will shape how investment takes place, and outlines the key parameters for policy towards the competitiveness and efficiency of the non-hydrocarbon economy.

The high cost of development and production means that almost all of these reserves are very likely to be exported as liquified natural gas (LNG) to make gas production at scale commercially viable.[2] Even a small share of those export volumes going as a 'domestic market obligation' for sale in Tanzania is large relative to the current domestic market. In addition, there is a smaller collection of shallow-water and onshore natural gas deposits, which are in the process of being connected to an onshore pipeline to link them to the gas network, and gas-fired power generation, in Dar es Salaam.

The main focus of this chapter is on the policy that will shape the opportunities arising from large-scale offshore gas for LNG. To frame policy choices for managing hydrocarbons, we set out projections of the projects and their key economic impacts. There are two main impacts: the first comes during the investment in development, the second from the broader macroeconomic consequences for the balance of payments and the public finances once offshore gas is in production.

The array of policy implications is complex, and many of the specifics will be touched upon elsewhere in this volume. The first big economic impact is from investment. At the same time the quality of future policy to manage the revenue will be shaped by the quality of advance preparation. Careful decisions on how much new revenue to spend depends on whether the public sector will have already built the institutional capability to save and then spend well. In addition, the development of the legal, regulatory, and administrative framework within which hydrocarbon investment and production would take place—sometimes called the 'authorizing environment'—is a critical determinant of whether, how, and when investment in hydrocarbons happens. Overall, the management of hydrocarbons entails work in parallel areas.

Section 3.6 of this chapter reviews Tanzania's policy options. We argue that making, and then implementing, the policy decisions that will condition the broad impact of hydrocarbons will be successful not just in terms of the resulting scale and efficiency of the hydrocarbon sector, but principally in terms of the impact these policies have on the vibrancy, growth, and development of the *non*-resource economy of Tanzania.

3.2 The Economic Impact of Hydrocarbons

A new discovery of hydrocarbons increases natural assets and national wealth. But for hydrocarbons to have a positive impact on Tanzania's 'path to prosperity' they need to be transformed: from stock to flow; from sub-soil mineral to money; and from a state-owned asset to a flow of benefits to private citizens. As illustrated in Figure 3.1, this is a complex sequence, with a 'weakest link' problem. Each transformation has to work if a sub-soil hydrocarbon asset is to end up in a higher flow of private benefits; one failure compromises the opportunity.

There are also potentially significant benefits to the economy from externalities to some of the key transformations themselves. If the skills can be developed, there could be jobs during construction; if there are national firms with the capabilities to deliver to time, scale and quality, then there could be new business opportunities for Tanzanian firms in the gas industry supply chain. Both of these things depend on careful preparation and appropriate policy.

The macroeconomic impact from transforming a sub-soil mineral asset comes first from monetizing the mineral—often by exporting it—and then, second, from revenue for the government, treated in the accounts as a flow of receipts. The decisions that shape public saving and consumption choices, and the allocation of spending and any accumulation of public assets determine the impact on private living standards.

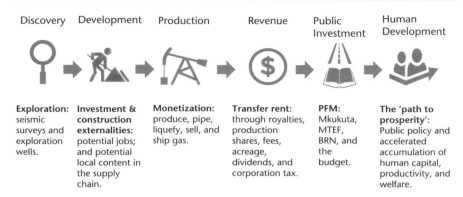

Figure 3.1. Asset transformation

Source: OPM (2013). DfID PEAKS Topic Guide: Extractive industries, development and the role of donors, September 2013.

These transformations and their externalities are complex, not only from a policy and an administrative perspective, but also from a political perspective. There are at least two political dimensions. First, there is already a problem of elevated expectations in Tanzania—including in Mtwara, which has been the onshore supply base for offshore exploration, where disorder has led to fatalities. The news of a massive hydrocarbon discovery can easily give people expectations of immediate personal wealth, regardless of how big the economic consequences might be, or when there might actually be some production. There has not been clear public communication on the possible scale of impact or the uncertainty surrounding when and how the projects might go ahead. Our projections (set out in Section 3.3) imply that production is at least a decade away, and will deliver government revenue in single digits of gross domestic product (GDP). Expectations that there will be an early and big impact are clearly going to be disappointed.

Second, increased in public revenue from hydrocarbons puts a point source of rent in the hands of government. Such rents have had a corrosive impact on the quality of public financial management and economic policymaking in other countries. But this is precisely the point when the very presence of those rents demands higher quality policy and financial management if the opportunity they present is to be seized.

3.3 A Potential Hydrocarbon Boom? If So: How Much? When?

The Ministry of Energy and Minerals (MEM) estimates total natural gas reserves at 55 trillion cubic feet (TCF).[3] These are significant volumes, though smaller than the 180 TCF reserves also recently discovered offshore Mozambique.[4] Tanzania therefore has material reserves of gas. In this section we set out when those reserves might be produced, and at what volumes.

Box 3.1. NATURAL GAS—TERMS AND UNITS

The natural gas industry uses a mix of units—for reserves, flows of gas at ambient temperature, and the mass of gas when slightly compressed and cooled in an 'LNG train' to –161°C. When it becomes liquid and can then be shipped in specially insulated LNG carriers to export markets.

The unit for reserves is conventionally 'trillion cubic feet' (TCF); for gas flows 'millions of standard cubic feet per day' ('mscuf/d'); while the units for LNG are usually millions of tonnes ('MMT').

In addition, gas is sometimes presented as 'barrels of oil equivalent' ('boe')—the equivalence is in terms of the energy, or calorific, content of the hydrocarbon. It provides a comparison between costs of processing and production of gas with those of oil.

Finally, the price of gas is usually expressed in terms of dollars per 'million British thermal units' ('mmbtu')—again a unit of energy or calorific content of gas.

For a set of conversion tables across the various units used in oil, coal, gas, and LNG, see the inside cover of the *BP Statistical Review of World Energy*, which is itself a useful source of global energy data: <www.bp.com/statisticalreview>.

3.3.1 *Scale: Gas in Tanzania*

Not all gas in Tanzania is the same. There are onshore or shallow-water fields, such as those at Songo Songo and Mnazi Bay, and there is a set of offshore deep water fields, such as those discovered by consortia led by BG Group and Statoil.

There are two main differences. First, they are different sizes: the deep-water offshore fields are bigger than the onshore or shallow water ones. The technically recoverable gas in Songo Songo is about 0.9 TCF; Mnazi Bay holds about 0.3 TCF.[5] Estimates vary for recoverable gas in deep-water offshore fields, but a significant part of the 55 TCF of reserves announced by the Ministry of Energy and Minerals are the deep-water offshore discoveries made since 2010. BG Group has confirmed reserves in their blocks of 15 TCF.[6] Statoil has confirmed reserves of 22 TCF.[7] Figure 3.2 maps the principal gas fields offshore Tanzania.

Another indication of scale can be provided by the volume of gas that goes through one LNG liquefaction plant, or 'train'. Most modern LNG trains process around 3–5 million tonnes (MMT) of LNG each year, which is equivalent to a flow of about 500–700 million standard cubic feet per day (mscuf/d). That is up to ten times the flow of gas into power production in Tanzania in

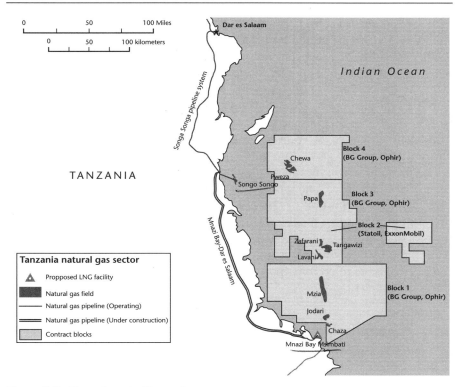

Figure 3.2. Natural gas in Tanzania
Source: US Energy Information Administration.

2013. The current expectation is that the discoveries so far reported could support at least two trains of LNG in a first phase with two more in a second phase. In the projections in this chapter we assume a volume of LNG production of 10 MMT per year from each of the two main offshore gas production projects, with the second phase of an LNG plant producing a total of 20 MMT for export.

The second difference relates to the first, and it is the time and costs involved in bringing each sort of gas field to production. Big deep-water fields take longer to bring to production once a 'Final Investment Decision' has been taken, and they cost more: between around two-thirds higher to double the cost. To give a rough comparison—again as a matter of an order of magnitude rather than precise estimates for anything specific in Tanzania—the 2013 estimated cost of bringing deep-water gas ashore was up to US$7/mmbtu (million British thermal units); gas from the shallow-water on the continental shelf costs about US$1–2/mmbtu less, with onshore gas costs up to about US $4/mmbtu.

As well as having lower unit costs, the time it takes to bring onshore or shallow-water gas to production is significantly shorter than deep-water gas, mainly reflecting the fact that the scale and engineering involved is easier— which is part of the reason why it is lower cost—and production is starting in 2015. Maurel et Prom and Wentworth started to deliver gas from Mnazi Bay into the new pipeline to Dar es Salaam in August 2015, and could produce up to 80 mscuf/d in 2015/16, and up to 130 mscuf/d in 2016/17. This gas is principally intended for power generation, under an agreement with the Tanzania Petroleum Development Corporation (TPDC).

The minimum volumes of shallow-water gas production needed to cover the initial capital investment over a reasonable period of time are also smaller. This idea of a minimum, or 'anchor', volume for production, below which investment would not make commercial sense, helps explain why large volumes of deep-water gas are needed for any production at all, and that given the scale of production volumes required to justify the investment, the majority of the gas will have to go for export where there is the demand for gas at world prices in sufficient volumes.

3.3.1.1 POTENTIAL DOMESTIC USE

As well as the increased supply of gas from Mnazi Bay there are 'domestic market obligations' included in the contracts for deep-water gas. That means that some minimum percentage of gas, probably between 5 and 10 per cent of production, could be sold into the domestic market, if required, at an agreed price. That may initially appear to be a low percentage of production for the domestic market, but the volumes of gas needed to make an LNG export project work commercially are so big, that 5 per cent of a medium-sized two-train LNG project would be roughly the equivalent of two-thirds of total current gas production, and broadly equivalent to all the gas currently used each year in power generation.

Increased production from the shallow-water, and onshore gas reserves will be both more immediate and lower cost when delivered to the domestic market than the gas delivered through the domestic market obligation for deep-water gas.

There is a range of potential uses for increased gas supply to Tanzania, including more gas into power generation. Just as not all gas reserves are created equal, not all domestic uses of gas are equal. It is the economics of the alternatives which mean that some uses are good supports for economic growth and human development, such as gas going into properly priced power generation, but others would likely destroy value or waste the investment such as, for example, a 'gas to liquids' plant in Tanzania. The key to identifying which uses add value for Tanzania is to examine the project economics, and to take care in using the price assumptions for valuing the costs and the benefits of alternative domestic uses of gas.

Perhaps the most straightforward gain to the domestic economy would come through reducing the cost of power generation. Until recently, Tanzania was producing up to 30 per cent of power from diesel generators, with imported fuel. Substituting a lower cost gas-fired power generation would be a potentially significant gain. In part, the gain would accrue to the public sector in reducing the losses previously accrued from the high costs of power generation not having been covered by the wholesale price of electricity. But beyond that, in principle, reliably delivered and consistently priced power would support growth. As noted in Section 3.3.1, the most immediate and lowest cost source of gas for power comes from the onshore and shallow water fields: Songo Songo and Mnazi Bay. To realize the potential support for growth requires a policy framework with the pricing structure that sustains investment in gas and power infrastructure and generating capacity.[8]

3.3.2 *Timing*

Although there are proven reserves of gas, it will be a long time before there is any production from the large offshore reserves. The combination of deep-water gas production projects and an LNG plant makes for a big and complex project, surrounded by a range of risks. If everything moved smoothly, without risk, then it would still take a long time to bring offshore gas reserves into production. Such a project goes through phases, illustrated in Figure 3.3, and Tanzania is now in the planning phase for developing discovered reserves. During planning, a final investment decision (FID) is taken. At that point a contractor may stop further work, or go ahead—with a range of possibilities on the phasing. The decision will depend on several considerations, including the risks the contractor faces, which we discuss in Section 3.5.1.

If the decision is taken to move ahead, then there is more work to be done, principally on design and engineering, before construction can start. This is all

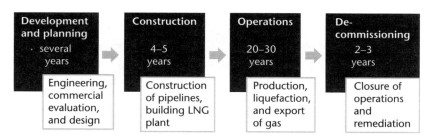

Figure 3.3. Timeline for risk-free LNG

part of the 'development' phase of the project. Construction encompasses both the sub-sea work to produce the gas and the initial processing facilities, pipelines, values, and other equipment to transport the gas to shore, as well as the LNG plant itself. Taken together it would take at least four to five years, if no risks materialized and the project ran smoothly. At this point, production would start, with an initial period when production ramps up, a plateau period with more or less constant volumes expected, and a final period of decline. In the projections we discuss in Section 3.4.1.1, we assume that the period of operations lasts thirty years. Once all the gas that can be produced commercially has been produced there is a phase of de-commissioning.

3.4 Project Impact

Most of the direct economic impacts of large-scale LNG production on jobs, skills, and potential local supply chains arrive earlier than the bigger, broader macroeconomic impact on government revenue. This is because they principally take place during construction—the phasing of the project and associated direct impacts are illustrated in Figure 3.8 (Section 3.5.3), which overlays the project timeline onto one of the key steps in asset transformation, which is bringing it above ground through production.

During the planning phase of these projects, the contractors and their subcontractors will have already created a few hundred jobs. By the end of 2014, Statoil estimated that around 600 Tanzanians had been employed directly, and indirectly through suppliers and vendors from their operations.[9] Table 3.1 shows the location of the near 1,000 jobs created by the BG-led consortium during exploration in 2012/13.

These jobs will also have had a modest induced impact through multiplier-type effects, as workers spend their higher incomes. There has also been a contribution to tax receipts, principally the income tax paid on employees' earnings. In addition, these companies have needed locally supplied inputs to

Table 3.1. Tanzanians employed in relation to Block 1, 3, and 4 during exploration, 2012–13

Location	Tanzanian employees
Dar-based staff	33
Dar-based contractors	355
Drilling rig (offshore)	72
Supply base (Mtwara)	500
Total:	960

Source: VSO (2014)

do their work: transport, housing, office space, and other office services. For example, the development of the port at Mtwara as a shore-base for off-shore exploration.

There is a potentially bigger employment impact during construction, when the project will need to hire thousands of people, mainly for construction of the LNG plant. Much of the work to fabricate and install the facilities for gas production will take place abroad, and is technically complex, requiring high levels of skill and experience. Similarly, the LNG facility itself will have much of the fabrication taking place in specialized fabrication-yards, such as in South Korea, and will likely be delivered to Tanzania in near-complete modules for assembly. But the site will still need preparation and construction work before the plant can be installed. The efficient lowest cost—engineering-style—solution would be to bring in expatriate labour with experience of building LNG plants in the Gulf. To increase the direct impact on Tanzanian jobs of these projects, a programme of skills development for nationals is needed, mainly in construction skills.

3.4.1 Macroeconomic Impact

Estimates of the scale and timing of production and the associated revenues can be made by modelling the cash flows surrounding each main production project and the project for building the LNG plant—but are very conditional on the risks and uncertainties set out in Section 3.5.1 In particular, gauging the scale of the macroeconomic impact critically depends on when it is assumed that production might start.[10]

The macroeconomic impact can be shown to be big: for example, the total capital expenditure expected during the life of an LNG project is comparable to total GDP in Tanzania in 2012. It can also be shown to be actually quite modest: annual revenue to government at peak will be a modest number of single digits of GDP and a few tens of dollars per person—material but not transformative. As we argue later in this section, the more immediate impact is the potential for jobs and business during the investment phase rather than the single-biggest macroeconomic impact of revenue during production.

This section sets out the projections of government revenues from the offshore LNG projects as the basis for calibrating direct and indirect economic impacts likely to arise—both in the sense of what happens first, and how big the impact might be.

3.4.1.1 PROJECTING CASH FLOWS
The starting point for such estimates is a set of assumptions about each project (see Annex A). These are part informed by publicly available

---

Box 3.2. INSTRUMENTS FOR REVENUE FROM HYDROCARBONS

There is a range of instruments for translating natural resources into public revenue. They have different implications for timing, risks-sharing, and the distribution of any rents associated with natural resources. Different countries use a range of approaches. Tanzania uses a mix of a royalty, a profit share, corporate income tax, and various fees and charges.

Royalty: this is usually a fixed percentage of sales revenues levied as soon as production starts. It can be administered relatively simply—subject to clarification on the point at which the sale is made, metering volumes and determining a price for tax purposes. It provides immediate revenue, but lowers the return to marginal investment.

Profit share: the post-royalty receipts from sales are allocated to the contractor to recover capital and operating costs, usually up to a ceiling in any period, with the remaining output or receipts designated 'profit gas' (or oil), and split between the state and contractor using an agreed formula, which may vary with price or returns to contractor. This stream of revenue increases once capital costs have been repaid. It is often a corollary of the contractor having taken the exploration, technical, and commercial risks associated with the project, and having financed the investment.

Corporate income tax (CIT): a conventional tax instrument, but one for which there is no a liability if there are provisions to carry forward losses incurred from an investment phase—as is the case with capital intensive projects.

Fees and charges: when combined with royalty, profit-sharing, and CIT, these are usually just an acreage fee for the area in each block under exploration or production.

Equity: in many countries the national oil or gas company holds an equity share in the consortium running exploration or production operations, which requires a commitment to contribute to the capital investment up front—unless financed at some cost by other consortium partners—but yields a dividend in due course.

(For more detail, see Daniel et al., 2010)

---

information which are partly estimates—there is not yet sufficient certainty on key variables, or transparency on key terms to be certain beyond reasonable estimates.[11]

Table 3.2 summarizes some of the projected sequencing of cash flows and activities, showing cash estimates (in 2012 US dollars), with production starting in year one, after eight years of preparation. The bottom part of the table shows a scaling by population and GDP on the optimistic assumption that production starts in 2020.

Because we have assumed that one project starts three years before the other, with the associated development of LNG capacity also taking place in two phases, and because there will be ongoing capital investment during the life of the project, the first ten years of production sees an annual average capital expenditure of almost US$3bn with operating costs of US$2bn each year.

The consortium only becomes liable for corporate income tax (CIT) once the losses associated with the initial capital investment have been accounted

Table 3.2. Summary of project and revenue projections

Annual averages to year:	0	10	20	30
Capex (US$bn)	1.9	2.9	0.6	0.0
Opex* (US$bn)		2.0	2.9	2.3
LNG production (MT)		14.0	20.0	16.0
Gross sales (fob, US$bn)		7.9	11.3	9.0
Government revenue(annual average, US$bn)		1.5	3.8	4.1
Scaling revenues:	2020	2030	2040	2050
Population (m)	56	73	95	124
GDP (US$bn)	67	130	253	490
GDP per person (US$)	1,209	1,797	2,668	3,959
Total government revenue (US$)		2	5	2
Revenue per person (US$)		28	51	18
Revenue (as percent of GDP)		1.6%	1.9%	0.5%

*excludes interest cost of debt
Source: Authors' calculations

for. It takes about ten years before a net profit is booked as liability for corporate income tax. This is also the point when the recovery of the cost of capital investment falls and profits on gas increases. It is likely to take ten years of production before both a CIT liability and a dividend for distribution from after-tax corporate profits are realized.

The net result is that after ten years of production, cumulative gross sales are accounted for mostly by the accumulated capital and operating costs, and payments of royalties and a distribution of profit shares. The cumulative total of gross sales—on the assumptions we have made—would be US$79bn over the first ten years of production. Cumulative costs will be US$64bn and payments to government US$15bn. Not all the costs will have been covered by the share of production set aside for cost recovery, and the contractor will have received a share of the 'profit gas'. But although it looks as if the government gets a small share of gross sales, the revenue to government is a large share of sales net of capital costs. At the same time, the contractor only starts to turn a net positive cumulative cash flow in year eleven of production at the earliest, and possibly as late as year twenty, depending on the precise terms on profit share that apply to each block.

We have presented project cash flows in terms of 2012 US dollars, but quite how big a macroeconomic impact they turn out to have depends on when the projects happen—the population and the GDP of Tanzania will grow over time. A dollar in 2012 is bigger in terms of absolute purchasing power, and relative to Tanzanian GDP, and population, than a dollar will be in 2020 or 2030. In addition, US$30bn over the life of the project means capital spending that takes place over at least twenty years—albeit with much of it needed early on to get production going. These sums constitute record-breaking inflows of foreign direct investment (FDI) but they will be financing equally record-breaking imports of specialized capital equipment and the skilled experienced foreign labour needed to make the projects work.

The single biggest macroeconomic impact in terms of dollars will eventually be delivered as revenue to government. This will start to arrive after production starts, possibly in ten years' time, and then royalty payments and some profit share will start to go to government. There is a significant increase in revenue once the capital costs have been paid off, but that takes around ten more years before revenue steps up—potentially twenty years from now. The sequencing of the main revenue streams is illustrated in Figure 3.4.

The way in which government receives revenue from these projects is through royalties, profit shares, corporate income tax, and dividends from the state-held equity in the project. These come in phases: royalties are due immediately after production starts, and we assume that there is a 5 per cent royalty rate on gross sales from the upstream gas production in to the LNG plant. Up to 70 per cent of the post-royalty gas is assigned to repay the accumulated costs of investment and operating costs. The 70 per cent cost recovery ceiling preserves at least 30 per cent of post-royalty gas for profit-sharing between the contractors who have invested in the project and the government. The percent shares vary according to the volume of production, and according to contract terms. There is likely to be a mix of terms applied to

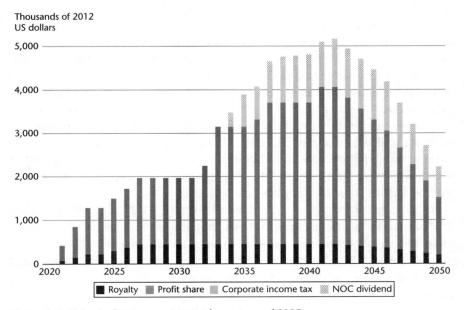

Figure 3.4. Principal revenue streams from gas and LNG
Source: Authors' calculations.

each block in Tanzania. We used the model production sharing agreement (PSA) terms as well as that part of the terms in the leaked Statoil PSA (as in the assumptions set out in Annex A). Once the initial costs of capital investment have been repaid, more of the gas is shared as profit gas between the contractor consortium and the government.

The scaling of revenue to government is therefore critically affected by when we assume production will start. In the projections we are presenting in this chapter, we assume that production starts from the first upstream project in 2021, and from the second in 2025, at which point the volumes of LNG rise from 10 MMT a year to 20 MMT. We have based this assumption on the idea that the final investment decision might be in 2017 and that there will be no difficulties during the construction phase, which then gets accelerated to take only four years—in effect, a risk-free scenario. This is certainly optimistic: as we have asserted already in this chapter, there are a number of technical, commercial, and market, as well as legal and regulatory risks; FID will probably take longer—with the take-over of BG Group by Shell, approved by shareholders in early 2016, unlikely to accelerate the decision—and construction is going to take at least four to five years; so a more balanced projection might be for first gas production in 2025 for the first phase.

Nonetheless, working with a 2021 start date, to provide an initial sense of the scale and thus macroeconomic impact of revenue to government, we use the UN projections of population to look at annual revenue per person, and we make a basic projection of GDP to look at revenue as a ratio to GDP.

Tanzania's population was just under 50m people in 2015.[12] The 2015 low fertility variant of UN population projections imply an increase to around 56m in 2020 and 73m in 2030—an increase of 50 per cent in fifteen years.

Our straightforward approach to projecting GDP gives us an annual average GDP growth of 6.8 per cent through to 2050.[13] On that basis, Tanzania's GDP would go from around US$48bn in 2015 to almost US$67bn in 2020.[14] By 2030, at an average growth of 6.8 per cent, GDP will have almost doubled over ten years to reach US$130bn. Against these projections, and using what we consider to be an optimistic start date of production in 2021, by 2030 revenue of US$2bn each year is equivalent to US$28 per person, and 1.6 per cent of GDP. While revenue in 2040 would be two and a half times higher in dollar terms, it is less than twice as much per person, and only a modestly higher ratio to total GDP at 1.9 per cent of GDP.[15]

The bias in the ratio to GDP is downwards: these may be overestimates of prospective GDP growth. On the other hand, a higher ratio to GDP for these dollar projections would imply lower growth in the rest of the economy, which is a less desirable outcome. It would be a hallmark of successful management of the impact of hydrocarbons for GDP growth to be sustained at the average of the last ten years over the next thirty-five or so years.

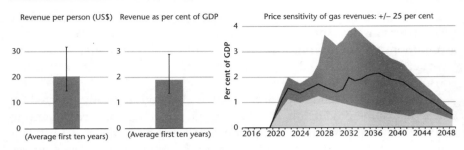

Figure 3.5. Revenue projections
Source: Authors' calculations.

The charts in Figure 3.5 illustrate these projections. The first two panels show revenue per person and then revenue as a share of GDP just for the first ten years of production (that is, the ten years from 2021). The error bars illustrate what happens to these ratios if gas prices are 25 per cent higher or 25 per cent lower than the baseline case of LNG prices of US$11.50/mmbtu (fob). The third panel also shows the ratio of revenue to GDP, with the range of sensitivity to prices being higher or lower by 25 per cent, but over the assumed thirty-year life of the projects. To put these numbers further into context, in 2012 Official Development Assistance (ODA) to Tanzania was US$59 per person, equivalent to 6.1 per cent of GDP, i.e. off the scale of the two left-hand panels of Figure 3.5.[16] To provide another comparison: 2 per cent of GDP is less than two-thirds of the overall fiscal deficit (*after* grants) of 3.3 per cent of GDP in fiscal year 2013/14.[17]

This revenue will be volatile: in the right-hand panel the ratio of revenue to GDP is rarely the same two years in a row, yet the assumptions we have used to build these revenue projections are flat in terms of price and the plateau level of gas production—of course we have assumed that GDP will grow continually. The jagged profile of revenue with constant prices and largely constant volumes reflects the phasing-in of revenue instruments as well as the two phases in the development of LNG exports. But it does not provide for any year-to-year volatility in prices, which will doubtless be a feature of a long-lived gas field, and will be an added complication to careful public financial management.

These ratios provide something of a reality check on the probable impact of new hydrocarbon revenues. They will be significant—additional government revenue of around 2 per cent of GDP is indeed material—but not of themselves transformative. The revenues represent a potential increment to aggregate demand. In addition to careful management of the public finances to turn revenue into effective public investment, the primary determinant of a positive economic impact is the policy that enables Tanzanians to have the skills to take up employment opportunities, and firms in Tanzania to have the investment in the capabilities needed to take up business opportunities, during the investment phase of these projections. In other words, for the supply response to incremental aggregate demand to be in Tanzania.

3.5 Policy Choices

We have outlined the possible scale and timing of both the investment needed to transform new natural assets so that hydrocarbons provide some positive assistance on the path to prosperity, and of the economic impact of the investment projects and the revenue that will follow. The policy choices that will facilitate these transformations have several dimensions. We first review some of the policy and administrative choices along the path to an FID, before turning to the policies that make the most of significant investment in natural gas and then decisions upon which good macroeconomic management of new revenues will depend.

3.5.1 *The Path to 'Final Investment Decision'*

Before the complex engineering and sophisticated fabrication and construction needed for production can be tackled, there is a set of risks and uncertainties which will also take time to resolve before an FID can be taken. These include market risks, the technical risks, and engineering challenges. In addition, the contractors who will mobilize significant private investment need a feasible set of legal, regulatory measures, and commercial agreements to be in place. From the policy perspective, that need equates to a coherent 'authorizing environment' to hold together the same set of laws, regulations, and well-managed government agencies needed for Tanzania to benefit securely from new investment in hydrocarbons.

3.5.1.1 MARKET RISKS
Market risks are faced by the contractors, who will need to sell LNG in international gas markets in order for them to be able to earn a return on their investment and to generate public revenue. These risks are naturally hard to evaluate because the market for LNG from Tanzania is at least ten years in the future. The commercial appraisals that contractor companies will do will use projections of volumes, prices, and costs as part of the evaluations of the business case that contribute to FID. The underlying market analysis has some consistent elements, however: demand, alternative competing supply to meet that demand, and prices.

The demand for lower-carbon energy for power generation and transport can be expected to be sustained if economic growth in Asia, and in China in particular, is sustained. In 2015 Chinese economic growth slowed; but is more likely to recover than stagnate in the long-term. China currently uses relatively little gas but lots of coal, and so growth in gas demand might be expected to be strong and sustained, subject to pricing and the domestic politics of coal and pollution in China. As well as being lower in carbon intensity, natural gas is also a cleaner fuel for power generation, with a concomitant contribution to lower air pollution. In general, as countries become better off, the premium on the environment, including clean air, goes up, and can be expected to be reflected in a higher relative price for a cleaner fuel.

There are alternative sources of supply to East Asia. These include a pipeline of gas from Siberia that would skirt Lake Baikal, and be delivered under an agreement between China and Russia. The surge in production of 'unconventional' or 'tight' gas in the US has stopped imports of LNG into the US, which has in turn increased LNG supply to the rest of the world. In addition, there is the possibility that the US may start exporting gas, which would be a further supply shock to what is an increasingly integrated global LNG market. In any case, there is also additional new LNG supply, much of it from Australia likely to go to East Asia and expected over the next five to eight years. Any East African LNG, from both Mozambique and Tanzania, would probably arrive later, and could then be well placed to meet any further increases in demand.

However, the prospects for LNG supply meeting this future demand hinges on prices. Coal in China is polluting, but significantly cheaper than LNG. The best prices for LNG in East Asia are currently in Tokyo for import into Japan, in part a legacy of increased LNG consumption following TEPCO nuclear power stations failing safety standards in 2002, being damaged by the tsunami of 2004, and the Fukushima disaster of 2011.

Strong prices for LNG have also reflected a convention of pricing LNG using a formula related to the oil price. Until oil prices fell in the second half of 2014, they had been high by historical standards and that was reflected in LNG prices. Lower oil prices present two market risks for LNG. First, they pull oil-linked LNG prices down, which influences expectations of the prices that an LNG project would expect, and reduces the commercial attractiveness of the LNG investment. If oil prices go back up, then the link between oil prices and LNG will come under renewed pressure, not least from China for so long as coal remains relatively cheap. Second, lower oil prices have squeezed the free cash flow of multinational energy companies raising the opportunity cost of the capital needed to make the LNG investment.

3.5.1.2 TECHNICAL RISK AND ENGINEERING CHALLENGES
There are, broadly, two technical risks: geology and engineering, and we have little to say on either other than to acknowledge that these risks are potentially

significant for a technically feasible project, not least because technical complexity implies a risk of higher costs.

The geological risks relate to gaps in the understanding of the gas reservoirs that remain even after the discoveries have been appraised for scale, and for other reservoir characteristics, such as temperature and pressure. Natural gas around the world is not uniform, and comes in different mixtures of butane and propane, with differing mixes of associated liquids and impurities; and the reservoirs are different shapes with different geological characteristics. The properties of each reservoir may only be fully understood as it goes into production, and gaps in geological knowledge constitute a risk that the assumptions for volumes and rates of production turn out not to hold.

On the technical engineering risks, consider that the gas for LNG is around 80–100 km offshore, and up to 4 km below the surface of the sea, and that there is a sea-bed canyon of the scale of the Grand Canyon, between the gas fields and the shore that a sub-sea pipeline will need to cross, and the significance of the challenges becomes evident. They can all be overcome, but the key to engineering is efficiency: whether they can be overcome at a feasible cost. The risk for these projects is that it might take a long time for engineering skill and experience, and technology, to deliver the solution that is efficient, both in engineering and commercial terms.

3.5.1.3 LEGAL AND REGULATORY MEASURES AND COMMERCIAL AGREEMENTS

The legal and regulatory environment in which gas production and LNG investments would be made is incomplete. However, in a significant step forward in defining the legal environment for investment in LNG, the Petroleum Bill, 2015, has received presidential assent, having been hotly debated in the National Assembly in July 2015. The new Act is a major piece of legislation which expands the provisions regulating upstream petroleum operations that initially were governed by the Petroleum (Exploration and Production) Act, Cap. 328 (PEPA), and also includes mid- and downstream petroleum product supply operations (that were regulated by the Petroleum Act, Cap. 392). In addition, it provides regulation of the mid and downstream natural gas activities. Some of the salient features of the Act include:

- Establishing the 'Oil & Gas Advisory Bureau' under the President's Office to advise the Cabinet on strategic matters of the petroleum industry;
- Establishing the Petroleum Upstream Regulatory Authority (PURA);
- Designating the Tanzania Petroleum Development Corporation (TPDC) as the National Oil Company (NOC);
- Providing exclusive rights to TPDC of exploration licenses and collecting natural gas from producers and distributing to customers;

- Identifying revenue sources and obligations of license holders and contractors to pay royalty, fees, income taxes, and other taxes including capital gains tax;
- Measures intended to strengthen Tanzanian participation in the petroleum value chain.

The Act is therefore the cornerstone for all activities of the oil & gas sector in Tanzania. However, several sections would benefit from further refinement in order to provide feasible solutions and the required clarity to the broader legal framework, and we cite a few such examples in what follows.

Investing partners are currently evaluating a joint LNG plant, which together with other offshore developments forms an integral part of a gas/LNG value chain. The nature and operation of an export LNG plant is distinct from traditional downstream activities such as transportation or distribution and sale of natural gas for the domestic market. It is essential that large integrated gas projects that span upstream and midstream should have a single regulator to ensure consistent regulation and effective project execution and operation of the gas/LNG value chain. However, in the Act, construction and operation of export liquefaction facilities (and other activities related thereto such as gas processing, storage, and jetties/marine facilities) are considered part of the midstream and downstream regulated activities alongside domestic transportation, and distribution, and the sale of gas to the market in Tanzania.

The Act also provides exclusive rights over the natural gas midstream and downstream value chain to the National Oil Company. This provision might not be beneficial for an efficient development of gas resources particularly in areas where the NOC clearly currently has no capacity and expertise, for example in liquefaction. In a gas/LNG value chain, the upstream contractors should be allowed to undertake liquefaction (construction and operation of an LNG plant) in line with their upstream participation interests. Such aligned participation secures common incentives in the value chain (between owners and users of the LNG plant), which is important to ensure cost-effective execution and operations. It also provides for a financially strong partnership that is able to attract the required financing for these large investments.

For the LNG project to proceed, it is important that the government enters into a Host Government Agreement (HGA) with the IOCs covering regulatory and other government consents and the commercial terms and framework for the LNG project. Such HGAs, supported by project specific legislation are common practice for LNG projects. Ideally, the Act should have provided the Minister responsible for the sector with powers to enter into an HGA with the approval of Cabinet.

Moving forward, it is essential that these and other shortfalls in the Act are addressed to encourage and create favourable conditions for IOCs to invest in

Tanzania so as to ensure a successful future for the oil and gas industry. The alternative is likely to be further delay in realizing FID, investment, and eventual revenue for government.

In addition to the broader legal framework provided by the Petroleum Act 2015, there are some specific laws, regulations, and contracts needed for a large-scale LNG project to start. These are all part of the broader 'authorizing environment' that the government would need to have in place for the country to make the most of the opportunity offered to it by a new natural resource asset. This context is sketched in Figure 3.6, which illustrates how different laws, regulations, and government agencies shape the transition from sub-soil asset to a contribution to human development.

For a contractor to commit to the initial 'Front-End Engineering and Design' (FEED) phase of planning, and then to FID, there needs to be a reasonable degree of certainty on the laws, regulations, and commercial agreements that will govern the project. This is not yet the case in Tanzania.

Among the gaps, from a contractor perspective for their investment in the FEED phase to start, are:

- A form of LNG plant 'Host Government Agreement'
- LNG Site Lease Agreement and LNG Marine Rights Agreement
- Project Development Agreement between project sponsors (TPDC and IOCs) on co-operation for FEED and beyond.

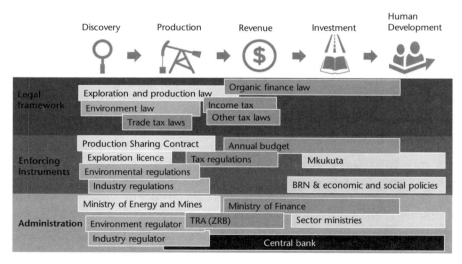

Figure 3.6. The authorizing environment for the transformation of a natural asset

Source: OPM (2013). DfID PEAKS Topic Guide: Extractive industries, development and the role of donors, September 2013.

- Upstream Implementation Arrangements by block, including 'Domestic Market Obligations' (DMO) terms and conditions.

And for a contractor to move through concluding their FID, they would also look to have in place the laws, regulations and agreements for:

- Commercial structure and tariff systems;
- Regulatory and fiscal framework conditions;
- Implementing legislation;
- Future expansions;
- Governance, approvals and permitting;
- Stability of terms.

3.5.2 Policy Coordination and the 'Authorizing Environment'

Too often the transformation of resource wealth into prosperity fails not because of a lack of the correct policies, but because of a weak underlying system of governance. Implementation of polices and strategies in the oil and gas sector, will require coordination and an authorizing environment across a range of different Government institutions. Currently, the Ministry of Energy and Minerals (MEM) is the lead policy and administrative institution and plays a coordinating role with other institutions in the sector, many of which are its affiliates. Working alongside MEM, the nationally-owned petroleum company TPDC is the national partner in all petroleum ventures. The potential conflict of interest given that still it holds policy and regulatory roles in addition to its commercial role, is being addressed through restructuring of the company to take on a purely commercial role, and portioning off its upstream regulator role to a new independent regulatory body, the PURA. The Energy and Water Utility Regulatory Authority (EWURA) role is confined to midstream and downstream regulation.

Looking towards taxation and revenue collection, the Ministry of Finance (MOF) is the lead policy institution, but MEM and TPDC also play an important role in setting royalty and profit sharing terms on the project level. The Attorney General is also involved in negotiation and devising contracts. In terms of revenue collection, several institutions have roles to play over different components. Among the institutions involved, the Tanzania Revenue Authority (TRA) collects income taxes from gas companies, while MEM collects the large share of non-tax revenues from petroleum activities via TPDC including royalties, licence fees, application fees and annual rent, and profits from oil and gas. The MOF collects revenues from equity holdings, and local authorities collect a local service levy from mining companies. Tax audits are carried out by the TRA. These institutions play similar roles in relation to all other economic agents in the economy.

Coordination on environmental and community issues is also complex. The Vice President's Office (VPO) is the lead policy institution in this domain, and has to coordinate with MEM, and the national agencies on policy issues. Compliance and enforcement of law is implemented by the National Environment Management Council (NEMC), in coordination with local authorities. Meanwhile the Ministry of Labour and Employment, lead on formulation of labour, labour market, social security, and employment policies, while the Ministry of Lands, Housing and Human Settlements Development has to approve land allocations for extractives use.

Two key challenges pervade when it comes to coordination on the full range of issues required to harness natural gas for development. First, the fact that many of these institutions lack the authority to convene high-level decision makers from partner institutions on a regular basis means that they tend to operate in an environment of inadequate information. Second, without high-level oversight to direct activities, there has been no one to oversee organizational roles and responsibilities, opening possibilities of 'mission creep' where institutions work beyond their mandate, sometimes leading to potential conflicts of interest; while lack of engagement or inaction has meant that other institutions are not doing the work that they should be. Coordination challenges and complexity are most acute when one considers the relationship between oil and gas and wider economic issues. The key institutions in this realm include the President's Office Planning Commission (POPC), the body which develops Tanzania's national planning framework centred on the Five-year Development Plan (FYDP), and MOF which manages the national budget, and the financing framework for the Medium-Term Expenditure Framework (MTEF). Strengthening the coordinating agencies and institutions is critical if natural gas resources are to effectively integrate within the wider economy.

3.5.3 *The Investment Phase: Jobs, 'Local Content', and Growth*

There has already been a positive impact from contractor companies' exploration programmes on employment and PAYE in Tanzania. But a bigger impact on demand for goods and services supplied within Tanzania, and the biggest impact on jobs, will come during construction. That investment will be financed by FDI which will be bigger than FDI has been in the past (as discussed in Section 3.3), almost all of which will finance a significant increase in imports. This means big shifts in the balance of payments, which are illustrated in Figure 3.7.

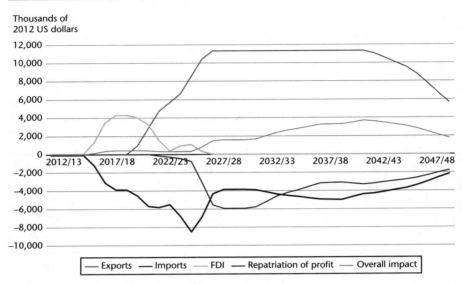

Figure 3.7. LNG in the balance of payments
Source: Authors' calculations.

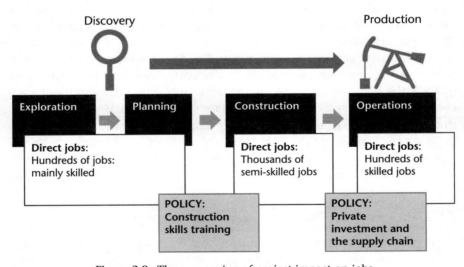

Figure 3.8. The sequencing of project impact on jobs

To gauge the scale of the direct impact on jobs during construction we look at rough estimates of the semi-skilled and skilled jobs that could potentially be filled by Tanzanian nationals during construction, and the magnitude of the potential increment to domestic demand for goods and services that could be associated with significant FDI during construction (Figure 3.8).

3.5.3.1 JOBS AND SKILLS

The starting point is that most people in the labour force in Tanzania are low-skilled. Moyo et al. (2010) analysed Tanzania's vision for achieving middle-income country status and compared the skills composition of Tanzania's labour force and the labour force of a median middle-income country. The predominantly rural and agricultural nature of Tanzania's workforce means that more than 80 per cent of the work force is low-skilled. To put this in more specific context, national data shows that of the around 900,000 15–24-year-olds that entered the labour market in 2010/11, 14 per cent did not complete primary school, 44 per cent finished primary but did not transition to secondary, and an additional 38 per cent went to secondary school but did not reach or finish Form IV. Only 4 per cent went beyond 'O'-level.[18] A significant improvement in educational attainment and skill levels, and therefore potential productivity, is essential if Tanzania is to come close to the skill levels, and productivity, of a median middle-income country.

This has two implications for building skills as part of the construction phase of an LNG plant. First, the low starting point makes it hard to find people who are prepared for further training and skill development to move from being low-skilled to semi-skilled. Second, at the same time, even modest increases in skills can make significant contribution to the development of skill levels in Tanzania, given the low starting point.

There has already been work done to analyse the challenges of appropriate skills development given the prospects for more jobs from investment in hydrocarbon production. In 2014, an assessment of vocational and educational training needs by the Voluntary Service Overseas (VSO) organization in partnership with the Vocational Education and Training Agency (VETA), the official vocational skills training agency of Tanzania, supported by a phalanx of energy companies concluded that: (i) those graduating as part of the existing set up are not directly employable; (ii) the trades currently being taught are not the ones that will be needed; (iii) the quality of training is constrained; (iv) VETA programmes have to cover additional training to compensate for weaknesses in the school system; (v) workshops and equipment are variable in quality and usually out of date; (vi) there are too few opportunities for industrial placements; and (vii) the accreditation process puts too little weight on the accumulation of practical skills.[19]

With almost a million new entrants to the labour force each year, the training for the estimated 4,500–5,000 directly created new jobs during the construction phase shown in Table 3.3 is clearly not sufficient to address the challenges of a low-skilled labour force. However, most of the areas in which training would be needed to fill the jobs created as part of the investment in hydrocarbons are not sector-specific. The VSO assessment showed that a significant number of the skills needed are transferable. These include

Table 3.3. Indicative estimates of direct labour demand by project phases

Skills level	Examples	Sourcing	Planning	Construction	Operations
University graduates	Sector-related Engineering, Earth and Marine sciences, Management, Finance, Accountancy, Legal services, etc.	International workforce and suitably qualified Tanzanians—university qualifications as a minimum	150	350	200
Highly skilled and professional certified technicians (e.g., advanced technical education and training, TET)	Electronics, Electrical Engineering, Plumbers, Instrument and Machine Operators, Welding Specialists, Metallurgy technicians, other specialist technicians, etc.	International workforce and suitably trained Tanzanians—advanced TET training based on successful completing of secondary education at a minimum	+offshore drilling	1,000	80
Certified Occupations and Crafts (e.g., VET graduates)	Scaffolding, basic Electricians, Plumbing, Welding, Metalwork, Carpentry, Vehicle maintenance, Catering and Hospitality	International workforce and suitably trained Tanzanians—training based on successful completion of lower secondary education as a minimum, or primary education with relevant work experience	+offshore drilling, +on shore base	2,000–2,500	Required sporadically for maintenance of equipment
Lowest level of skilled labour	Logistics/drivers, Security guards, Housekeeping and Catering, basic construction skills.	Tanzanians—training based on targeted short training courses; have to meet in basic sector relevant requirements, including English language proficiency, health and safety awareness	+drilling, base camp labour	400–700, + camp labour, +security guards	+ security guards, drivers, camp labour

Source: VSO (2014); 'BG Tanzania Preliminary Labour Demand Study' (2011), unpublished document, internal estimates.

the skills needed in metal work, building works, civil engineering and infrastructure, mechanical work, and electrical work.[20]

In addition, the development of skills for more people that just needed for construction on the LNG site would strengthen the indirect impact of a resource-led boom. A construction boom follows a natural resource boom when increased income is invested in non-tradable capital. When the supply of buildings is inelastic, then the real estate boom is in prices, but when there is skilled labour, and materials are available, then the boom is in buildings. Training programmes that endow workers from across Tanzania, not just from the region where the LNG plant will be built, with construction skills, will lower the unit cost of fixed capital by helping make the supply of buildings more elastic.

There is some urgency in stepping up efforts to raise skill levels in Tanzania. This is not driven by the imminent investment in hydrocarbons, but rather by demographics: there is a rising number of young people entering the labour force burdened by the failure of schools to equip them with education and skills. A top priority then is to address this 'learning crisis'; and to raise skills in the labour force by addressing shortfalls in the current system for technical and vocational skills training. The priorities highlighted in the 2014 assessment included: (i) strengthening the VETA curriculum; (ii) improving the trade testing; (iii) better equipping prospective VETA students with grants for 'bridging funding'; (iv) enhancing teacher training; (v) strengthening the practical training elements of technical and vocational education. Across all these measures is the need for an appropriate involvement of industry—and not just in the hydrocarbon sector.

3.5.3.2 JOBS AND LOCAL CONTENT

Efforts to develop individuals' skills can be thought of as being on the supply-side of the labour market. Efforts to develop 'local content' in the supply-chain for major extractive projects seeks to create jobs on the demand-side of the labour market. Combined, both push towards an increase in the capacity and flexibility in the economy to respond to the increase in aggregate demand presented by investment in hydrocarbons, and then the spending from revenues, with a supply of goods and services that will constitute a positive impact on growth.

In particular, labour productivity, and so prosperity, is not just a function of an individuals' skill, but of the capabilities of the firm, or organization, within which that individual works. Accumulating such 'firm capabilities' is a central challenge of industrialization and modernization. It entails not just private investment in firms, but access to technology, and the organizational capabilities needed to combine diverse inputs to add value. When thinking carefully about economic growth and prosperity in these terms, it is clear that legislating for specific shares of 'local content' is not the same as building productive capable firms.

The usual approach to local content is a regulation that commands a certain share of absolute level of spending on goods and services be directed towards 'local' firms. This has one major difficulty, and in practice is not strongly linked to sustained job creation. The problem is in the meaning of 'local'. A firm registered in-country, and indeed majority national-owned, may be simply a licensee of a foreign firm, and in effect just an importer. In other words, defining 'local' in terms of the ownership of a supplier does not mean that the opportunity for developing national firm capability is being realized.

For example, in Zambia, some 80 per cent of spending on inputs for the major mines consists of 'local' transactions, and almost all inputs to mining are imported.[21] At one level, 'local content', as measured by the share of input spending or by a dollar amount of spending is very high. In a more meaningful assessment, local content is not as high as those indicators suggest because so much of that spending is on imports.

Of course, for a capital and technology intensive sector, technically sophisticated inputs need to be imported. But at the margin, there will be inputs that could be locally supplied in time. But what it takes is a focus on the development of the necessary firm capabilities to deliver reliably to quality specifications and in sufficient volumes, not a focus on the share of locally-purchased inputs or an absolute value of local spending. This re-defines the challenge and opportunity of 'local content' policies. They become complements to government policy on private investment and job creation more broadly; indeed, this is key to the growth and development of the non-hydrocarbon economy of Tanzania in general.

The 'Enterprise Map of Tanzania' (Sutton and Olomi, 2012) provides a review of key firms in the principal industrial sectors in Tanzania; it surveys Tanzania's industrial sectors (agribusiness, manufacturing, and construction) focusing on leading firms, and covers fifty large firms in detail which are representative of Tanzania's industrial capabilities in 2012—focusing on what they produce and how they developed their capabilities. It thus provides a foundation for thinking where there is scope for developing firm capabilities in response to the demand for inputs from investment in hydrocarbons. The conclusion that the authors arrived at is that the prospect of investment in hydrocarbons is indeed an opportunity to significant boost capabilities, and medium-term growth in Tanzania, but likely only for a few key firms.[22]

3.5.3.3 THE IMPACT ON GROWTH

If jobs are created during the investment and construction phase of the LNG project, and there is some local value-added in the supply chain for hydrocarbon investment and production, then the positive economic impact will be deeper and broader than if hydrocarbons remain a capital-intensive high-technology, high-skill enclave. This is the most immediate opportunity. But, as we have argued, it is not sufficient to legislate for more jobs or more local value-added: the jobs will only be filled if there are skilled people, and the local value-added needs a supply base in domestic industry, which in turn depends on private investment in industry.

The impact on growth in Tanzania therefore hinges critically on whether there are sufficiently skilled people in the workforce to take up job opportunities, and firms which already have sufficient capability to get in to the supply chain. These are determined by schooling and training, and by the current firm capabilities in Tanzania. At the time of writing, neither is particularly good. However, with hydrocarbon investment probably some way off, there is scope to step up the level of skills for labour and to unleash private business investment to strengthen firm capabilities. Both are necessary for a positive impact on growth and prosperity from hydrocarbons. The policy measures that deliver skills and investment are the same with an urgency to sustain growth, regardless of whether there is an emerging opportunity from hydrocarbons.

3.5.4 *The Production Phase: Government Revenue*

After around a decade production will be ramping up, and government revenue will then start to increase. As shown in Section 3.4.1.1., the lag in revenues is due to the phase of cost recovery that reduces the gas set aside for profit sharing between the contractor and the government, and which delays the contractor liability to corporate income tax.

In looking at the fiscal impact of new gas revenues, we started with estimates of the revenues themselves. These were illustrated in Figure 3.4 showing the main sources of new government receipts from gas and LNG production.

However, the broader fiscal impact—and by extension the impact on public investment and Tanzania's prosperity—is more complex. The macroeconomic stance of the budget will partly need to reflect the challenges of managing the monetary and macroeconomic effects of big changes in the balance of payments (as illustrated in Figure 3.7). There will also be a sequence of other public financial management challenges. A stylized decision tree to illustrate those policy choices is in Figure 3.9.

There are two initial policy choices once revenue starts to flow. Macroeconomic stability is conditioned on how much out of gas revenue gets spent and how quickly. This is partly related to the aforementioned challenges of macroeconomic absorption, but also to the monetary impact of the cash flows associated with the gas and LNG projects. But before any revenue comes in, so long as there is a decision to invest, there will be scope to borrow in advance and bring forward revenue.

3.5.4.1 BORROWING IN ADVANCE

The record with sovereign borrowing from international capital markets of relatively poor but resource-rich economies is not strong. Most recent

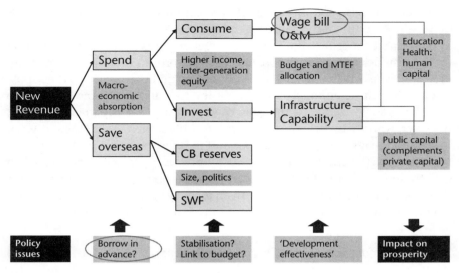

Figure 3.9. Macroeconomic policy choices
Source: Drawn from Henstridge et al. (2015).

examples include Ghana and Zambia. Debt finance has contributed to some investment, but at the same time, both have had fiscal crises. Ghana entered an IMF programme after long negotiations in 2015, and Zambia had started but not completed negotiations in 2014.

The charts in Figure 3.10 show one scenario for borrowing in advance. A credit of US$5bn which contributes US$625m to spending each year over a period of eight years, and is paid back over ten years after a grace period of six years, but with interest charged on the outstanding balance of 5 per cent per year, offers increased revenue earlier on than would be possible by just waiting for gas revenue to come on stream. The costs of the debt then depress the financing available once gas revenue does start to flow. The right-hand panel shows the consequences for the public debt-to-GDP ratio, and the public investment to GDP ratio for Tanzania under this scenario, and provide a comparison with possible equivalent scenarios for Uganda and Sierra Leone taking out debt to bring forward revenue from prospective revenues from oil and mining, respectively.[23]

While there are economic and political reasons in principle to bring revenue forward, whether or not it contributes to accelerated growth hinges on whether in practice the increment to investment delivers an economic and social return. There is not a convincing track record yet emerging from sovereign borrowing over the last decade. Work on investment in Uganda, under more or less comparable circumstances to those faced by Tanzania, shows that allowing for inefficiencies in making investments, and under-provision for operations and maintenance, it would be a mistake to try too much too soon before the benefits for growth are compromised.[24]

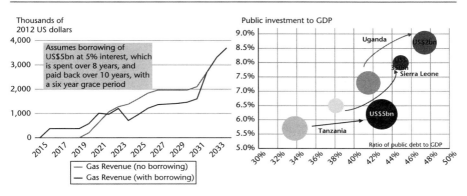

Figure 3.10. Scenario for borrowing in advance
Source: Authors' calculations, based on the scenarios in Henstridge et al. (2015).

3.5.4.2 PUBLIC SECTOR PAY

One of the main ways in which newly resource-rich countries have increased immediate consumption has been sharp increases in public sector pay. This has been true of Ghana in the wake of commercial oil discoveries, and of Zambia with high copper prices. In both countries electoral cycles played some part.

The cost of any given increase in average is relatively straightforward to calculate in relation to the expected revenue from producing natural assets over the medium-term. We chose the period 2015–30 and modelled the increase in pay as a step increase in 2015 and then a rise in line with the growth of GDP. In striking contrast to this scenario in Uganda and Sierra Leone, for Tanzania the numbers show that the scope for any significant increase in public sector pay is very limited. A real increase of 20 per cent in 2015, followed by increases in line with the growth in real GDP would exhaust all the expected revenue to 2030, as illustrated in Figure 3.11.

3.6 Conclusion

The management of hydrocarbon resources to support Tanzania on the path to prosperity entails a range of legal, regulatory, administrative, and policy challenges. We have used a set of projections of the investment in, and then the production of, hydrocarbons to frame those challenges. The first opportunity comes during construction with the potential creation of thousands of jobs. During investment and then during operations there is potential for national firms to be part of the international supply chain for the hydrocarbon industry. During production the single biggest impact will eventually be from revenue to government; however, this is not imminent: production is unlikely to start before the end of this decade and may be ten years away. The need to reimburse

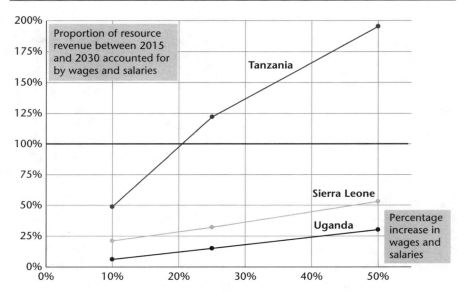

Figure 3.11. Scope for increased public sector pay

capital costs means that significant profit-sharing takes around a further five years or more, as does liability for corporate income tax. If the non-hydrocarbon economy has continued to grow in the meantime, then as a ratio to GDP, new revenue from gas will be of the order of two per cent of GDP—depending on gas prices—but unlikely to be more than single digits of GDP.

The suite of policies that will help realize the opportunity of hydrocarbons include skills programmes to support national job creation, supply chain development programmes to support increased local content, and a sequence of fiscal policy decisions that will sustain the transformation from natural asset to increased prosperity.

At the same time, the array of supporting policies is also critical to make the most of the opportunities of hydrocarbons. Significantly improved skills, stronger firm capabilities, and a configuration of macro-policies consistent with sustaining macroeconomic stability are, in any case, likely to be import-ant for the continued growth of the non-resource economy, and critical for making the most of hydrocarbons.

Acknowledgement

The authors are very grateful to Christopher Adam, Evelyn Dietsche, Simon Hunt, and Alan Roe for comments on earlier drafts of this chapter and acknowledge that the views and any errors or omissions in the chapter are entirely their own.

Modelling assumptions	BG Group	Statoil	Midstream LNG	Units	Source/notes
Pricing					
Price	10	10	10	US$/mmbtu	Reuters (22 November 2013)
Netback charge	1	1	1		OPM assumption: for transport and processing
FOB price of LNG	11.5	11.5	11.5	USD/mmbtu	OPM assumption ($16/mmbtu CIF in Tokyo as per WB forecast, less transport costs)
Production and timing					
Reserves	15	22		TCF	Company press releases and Richmond Energy Partners
Production start date	2021	2025	2021		Assumption as in IMF (2014) and OPM (2013)
Peak production year	2024	2028			OPM (2013)
Peak production	10	10	20	MMT LNG	1,325 mmscufd required to produce 10m tonnes of LNG/year, Reuters (22 November 2013)
Years of peak production	20	20			OPM assumption
Years of decline	10	10			OPM assumption
Capex and opex					
Total investment cost (capex)	20	20	10	US$bn	OPM assumption
Share of capex in pre-production phase	50%	40%	50%		OPM assumption
Number of years in pre-production	4	4	3		OPM assumption
Share of capex in ramp-up phase	20%	40%	50%		OPM assumption
Number of years in ramp-up phase	2	2	7		OPM assumption
Share of capex in steady-state phase	30%	20%			OPM assumption
Number of years in steady-state phase	18	18			OPM assumption
Opex (variable costs)	2.5	2.5	0.5	US$/MMBtu	OPM assumption
Financing and fiscal					
Gov. shareholding in upstream (gas extr.)	12.5%	10.0%			OPM assumption
Cost recovery ceiling	70%	70%			As per 'modified gas terms' described in Deloitte (2013).
CIT rate (upstream)	30%	30%	30%		Deloitte (2013)
Royalties	5%	5%			Article 20 A in MPSA states 12.5%, but 5% under 'modified gas terms' (Deloitte, 2013)
Production sharing (NOC share)					
Basis for calculating				mmscuf/day	Daily gas production sliding scale. - For BG Group: breakdown p.30 on 2008 Model PSA, based on production rate (MMSCFGPD) - For Statoil: Based on leaked Statoil PSA Addendum (<http://www.resourcegovernance.org/sites/default/files/Tanzania_Statoil_20140808.pdf>)
First threshold: zero to	20 / 60%	299.999 / 30%			
Second threshold	40 / 65%	599.999 / 35%			
Third threshold	60 / 70%	899.999 / 38%			
Fourth threshold	80 / 75%	1199.999 / 40%			
Fifth threshold	100 / 80%	1499.999 / 45%			
Sixth threshold	10,000 / 85%	10,000 / 50%			

Annex 3B. Mapping gas and LNG into macroeconomic accounts

	2015	2020	2025	2030	2035	2040	2045	2050
	(Thousands of 2012 US dollars; unless otherwise specified)							
1. Project investment and operating cost assumptions								
Capex (gas)	0	2,500	4,333	556	556	556	0	0
Opex (gas)	80	125	1,612	2,418	2,418	2,418	2,088	1,099
Capex (LNG)	0	1,667	714	0	0	0	0	0
Opex (LNG)	0	0	329	493	493	493	426	224
Total	**80**	**4,292**	**6,988**	**3,467**	**3,467**	**3,467**	**2,514**	**1,323**
to Imports	**64**	**3,850**	**6,095**	**2,829**	**2,829**	**2,829**	**2,011**	**1,059**
to GDP	**16**	**442**	**893**	**638**	**638**	**638**	**503**	**265**
Memorandum items:								
Total investment (gas)	0	2,500	4,333	556	556	556	0	0
Total investment (LNG)	0	1,667	714	0	0	0	0	0
Total investment	**0**	**4,167**	**5,048**	**556**	**556**	**556**	**0**	**0**
2. Cashflow and revenue								
Gas (gross sales)	0	0	6,575	9,863	9,863	9,863	8,518	4,483
Transportation costs	0	0	658	986	986	986	852	448
Netback sales of gas	**0**	**0**	**5,918**	**8,877**	**8,877**	**8,877**	**7,666**	**4,035**
less royalties	0	0	296	444	444	444	383	202
less cost recovery	0	0	3,935	5,903	4,494	2,973	2,088	1,099
less contractor profit share	0	0	492	1,007	1,235	2,200	2,272	1,421
less government profit share	0	0	1,194	1,523	2,705	3,260	2,923	1,313
Balance:	0	0	0	0	0	0	0	0
IOCs								
Cost recovery	0	0	3,935	5,903	4,494	2,973	2,088	1,099
Profit share	0	0	492	1,007	1,235	2,200	2,272	1,421
less opex (lifting + transport costs)	80	125	1,612	2,418	2,418	2,418	2,088	1,099
less capex	0	2,500	4,333	556	556	556	0	0
less corporate tax	0	0	0	0	605	595	673	426
less NOC dividend	0	0	0	0	141	145	163	102

	2015	2020	2025	2030	2035	2040	2045	2050
Balance:	-80	-2,625	-1,517	3,937	2,009	1,460	1,435	893
o/w FDI	80	2,625	1,517					
o/w remittances				-3,937	-2,009	-1,460	-1,435	-893
Government revenue (gas)	0	0	**1,490**	**1,967**	**3,894**	**4,444**	**4,143**	**2,043**
LNG (sales)	0	0	7,562	11,342	11,342	11,342	9,796	5,156
Cost of gas (netback sales from upstream)	0	0	5,918	8,877	8,877	8,877	7,666	4,035
Net sales	0	0	**1,644**	**2,466**	**2,466**	**2,466**	**2,130**	**1,121**
less opex	0	0	329	493	493	493	426	224
less capex	0	1,667	714	0	0	0	0	0
less corporate tax	0	0	0	0	0	285	256	134
less dividends (govt.)	0	0	0	0	0	80	72	38
Balance:	0	-1,667	601	1,973	1,973	1,608	1,377	724
o/w FDI		1,667						
IOC net cashflow (LNG)	0	-1,667	-601	-1,973	-1,973	-1,608	-1,377	-724
Government revenue (LNG)	0	0	0	0	0	**364**	**327**	**172**

Economic impact summary

(Thousands of 2012 US dollars; unless otherwise specified)

Balance of Payments	2015	2020	2025	2030	2035	2040	2045	2050
Exports	0	0	7,562	11,342	11,342	11,342	9,796	5,156
Imports (from costs + impact on GDP)	-64	-3,850	-6,095	-2,829	-2,829	-2,829	-2,011	-1,059
IOC dividend/profit repatriation	0	0	-601	-5,909	-3,982	-3,068	-2,812	-1,617
FDI	80	4,292	1,517	0	0	0	0	0
Overall balance:	16	442	2,383	2,604	4,532	5,446	4,973	2,480
(as per cent of baseline GDP)	0.0%	0.7%	2.5%	2.0%	2.5%	2.2%	1.4%	0.5%

Monetary impact	2015/16	2020/21	2025/26	2030/31	2035/36	2040/41	2045/46	
Change in NFA	315	2,199	3,020	5,168	7,878	10,473	12,880	
Change in private sector credit	1,268	1,427	3,165	4,803	8,722	14,716	25,165	
Change in credit to government	-219	-391	-501	-1,889	-3,041	-3,386	-3,231	
Change in Broad Money (M3)	1,363	3,235	5,684	8,082	13,559	21,803	34,814	
Broad Money growth	12%	15%	13%	11%	11%	11%	10%	

(continued)

Annex 3B. Continued

	2015	2020	2025	2030	2035	2040	2045	2050
	(Thousands of 2012 US dollars; unless otherwise specified)							
Fiscal impact	2015	2020	2025	2030	2035	2040	2045	2050
Total government gas & LNG revenue	0	0	1,490	1,967	3,894	4,808	4,470	2,215
Incremental non-resource revenue	0	0	858	456	837	1,008	840	0
Total additional revenue	0	0	2,348	2,423	4,731	5,817	5,310	2,215
as per cent of baseline GDP	*0.0%*	*0.0%*	*2.5%*	*1.9%*	*2.6%*	*2.3%*	*1.5%*	*0.5%*
Real impact: GDP/GNI	2015	2020	2025	2030	2035	2040	2045	2050
Baseline GDP	48,108	67,210	93,634	130,412	181,585	252,771	351,773	489,597
Domestic component of capex and opex	16	442	893	638	638	638	503	265
Indirect component impact of capex and opex	16	442	893	638	638	638	503	265
Gas + LNG direct increment to GNI	0		5,020	2,522	4,450	5,364	4,470	2,215
Gas + LNG indirect increment to GNI	0	0	5,020	2,522	4,450	5,364	4,470	2,215
Total impact on GNI	32	883	11,826	6,320	10,175	12,003	9,946	4,960
as per cent of baseline GDP	*0.1%*	*1.3%*	*12.6%*	*4.8%*	*5.6%*	*4.7%*	*2.8%*	*1.0%*
Scenario GNI	48,140	68,093	105,461	136,731	191,760	264,774	361,719	494,557
Scenario GNI growth	*7.2%*	*6.8%*	*9.1%*	*6.5%*	*7.0%*	*6.5%*	*6.5%*	*6.5%*

Notes

1. Tanzania is already resource rich, producing 40 tonnes of gold in 2014, which dominated exports, and made it the fourth largest producer in sub-Saharan Africa.
2. Because of high fixed costs for offshore gas production at scale—an 'anchor volume' for the project—is needed to ensure commercial viability.
3. This estimate from the 2015/16 Budget Speech. See also: <http://mem.go. tz/energy-sector/> (accessed 5 June 2016).
4. These are reported reserves numbers for Mozambique, see <http://blogs.wsj.com/ frontiers/2014/09/04/tanzania-looks-to-review-gas-and-mining-sector-agreements/> (accessed 5 June 2016).
5. Sources: Songo Songo: MEM: <https://www.chathamhouse.org/sites/files/ chathamhouse/public/Research/Africa/260213presentation.pdf> (accessed 5 June 2016); Mnazi Bay: Wentworth Resources: <http://www.wentworthresources. com/tanzania.php> (accessed 5 June 2016).
6. See <http://www.bg-group.com/111/media/press-releases/> (accessed 5 June 2016).
7. See <http://www.statoil.com/en/NewsAndMedia/News/2015/Pages/30Mar_ Tanzania.aspx> (accessed 5 June 2016).
8. The opportunity from lower cost power is discussed in Venables (2012).
9. See Statoil: 'Tanzania Gas Project: from Discovery to Gas Sales'. Available at: <http://www.statoil.com/en/NewsAndMedia/Events/EAPCE2015/Downloads/ Tanzania%20gas%20project%20-%20From%20discovery%20to%20gas%20sales. pdf> (accessed 5 June 2016).
10. Such estimates will have been made in at least three versions: one in an OPM study for BG Group (2013) on their volumes only; one by the IMF as a background paper for an Article IV report (2014); and one by OPM for an AfDB-BMGF Flagship report (AfDB, 2015), which also combines Statoil and BG volumes; we are drawing upon and updating that work in this chapter. The updates include the use of the 2015 UN population projections and the revised national accounts for Tanzania as ways to scale potential revenues.
11. The exercise presented here is set out in greater detail in the background papers to AfDB (2015), in particular Henstridge et al. (2015).
12. Based on the estimates in the 2012 population census.
13. To project GDP we use UN demographic projections to derive the growth of the labour force, and then simply assume that the average growth in labour productivity of the last ten years is sustained. Those who will enter the labour force over the next fifteen to twenty years have already been born, which gives those projections some demographic foundation. Whether the trend on average labour productivity will be sustained hinges on a broad range of factors, among which is the quality of management of potential hydrocarbons.
14. These estimates reflect the 2015 revision in national accounts, which updated the base year to 2007, and used fresh survey data in estimating the national accounts, which in turn led to an upwards revision of the level of GDP by 27.8 per cent. Accordingly the ratios of dollar LNG revenue in this chapter are smaller than the calculations presented in AfDB (2015).

15. This is a comparable order of magnitude to an earlier exercise that looked at the scale and timing of possible oil revenues in Uganda. See Henstridge and Page (2012).
16. ODA data from the OECD: <http://www.oecd.org/dac/stats/> (accessed 5 June 2016).
17. See IMF (2015).
18. See <http://blogs.worldbank.org/africacan/youth-in-tanzania-a-growing-uneducated-labor-force> (accessed 5 June 2016).
19. VSO (2014).
20. See VSO (2014), Table 3.
21. ICMM (2014).
22. See <http://personal.lse.ac.uk/sutton/tanzania_final.pdf>. At the launch of the 'Enterprise Map of Tanzania' in Dar es Salaam in 2012, John Sutton argued that the integration of the domestic industrial sector with hydrocarbon supply chains will have a huge pay-off to medium-term growth, and that 'No single issue in enterprise policy is more important right now . . .'.
23. See Henstridge et al. (2015) for equivalent analysis of Uganda and Sierra Leone.
24. See Adam et al. (2014).

References

Adam, C. S., Bevan, D. L., and Ohlenburg, T. (2014). 'Public Investment and Growth in Uganda', IGC Working Paper, November 2014.

AfDB (African Development Bank) (2015). 'Delivering on the Promise: Leveraging Natural Resources to Accelerate Human Development in Africa', a joint report of the African Development Bank and the Bill and Melinda Gates Foundation. Available at: <http://www.gatesfoundation.org/What-We-Do/Global-Policy/Natural-Resources/> (accessed 5 June 2016).

Daniel, P., Keen, M., and McPherson, C. (2010). 'The Taxation of Petroleum and Minerals: Principles, Problems, and Practice', IMF, Washington, D.C.

Deloitte (2013). 'Oil and Gas Taxation in Tanzania', updated 2016. Available at: <https://www2.deloitte.com/content/dam/Deloitte/global/Documents/Energy-and-Resources/gx-er-oil-and-gas-tax-guide-tanzania.pdf> (accessed 3 August 2016).

Henstridge, M. and Page, J. M. (2012). 'Managing a Modest Boom: Oil Revenues in Uganda', OxCarre Research Paper 8/12, Oxford.

Henstridge, M. and Travis, N., with Slaven, C. and Rai, S. (2015). 'Natural Resource Revenues and Macroeconomic Policy Choices', background paper to BMGF/AfDB Flagship Report: 'Delivering on the Promise: Leveraging Natural Resources to Accelerate Human Development in Africa'.

ICMM (International Council on Mining and Metals) (2014). 'Enhancing Mining's Contribution to the Zambian Economy and Society', republished as 'Mining: Partnerships for Development Toolkit'.

IMF (International Monetary Fund) (2014). 'United Republic of Tanzania: Selected Issues', CR: 14/121, IMF, Washington, D.C.

IMF (2015). 'Staff Report: Republic of Tanzania: Second Review under the Policy Support Instrument', CR: 15/181, IMF, Washington, D.C.

Moyo, M., Simson, R., Jacob, A., and de Mevius, F.-X (2010). 'Attaining Middle-Income Status: Tanzania: Growth and Structural Transformation Required to Reach Middle Income Status by 2025', IGC Working Paper, Dar es Salaam.

OPM (Oxford Policy Management) (2013). 'Impact of LNG in Tanzania', report for BG Group presented at a workshop for government, August 2013, available on request.

Sutton, J. and Olomi, D. (2012). 'An Enterprise Map of Tanzania', International Growth Centre, London.

Venables, A. J. (2012). 'Tanzania's Resource Challenge', paper prepared for International Growth Centre seminar on 'Harnessing the gains from natural gas: opportunities and challenges for Tanzania', Dar es Salaam.

VSO (Voluntary Service Overseas) (2014). 'Pathway to Vocational Employment in the Emerging Tanzanian Gas Sector—a Collaborative Assessment of Vocational and Educational Training Needs', a report by VSO with VETA, Dar es Salaam.

4

Transforming Dar es Salaam into a City That Works

Paul Collier and Patricia Jones

4.1 Introduction

Urbanization is central to the national growth process. As countries develop, workers move from rural areas to urban areas for jobs that are productive and therefore better paid. Not only do the people who migrate to cities gain, those who remain in rural areas also become better off: they have more land per person, and their produce fetches better prices in urban markets.

As shown in Figure 4.1, most countries reach an urbanization rate of about 40 per cent before achieving upper middle-income status (countries with a gross domestic product [GDP] per capita of more than US$2,505 but less than US$12,125) while high-income countries have urbanization rates of 70 per cent to 80 per cent (World Bank, 2013).

Tanzania—like other countries in sub-Saharan Africa—is urbanizing rapidly. Its rate of urbanization is slightly higher than the sub-Saharan Africa average but not as high as that of other developing regions such as East Asia (Figure 4.2).

Since 1967, Tanzania's cities have become home to more than 30 million new residents (Wenban-Smith, 2014). Dar es Salaam—Tanzania's primate city—has experienced the largest increase in population (see Table 4.1). Between 2002 and 2012, its population grew by more than 6 per cent per annum, with over 70 per cent of this increase being accounted for by in-migration from other regions (Wenban-Smith, 2014). Although Dar es Salaam is no longer Tanzania's political capital (Dodoma became the national capital in 1973), it remains the country's largest city, both in terms of population and business activity.

Tanzania is 30 per cent urban today and will be 50 per cent urban by the year 2030. Since the national population will also increase substantially,

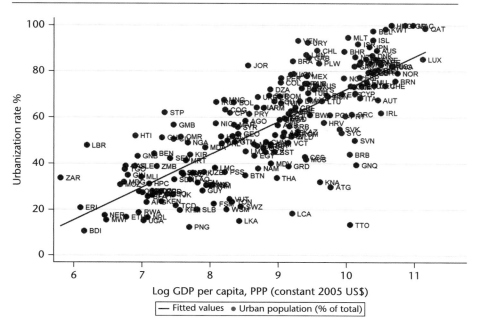

Figure 4.1. Urbanization and economic development
Source: World Development Indicators, authors' calculations.

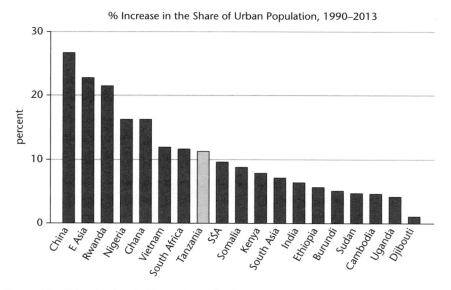

Figure 4.2. Urbanization in Tanzania and other countries
Source: World Development Indicators, authors' calculations.

Table 4.1. Urbanization in Tanzania across time

Tanzania	1967 Census	1978 Census	1988 Census	2002 Census	2012 Census
Mainland Urban Population (Growth rate % p.a.)	685,092	2,257,921 (11.5%)	3,999,882 (5.9%)	7,554,838 (4.7 %)	12,701,238 (5.3%)
- of which Dar es Salaam (Growth rate % p.a.)	*272,821*	*769,445 (9.9%)*	*1,205,443 (4.6%)*	*2,336,055 (4.8%)*	*4,364,541 (6.5%)*
Mainland Total Population (Growth rate % p.a.)	11,975,757	17,036,499 (3.3%)	22,507,047 (2.8%)	33,461,849 (2.9%)	43,625,354 (2.7%)
Urbanisation (%)	5.7	13.3	17.8	22.6	29.1

Source: Wenban-Smith (2014).

Tanzania's urban population is expected to triple in size over the next thirty-four years. This means that only one-third of the urbanization infrastructure that Tanzania will need by 2050 has already been built. Yet it has taken around a century to build that existing third. The challenge facing the society between now and 2050 is thus to build twice as much as has yet been built but in just one-third of the time.

But it will not even be enough to do six times more than what has been done. As we show, Tanzania's urbanization to date has not generated the physical conditions in which ordinary workers can be productive, and ordinary households can live in decent surroundings. That so much is left to be built is a huge opportunity to do things better but this depends upon understanding what has gone wrong to date.

In this chapter we set out the potential of urbanization, present new evidence that Dar es Salaam is not yet realizing this potential, and discuss the policies that could promote change. We focus on Dar es Salaam because it is Tanzania's primate city. Currently, Dar es Salaam accounts for 40 per cent of the country's urban population, 17 per cent of GDP, and 70 per cent of all taxes (World Bank, 2015).

4.2 Connectivity and the Miracle of Urban Productivity

The starting point in understanding what has gone wrong is to see how a successful city raises the productivity of its workforce. It does so through enabling firms to achieve *scale* and *specialization*. The simplest benefits of scale are technological: for example, a large boiler is more efficient than a small one. Specialization enables skills to develop. Skill develops through time spent doing the same task, a process known as 'learning by doing'. Probably the most important component of the miracle of productivity that cities enable is that by specializing on a single narrowly defined task, a worker is able to concentrate learning on acquiring the corresponding narrowly defined skill. As a result, the workforce accumulates far more human capital than if it were unspecialized. Scale and specialization interact. At low volumes of production a task that requires only a small proportion of the total work time will not warrant having anyone dedicated to it. Hence, the larger is the scale of production the more specialized each worker can be. Scale and specialization apply not just within individual firms, but to the market as a whole. Scale enables more firms to co-exist, and so makes markets more competitive. Competition is a spur to *dynamic* efficiency: firms struggle to innovate in order to get ahead of rival firms.

Scale and specialization both have important spatial implications. Technological scale can only be realized if the product is produced in one place. Market scale economies can only be realized if many producers are able to reach a common large group of consumers. Specialization in a particular skill is only possible if many complementary skills can be mustered together in the same location. The common spatial requirement for these conditions is *connectivity*. Producers must be sufficiently well-connected with consumers that both can transact in markets that are specialized yet competitive; workers must be sufficiently well-connected with firms that both can transact in such markets. Since people both consume and work these distinct transactions share a common need: *connectivity between households and firms*.

A successful city provides good connectivity. It can be achieved in two different ways: the distance between households and firms can be reduced, and the cost of transport per unit of distance between them can be reduced. These two approaches require different actions but they are complements not alternatives. Reducing the distance between households and firms involves increasing their density of occupation: firms and households cluster more closely together. Reducing the cost of transport per unit of distance involves investment in transport infrastructure, such as roads and rail lines, and transport services such as bus companies. Although these are distinct, over a range they are complements. As the density of occupation in any two locations increases, there is more scope for reaping scale economies in transport links between them. However, for any given transport technology, at some point increases in density start to increase the unit cost of transport. This is due to congestion, the most evident example being a traffic jam.

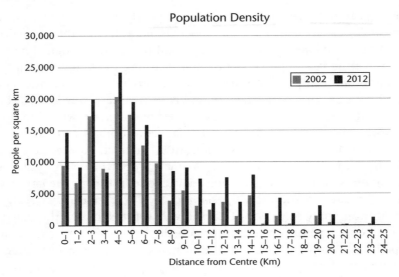

Figure 4.3. Population density in Dar es Salaam, 2002 and 2012
Source: Census 2002 and 2012.

In summary, *productivity depends upon connectivity, and the two inputs into connectivity are density and transport*. So how well has Dar es Salaam been doing in respect of density and transport?

Near the central business district (CBD), the average population density of Dar es Salaam is about 20,000 people per square kilometre (Figure 4.3). This is much lower than in more successful developing country cities. For example, by 1980 Jakarta's CBD was more than double this density, while in Shanghai and other large Asian cities it has exceeded 100,000 people per square kilometre. Although the population of Dar es Salaam is growing, the extra people are accommodated predominantly by the city spreading outwards rather than by higher density. Figure 4.3 shows where the extra population located during 2002/12.

As to transport in the city, a useful indicator is how people get to work. The most common mode of transport to work is on foot. According to the Measuring Living Standards within Cities data, 43 per cent of household heads walk to work (Figure 4.4). One implication is that many workers are only able to seek jobs in those areas of the city within walking distance of their homes. Thus, Dar es Salaam is currently not benefiting from the potential productivity gains of an integrated urban labour market.

More fundamentally, it is not generating the productive jobs that follow from firms being able to achieve scale and specialization. Most people (87 per cent) work in micro enterprises (World Bank, 2014). Such small firms cannot generate high productivity even if they cluster together in densely populated

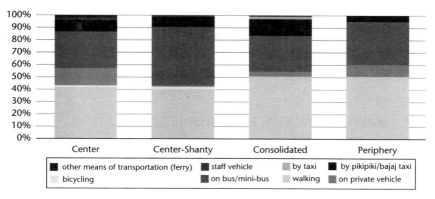

Figure 4.4. Means of transport to work
Source: World Bank (2015).

areas. While our data do not allow us to investigate changes over time, we find that for micro, small, and medium-sized firms, worker productivity is *not* correlated with density. As a result, around half of all the owners of small-scale businesses, (let alone their employees), say that they would accept a fulltime, salaried job if offered one (Financial Deepening Trust, 2012). Given the shortage of wage employment in larger, more productive firms, these individuals have no choice but to earn a living through self-employment. To the limited extent that Tanzanian cities have provided connectivity it has helped larger firms to be more productive. We find that in contrast to the lack of a relationship between productivity and density for smaller firms, for those which are larger and formal, (those with over a hundred employees), productivity increases as cities get larger. The problem is not that good connectivity does not deliver productivity in Tanzania, but that connectivity is so inadequate that few large firms can survive.

The density and transport which a city needs to support productive firms are the result of investments in physical structures. There are three distinct types of structures, each undertaken by a different type of investor: households invest in residential property, firms invest in commercial property, and government invests in infrastructure. Each type of investment involves thousands of decisions by many different people, but the pay-off to each particular investment depends upon what other investments are made. This interdependence requires some mechanism for coordination of the thousands of decisions involved. There are two processes for achieving this coordination: active markets in urban land and credible planning. Sometimes they are posed as alternatives, but this is a mistake: they are complementary. Markets alone cannot satisfactorily resolve the indeterminacy that follows from interdependence, while planning alone cannot possibly cope with the vast amount of information required for so many different decisions. Tanzanian urbanization has not suffered from an imbalance between active land markets and credible planning, but from an acute shortage of both.

4.3 Connectivity and Firm Productivity: New Tanzanian Evidence

Inadequate investment in connectivity inhibits the miracle of productivity. One consequence is that firms struggle to compete internationally and this may have contributed to Africa's lack of success in global manufacturing. Since 1980, Africa's share of world output of both manufactured goods and trade has declined (UNIDO, 2009). Between 1995 and 2008, employment growth in manufacturing was only about 3 per cent in Africa whereas it was more than 6 per cent for other developing regions (Page, 2011).

In other regions urbanization and industrialization have tended to go hand-in-hand (Figure 4.5). Manufacturing continues to grow until urbanization reaches about 60 per cent and manufacturing comprises about 15 per cent of GDP.

This pattern of development, however, not been followed by Tanzania, and indeed not by most countries in sub-Saharan Africa (Figure 4.6). Instead,

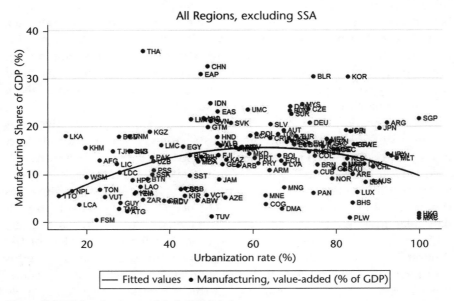

Figure 4.5. Urbanization and industrialization

Source: World Development Indicators, authors' calculations.

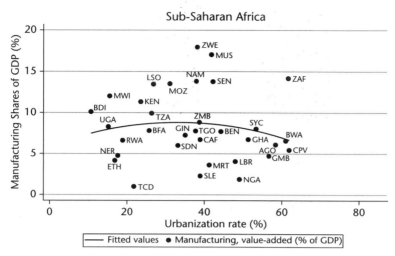

Figure 4.6. Urbanization and industrialization in SSA
Source: World Development Indicators, authors' calculations.

urbanization has occurred without industrialization. While Tanzania is slightly above the African average in terms of its manufacturing share, it lags behind other African countries like South Africa.

So what has been driving urbanization in Tanzania? Recent research by Gollin et al. (2016) suggests that the key driver has been rapid, natural resource development. In Tanzania, as in much of Africa, the natural resource sector has grown rapidly, due partly to new discoveries and partly to the increased prices of the recent super-cycle for existing resource extraction. This expansion has attracted workers into the sector from both agriculture and manufacturing. Meanwhile, the income generated from the resource sector has been spent disproportionately on manufactured goods that are imported, and services that cannot be imported. These services are produced in Tanzania's cities and account for the rapid urban growth. However, such cities are merely catering for consumer demand generated by the success of the resource sector, rather than themselves generating a miracle of productivity. Gollin terms them 'consumption cities' to contrast with the cities of East Asia in which growth is driven by industrialization.

Is this an accurate characterization of Tanzanian urbanization to date? To find out, we use new data on the productivity of Tanzanian firms. We draw upon two surveys: the World Bank Enterprise Survey data (2006/12) and the Micro, Small, and Medium Enterprise (MSME) Survey which was collected in 2010 by the Financial Sector Deepening Trust in collaboration with the Tanzanian Ministry of Trade and National Bureau of Statistics.

Gollin et al.'s hypothesis of the 'consumption city' is that urban growth is dominated by the services sector. This is indeed the pattern in Dar es Salaam: a large percentage of both formal and informal sector firms operate in retail trade and services. According to the most recent Business Register Survey (2011/12), 57 per cent of firms in the formal sector and 52 per cent of firms in the informal sector are engaged in wholesale or retail trade. This percentage rises to almost 75 per cent when food service is included. Consistent with Dar es Salaam being a 'consumption city', manufacturing accounts for only 6 per cent of formal sector firms and 1 per cent of micro and small firms. Furthermore, this percentage has decreased over the past decade. Back in 2003/05, the figure for formal sector firms was 10 per cent (Business Survey 2003–05 [National Bureau of Statistics, 2006]).

According to the MSME data, there are 405,902 micro, small, and medium enterprises in Dar es Salaam, with over 800,000 people working in them. Most of these enterprises are one-person establishments with no paid employees that are run at the household level. These firms trade mainly in retail and food services (Figure 4.7), and their turnover rate is high. For example, more than 30 per cent of these firms had exited the market during the two years prior to the MSME survey.

Around a third of all informal enterprises are located at the owner's own house, and a further 20 per cent are located in a house that the business owner rents. Thus over half of all informal sector firms are located in residential areas (Figure 4.8). Most of the others are located by the roadside or operate as mobile businesses which move across the city from day to day. Only 17 per cent are in fixed markets, commercial, or industrial areas. Perhaps not surprisingly, the geographic market which these firms serve is limited. More than 70 per cent report that 'most of their customers live within the same ward as where their firm is located'.

Inevitably, firms that are this small cannot reap the potential of urbanization for productivity gains. We find that their productivity is not correlated with either density or transport connections (as measured by access to roads). More specifically, to examine the relationship between urban characteristics and firm productivity, we estimate the following productivity equation:

$$lny_{idr} = \beta_0 + X_{idr}\theta + Z_{idr}\gamma + U_d\delta + v_r + \epsilon_{idr} \qquad (4.1)$$

where y is the monthly sales per worker of the ith firm which is located in urban district d and region r, X is a vector of the business owner's characteristics (e.g., age, gender, years of education, etc.), Z is a vector of firm characteristics (e.g., number of paid employees, industrial sector, firm age, etc.), δ is a vector of urban district characteristics, v_r are regional fixed effects, and ϵ_{icr} is an error term. Our focus is on the estimated coefficients for the urban characteristics, δ. We include six of them and restrict our sample to firms which operate

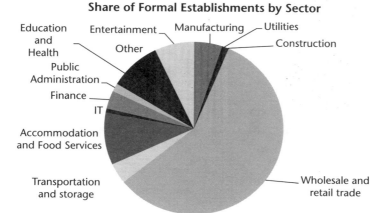

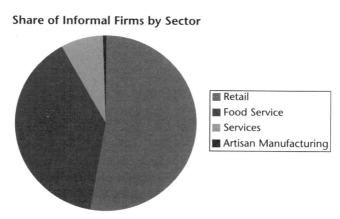

Figure 4.7. Share of firms by sector
Source: Authors' calculations based on Business Register Report 2011/12
(National Bureau of Statistics, Tanzania) and MSME Survey (FSDT 2012).

in urban districts of which there are twenty-four in Tanzania. Our six characteristics are population density (logged); the growth of night lights 2005/10;
and four distances: to the nearest paved, trunk road, to the nearest paved,
regional road, to the coast, and to Lake Victoria.

We distinguish between two types of entrepreneurs: true and reluctant. We
proxy 'true' entrepreneurs as those business owners who reported that they
started their business because they 'saw a profitable market opportunity', or
'wanted to try a business idea', or 'believed they could make more money
working for themselves than someone else'. 'Reluctant' entrepreneurs are
simply those who cited any other reason for starting a business. For example,
12 per cent of business owners reported that they started their business because
they had 'no better option'. Such business owners are not entrepreneurs in the

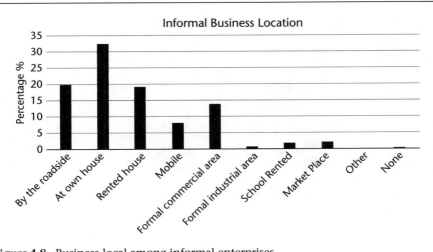

Figure 4.8. Business local among informal enterprises
Source: MSME Survey (FSDT 2012).

true sense—that is, individuals who see a market opportunity and capitalize on it. Rather, they are struggling to survive.

When we run the equation on the sample of 'reluctant' entrepreneurs, none of these urban characteristics is significant. By contrast, when run on the sample of 'true' entrepreneurs, we find that proximity to a paved road and access to electricity are both positively correlated with firm productivity and significant at the 5 per cent level. Population density, however, remains insignificant. We then introduced another probable influence on productivity, namely education. We investigated whether education enabled entrepreneurs to take advantage of the greater market opportunities provided by population density. For this we added a further term which inter-acted the entrepreneur's level of education with the population density of his district. This new term was indeed positively associated with firm productivity (and significant)—but again only for the sample of 'true' entrepreneurs. Thus, even for small firms, as long as they are run by entrepreneurs who are educated and motivated, productivity is enhanced by connectivity (through both density and transport). This is the case even when controlling for the capital intensity of the firm, the industry that it is in, and the entrepreneur's other personal characteristics. An implication is that connectivity can benefit small firms as well as large ones. But the benefits for small firms depend upon a higher level of education than is currently common, and a more selective entry into entrepreneurship. This in turn depends upon more jobs being generated by large firms that provide a better alternative for 'reluctant' entrepreneurs.

4.4 Livability: Evidence for Dar es Salaam

Well-functioning cities are not only productive places for firms, they are also pleasant places for people to live. So how livable is Dar es Salaam? We take several measures of livability, drawing on the Tanzanian Budget Surveys, the Tanzanian National Panel Survey, and the Measuring Living Standards within Cities Survey of the World Bank. The evidence suggests that Dar es Salaam still has a long way to go before the majority of its residents have access to basic services and affordable housing. According to the latest Population and Housing Census (2012), the city has 4.4 million inhabitants. It accounts for 40 per cent of Tanzania's urban population, 17 per cent of its GDP, and 70 per cent of its taxes (World Bank, 2015).

Due to its implications for health, probably the single most important measures of livability concern water: both the disposal of human waste, and the supply of drinking water. Most households in Dar es Salaam (58 per cent) share their toilet facilities. This is considerably higher than in other urban areas at 46 per cent (Tanzania National Panel Survey 2010/11). Not only do most households share toilets, but they rely upon unventilated pit latrines (Figure 4.9). Having more space, rural households have better access to sanitation than urban households with only 20 per cent sharing a toilet.

As to drinking water, less than half of households have access to piped water, and this is mostly shared. Over 40 per cent of households report that their main source of water is the water pipe at a neighbour's house (Measuring Living Standards within Cities Survey (MLSC)). Strikingly, access to piped water has sharply declined over the past decade (see Figure 4.10).

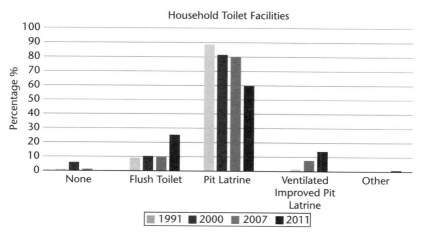

Figure 4.9. Household sanitation in Dar es Salaam
Source: Household Budget Surveys.

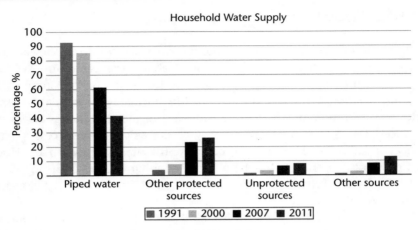

Figure 4.10. Household water supply in Dar es Salaam
Source: Household Budget Surveys.

The city authorities have not yet managed to reconcile livability with density. In the high density areas of the city—the shanty areas—80 per cent of households share toilet facilities and 51 per cent share a water source. In contrast, on the periphery of the city, where density is much lower, access to basic services is better. There, only 36 per cent of households share toilet facilities (World Bank, 2015).

A further important measure of livability is the quality of the housing stock. In Dar es Salaam, 60 per cent of residents now live in slums, defined as areas characterized by some combination of poor quality housing, over-crowding, and inadequate access to clean water and sanitation (UN Habitat, 2010).

4.5 Public Policies that Deliver Connectivity: Land Markets and Credible Planning

Evidently Dar es Salaam is not yet a city in which plenty of firms can be productive, and ordinary people are able to live in decent conditions. But by 2050 Dar es Salaam may well be three times its present size, and this expansion is an opportunity to reshape the city. We have suggested that making Dar es Salaam a productive city requires enhanced connectivity. In turn this requires both greater density of firms and households, and better transport links between them. Coordinating the thousands of investment decisions involved in achieving connectivity depend upon active land markets and credible planning. Each of these requires strong public policies.

Land markets depend upon an efficient process of registering and exchanging land titles: Tanzania lacks such a system. Many households do not have tenure security and therefore worry about possible eviction. Around 80 per cent of all the buildings in Dar es Salaam are situated on unplanned land (Kironde, 2009). Lacking both secure title and supporting infrastructure, there has been little incentive to make substantial investments in these buildings. As a result, Dar es Salaam is overwhelmingly a single-storey city, and so even the modest levels of density achieved near the city centre come at the price of overcrowding. Lacking the floor space that would be provided by multi-storey building, the shanty areas are very crowded without being very dense.

Secure titles will need to be complemented by active markets in land and homes. Land near the city centre needs to change use from single-storey homes to business premises and multi-storey housing; people will only search for jobs in a wider area of the city if they can readily relocate.

Credible planning depends not upon drawings done by architects, but upon laying down physical infrastructure that decisively defines patterns of future land use by means of roads, water, power, and sewerage. Yet Dar es Salaam has little planned land. While many factors are likely to be involved, there is little doubt that the city's regulatory framework plays a major role. Acquiring planned land in Dar es Salaam is not easy. Individuals must comply with at least three forms of regulation. First are *administrative procedures* (steps that individuals have to take in order to apply for and acquire planned land); next are *planning standards* (requirements—like minimum plot size); and finally, *planning regulations* (rules that restrict land from certain types of development). In many cases, these regulations make it economically infeasible for urban residents to acquire planned land, forcing them to seek alternative land sources. Planning standards, for example, require that urban plots be at least 400 square metres, which, given current land prices, is beyond the budget of most Tanzanians.

To try to alleviate this problem, the government initiated a large, planned land delivery project in 2002 which became known as the 20,000 Plots Project. The project eventually turned out nearly 35,000 plots in twelve locations, consuming some 75,816,731 square metres of land. However, it had weaknesses. Despite the poor living conditions for ordinary people it targeted mainly middle and high income households. Despite the need for density, it contributed to Dar es Salaam's sprawl, a process which we have already seen from Table 4.1, which showed the changes in population density at different distances from the city centre. Most of the 20,000 plots were developed in peri-urban areas and had large plot sizes. Figure 4.11 shows their location. Despite it now being over ten years since the project was first implemented, many plots remain undeveloped, and those that have been developed tend to have expensive houses.

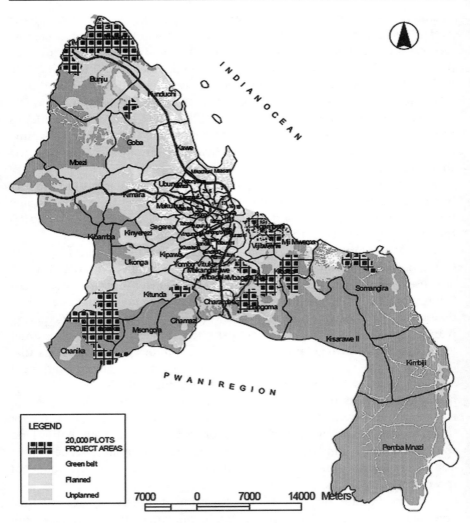

Figure 4.11. Map of the locations of the 20,000 plot areas
Source: UN Habitat (2010).

Despite these limitations, the Ministry of Lands has chosen to replicate the 20,000 Plots Project, extending loans to the three municipalities of Dar es Salaam so that they can implement similar schemes. Planned land use schemes have been carried out in areas of Gezaulole (Temeke), Kinyerezi (Ilala), and Mivumoni (Kinondoni). Municipalities have also taken out loans from financial institutions to assist them in their development. The Kinyerezi scheme, however, has stalled due to disagreement between the municipality and land owners. A further large new housing project has taken place in

Kigamboni which, though near the city centre, is not easily accessible. The area lies on the eastern shore of Dar es Salaam (across the harbour from the CBD) and can only be reached by ferry or car. Both options are time consuming: there are long waits for the ferry and the overland car route can take two hours. A bridge is being constructed across the harbour, financed largely by the National Social Security Fund (NSSF), and this will connect Kigamboni to the CBD. It is likely to have a fundamental impact on the spatial development of Dar es Salaam.

While these government projects were intended to increase the supply of planned land, severe shortages still persist. If it is not possible radically to speed up the public preparation of land, a more minimalist approach would be to auction land to commercial developers, with conditions attached concerning the infrastructure which they must provide and the time by which it must be completed. Recall that the preparation of urban land must proceed far more swiftly than it has to date.

The infrastructure needed for connectivity and decent living conditions is partly for livable density and partly for transport links. That for density is site preparation such as beneath-ground water, sewerage, and power. That for transport links is the local road grid, the arteries that connect localities to the CBD, and a dedicated mass transit system such as Bus Rapid Transit (BRT). A BRT system is now being retrofitted to cover parts of Dar es Salaam, but it would have been far easier to install, in terms of both politics and cost, if it had been done in advance of settlement.

Despite government initiatives, Dar es Salaam and other cities have become increasingly short of the infrastructure needed for connectivity and decent living conditions. Yet with an effective tax system, its cost can be fully recovered. The productivity that connectivity generates is reflected in higher land values for those locations at which firms can operate productively and households can live within reach of productive work. Taxing this appreciation in land values, both directly and through annual charges on land ownership, provides a simple means of financing infrastructure. Yet to date, land appreciation in Dar es Salaam has been captured by well-connected individuals rather than by society as a whole.

4.6 Conclusion

Tanzania is urbanizing fast but it is still only about one-third of the way through its urbanization process. This gives policy makers a window of opportunity to design new policies which avoid the mistakes of the past. From global experience, we know that urbanization can bring large benefits: by enabling firms to reap the productivity gains of scale and specialization it makes ordinary workers better off. Cities perform this miracle of productivity by providing good connectivity between firms and households. Connectivity depends partly upon high density of settlement, and partly upon good transport links within the city and to national and international markets. But high density threatens to reduce livability unless floor space per hectare is increased by constructing buildings that have multiple storeys. Both transport links and building height require large investments. The myriad decisions that underpin these investments need to be coordinated through active land markets and planning that is made credible by advance public investment in pertinent infrastructure. Both land markets and public investment require strong public policies.

The evidence that we have presented suggests that even to date such limited connectivity as has been achieved has enhanced firm productivity. But connectivity has been far too limited to provide an environment in which many large firms can prosper. The most common means of getting to work is on foot, and in receiving and making the deliveries intrinsic to the functioning of large firms, they face traffic gridlock. As a result there are very few jobs in large firms. Most urban workers have no option but to try to be small-scale entrepreneurs despite lacking the motivation and education to succeed. Such tiny, ill-managed firms cannot harness even the limited potential for scale and specialization feasible with current urban connectivity since they lack the necessary 'organizational capital'.

The evidence also suggests that, as in much of urban Africa, living conditions in urban Tanzania are very poor. In some respects they are worse than in rural areas, and also worse than Asian cities. The cost of African urban labour is often higher than in other developing regions that are competitors for the location of global manufacturing (Gelb et al., 2013; Iarossi, 2009). The need for firms to compensate for poor living conditions by offering higher wages may account for the higher cost of labour. If so, poor living conditions feed directly back onto the economy, inhibiting industrialization.

So, what needs to be done to transform Dar es Salaam into a well-functioning city? Getting the right institutional and planning systems in place is critical. Much of the city's growth has taken place without effective planning by local government. Dar es Salaam, for example, had no master plan in place between 1999 and 2012. As a result, a large percentage of the city's roads are unplanned and not paved. While the government published a new master plan in 2013, it will need to expand its revenue base significantly in order to carry out the planned investments.

Both Dar es Salaam and secondary cities in Tanzania need to develop clear investment plans that are funded through a variety of financial instruments. Recent improvements in revenue collection in Tanzania's medium-sized cities (utilizing modern, GIS-based, electronic systems) show promise, and similar efforts should be scaled up to all urban local governments. Inter-governmental fiscal transfers need to become more consistent, be linked with investment demand, and respond to performance metrics. In addition, taxing land appreciation is a fair and non-distortionary way of raising tax revenues. Building the capacity to tax valuable urban land links naturally to the need for a register of land ownership. In turn, clarity of land ownership is a pre-condition for an effective land market. Without such a market, the city is unable to evolve through changing uses of land as it grows. Partly because of this, much of the growth to date has been in outward sprawl instead of internal intensification. Looking towards the future, <u>plans should be put in place to reinvest the antici-</u><u>pated revenue from the gas sector into Tanzania's cities.</u>

Acknowledgement

This chapter is a part of a Global Research Program on Spatial Development of Cities, funded by the Multi Donor Trust Fund on Sustainable Urbanization of the World Bank and supported by the UK Department for International Development.

Appendix: City Size and Firm Productivity

Our results on small firms depend upon a single, cross-section of data. The correlations that we observe may reflect causal relationships but could also arise indirectly. Our evidence is consistent with what is known about the productivity benefits of connect-ivity from studies in other countries, but in itself it is not decisive. We can correct for some of these deficiencies by using new data from the World Bank Enterprise Surveys which enable the same firm to be studied at two different times: 2006 and 2012. With

Table 4.2. Firm productivity and city size

	(1)	(2)	(3)	(4)
Log (K/L)	0.273**	0.285**	0.161**	0.201**
	(0.02)	(0.02)	(0.05)	(0.05)
Log(L)	0.294	−0.374*	−0.134	−1.297**
	(0.08)	(0.09)	(0.12)	(0.32)
Log(POP)	0.073	−0.307	−0.039	−0.7210**
	(0.05)	(0.10)	(0.09)	(0.21)
Log(POP)*Log(L)	*	0.099**	*	0.164**
	−	(0.01)		(0.04)
Firm Fixed Effects	No	No	Yes	Yes
Time Fixed Effects	Yes	Yes	Yes	Yes
R-squared	0.41	0.42	0.17	0.34
Observations	288	288	288	288

Notes: Dependent Variable is the logarithm of annual sales per worker. Robust standard errors in parentheses. ** and * represent significance at the 1 per cent and 5 per cent level respectively.

these data we ask a simple question: 'Do larger cities in Tanzania increase firm productivity?' For this we estimate the following equation:

$$lny_{ict} = \beta_0 + \beta_1 lnk_{ict} + \beta_2 lnl_{ict} + \beta_3 lnPOP_{ct} + v_i + w_t + \epsilon_{ict} \qquad (4.2)$$

where y is the annual sales per worker of the ith firm which is located in city c at year t, k is the firm's capital–labour ratio, l is the firm's number of full-time employees, POP is the city population of the city where the firm is located, v_i are firm fixed effects, w_t are time fixed effects, and ϵ_{ict} is an error term. Our sample is comprised of 288 firms which are located in Tanzania's three largest cities (Dar es Salaam, Mwanza, and Arusha). We estimate the model with fixed effects (using a fixed effects estimator) and without (using an OLS estimator). In addition, we estimate equation (4.2) with an interaction term between $lnPOP$ and lnl. The results from our estimation analysis are listed in Table 4.2.

References

Financial Deepening Trust (2012). 'Micro, Small, and Medium Enterprises in Tanzania: National Baseline Survey Report', Dar es Salaam, Tanzania.

Gelb, A., Meyer, C., and Ramachandran, V. (2013). 'Does Poor Mean Cheap? A Comparative Look at Africa's Industrial Labor Costs', Center for Global Development, Working Paper 325, May.

Gollin, D., Jedwab, R., and Vollrath, D. (2016). 'Urbanization with and with Industrialization'. *Journal of Economic Growth,* 24(1): 35–70.

Iarossi, G. (2009). 'The Africa Competitiveness Report', World Economic Forum.

Kironde, L. (2009). 'Improving Land Governance in Africa: The Case of Tanzania', paper prepared for the workshop on 'Land Governance in Support of the MDGs: Responding to New Challenges', Washington, D.C., 9–10 March 2010.

National Bureau of Statistics (Tanzania) (2006). 'Business Survey 2003–05'. Volume 1: Dar es Salaam Report, Dar es Salaam, Tanzania.

National Bureau of Statistics (Tanzania) (2012). 'Business Register Report 2011/12: Tanzania Mainland.' Dar es Salaam, Tanzania.

Page, J. (2011). 'Can Africa Industrialize?' *Journal of African Economies* 21, AERC Supplement 2: ii86–ii125.

UN Habitat (2010). 'Citywide Action Plan for Upgrading Unplanned and Unserviced Settlements in Dar es Salaam', UN Habitat, Nairobi.

United Nations Industrial Development Organization (UNIDO) (2009). 'Industrial Development Report. Breaking in and Moving Up, New Industrial Challenges for the Bottom Billion and the Middle-Income Countries'.

Wenban-Smith, H. (2014). 'Population Growth, Internal Migration and Urbanization in Tanzania: 1967–2020: A Census Based Regional Analysis', IGC Working Paper.

World Bank (2013). 'Harnessing Urbanization to End Poverty and Boost Prosperity in Africa: An Action Agenda for Transformation', World Bank, Washington, D.C.

World Bank (2014). 'Tanzania's Economic Update: Who Wants a Job? The Magnetic Power of Cities', World Bank, Washington, D.C.

World Bank (2015). 'Tanzania Policy Note', mimeo, World Bank, Washington, D.C.

5

Trade, Logistics Infrastructure, and Regional Integration

Charles Kunaka, Olivier Hartmann, Gaël Raballand, and Rukia Shamte

5.1 Introduction

In March 2015, the Tanzanian President convened the first Central Corridor Heads of State summit in Dar es Salaam. In August 2015, an inter-state council of Ministers from Rwanda, Burundi, Tanzania, and Democratic Republic of Congo (DRC) was held to develop trade along the Central Corridor. It builds on the establishment of the Central Corridor Transit and Transport Facilitation Agency in 2006 and a specific non-tariff barrier (NTB) Monitoring Committee at National levels and at the East African Community (EAC) at the Regional Level.

The Government of Tanzania aims at increasing trade flows from and to Dar es Salaam, especially to the Tanzanian hinterland.[1] Amid major port and transport investment programmes ongoing or planned in the region, the Government of Tanzania aims at confirming its role of major maritime gateway for the entire East Africa region. Tanzania is seeking to pursue an export-led growth strategy that exploits its natural geographical location. As part of this strategy, the country and Dar es Salaam in particular have the opportunity to service both import and export trade into and out of the East Africa and Great Lakes region.

The port of Dar es Salaam has served as a trade gateway since 1867 when Sultan Sayyid Majid selected it as a caravan and commercial centre (Illiffe, 1979). Since then, the port has grown into the pre-eminent trade gateway for Tanzania, handling more than 90 per cent of its trade by volume, and for several neighbouring landlocked countries. The connectivity by land transport of the port to neighbouring countries evolved partly due to economic demands but also due to political developments. The initial push in the early twentieth century was by road and rail, especially to the west of Dar es Salaam, towards Lakes Victoria and Tanganyika. The southward connections received particular attention only in the latter half of the century, when a highway and pipeline to Zambia were developed in the late 1960s to provide Zambia with an outlet to the sea following the closure of the southern routes to South Africa passing through what was then Rhodesia. A railway link to Zambia was built in the early 1970s also for the same reasons and with funding from China.

However, in the decades that followed, Dar es Salaam lost traffic to competing corridors, namely the Northern Corridor for the landlocked countries in East Africa and a reopened Southern Corridor (now North–South Corridor) to South Africa and its ports, for Zambian and DRC traffic. Relatively poor volumes and performance persisted until the early 2000s when the authorities started introducing major reforms to the management of the port and rail and invested large amounts in rehabilitating the national and regional road networks to neighbouring countries. It is these developments in the core logistics infrastructure and systems that hold the key to the growth prospects of the port to serve as a logistics hub.

Over the last five years, Tanzanian Government and the Central Corridor Member States have taken some measures to improve the flow of traffic via the Dar es Salaam Port and along the corridors.[2] In 2013, the Government of the United Republic of Tanzania engaged a consulting firm to develop a monitoring strategy that would result in timely identification of potential growth factors and actions to be taken that would ensure achievement of trade along the Central Corridor. This resulted in a programme called 'Big Results Now' (BRN).

Port competition is developed in the Eastern and Southern sub-regions: the entire Eastern and Southern Africa is connected to the rest of the world through four main regional gateways: Djibouti, Mombasa in Kenya, Dar es Salaam in Tanzania, and Durban in South Africa.[3] The regional growth potential is high since the total regional population of Rwanda, Burundi, Zambia, Uganda, Malawi, and the Democratic Republic of Congo, currently estimated at 200 million people, is expected to double every twenty-five years with the current rate of growth with subsequent required trade outlets.

This chapter explores the potential for Tanzania/Dar es Salaam to exploit its geographical advantage and discusses the economic and political economy challenges, in the short and medium term, that need to be addressed to realize this vision.[4] Moreover, it estimates the benefits of traffic in transit for Tanzania, especially in Dar es Salaam region. Finally, it identifies some possible actions in order for Tanzania and Dar es Salaam in particular to attract more traffic in transit.

In terms of the main messages, container traffic will soon exceed the capacity limits of the port of Dar es Salaam, for which traffic in transit accounts for approximately one-third of the total container traffic. The increase in traffic in transit seems to be mainly due to captive markets in East and Southern Africa. Because of international shipping lines strategies, the prospects for Dar es Salaam Port to become a transshipment hub are bleak in the short and medium term. However, overall traffic at the port of Dar es Salaam continues to grow, which will likely lead to a lack of capacity in the upcoming years.[5] But the Government should be careful about investing excessively in ports and roads because, even though investments in logistics are important for the Tanzanian economy to remain competitive, transport and logistics in transit have a limited potential for job creation as port activities are mainly capital-intensive.

5.2 Dar et Salaam Port Traffic Comparisons and Trends

This section presents Dar es Salam in a global and regional context before analysing the major traffic trends for Dar es Salaam Port.

5.2.1 Dar es Salaam Competitive Environment and Traffic Flows Comparisons

On a global scale, Dar es Salaam is a 'small' port because it accounts for less than 5 per cent of Dubai port container traffic, 20 per cent of Durban traffic, or even 60 per cent of Mombasa traffic (see Figure 5.1).

Dar es Salaam Port is the fourth largest in East Africa, after Durban, Mombasa, and Djibouti, according to the Port Management Association of Eastern and Southern Africa (PMAESA). Dar es Salaam is not the only maritime gateway for the landlocked countries of Eastern and South-Eastern Africa: Mombasa and Durban also compete to serve the hinterland.[6]

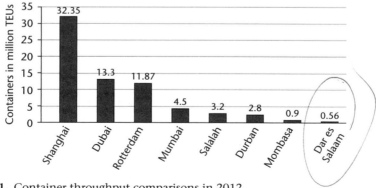

Figure 5.1. Container throughput comparisons in 2012
Source: EAC (2014).

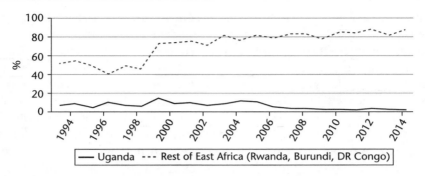

Figure 5.2. Share of Dar es Salaam in East Africa transit trade
Source: Kenya Ports Authority (KPA) and Tanzania Ports Authority (TPA) data.

Competition is, however, somewhat limited, as there is a preferred gateway for subsets of countries, rather than pure substitutability between ports. The South-Eastern Africa region (Malawi, Zambia, and Southern DR Congo) is shared by Dar es Salaam and Durban; the North-Eastern Africa region (South Sudan mainly) is exclusively served through Mombasa, and on the common East Africa hinterland, Uganda is primarily relying on Mombasa, while Rwanda, Burundi, and DR Congo are primarily relying on Dar es Salaam.

The growth of the traffic in Dar es Salaam has been driven by the growth of the Tanzania economy and the hinterland. Figure 5.2 shows that the respective market share versus Mombasa remained quite static over time.

5.2.2 Increasing Flows in Transit at the Port of Dar es Salaam

The port of Dar es Salaam serves a vast hinterland that extends well beyond the borders of Tanzania, as transit traffic represents one third of the activity of the port, reaching 4.6 million tons in 2014 for a total port throughput of 14.7 million tonnes (see Figure 5.3). The transit cargo comprises mostly petroleum products and containerized goods, and practically equal shares. In terms of geography, the hinterland of the port of Dar es Salaam comprises, from north to south, Uganda, Rwanda, Burundi, the eastern and southern parts of DR Congo, Zambia, and Malawi (see Figures 5.4 and 5.5).

The port of Dar es Salaam has been playing the role of a maritime gateway (see Box 5.1) for Eastern and South-Eastern Africa for several decades. The share of transit in the container activity has been fluctuating from above 40 per cent in the early 1990s to reach a low of 25 per cent in the early 2000s, to stabilize around one-third in the recent years (see Figure 5.6). In the meantime, the container traffic increased at an average annual rate of 9.1 per cent from 65,000 TEUs (twenty-foot equivalent units) in 1992 to 430,000 TEUs in 2014.

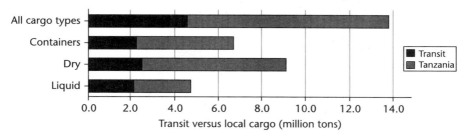

Figure 5.3. Traffic 2014 in Dar es Salaam—transit versus local cargo (million tons)
Source: Tanzania Ports Authority (TPA) data.

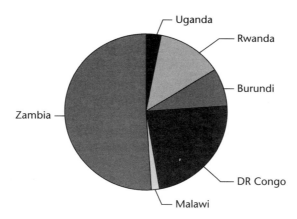

Figure 5.4. Transit for petroleum products in 2014
Source: Tanzania Ports Authority (TPA) data.

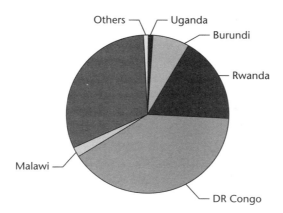

Figure 5.5. Transit for containers in 2014
Source: Tanzania Ports Authority (TPA) data.

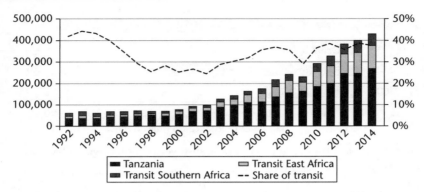

Figure 5.6. Evolution of transit and local containerized traffic in Dar es Salaam
Source: Tanzania Ports Authority (TPA) data.

Box 5.1. A QUESTION OF VOCABULARY—TRANSSHIPMENT HUBS, LOGISTICS HUBS, AND MARITIME GATEWAYS

The notion of a logistics hub refers to a node in a network. When applied to ports and shipping, however, it frequently evokes the notion of transshipment, a specific function in a shipping network. This function can be mirrored in the hinterland on the maritime side of the port.

To distinguish between the two notions, a different vocabulary is being used in this chapter, consistent with the commonly accepted designation of ports in the specialized literature:

- Hub (sometimes transshipment hub), refers to nodal position in a shipping network organized with main lines connecting in selected hub ports with a network of feeder or other intersecting main lines;
- Maritime gateway, refers to a port serving a large regional hinterland extending beyond the national boundaries.

These two functions may coexist in a given port, or a port can perform either one of the functions, or neither for secondary ports. An example of a pure transshipment hub is Salalah in Oman, examples of pure gateways are Dar es Salaam and Mombasa, and Durban is an example of a port combining the two functions.

5.2.3 *Dar es Salaam Benefits from Captive Markets*

The Eastern Africa hinterland is an important market for the ports: out of a total containerized trade generated by East Africa surpassing one million TEUs in 2014, it divided into two-thirds for the coastal countries, and one-third for the landlocked countries. When empty container moves are included in the throughput, the total container activity in East Africa is over 1.6 million TEUs (see Figure 5.7). Despite a smaller economy than its neighbour Kenya, Tanzania managed to attract half of the trade generated by the hinterland.

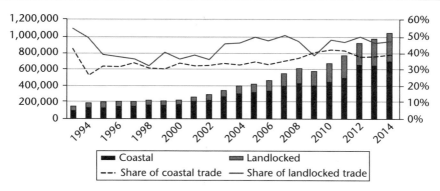

Figure 5.7. East Africa containerized trade and share of Dar es Salaam
Source: Kenya Ports Authority (KPA) and Tanzania Ports Authority (TPA) data.

Table 5.1. Distance comparisons for DRC, Zambia, and Malawi

	Distance to Dar es Salaam	Distance to Durban
Lubumbashi (DR Congo)	2,040 km	2,674 km
Ndola (Zambia)	1,811 km	2,445 km
Blantyre (Malawi)	1,785 km	2,270 km

Source: Google maps calculation

Table 5.2. Container freight rates in Dar es Salaam, 2010–12

	2010	2011	2012
20' container from Asia	US$1,250	US$675	US$788
20' container to Asia	US$520	US$350	US$450

Source: Tanzania Surface and Maritime Transport Regulatory Authority (SUMATRA)

The South Eastern Africa landlocked countries are closer to Dar es Salaam than to Durban, but when the shipping freight rates are included in the equation, what is lost on the land transport may well be gained in the sea leg. In the early 2000s, severe over-capacity on the Asia South Africa trade route led to intense competition among shipping lines, and freight rates out of Durban were as low as US$300 for a twenty-foot container to Shanghai. On the other hand, the East Africa market was much more modest, with less competition, and freight rates were higher. At that level of price on the maritime leg, it was making economic sense to take the long route to Durban (see Table 5.1).

With the traffic growth in East Africa, competition increased and freight rates decreased, while on the South Africa route, shipping lines managed to raise freight levels (see Table 5.2). The differential closed, and inland transport regained its importance as the main determinant of the routing of cargo. With shorter distances, and fewer borders to cross, Dar es Salaam regained its importance as maritime gateway of choice for the landlocked countries of South-Eastern Africa.

5.3 Which Obstacles Should be Overcome for Dar es Salaam to Strengthen Its Regional Gateway Role?

5.3.1 *Are There Any Prospects for Dar es Salaam for a Transshipment Hub?*

This section assesses the prospects for Dar es Salaam to become a transshipment hub in the short to medium term. It concludes that the prospects are bleak mainly due to shipping lines strategies, which are unlikely to change soon. Haralambides et al. (2011) had found a similar result based on an estimated model explaining that a new port in Tanzania could only function as a 'regional lower-tier hub' due to its distance from the arterial maritime container trade routes and to other organizational problems. Dar es Salaam is comparable in size to Abidjan or Dakar, which have a container throughput around half a million TEUs, but smaller than, for instance, Mombasa, Durban, or Lagos, all above one million TEUs. Its growth has been at the pace of the economic development of its hinterland, and its competitive advantage versus the other maritime gateways has not really improved. Dar es Salaam Port has not been able to significantly gain market share over its competitors. As for the prospect of growth by attracting transshipment traffic, the present conditions in which the shipping lines serve East Africa are not conducive to the emergence of regional transshipment hubs. This lack of prospects is therefore not specific to Dar es Salaam.

East Africa is very close to the Mid-East transshipment hubs on the Europe–Asia trade lane, tilting the balance between direct services and connections through feeder services in favour of transshipment solutions. On the Europe–East Africa trade route, the conversion to feedering was triggered by the Maersk line in 2002 and adopted by MSC (Mediterranean Shipping Company) and the former BEACON conference partners followed. On the Asia–East Africa route, however, there is still a mix of direct and transshipment services, with the main carriers even combining the two options in their offer.[7] With a limited number of gateway ports and small secondary ports, transshipment needs within the region are extremely limited, and as a consequence, no transshipment hub has developed in East Africa (see Figure 5.8 for transshipment trends for the ports of Dar es Salaam and Mombasa).[8]

This lack of diversity in the nature of the shipping lines serving East Africa translates into low scores in the Liner Shipping Connectivity Index (LSCI).[9]

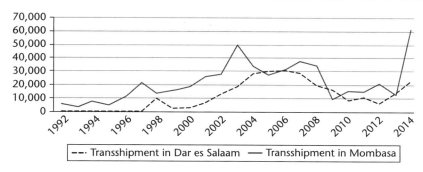

Figure 5.8. Transshipment traffic in the ports of Dar es Salaam and Mombasa
Source: Kenya Ports Authority (KPA) and Tanzania Ports Authority (TPA) data.

In the Western portion of the Indian Ocean, there are already major hubs, notably in Oman, with Salalah, the transshipment hub development by Maersk on the main east–west shipping lane. Further south, Durban and Coega in South Africa are regional hubs for the north–south trade lanes linking Africa with Asia and Europe. The LSCI for Tanzania and the neighbouring countries with an existing hub or a potential for transshipment hubs are illustrated in Figure 5.9. Oman and South Africa have the highest connectivity, due to the status of their hub ports, followed by Mauritius and Djibouti. Kenya and Tanzania have relatively low indexes of connectivity, being primarily gateway ports, served primarily through secondary lines connected via a regional hub port, either in the south or in the north.

5.3.2 What Are the Remaining Obstacles for Dar es Salaam Port to Develop?

The port of Dar es Salaam is a medium to large port, which should aim at remaining a regional maritime gateway but not a transshipment hub. The development of the port of Dar es Salaam rests on strengthening its position on its hinterland. That assumes overcoming operational constraints at the port, but also improving the connection to the hinterland. This section discusses the port performance and then analyses port dwell time, which is what matters most for importers/exporters.

5.3.2.1 OPERATIONAL CHALLENGES AT THE PORT

As far as container traffic is concerned, Dar es Salaam Port performance has slightly improved in the last years and performs acceptably. Container ships are handled at the container terminal operated by the Tanzania International Container Terminal Services (TICTS), or on the TPA (Tanzania Ports Authority) conventional berths, since the exclusivity clause granted to TICTS in the

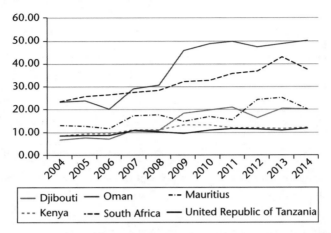

Figure 5.9. LSCI for selected countries of the Western Indian Ocean coastline
Source: UNCTAD (LSCI 2014).

Box 5.2. TICTS (TANZANIA INTERNATIONAL CONTAINER TERMINAL SERVICES)

The container terminal comprises berths 8, 9, 10, and 11. The concession in 2000 was for the three container berths, 9, 10, and 11, but berth 8 was added to the concession perimeter on 1 January 2009. The terminal characteristics are as follows:

- Four berths on a 750m long quay, with a depth of 12.2m;
- 7 ship-to-shore gantry cranes (last two were delivered in August 2014);
- An 18.75 hectares container yard equipped with nineteen RTGs (rubber tyre gantry cranes) for a capacity of 11,500 TEUs and an annual capacity of 500,000 TEUs.

The initial concession agreement was for a duration of ten years. Given the relatively short span for the concession, the slow traffic growth during the 1990s, and the capacity reserves of the terminal (rated at 120,000 TEUs per year for a traffic around 80,000 full TEUs), the contract did not foresee a high level of investment. However, when the concession was modified in 2005 and extended by fifteen years (in addition to the original ten years), traffic had started to pick up, and it was clear that the terminal capacity would be insufficient before the end of the concession, and that more signifi-cant investments would become necessary to expand capacity.

---

original concession was removed in 2009 (see Box 5.2). TICTS handles 80 per cent of the container traffic of Dar es Salaam Port.

Performances at the TICTS terminal are acceptable, with a minimum of 25 net moves per hour on the ship-to-shore (STS) cranes. Performances at the TPA terminal are much lower, comparatively, but the differences are explained by the nature of the equipment, and the characteristics of the ships and calls. Mobile cranes or ship's gear, combined with lower volume

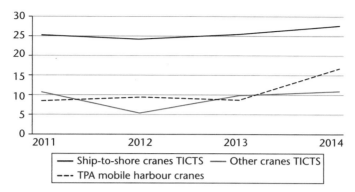

Figure 5.10. Crane productivity in Dar es Salaam, net moves per hour
Source: Tanzania Ports Authority (TPA) data.

calls, do not allow for the higher level of productivity that can be attained by STS cranes. When compared with similar equipment, TICTS and TPA productivity are close (see Figure 5.10).

Despite acceptable levels of performance, the port of Dar es Salaam experiences capacity constraints. At the time of the concession, the container terminal had a theoretical annual capacity of 250,000 TEUs. Through various measures,[10] it has been able to increase capacity to 500,000 per annum without major infrastructure work.

With increased volumes to handle, the port reaches saturation, and minimal surges in the traffic can have severe consequences for the shipping lines. The risks of operating near capacity limits were dramatically illustrated by the escalation of delays for container ships before a berth at the terminal became available (see Figure 5.11). Queues formed, and ships had to wait up to ten days on average (some much longer) before offloading their containers. With daily charter rates for ships of 2,500 TEUs capacity around US$15,000 per day,[11] such delays were unacceptable for shipping lines. The situation returned to more acceptable levels in 2012, but persisted on the TPA berths. The slight increase in the occupancy level of the berths at the end of 2013 triggered a similar, although less severe, increase in the delays. With the additional handling equipment delivered in 2014, the risks of saturation are lower, but traffic growth will soon erase increased capacity.

5.3.2.1.1 The Dwell time Problem of Cargo (in Transit)

Overall, dwell time for cargo, despite improvements, remains too long for a worldwide standard (but relatively better than in sub-Saharan Africa in transit).[12] It is especially long for cargo in transit. The slow documentation process, poor

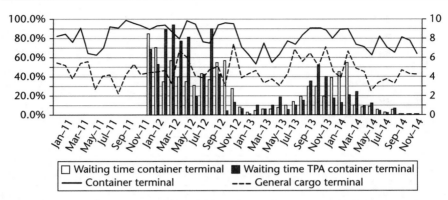

Figure 5.11. Berth occupancy and pre-berthing delays at the container berths
Source: Tanzania Ports Authority (TPA) data.

multimodal transport and some private sector strategies all contribute to explain why cargo dwell time remains so long.

The Port of Dar es Salaam experienced long dwell time (between five and twenty days for most shipments) with a significant problem with congestion during 2008 resulting from a combination of factors, which can be detrimental to increased flows from/to hinterland countries. Data from 2008 (see Table 5.3) showed a pattern that still prevails today, that dwell times especially for cargo destined for DRC, Burundi, and Zambia stayed longer in the port compared to local cargo, and cargo going to Uganda and Rwanda.

Lengthy cargo dwell time in a port can have costly implications in terms of space utilization and investment requirements and will be addressed in Section 5.4 estimating the costs/benefits of cargo in transit.

Long cargo dwell time is a pervasive problem in many ports in Africa, with both complex causes and a severely detrimental impact on trade. Research by the World Bank suggests that, beside institutional inefficiencies and deficient infrastructure, political economy factors contribute, at times significantly, to the delays at sub-Saharan African ports (Raballand et al. 2012).[13] Port users also play a role, as they may delay in submitting documents or making payments resulting in lengthy dwell times.

The dwell time also reflects the (in)efficiency of the transit process. Transit regimes are designed to safeguard leakage of goods into a transit economy without the payment of duties and taxes. They are regulated by customs administrations and may involve the lodgement of necessary guarantees. In many countries the process of initiating transit can be time consuming and costly, resulting in additional delays to cargo.

In additional to lengthy stays, the cargo dwell times are also marked by high levels of variation, which indicate that the clearance process is unpredictable.

Table 5.3. Aggregate delay between unloading from vessel and final delivery to the client in Dar es Salaam Port, September–November 2008

Maximum	107	119	113	112	70	80	56
Minimum	0	0	0	0	0	0	0
Mean	13	15	15	16	11	16	11
Median	9	12	13	13	7	15	7
Standard deviation	13	13	12	13	11	12	12
Total traffic	302,840	118,180	50,060	27,600	21,000	14,880	2,760

Source: Raballand et al. (2012)

Empirical evidence does suggest that unreliability increases logistics costs, as firms are forced to maintain high inventories to minimize the risk of stock-outs. Addressing the problem of lengthy dwell time requires that the port operators as well as trade regulatory authorizes in Tanzania continue to work closely with all neighbouring countries to improve the efficiency of the clearance and removal processes.

Currently, dwell time for local containers is approximately at six days according to container operators but remains much longer for transit containers (see Figure 5.12). However, average dwell time hides a much longer stay in the port area than official statistics, because most local containers are shifted to off-dock facilities (established around 2009).[14]

Rather than reforming the documentation process to reduce release time, the quick fix solution adopted was to shift containers to nearby facilities to reduce the pressure on the yard. This improved container operations within the terminal but did not address the problem of long delays for procedures. Moreover, additional handling and shunting of the containers within the Dar es Salaam metropolitan area increases costs.

Even though improvements have been recorded at Dar es Salaam, reducing by 20 per cent both the mean and the standard deviation of dwell time would lead to a significant improvement of the volume to capacity ratio of 38 per cent. Standard deviation mainly derives from private sectors' strategies.[15] Moreover, for several years, the incentives structure of Dar es Salaam Port has been biased in favour of using the port as a storage area, noted in Jensen et al. (2010).[16]

Based on the available statistics and discussion with stakeholders, it is possible to disaggregate the contribution to average dwell time according to three groups of importers.

- The first are the more organized importers who seek to minimize the cargo dwell time, primarily large importers with scheduled dates for cargo delivery. They use the larger shipping lines and freight forwarders/customs brokers in order to reduce the uncertainty of time required to clear cargo.

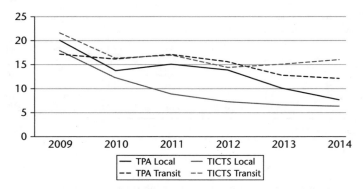

Figure 5.12. Container dwell time in Dar es Salaam
Source: Tanzania Ports Authority (TPA) data.

Their dwell time is normally 3–5 days. This group accounts for about 30–35 per cent of the local import and inbound transit containers.

- The second group is importers who experience difficulties in clearing cargo. Their cargo includes imports that require various permits, are unfamiliar to the customs officials, or are from countries subject to greater scrutiny. This group also includes importers who distribute their cargo to different locations and do not have a central warehouse, whose boxes are delayed in being transferred to the ODCYs (off-dock container yards)[17] or who require special transport services. Finally it may also include medium-size traders who are regular importers of certain goods but do not sell their goods until the cargo has arrived. These importers have a dwell time ranging from 6 to 21 days, but concentrated in the range of 7–14 days and are estimated to account for 40–50 per cent of the shipments.

- The third group is importers with long-stay cargo. These include small traders with cash flow problems and importers of duty-exempt cargo and abandoned cargo. The dwell time for this cargo exceeds 21 days. They account for only 15–25 per cent of the cargo but have an average dwell time of 40–45 days.

5.3.2.2 OPERATIONAL CHALLENGES ON THE HINTERLAND

The port is an important node, but the efficiency of a logistics chain depends on several other links and land connections on the hinterland are equally important for the landlocked countries relying on Dar es Salaam to connect with their overseas markets and sourcing regions. Although both corridors served by Dar es Salaam boast intermodal options, a closer look on the actual levels of activity on the railway lines shows that road transport is the only mode. Figure 5.13 shows the steady decline of the two railways over the years.

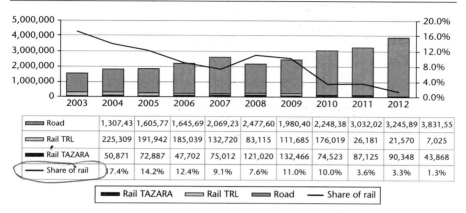

	2003	2004	2005	2006	2007	2008	2009	2010	2011	2012
Road	1,307,43	1,605,77	1,645,69	2,069,23	2,477,60	1,980,40	2,248,38	3,032,02	3,245,89	3,831,55
Rail TRL	225,309	191,942	185,039	132,720	83,115	111,685	176,019	26,181	21,570	7,025
Rail TAZARA	50,871	72,887	47,702	75,012	121,020	132,466	74,523	87,125	90,348	43,868
Share of rail	17.4%	14.2%	12.4%	9.1%	7.6%	11.0%	10.0%	3.6%	3.3%	1.3%

Figure 5.13. Evolution of the modal share rail–road in Tanzania
Source: EAC (2014).

For the lake transport, which was largely the continuation on the lake of the rail transport, the situation is similar.

In order to revive the railway, a concession agreement for a duration of twenty-five years was signed in September 2007 for the take-over of the operations on the TRL line.[18] However, in 2011, the Government of Tanzania revoked the concession. Total cargo transported by rail has become close to 0: out of Dar es Salaam in 2014, total transported cargo was less than 11,000 tons, and exactly 114 TEUs. The trend is attributable to the fact that many of the regional railway systems in Eastern Africa are not functioning as they should, in virtually all aspects since they are marred by underinvestment, poor reliability, high accident and failure rates, high costs, low volumes, and management problems. Lack of sufficient wagons and locomotives leads to high tariff rates, which in turn leads to further loss of traffic to other modes of transport thereby creating a vicious circle of poor performance.[19]

5.4 The Politics and Economics of Dar es Salaam Port

This section presents the costs/benefits of being a regional gateway and then gives some estimates on the costs and benefits for Tanzania to be a major outlet for traffic in transit in East and Southern Africa.

5.4.1 *The Benefits and Costs of a Regional Gateway*

There are several channels through which the evolution of a logistics node (port, country, etc.) into a hub are transmitted. Some channels are direct, through fiscal outlays or flows of revenues, or indirect in the form of increased

Table 5.4. Possible advantages/costs of traffic in transit

a. Infrastructure costs	Improved quality of infrastructure resulting in operational efficiency, reliability and lower costs	Either oversized infrastructure or congestion
b. Logistics services	Improved quality of logistics services— greater reliability and cost efficiency	Distorted markets and market fragmentation, resulting in poor reliability and high costs
c. Environmental and social costs	Jobs growth	Social hazards, disease transmission Increased carbon emissions
d. Regional spillover effects	Growth in centres along major corridors or around logistics nodes	Increased regional disparities
e. Political impacts	Increased regional integration	Risk of overdependency on a limited number of trade routes or users posing risk when there is diversion

Source: Author data

trade, participation in regional or international value chains, environmental or social effects and changes in diplomatic and political relations between countries. The net benefit of evolving into a hub is the sum of the various effects, positive and negative. The various effects can be grouped into five main categories (see Table 5.4).[20]

In order to develop and operate as a hub, there are costs associated with providing and maintaining port, road, rail, and other related infrastructure. The main issue is whether the direct and indirect returns from such additional costs are justifiable or whether consumption costs can be recovered from users. In those instances where infrastructure is under-utilized and there is spare capacity, revenues could be well above the marginal cost of providing additional services. Investing in additional capacity to handle a higher volume of traffic on the other hand may result in under-utilization. Additional capacity can be financed by users through user tariffs or some other cost recovery mechanisms. This is often the case with road transport where fuel taxes, tolls, or other mechanisms are common to recoup infrastructure development and maintenance costs. In East and Southern Africa both COMESA (Common Market in East and Southern Africa) and SADC (South African Development Community) have defined harmonized principles for road infrastructure costs recovery which are widely used. The proportion of transit traffic assessed over a long period can give some insights into the impact on port efficiency and utilization of resources of handling transit traffic.

Logistics services have a dual role in hub operations, through their impact on trade in goods and as tradable services in themselves. Logistics services include supply chain consulting services and transportation management services, transportation services, fleet maintenance and repair, packaging services, clearing and forwarding, and warehousing. Given that the logistics sector typically has increasing returns to scale, greater volumes of traffic

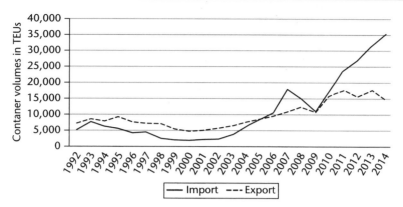

Figure 5.14. Zambia trade volumes through Dar es Salaam Port
Source: Tanzania Ports Authority (TPA) data.

normally result in reduced unit costs, greater connectivity, and quality of services.

Increasingly, Tanzania generates a higher volume of traffic than the land-locked countries that use its ports, roads, and railways. Therefore, there has been a corresponding growth in logistics services sector. As a result of this trend and partly also of geography and other factors, Tanzanian trucking and clearing and forwarding services dominate the major corridors connecting to the port. For example, while the volume of Zambian traffic passing through Tanzania has grown strongly in recent years (see Figure 5.14) most of the traffic is carried by Tanzanian registered trucks. This is due to several factors including traffic imbalances where there are more Zambia imports than exports, as well as practices that distort competition between the fleets of the two countries (permit regime, infrastructure cost recovery formula, and differences in technical standards for trucks). Consequently, operations on the corridor to Zambia and DRC are dominated by Tanzanian trucks for bilateral trade.

Logistics hubs attract various other types of activities of a social nature and experience different types of environmental impacts, both positive and negative. The provision of various logistics services comes with increased employment of drivers, support staff, repair facilities, insurance, demand for financing facilities by local banks, accommodation, and filling stations. Some of these activities will have associated social costs and risky behaviours. However, recent analysis in Djibouti, which is predominantly a transit coun-try for Ethiopia, found that the prospects for employment creation were limited (World Bank, 2012). The analysis concluded that transport and logis-tics in a transit context has limited potential for job creation, largely since port activities are capital-intensive, while ever improving supply chain efficiencies have reducing marginal job creation potential with an increase in trade volumes. Some of the same patterns apply to Tanzania, though as noted elsewhere, the dominance of Tanzanian operators in trucking services have resulted in some employment creation.

In Southern Africa, major trade routes were the initial main transmission lines for HIV (Human Immunodeficiency Virus) and economic centres within such routes had significant concentrations of prevalence. Other activities that may also be detrimental to society include smuggling and in some cases the illicit flows of arms. In addition to social impacts, logistics nodes in Africa often also suffer from high levels of congestion and carbon emissions.

The development of transit infrastructure and transport links may also provide the opportunity for close economic and trade links between countries. Industries developed in the coastal country may have a competitive advantage in the markets of the inland country. Transit is often costly and acts thus as a tax on non-regional trade, especially imports. Essentially, the inland country is brought within the economic sphere of influence of the coastal country. This would appear to be the case between Tanzania and some of its neighbours, such as Burundi and eastern DRC.

Clearly, however, the importance of the trade benefits depends upon the relative state of industrial development within the coastal and inland countries. Kenya has a relatively developed consumer product manufacturing base and is a significant source of Uganda's imports. Tanzania, on the other hand, has a very limited industrial sector and has not become an important supplier of the Ugandan market, despite the development of transit links. When properly exploited, strong transit links can thus effectively increase the economic market of a coastal country.

Transit provides political leverage and the more important the transit route to the inland country, the greater the political leverage. Landlocked countries dependent on transit through coastal neighbours are in a very weak position.[21] The power may be more the potential rather than its actual use. However, there are risks on both sides that have to be accounted for as illustrated by the two examples involving Tanzania (Sections 5.4.1.1 and 5.4.1.2).

Transit traffic can generate not only additional revenues but also additional risks for a country port, especially when the routing of such traffic is volatile. Investing in additional capacity to handle transit traffic may result in under-utilized capacity, if the transit traffic shifts to an alternative route. A prominent example of such a dynamic is Eritrea, which had just invested in additional container handling equipment for the port of Assab, when Ethiopian traffic shifted to Dijbouti overnight in 1998, leaving Eritrea with a port with no traffic and container handling equipment without containers. This case serves to illustrate the close link between politics and transit traffic.

Increasingly in East Africa there is also competition between different corridors serving the landlocked countries. The rivalry between the Northern and Central Corridors in East Africa probably did more to benefit the position of the landlocked countries than most official agreements. For example, TPA now advertises its services in various economic centres across the region, for example in Kinshasa in DRC. Such pressure to improve the competitiveness of transit routes may also benefit national traffic, through increased efficiency at the ports.

5.4.1.1 EXAMPLE 1

In the 1980s, a civil war was in full swing in Mozambique, disrupting trade routes with neighbouring countries. For Malawi, the only available alternative to going through Mozambique was a long route to the port of Durban in South Africa which passed through Zambia and Zimbabwe (a distance of 3,500 km from Blantyre). Estimates are that in 1984 total losses to the economy from using this route were equivalent to 20 per cent of the value of all exports. An alternative route had to be opened on an urgent basis. This was the route to the Port of Dar es Salaam. Opening the route involved construction of a dry port at Mbeya in Tanzania; improvements of the road between Mbeya and the main centres in Malawi; construction of fuel transshipment facilities at Mbeya; provision of fuel railway tankers and ordinary wagons; and construction of a border post and weighbridges.

The new route was a success, at least in the short term, so that by 1993, the Dar es Salaam route carried close to 20 per cent of Malawi's external trade, and was particularly important for fuel imports which increased from 1 per cent in 1986 to around 40 per cent of all fuel imports by 1994. However, once peace returned to Mozambique in 1992, followed by independence in Zimbabwe and the end of the apartheid in South Africa in 1994, the political reasons to avoid the southern routes were eliminated, and traffic on the Dar es Salaam route fell sharply. Currently, only fuel and small volumes of other products are shipped through Tanzania.

5.4.1.2 EXAMPLE 2

Following the Kenyan elections in late 2007, there was an outbreak of violence that disrupted the flow of traffic on the Northern Corridor. This corridor links the Port of Mombasa in Kenya and the landlocked countries of Uganda, Rwanda, Burundi, and eastern DRC. It is by the far the dominant trade route for Uganda, handling 98 per cent of import trade traffic and 80 per cent of export (by land) trade traffic. The interruption of traffic therefore meant that there was a huge amount of capital at risk for Uganda, and an alternative had to be found quickly.

Fortunately, such an alternative already existed in the form of the Central Corridor that connected the country to the Port of Dar es Salaam in Tanzania via a multimodal route comprising road, rail, and lake transport (approximately 1,150 km long). However, when compared to the Northern Corridor the route suffered from poor operational performance, and delays at border crossing points, intermodal terminals, and in the Port of Dar es Salaam. In addition, Ugandan shippers have developed relationships and invested in facilities in Kenya to handle their traffic. This meant that the route would attract traffic only as long as the Northern Corridor faced disruptions.

Where very large coastal countries provide transit to small inland countries, the political benefits of transit may be more important than the economic benefits, which may be trivial to the coastal country. There are also instances where it can be argued that the reverse is true. A large inland country may try and use its transit traffic as a bargaining lever with a small coastal country, as with Russia and transit through the Baltic states. The examples of the inland country having the scale to use its transit traffic as a political lever may, however, be limited—though Ethiopia and Djibouti are other such examples.

5.4.2 *Some Estimates of the Cost/Benefit and Employment Effect of Traffic in Transit*

This section estimates the benefits and costs of traffic in transit for Dar es Salaam Port. Moreover, it gives an estimate of the possible employment impact of the port and trucking industry. Based on our results, port revenues bring important revenues for Dar es Salaam Port as long as port capacity exists. In terms of the employment impact, this sector remains quite marginal (even when indirect and induced impact are taken into account), which can be explained by the fact that logistics/port activities are mainly capital intensive.

5.4.2.1 ESTIMATES OF PORT REVENUES/COSTS RELATED TO TRAFFIC IN TRANSIT

The main benefits for Dar es Salaam Port derive from various port and handling charges. With traffic of almost 200,000 TEUs a year, almost 40 million USD are collected from traffic in transit in Dar es Salaam Port. This is not negligible for Dar es Salaam activity and revenues flows. However, the negative impact of such flows are also quite numerous and costly, such as congestion costs and their environmental costs and also road maintenance costs. Due to lack of data availability, it has been difficult to estimate those costs with precision.

The problem of the congestion impact of traffic in transit due to long dwell times is also usually neglected since it remains difficult to estimate. However, this can be very costly for a port. In a container port, the number of slots in the terminal and in the yard is fixed and expensive to develop (around US$1,000 per square metre to build or over US$20,000 for a container).

In the case of Dar es Salaam Port, due to bad incentives and long dwell times for traffic in transit, the latter contributes greatly to port congestion. With traffic of almost 200,000 TEUs a year and with an average dwell time of fifteen days, traffic in transit almost contributes fully to the congestion of the port by taking approximately of 60 per cent of the container yard capacity (whereas it only accounts to 40 per cent of total container traffic).[22] For several years, to avoid yard congestion, Dar es Salaam Port has transferred containers to inland container depots (ICDs) when the yard utilization reaches 60 per cent (Mwasenga, 2012).

Therefore, even though Dar es Salaam Port capacity is better utilized thanks to traffic in transit and generates several dozens of millions of USD a year, there are costs attached to it that are not negligible for Tanzania.

5.4.2.2 ESTIMATES OF THE EMPLOYMENT IMPACT

Port impact studies are the most widespread methodology to assess the economic effects of a port. Three types of effects (direct, indirect, and induced) can be distinguished:[23]

- *Direct effects* occur within the land transport or port sectors;
- *Indirect effects* occur in the sectors with backward linkages to the transport sector through the supply of intermediate inputs;
- *Induced effects* refer to the chain reaction brought about by the increase in labour remuneration and additional revenues that is injected in the economy by of private or public spending.

It is difficult to use this methodology for two main reasons: (i) Port impact studies limit the assessment to the port and do not include the traffic in transit. Impact studies were developed in the US for assessing only port-related activities. However, traffic in transit consists of land transport (by road or rail) in addition to port-related activities. (ii) Data availability for Dar es Salaam is also insufficient. Therefore, it was necessary to rely on some benchmarks regarding the employment effect of port traffic in sub-Saharan Africa.

In a country like Djibouti, analysis showed that for traffic in transit of around 5 million tonnes, approximately 5,000 direct jobs and around 12,000–15,000 jobs were generated in total, by including indirect and induced jobs (World Bank, 2013). Since the global container operator in Dar es Salaam uses the same equipment/technology as in Djibouti and traffic is rather similar (around 4 million tonnes), the total number of jobs at Dar es Salaam Port generated by traffic in transit is unlikely to exceed 15,000 jobs.

Table 5.5. Estimate of total employment generated by trucking industry

	Trucks	Total/drivers	Drivers/truck	Employment/truck	Total employment
Tanzania	12,356	1.89	1.18	2.23	27,554

Source: Trucking Surveys Tanzania (CCTTFA, 2012)

Alongside the port, the trucking industry generates approximately over 20,000 direct and indirect jobs (see Table 5.5 for detailed data of the total employment generated by the Tanzanian trucking industry). Customs data on the main Tanzanian land borders (Kenya excluded) shows that the share of Tanzanian trucks is 89 per cent on all cargo types, and 94 per cent for containers.[24] More than 75 per cent of the Tanzanian trucking companies are involved in international transport. Considering the job structure of the Tanzania trucking companies,[25] the ratios between trucks, drivers, and other jobs applied to the large truck fleet in Tanzania indicate that a total of more than 27,000 jobs are linked to the trucking industry, with a vast majority of them linked to transit traffic.

Overall, for what is probably the most important employment generation activities, port and trucking, less than 40,000 jobs derive from traffic in transit. It means that it represents less than 0.2 per cent of total active population in Tanzania.

5.5 Trade Logistics: Investing in the Future Competitiveness of the Port of Dar es Salaam

5.5.1 Which Port Investments in the Future? The Importance of Corridor Competitiveness

Dar es Salaam Port has faced a steady traffic growth in the last years due to economic growth in the region. Even though dwell time would reduce significantly, investments in port capacity should be needed in at least in the medium term. Lack of investments in infrastructure has been brought to attention to policy makers in many SSA countries, including Tanzania (Shkaratan, 2012). Until now, most investments in the Port of Dar es Salaam were modest, mainly for handling equipment. For instance, to avoid future congestion after the tense situation in 2011–12, TICTS ordered additional handling equipment early 2014: two STS cranes, and additional rubber tyre gantry cranes (RTGs) and yard handling equipment, but fundamentally, the issue is that the terminal has reached its capacity limits.

But quay productivity is not the only constraint to capacity. The yard capacity is also a critical factor. The current annual capacity of 500,000 TEUs is based on an average dwell time of eight days (11,500 slots, which must be used over forty times per year).

The development of Dar es Salaam Port should include the widening of the entrance channel, improving both berth depth and the sufficient turning basin together with the creation of a new plan for the Port layout.[26]

5.5.2 What Should Be Done by Tanzania to Improve Growth and Economic Impact in Dar es Salaam?

Port, road, and rail capacity developments are being developed or planned but how to develop and manage new facilities will be even more important. Efficient port operations depend on the cooperation of players in the supply chain (Farrell, 2009; Raballand et al., 2012). The documentation process in Dar es Salaam Port (especially transit) needs to be streamlined. Off-dock container yards are not the long-term solution. Farrell (2009) had demonstrated that clearance processes (what she called 'soft cargo handling processes') imposed constraints on the speed at which containers could be handled and reduced the responsibility of the container terminal for port efficiency. One of the key priorities should be to improve the dwell time of those containers spending more than twenty days in the port. In this regard, the port of Dar es Salaam should adjust free time for cargo in transit to ten days in order to give an incentive for customs brokers and freight forwarders not to use the port as a storage area.

Although the port hinterland (mainly Mombasa and Dar es Salaam) is partly distinct, improvements in the land connections will sooner or later blur the lines between the ports, particularly if Bagamoyo is developed. Thinking on a regional scale will be necessary. In South Africa, the ports are considered as a system, and the development of each port is not considered independently, but as part of a whole. The same approach should be adopted in East Africa, with the EAC playing a greater role than it does at present.

Finally, Dar es Salaam Port development is likely to further increase traffic congestion. With around 2,000 TEUs in and out of the port everyday (plus additional movements created by the shunting to the ICDs), traffic is already congested. Night transfers (provided noise is not a nuisance) could help, but traffic planning and management for port traffic will have to be severely amended.

Annex 5.1. Timeline of key events at Dar es Salaam Port and on main corridors (2000–15)

Date	Event
2000	Three out of four container berths concessioned for ten years to a consortium led by Hutchison Port Holdings, operating as Tanzania International Container Terminal Services (TICTS)
2003	Dar es Salaam Corridor constitution signed among Tanzania, Malawi, and Zambia
2005	Tanzania Ports Authority (TPA) established as landlord port authority
2005	TICTS concession modified and extended by fifteen years
2006	Central Corridor Transit Transport Facilitation Agency (CCTTFA) established
2007	Central Corridor railway line concessioned to RITES operating as Tanzania Railways Limited (TRL)
2007	Port suffers from severe congestion—presidential committee established
2007	ICDs and CFSs developed to relieve port congestion
2008	TRA accepts submission of partial ship manifests
2009	Berth 8 included in TICTS concession and exclusivity rights for containers cancelled
2010	TRL railway concession cancelled—railway reverts back to state ownership
2010	CCTTFA becomes operational
2013	Improvements in port performance included specifically in Big-Results Now (BRN) initiative of the Government of Tanzania
2013	Work starts to expand port by building two new berths—based on BRN
2014	One stop border posts established between Tanzania and respectively Burundi, Rwanda, and Uganda
2014	Port stakeholders sign MoU on 24/7 operations
2015	Heads of State summit on Central Corridor—emphasis on development of trade along the corridor

Annex 5.2. Costs/benefits of a port in a given country

There are eight main areas where Tanzania faces costs and derives benefits from handling transit traffic. These are:

a) The port of Dar es Salaam where an estimate has to be made as to what the marginal cost and benefit is of handling transit traffic;

b) Contribution of transit to congestion in the vicinity of Dar es Salaam;

c) Road infrastructure to and from the port to neighbouring countries;

d) Road trucking services, where transit traffic contributes to employment creation and also to the fuel levy for maintenance of roads;

e) Rail services;

f) Clearing and forwarding services;

g) Provision of other logistics infrastructure and services including storage facilities;

h) Border infrastructure and systems.

Notes

1. The linkages between the port of Dar es Salaam and its hinterland are through two main intermodal corridors: (i) the Central Corridor radiating to Uganda, Rwanda, Burundi, and the eastern part of DR Congo with road, rail (through the Tanzania Railways TRL on the 1.000 meter gauge) and lake connections (Lake Victoria and

Tanganyika), and (ii) the Dar Corridor radiating to Zambia, Malawi, and the southern part of DR Congo, with also road, rail (TAZARA railway on the 1.067m gauge, same as for Southern Africa), and pipeline (TAZAMA) connections.

2. The major events over the past decade and a half are in Annex 5.1.

3. The other ports along the coast line are either specialized on bulk traffic, such as Maputo and Richards Bay, or play a limited role for container trade.

4. Traffic imbalance in import and export traffic flows are such that most of the constraints are faced with imports. In most instances transport prices for exports are discounted due to a lack of exports from the hinterland. Moreover, there is a greater availability of empty boxes in the hinterland. Therefore, the most important logistical constraints/prices are borne by imports through Dar es Salaam.

5. One avenue is the expansion of the port of Dar es Salaam, jointly supported by the World Bank and TMEA; a second one is a greenfield port development in Bagamoyo, supported by the Government of China; and a third is the expansion of the port of Tanga. This chapter will focus more on Dar es Salaam Port since it is the main port of entry for Tanzania.

6. (i) the Northern Corridor, originating from the port of Mombasa in Kenya, serves the same hinterland countries than the Central Corridor, and (ii) the North–South Corridor, which prolongs the Dar Corridor to Durban, serving Zimbabwe, Zambia, Malawi, and DR Congo.

7. Both feeder services and direct services are operated with what has become the feedermax vessel, averaging 2,500 TEUs.

8. The limited level of transshipment taking place in Dar es Salaam and Mombasa peaked in the mid-2000s when both ports were reaching capacity limits due to congestion. At that time, shipping lines were frequently cancelling one of the two ports in the loop, repositioning the containers to the destination ports using feeder vessels that were less costly than the main line vessels.

9. The LSCI was developed by UNCTAD as an empirical measure of how countries are integrated into the world-wide shipping networks, based on a combination of container traffic and characteristics of the shipping lines serving the its ports.

10. Capacity was increased through (a) denser stacking on the yard and its extensions, (b) the addition of a fourth berth in the concession, (c) additional quay handling equipment, (d) the transfer of containers to off-dock yards, and (e) 24/7 operations through the MoU signed in February 2014 by port stakeholders.

11. Hamburg Shipbrokers' Association's New Contex, reporting charter rates for several typical sizes of container vessels.

12. For a benchmark, see Raballand et al. (2012).

13. This was also confirmed for Dar es Salaam by Morisset et al. (2013).

14. Official statistics stop the clock when cargo exits the container gate and therefore off-dock facilities mask longer dwell times. Transit containers usually remain in the terminal yard until their delivery for transport to the hinterland, hence the longer dwell time for transit.

15. For more details on the importance of importers' strategies, Beuran et al. (2012) demonstrated with firms surveys how they contribute to longer dwell times in sub-Saharan Africa.

16. A storage fee reform was carried out in 2009 with the reduction of free days for storage fees from fifteen to ten days for Tanzanian traffic and storage fees were doubled.

17. This is an off-dock private facility offering services for handling and temporary storage of import/export laden and empty containers carried under customs control.

18. The railway operator was a joint venture between RITES of India, with a controlling stake of 51 per cent and the Government of Tanzania. However, in the years preceding the concession, the railway infrastructure and rolling stock had deteriorated, and the expected revival did not materialize.

19. Under the current BRN investment in railway, i.e. locomotive, rolling stock, and the overall rehabilitation of the central line, as agreed by presidents of the five related members of the TTFA countries, a positive trend reversing the limited use of railway could be expected to gradually pick.

20. Annex 5.2 describes in detail the main questions to address to estimate the overall impact of investments in logistics.

21. For more details, see Arvis et al. (2010), chapter 5.

22. This figure derives from the following formula: (yearly traffic *average dwell time)/ (number of yard slots * 365). The number of slots is 11,500 and we used an average dwell time of fifteen days.

23. It is difficult to assess accurately these impacts due to data availability. First, it is difficult not only to disentangle the three types of effects (especially between indirect and induced effects) but also to estimate accurately the various effects. Indeed, indirect and induced effects are not homogeneous: several sectors can benefit from these types of effects at various levels. Consequently, the multiplier can be difficult to estimate correctly.

24. Analysis Tanzania Revenue Authority (TRA) data for Customs Declarations on the period October 2012–March 2013.

25. Central Corridor Trucking survey, 2012.

26. TPA has a plan to construct Berths 13 and 14, with a primary objective of increasing the capacity of Dar es Salaam Port by between 500,000 and 650,000 TEUs to a total capacity of around 1.2 million TEUs per annum. A feasibility study for these new container berths at Dar es Salaam Port was completed in January 2009, The berths would accommodate Panamax vessels with capacity to take 4,800 TEUs ships. The project requires constructing a 750 m quay-wall with a depth of 13 m draft and a yard area of approximately 10,000 square metres designed for operation of RTGs. The Tanzanian Government committed a total of US$211 million for the development and upgrading of Dar es Salaam Port for the following:
    i) Strengthening and deepening of the seven General Cargo Berths,
    ii) Establishing Conveyor Belts for existing Silos within the port Area,
    iii) Development of Berths No. 13 and 14,
    iv) Dredging the entrance to enable bigger ships to dock at the port of Dar es Salaam.

References

Arvis, J.-F., Raballand, G., and Marteau, J.-F. (2010). *The Cost of Being Landlocked: Logistics Costs and Supply Chain Reliability.* Washington, D.C.: World Bank.

Beuran, M., Mahihenni, M. H., Raballand, G., and Refas, S. (2012). 'The Impact of Demand on Cargo Dwell Time in Ports in SSA'. World Bank Policy Research Working Paper 6014.

CCTCFA (Central Corridor Trade and Transport Facilitation Agency) Internal report (2012).

Farrell, S. (2009). 'Factors Influencing Port Efficiency: A Case Study of Dar es Salaam'. Paper presented at a conference of the International Association of Maritime Economics, Copenhagen, 24–26 June.

Haralambides, H., Veldman, S., van Drunen, E., and Liu, M. (2011). 'Determinants of a Regional Port-Centric Logistics Hub: The Case of East Africa', *Maritime Economics & Logistics* 13: 78–97.

Illiffe, J. (1979). *A Modern History of Tanganyika.* Cambridge: Cambridge University Press.

Jensen, J., Rutherford, T. F., and Tarr, D. (2010). 'Modeling Services Liberalization: The Case of Tanzania', *Journal of Economic Integration* 25(4) (December): 644–75.

Morisset, J., Moret, C., and Regolo, J. (2013). 'How to Push Efficiency Enhancing Reforms at the Port of Dar es Salaam?', Trade policy note 35, World Bank, Washington, D.C.

Mwasenga, H. (2012). 'Port Performance Indicators: A Case of Dar es Salaam Port', presentation at the Ad Hoc Expert Meeting on Assessing Port Performance in Geneva.

Raballand, G., Refas, S., Beuran, M., and Isik, G. (2012). *Why Does Cargo Spend Weeks in Sub-Saharan African Ports? Lessons from Six Countries.* Washington, D.C.: World Bank.

Shkaratan, M. (2012). 'Tanzania's Infrastructure: A Continental Perspective', World Bank Policy Research Working Paper 5962, World Bank, Washington, D.C.

World Bank (2012). 'Transport and Logistics in Djibouti: Contribution to Job Creation and Economic Diversification', Policy Note. World Bank, Washington, D.C.

World Bank (2013). 'Transport and Logistics in Djibouti: Contribution to Job Creation and Economic Diversification', Report no. 75145, World Bank, Washington, D.C.

6

Agricultural Transformation in Tanzania

Linking Rural to Urban through Domestic Value Chains

Douglas Gollin and Radhika Goyal

6.1 Introduction

Agriculture remains one of the most important sectors of the Tanzanian economy. The sector accounted for about 30 per cent of the country's measured gross domestic product (GDP) in 2013 and employed approximately three-quarters of the workforce (World Bank, World Development Indicators; Food and Agriculture Organization of the United Nations, FAOSTAT).[1] Agriculture also plays a significant role in terms of the country's external balance, generating about one-third of exports (UN COMTRADE [United Nations Commodity Trade Statistics Database] data, compiled by the Observatory of Economic Complexity).[2]

But as this chapter documents, agriculture remains a low productivity sector in Tanzania. Even a cursory comparison of the labour employed in agriculture and the output produced suggests that agriculture is on average a low productivity sector. If the aggregate data are taken literally, a strictly arithmetic logic suggests that output per worker in agriculture is only about one-sixth the level of output per worker in the rest of the economy. This 'agricultural productivity gap' (as in Gollin et al., 2014) implies that a large number of people are employed in a sector with very low labour productivity. A large productivity gap does not necessarily imply inefficiency (e.g., due to sector-specific factors of production or differences in equilibrium capital–labour ratios across sectors), but it does point to the reasons why structural transformation stands as a policy issue of central concern. The magnitude of the productivity gap raises questions about whether it might be possible to achieve significant gains in aggregate income by moving workers from agriculture to non-agriculture.

The low labour productivity of Tanzanian agriculture is closely related to a structure based primarily on traditional smallholder farmers. The sector is comprised of approximately 5.8 million farms, of which 73 per cent are smaller than 2.5 ha. Of the slightly smaller set of 3.5 million farms growing only crops, only 6 per cent are 5 ha or larger (National Bureau of Statistics, 2011: 8–9). Few purchased inputs are used; in the 2007/08 national agricultural survey, only about 10 per cent of households growing crops in the primary *masika* rainy season reported using inorganic fertilizer. Even these households used inorganic fertilizer on only a portion of their land: 7 per cent of *masika* cropland was treated with inorganic fertilizer.[3] Relatively small fractions used other kinds of improved technologies: 24 per cent reported using improved seeds, 7 per cent practised irrigated farming, and 14 per cent used other agricultural chemicals. In terms of mechanization, 14 per cent used ox ploughs; less than 1 per cent used tractors, disc ploughs, or power tillers (National Bureau of Statistics, 2011). Thus, most farmers use few inputs beyond their own labour and land.

Most of the country's small farms produce food crops for subsistence consumption and local markets. Maize is the most important crop, accounting for about 6 million ha, which is about three-quarters of the total area under cultivation, as estimated in the National Panel Survey Wave 3 for 2012/13. Of the remaining area, nearly half is devoted to rice production. Maize is a crucial subsistence crop. About 71 per cent of the farm households that produce maize do not sell any of it; almost half of the households growing paddy rice sell none of it. In fact, 40 per cent of farm households sell *none* of what they produce. They may instead work off-farm, possibly in wage labour, to earn money for those necessities that cannot be produced on the farm. Of the farmers who do sell some of their output, in addition to staple foods, many farmers find it profitable to produce and sell small quantities of non-perishable crops intended for eventual export. Coffee and tobacco are the two largest single agricultural exports; many others are produced in small quantities.

The low productivity of Tanzania's agriculture sector makes it a major focus for development policy. It is difficult to visualize any development process in Tanzania that does not involve significant transformation of the agriculture sector. Transformation will involve long-run changes in the size, structure, productivity, and market orientation of farms. But what will be the drivers of agricultural transformation? It is often assumed that transformation depends on improvements in agricultural productivity and in changes that take place on farms. This chapter will argue that structural transformation in Tanzania may also arise from other sources—including from changes that take place at some distance from the farm.

In particular, an emerging demand from urban consumers has the potential to drive transformation—but only if urban markets can be connected to rural sources of supply. At present, these links are weak. Urban consumers in Tanzania, like those elsewhere in the world, demand processed and prepared foods, rather than the unprocessed staple foods that are produced on Tanzanian farms. At present, their demands are met largely through imports of processed and semi-processed foods, rather than through domestic supply. In 2014, processed and semi-processed foods together accounted for over US$800 million in imports, more than double the imports of primary bulk commodities (UN COMTRADE data).[4]

Connecting Tanzanian farms with this growing urban demand will not be driven by increases in agricultural productivity so much as by growth in agro-processing industries, distribution systems, packaging, storage, branding, and retailing. Without these changes, Tanzanian farms will remain unable to produce the types of products that are preferred by urban consumers. In that case, the market opportunities for farmers could actually shrink, rather than grow, as urbanization proceeds.

This chapter begins by summarizing the status and trends of Tanzania's agricultural sector. It will then review the historical development of the sector and of agricultural policies in Tanzania. From there, it will turn to the changing urban demand and the missing links in the processing and retailing sectors. Finally, the chapter will turn to the implications and conclusions for policy.

6.2 Production Trends and Challenges

Agricultural production in Tanzania remains at low levels and has grown slowly in recent years. Crop yields for major crops remain low in comparison to Kenya and Uganda, and far below those attained in South Africa, though higher than Mozambique (Table 6.1). Maize yields in Tanzania show a statistically flat trend since 1990, and production has risen only because of an annual growth rate of 4.8 per cent in the maize area harvested.[5] Yields of paddy rice have grown slightly better, at 1.4 per cent annually since 1990, but even this rate remains well below the rate of population growth. Again, the major increases in production have come from area expansion; the area harvested in rice has grown at a rate of 5 per cent annually since 1990.

Thus, production of maize and rice—the major cereal staples, accounting for more than one-third of calorie consumption for Tanzania—has kept up with population growth primarily through expansion of area. With a limited

Table 6.1. Long-term patterns of cereal yield

	Cereal Yield (kg/ha)							
	1970	1980	1990	1995	2000	2005	2010	2013
Kenya	1,278	1,242	1,562	1,753	1,375	1,646	1,710	1,727
Uganda	1,363	1,491	1,498	1,571	1,539	1,574	1,978	2,143
Mozambique	1,000	596	477	653	868	529	1,028	818
South Africa	1,187	2,017	1,877	1,422	2,755	3,314	4,143	3,725
Tanzania	574	1,020	1,507	1,702	1,442	1,102	1,648	1,418

Source: World Development Indicators, The World Bank (accessed August 2015).

amount of suitable land available for further expansion of cultivation, Tanzania cannot expect the same patterns to continue over the years ahead. Agricultural land now encompasses 42 per cent of the total land area, and the scope for continued area expansion is not large, particularly if environmental amenities and wildlife habitat are to be maintained.

The highest rates of production growth have been in export crops such as sugar, tea, and tobacco. These crops account for relatively small fractions of the total area, and they benefit from high prices compared with food staples. Demand from the global market has led to annual average growth rates of production since 1990 of 6.9 per cent for tobacco, 4.4 per cent for sugar, and 2.5 per cent for tea. The story does not hold true for coffee, however. Production of coffee—which remains Tanzania's second-leading export crop, after tobacco—has stagnated over the past half century, with total production growing only at 1.1 percent annually since 1990; and over the half century since 1960, growth in coffee production has been a meagre 0.3 per cent annually (Figure 6.1).

Tanzania's low productivity growth in agriculture, when combined with continuing rapid population growth and shifting demand, has led to a steadily increasing import bill. Net imports of cereal grains accounted for as much as 15 per cent of total supply in 2011 before falling to around 10 per cent in 2013—compared with less than 1 per cent in 1990 (FAOSTAT Food Balance Sheets).

The constraints to increased agricultural production are numerous. Proposed explanations for the lack of agricultural transformation include structuralism, state failure, market failure, and policy failure. Many studies suggest that farmers lack access to improved technologies, either because no appropriate technologies exist or because of difficulties with information and extension. Input supply and distribution also remains a major problem, with implications for farmers' access to seed, fertilizer, and other agricultural chemicals. Many farmers may also face credit constraints and other finance-related problems, such as lack of access to secure savings and insurance products. Other

Thousand Tons

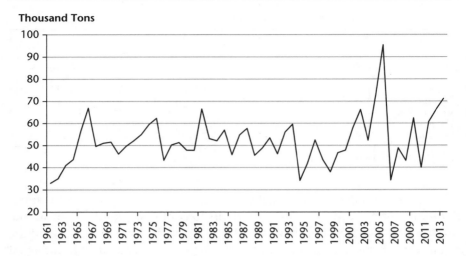

Figure 6.1. Coffee production in Tanzania

Source: Food and Agriculture Organization of the United Nations (FAOSTAT) statistics database, accessed September 2015.

constraints stem from a lack of rural infrastructure (e.g., roads, irrigation facilities, electrification, warehousing) and from policy failures related to market development and competition. In some settings, insecure land tenure and confusion over land rights may also affect production. Agricultural research and technology generation remain areas of clear underinvestment, with current expenditure on agricultural research as a proportion of agricultural GDP (a measure of research intensity) at 0.3 per cent, which is less than half the SSA average of about 0.75 per cent, and one-third the level attained in many other developing countries (Government of Tanzania, 2005). The low levels of research have contributed to a relatively low overall rate of modern variety diffusion. Recent estimates suggest that only about one-third of maize area and one-sixth of rice area were planted with improved varieties in 2010.[6] For some important crops, such as cassava, not a single PhD-trained plant scientist was engaged in crop improvement research in 2010; even for maize, only thirty-one full-time equivalent scientists were working in research. Coulson and Diyamett (2011) suggest that the national research system has been underfunded and has also failed to make effective use of links to resources emanating from the international research system, such as those of the Consultative Group for International Agricultural Research (CGIAR).

At the farm level, the responsiveness and relevance of the research and extension system to farmer needs has been questioned. As of 2005, data suggested that two-thirds of Tanzanian agricultural households had no contact with research and extension services (Government of Tanzania, 2005).

Although small farm sizes and low government expenditure on research and extension services are a hindrance to productivity growth, as suggested by Coulson and Diyamett (2011), the lack of rural infrastructure and poorly developed marketing systems also affect the take-up of agricultural technologies, leading to large spatial variations in incentives for farmers to adopt improved seeds or to use purchased inputs. In particular, farmers struggle with large distances to input dealers and poor infrastructure, and this poor mobility has halted productivity growth and market integration (Ndulu and Mutalemwa, 2002). Evidence from other countries shows that investment in roads and irrigation infrastructure would contribute significantly to crop production (Fan et al., 2005).

Another barrier to productivity is that most farmers are exposed to high levels of risk—chiefly from weather shocks. Most households are reliant on rain-fed agriculture, and they have little access to financial mechanisms that might allow them to smooth consumption or to manage income shocks. Insurance markets and credit markets are poorly developed (Winter-Nelson and Temu, 2005; Wetengere and Kihongo, 2012). Until recently, agricultural insurance products in Tanzania have been unavailable, with the exception of few pilot programmes (SFSA-SCBF, 2014).

The challenges of providing support for the agricultural sector are thus numerous and complex. These challenges remain in spite of a long history of government policies aimed at promoting productivity improvements in agriculture—and, in general, efforts to support agricultural development.

6.3 Policy History and Sectoral Background

Tanzania has a long and varied history of agricultural policies, ranging from the modernization-oriented approaches of its early postcolonial period to the more recent focus on smallholder food production. It is fair to say that these policies have not delivered much in the way of sustained sectoral transformation, which perhaps highlights the limited potential for driving transformation largely or exclusively from the supply side.

It is also worth noting that Tanzania's history of policies aimed at promoting transformation has undoubtedly left political scars that may affect contemporary discussions of the state's role in promoting transformation. As has been well documented elsewhere (Putterman, 1995; Edwards, 2014), the postcolonial focus of Tanzania's agricultural policy was on an effort to transform traditional agriculture completely and radically into a mechanized, capital-intensive, and technologically advanced activity. The government's *ujamaa* policies entailed a shift towards state control, with policies supporting collectivization and the systematic relocation of people into villages. By some measures, the policies succeeded in their immediate objective. For export crops, area under cultivation and yields increased in the 1960s. Prices for many commodities—both producer and consumer goods—were set by government authorities, and markets played a limited role. Marketing was controlled by parastatal marketing boards, which were of questionable efficiency. Producer prices, even for many export crops, were poorly integrated with reflected world prices (Gerrard et al., 1993).

From the mid-1970s through the early 1980s, there was a period of economic decline and slow growth caused in part by external factors: the oil price shocks of 1973 and 1979 and the war with Uganda of 1979–80, and in part by internal factors: the nationalization of industrial, financial, and trade concerns; structural reforms in the smallholder sector; and the lack of attention to incentives for output and productivity growth (Edwards, 2014; Lofchie,1988). Prices for both food and cash crops fell below world levels, due in part to implicit and explicit taxation, but there was a relative shift of prices in favour of food crops and an associated shift in production. Fiscal constraints led to the neglect of transportation facilities such as roads and ports, and to rapid depreciation of crop milling and processing facilities, and irrigation equipment (Gerrard et al., 1993).

Starting in 1984 and accelerating in 1986, economic reforms were introduced to allow market forces to play a greater role in the economy. From 1986 to 1993, the real exchange rate depreciated significantly, providing better incentives to exporters. Domestic food crop marketing was liberalized, with private traders gradually taking over the role of the cooperatives and crop authorities. From 1991 to 1995, fertilizer subsidies were phased out and markets were opened to private traders (Ministry of Industry, Trade, and Marketing, 2008). In the mid-1990s, the marketing and export of traditional export crops was liberalized and the commercial role of parastatal crop authorities scaled back.

From the mid-1990s to early 2000s, the government adopted a number of policies to revive the agricultural sector including the decontrolling of export crop prices in 1994/5 and formulation of a comprehensive marketing policy in 2001. Crop yields reached their peak despite falling share of government spending in the sector.

Liberalization of markets has remained incomplete, however. Although formal price controls have been disbanded, there has been a recurring tendency for the government to impose export bans at moments when prices are high—even when high internal trade costs mean that it might be more efficient for northern Tanzania to export to Kenya and southern Tanzania to import from Zambia. Most recently, an export ban was imposed in 2011–12, though the ban was rescinded at the end of 2012.

6.3.1 *Development Vision 2025*

Agriculture's role in Tanzania's development strategy has received renewed attention in the past fifteen years. In 1999, the Tanzanian government adopted the *Tanzanian National Development Vision 2025*, which had been developed under the auspices of the Planning Commission, to further progress towards achievement of middle-income country status by 'transforming from a low productivity agricultural economy to a semi-industrial economy led by modernized and highly productive agricultural activities which are effectively integrated and buttressed by supportive industrial and service activities in the rural and urban areas' (Tanzania National Development Vision 2025).[7] The ASDP was subsequently adopted in 2006 and remains a key agricultural policy initiative of the new century. Through the ASDP, the government has emphasized transformation of agriculture through accessibility and usage of farm inputs, strengthened crop research and crop extension services, increased number of crop extension workers, farmers' fields schools, agricultural mechanization, agricultural irrigation development, crop pest and diseases management. The implementation of ASDP was extremely slow, with many coordination problems (Greeley, 2007; Cooksey, 2012).

The African Union's CAADP (Comprehensive Africa Agriculture Development Programme) programme under the New Partnership for Africa's Development (NEPAD) led the government to expand the ASDP's scope and projected cost, establishing the *Tanzania Agriculture and Food Security Investment Plan* in 2011 which retained ASDP's emphasis on state-led agricultural development model with focus on inputs and productivity rather than markets and value chains.

Whilst policy continues to prioritize improving smallholder productivity and poverty reduction, it has also gradually moved towards encouraging large-scale commercial agriculture based on substantial foreign investments and land acquisitions. Thus, guided by the national vision, a Tanzanian private-sector-led agricultural strategy to modernize the sector known as *Kilimo Kwanza* (translated literally as 'farm first') was established in 2008. Furthermore, Tanzania is one of the first three countries to develop a cooperative framework agreement for the US government-led *New Alliance on Food Security and Nutrition* that was launched at a G-8 summit in 2012. As part of the agreement, Tanzania commits to policy reforms to create incentives for private sector, including agribusiness. Another recent initiative, the Southern Agricultural Growth Corridor of Tanzania (SAGCOT) has been adopted to develop the region's agricultural potential. With strong support of donor groups, the initiative has taken the lead in promoting private sector in the sector by encouraging alignment of interests of the state and over twenty global agribusiness interests to build public–private partnerships. Furthermore, in order to improve investment incentives, the government pledged in 2012 not to rely on periodic bans on staple food exports during times of poor harvest.

The development strategies of the past decade have thus focused considerable attention on agricultural policy. However, the agricultural growth rate continues to be low compared to the target of 6 per cent annual growth that was established in the Five Years Development Plan (2011/12–2015/16). In order to accelerate the pace of sustainable and inclusive economic growth, the government introduced the *Big Results Now* programme in 2013, with agriculture as one of the priority sectors. Under this initiative, the government envisioned a commercialization strategy for the agricultural sector to ensure nationwide food security and food self-sufficiency, while increasing incomes through viable internal and international trade by 2025.

Against this backdrop, we consider the important changes taking place in the structure of demand and the opportunities that this creates for transformation in the Tanzanian agricultural sector.

6.4 Emerging Urban Demand

In this section, we explore the changes in the structure of agricultural demand that has accompanied urbanization in Tanzania. The argument is that a growing urban population, along with changing consumption patterns for urban dwellers, has led to a significant shift in the demand for food. This emerging urban demand in turn creates important potential channels for growth.

Over the past half-century, Tanzania's urban population growth has been rapid—as has been true elsewhere in sub-Saharan Africa. From around 5 per cent of total population in 1960, the urban population share has surpassed 30 per cent in the past decade. That rising urbanization rate must also be viewed in the context of rising population, so the increase in the total urban population is even more striking—from 0.5 million in 1960 to 4.8 million in 1990 and 15.7 million in 2014 (Figure 6.2).[8]

The sheer increase in urban numbers creates a growth in demand for marketed surplus from rural areas. But in addition, urban consumers demand different products than rural consumers. In contrast to rural households, many urban households have higher incomes and have access to a broader range of goods. They have access to different fuels for cooking, and they face different monetary costs and opportunity costs in relation to fuel and to cooking and processing facilities. They also face different time costs; and typically, around the world, urban consumers exhibit preferences for foods

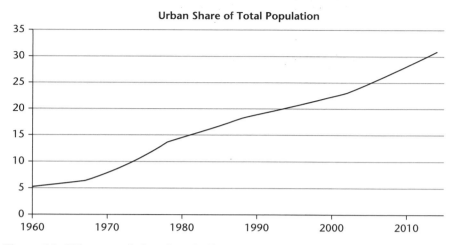

Figure 6.2. Urban population share in Tanzania
Source: The World Bank, World Development Indicators, accessed September 2015.

that require relatively little processing and cooking. Food consumed away from home represents a much larger fraction of total consumption for urban consumers; by one recent estimate, as much as one-third of consumption in Dar es Salaam takes place outside the home, implying major shifts in the patterns of what consumers eat and where they eat it (Cochrane and D'Souza, 2015).

This evolving demand from urban consumers explains many of the shifting patterns in the data on food and agriculture. One clear change is in the market for cereal grains. Like many other African countries, Tanzania has exhibited a growing dependence on imports of rice and wheat. This reflects an important structural change in food demand, with rice and wheat serving as alternatives, especially in urban areas, to maize and *ugali*. Urban consumers in many African countries appear to be switching to wheat and rice consumption as rapidly as their budgets allow.

In Tanzania, wheat accounted for 2.1 per cent of total calorie consumption in 1990; it now accounts for 5.5 per cent (FAO Food Balance Sheets).[9] Wheat is essentially a convenience food from the consumer's perspective. Urban consumers can purchase bread that is milled and baked at an industrial scale. This contrasts with root crops that need to be pounded and processed in the home, or maize that is either processed in the home or is purchased as ready-to-eat food from small-scale producers.

Rice is also a convenience food, at least relative to sorghum, millet, or root crops: it requires little processing and cooking times are short. Clearly there are also issues of social status attached to the consumption of bread and rice, but the sheer time demands of food preparation and cooking are a part of the explanation for their success. Cochrane and D'Souza (2015) estimate that in

Dar es Salaam in 2010/11, rice accounted for over 20 per cent of calorie consumption, compared with 11 per cent for all of mainland Tanzania.

Along with the rise in wheat and rice consumption, the data suggest a major decline in per capita consumption of starchy roots—nearly a 50 per cent decline since 1990. Although the data on root crop production are perhaps unreliable (as they are elsewhere in Africa, reflecting the difficulties of measuring yield and area), this would seem to suggest a meaningful decline in consumer demand for roots and tubers. In many other parts of the world, the data suggest that root crops are viewed as an inferior good at moderate levels of income, with consumers shifting to more preferred small grains as incomes rise.

Beyond these large-scale shifts in staple food consumption, there is also evidence that Tanzania's urban consumers are demanding a more diverse array of foods and an increased quantity of calorie-dense foods: sweetened products, processed beverages, oils and fats, and a range of processed and prepared foods. Since 1990, Food Balance Sheets show that Tanzania's per capita daily consumption of sugars and sweeteners have risen from 43 calories to 102 calories, and per capita daily consumption of vegetable oils has risen from 97 calories to 166 calories. These are national-level averages, and they conceal what is widely taken to be a major difference between rural and urban diets.

Although there is little detailed data comparing rural and urban diets, evidence suggests that farming households consume considerably less than non-farm households, and the data also point to substantial differences in composition. According to the Household Budget Survey and National Panel Survey, urban residents have decreased their consumption of traditional staple foods and increased consumption of meat products and beverages.

The changing consumption patterns of urban households show up in Tanzania's trade data. Because Tanzania's cities are well connected to international markets, it is often relatively cheap to procure 'urban foods' from international markets. As will be discussed below, domestic producers struggle to supply 'urban foods' in quantities and qualities sufficient to meet the emerging demand. This is compounded by the high costs of moving goods from rural areas to urban areas within Tanzania.

Given the growing demand and the relative ease of accessing urban foods from international markets, Tanzania's cities have grown dependent on imported foods. In 2014, Tanzania imported around US$1.24 billion of agricultural products, of which over 70 per cent were processed and semi-processed items. The leading processed agricultural goods were sugar and sweeteners, beverages, tobacco products, processed grains, and dairy products. The five leading semi-processed items were: vegetable oils, fatty acids and alcohols, flour (including soy flour), and non-sugar sweeteners (glycerol, sorbitol, and mannitol). Processed and semi-processed foods made up 6.9 per cent of total imports for Tanzania in 2014, and the average share for 2010/14 was 1.65 per cent of GDP.[10]

Can domestic suppliers meet the demand for processed and semi-processed foods over the coming ten to twenty years? This question depends not only on farm production, but also on the creation of value chains that lead from farm to consumer. Section 6.5 will argue that agroprocessing and food manufacturing—along with sectors such as packaging, distribution, and retailing—are substantially underdeveloped in Tanzania. The development of these agriculture-linked sectors may provide the key to agricultural transformation. Instead of a policy emphasis on farm production of crops, perhaps there are reasons to explore a new strategy that might highlight the opportunities to stimulate agricultural transformation through the development of these intermediate sectors.

6.5 The Missing Link: Rural–Urban Supply Chains

The preceding sections have argued that Tanzania's growing urban demand is not currently being matched by an increase in the supply of urban foods. Instead, urban food needs are being met to a large degree from imports—of rice and wheat, as starch staples, but also of various processed and prepared foods. This represents a lost opportunity for agricultural transformation in Tanzania. An important point to make is that the required transformation is not limited to the agroprocessing sector; it includes agricultural purchasing and trading, packaging, processing, storage, refrigeration, retail distribution, and retail sales. Investments in the processing sector alone are unlikely to achieve much impact. The challenge is not simply to turn fresh milk into yoghurt or fresh oranges into juice; it is to deliver these processed foods to consumer retail outlets in an efficient, low-cost manner, while meeting high quality standards and consistency.

In much of the rest of the world, the private sector has played a central role in developing the supply chains to link rural and urban markets—often with the support of public investments in key infrastructure and enabling institutions. Reardon and Timmer (2014) and Reardon (2015) document the ways in which 'midstream' elements of the food chain have played important roles in the development of urban food supplies in other parts of the developing world. A key insight is that the 'supermarket revolution' (Reardon et al., 2003; Traill, 2006) has only been one part of a much larger change in urban food supply chains.

For Tanzania, these sectors remain relatively undeveloped. Although agroprocessing stands as the largest sub-sector within manufacturing, for Tanzania, it employed only about 70,000 people in 2008 (Dinh and Monga, 2013)—a very low total in a labour force of 26.5 million. Most of the employment and production took place in very small firms, with only a few hundred firms having more than ten employees. As Dinh and Monga (2013) note, one constraint is on the agricultural supply side: few large farms are able to provide consistent supplies of high-quality goods in the volumes required by large-scale commercial processors.

Sutton and Olomi (2012) note that the history of food processing industries in Tanzania has been problematic, with many industries created under the import substitution regime in place after independence—but eventually shutting down under the competitive pressures accompanying liberalization in the 1990s. Sutton and Olomi note that the regulatory environment makes it difficult for food processing industries to get started and to grow. They write, 'Food processing is currently regulated by more than 17 different bodies, leading to multiple fees, a duplication of regulatory functions, delays, bureaucracy and corruption. This has made it extremely difficult for new and smaller firms to succeed in the industry' (Sutton and Olomi, 2012: 62).

Sutton and Olomi (2012) cite poor quality of agricultural inputs as a constraint to the expansion of this sector, with commodities often produced to a low standard and then damaged further in subsequent handling and trading. The absence of Reardon's 'midstream' is also discussed as a constraint, with packaging, distribution, and various kinds of standards and certification representing constraints. They cite the example of one firm that produces nutritionally enhanced flour aimed for niche markets; the owner sources ingredients from Netherlands, France, and South Africa in spite of the fact that all these ingredients are produced locally in Tanzania. There are local biscuit companies, but many rely on flour that is milled in Tanzania from imported wheat.

In some sectors, such as beverages and vegetable oil, there are successful industrial firms that draw on locally produced agricultural goods—often through contract farming and outgrower schemes. Sutton and Olomi (2012) estimate that 500,000 families were involved in oilseed production to serve this market, which would make for nearly one in ten farm households. But even here the potential is strong for further growth of firms serving the domestic market; FAO Food Balance Sheets for 2013 showed that 55 per cent of Tanzania's supply of edible oil came from imports.

The continued growth of this sector will depend on the effectiveness with which farmers and rural communities can be connected with urban markets. This is partly an issue of transportation infrastructure, but perhaps equally important is the need for effective systems of sourcing, packaging, processing, distribution, and logistics. There are indeed some companies that are capable of performing these tasks, but it is worth noting that in many parts of the developing world, it has been supermarket chains that have played the key role in developing these capabilities. In particular, the multinational supermarket chains—such as the South African, Turkish, and European retailers—have enormous expertise in developing supply chains, all the way back from retail outlet to farm. These companies understand how to source fruit and vegetables, locally, but also dairy, vegetable oil, and a range of processed foods that can be produced from locally supplied ingredients. In Tanzania, this might in the first instance include rice, bread, and prepared maize flour for *ugali*.

Reardon (2011) notes the importance of foreign direct investment (FDI) in the development of the supermarket and retail sector in Asia's developing countries. He argues that FDI has stimulated the development of this sector in many Asian countries—though it has been accompanied by growth in the domestic 'modern retail' sector. The foreign chains bring strong expertise in identifying and meeting consumer demand and in developing locally sourced sources of supply. Reardon (2011) argues further that policy liberalization has been important for FDI in the retail sector in some countries with long histories of restricting foreign-owned retailing.

Neven and Reardon (2003) argue that supermarkets play a vital role in driving agricultural transformation by serving as 'demanding customers' and make the argument that they are 'at the forefront of the modernization process'. By insisting on a range of quality standards, consistency of supply, and volume, supermarkets drive transformation along the entire supply chain—including ultimately to the farm level.

Within Tanzania, the supermarket sector remains small, in spite of its potential for growth.[11] Relative to Kenya and South Africa, Tanzania has a relatively modest number of chains. Nakumatt and Uchumi are the two largest chains, but between them operated only ten stores as of early 2014, compared to sixty-four that they operated in Kenya. As urban demand continues to grow, the question will not be whether or not supermarkets expand in Tanzania; the issue will instead be the extent to which the supermarket chains are willing and able to source materials locally and to extend their supply chains into rural Tanzania (rather than sourcing from existing suppliers in Kenya or abroad). Policies and government investments will undoubtedly matter for how this process unfolds.

6.6 Implications for Policy

In Tanzania, as in most African countries, agricultural policies have historically focused on the production side of farming. Agriculture ministries view processing and downstream activities as falling outside their areas of responsibility. Crop and livestock production tend to remain the focus of policy activity. Policies such as the Agriculture Sector Development Programme (which ran from 2006 to 2013) and the subsequent Tanzania Agriculture and Food Security Investment Plan (TAFSIP) placed a focus on subsidizing agricultural inputs, including credit. Little attention was given to the processing sector. The more recent *Kilimo Kwanza* (KK) programme introduced a public–private partnership for increasing food production and for supporting agricultural processing. Both TAFSIP and KK have tended to shift government resources towards direct support for farms and agribusiness. The policy agenda has also been caught up in discussions of the Southern Agricultural Growth Corridor of Tanzania (SAGCOT). The growth corridor strategy envisions concentrating government investments in infrastructure—both roads and electrification—in a relatively narrow geographic area as a way to give support to commercial production in that region.

Lost in this conversation is any real emphasis on demand for agricultural goods. This chapter argues that neither farm production nor processing can be pursued effectively except as part of a strategy that begins from the demand side. For Tanzania, demand comes from both foreign consumers and domestic (largely urban) consumers. For some goods, Tanzania has a clear comparative advantage as an agricultural exporter. But an agriculture strategy that focuses on exports will overlook an important and growing source of demand, which is the rapidly increasing urban population.

Although the domestic market is small relative to the *potential* world market, it is large in terms of the orientation of domestic production. Reardon (2015) estimates that 90–95 per cent of domestic food consumption in developing countries comes from domestic supplies. Even with poor roads and transport infrastructure, this suggests that domestic production has a significant relative advantage in the domestic market. Moreover, an agriculture strategy targeted to Tanzania's urban demand offers a number of advantages relative to a focus on international markets. Domestic demand is not susceptible to exchange rate movements or foreign economic crises, and at least in principle it has an advantage in terms of the proximity and potential immediacy of supply. As retailers shift towards 'just-in-time' strategies and seek to minimize inventory, domestic sources of supply can be very attractive. This demand creates incentives for private investment in storage and in production technologies such as irrigation that allow for steady and smooth supplies.

The policy levers are both simple and complex. Reardon (2015) writes about a set of 'policy meta conditioners' that lead to transformation of the domestic market. These include direct public sector investments in 'hard and soft infrastructure' (which he interprets as including roads, electrification, wholesale markets, commercial regulations, and public standards) as well as policy interventions that include both state investments (e.g., in warehousing and storage) and support for private investments through liberalization and privatization. He further notes that FDI has been a particularly important source of investment in the 'midstream' agricultural economy; encouragement of FDI in this area is another potential direction for government policy.

For the most part, however, lessons from other countries suggest that the government's primary role has not been to invest directly in plant or equipment for agri-processing, nor has it simply been to push on the production side of the economy through agricultural research and extension. Although these investments have a place in the portfolio, the key lessons are to liberalize and encourage FDI in the retail and midstream sector and to invest in physical infrastructure (e.g., roads and electrical grid) and institutional infrastructure (e.g., transparent systems of standard setting and quality assessment; appropriate regulation and deregulation of domestic transport; support for systems of warehouse receipts).

This relatively limited role for government does not imply that complete liberalization is the answer. Consider the example of the domestic transport sector. There is some evidence (e.g., Center for Economic Prosperity, 2010) that domestic regulations have led to a system in which checkpoints and weighing stations create major delays and costs in the domestic transport of food and agricultural goods. These bottlenecks also create insidious incentives for petty corruption. The underlying regulations are arguably justified: overloading of trucks creates safety hazards and leads to damage of roads. But there may be ways to create smart regulations that achieve the desired policy goals without generating unnecessary costs. For example, trucking companies that consistently meet safety and weight standards might be allowed to qualify for 'fast track' movement through weigh stations and check points—a status that they risk losing if they are caught in violations.

Similarly, complete liberalization also has the potential to give rise to market power and concentration in the trucking industry, where domestic routes can sometimes be carved up and divided among cartels. Encouraging competition in this sector—and aggressively limiting the tendency of firms to form cartels and drive up prices—can be important for unleashing the transformation of the sector.

6.7 Conclusions

This chapter has argued that a transformational agricultural policy for Tanzania must move beyond the level of the farm. Transformation cannot be achieved simply from investments on the production side—whether in smallholder agriculture or through the promotion of large commercial farms. Instead, transformation is likely to emerge through linking the agricultural sector to the demand from urban consumers. Although the urban market is still small, it is growing rapidly, both through the expansion of urban populations and through the shift in urban diets. Linking urban demand to domestic farm production will require the development of an array of intermediate sectors—food processing, storage, packaging, distribution, and retailing, to name a few. The government does not have a large role in direct interventions to support these intermediate sectors, but it can and should play a crucial role in providing physical and institutional infrastructure to support the development of these intermediate sectors. Through an approach of this kind, there is potential to bring about significant and meaningful transformation of Tanzania's agricultural economy.

Acknowledgements

We have received valuable comments and insights from Chris Adam and Anne Laski. The views expressed here are those of the authors as individual researchers and do not reflect the official views of any institutions with which we are affiliated.

Notes

1. Estimates of the agriculture share of GDP differ slightly depending on the source, depending in part on how the sector is defined.
2. Data for 2012 available at: <https://atlas.media.mit.edu/en/> (accessed 30 August 2015).
3. The figures for the short *vuli* rainy season were even lower: 7.2 per cent of households used inorganic fertilizer, on a total of 4.0 per cent of the land planted in *vuli*.
4. The categories of primary bulk commodities, semi-processed, and processed foods are defined as in Regmi et al. (2005).
5. It is worth noting, however, that the data on area harvested show a scarcely credible doubling of maize area between 2001 and 2003, which seems likely to reflect a change in collection methods or a break in the data series rather than an actual increase in area harvested. The jump does not reflect a single-year anomaly, either; the same increase shows for the average of the five-year period from 2003 to 2007 relative to the average from 1998 to 2002.
6. Data drawn from the DIIVA database at: <http://www.asti.cgiar.org/diiva> (accessed 8 June 2016).
7. Document available at: <http://www.tzonline.org/pdf/theTanzaniadevelopmentvision. pdf> (accessed 27 September 2015).
8. It is worth acknowledging that urbanization numbers are subject to measurement errors and to the difficulty of defining urban areas. These figures are taken from the World Development Indicators (accessed September 2015).
9. Cochrane and D'Souza (2015) report a detailed study of Tanzanian diets based on National Panel Survey data. The household survey data give results that differ in

significant ways from the Food Balance Sheets (FBS), which are based largely on estimates of production, imports, exports, and various losses and uses of commodities. Both methods have their advantages and disadvantages; household surveys may underestimate the consumption of goods such as alcohol and food away from home, which may be better picked up in national statistics. By contrast, the FBS data rely on production estimates that are themselves problematic. It is worth noting that Cochrane and D'Souza find a similar displacement of maize by rice, especially in Dar es Salaam. They find lower calorie shares devoted to wheat, although it seems possible that 'bread' may fall into their category of 'other' foods.

10. Data from COMTRADE and World Development Indicators, The World Bank (accessed August 2015).
11. A recent consultancy report by A. T. Kearney ranked Tanzania as one of the five most attractive retail markets in Africa, based on 2012 data in their African Retail Development Index: <https://www.atkearney.com/consumer-products-retail/african-retail-development-index/full-report> (accessed 8 June 2016).

References

CEP (Center for Economic Prosperity) (2010). *Road Blocks on Tanzania's Main Truck Routes*. Dar es Salaam: CEP.

Cochrane, N. and D'Souza, A. (2015). 'Measuring Access to Food in Tanzania: A Food Basket Approach. EIB-135', U.S. Department of Agriculture, Economic Research Service, Washington, D.C.

Cooksey, B. (2012). 'Politics, Patronage and Projects: The Political Economy of Agricultural Policy in Tanzania', Working Paper, Future Agricultures.

Coulson, A. and Diyamett, B. (2011). 'The Capacity and Uptake of Agricultural Research in Tanzania: A Scoping Study', IGC mimeo.

Dinh, H. T. and Monga, C. (2013). 'Light Manufacturing in Tanzania: A Reform Agenda for Job Creation and Prosperity', World Bank, Washington, D.C.

Edwards, S. (2014). *Toxic Aid: Economic Collapse and Recovery in Tanzania*. Oxford: Oxford University Press.

Fan, S., Nyange, D., and Rao, N. (2005). 'Public Investment and Poverty Reduction in Tanzania: Evidence from Household Survey Data', DSGD Discussion Paper No. 18, IFPRI, Washington, D.C.

Gerrard, C., Ansong, G., and Posehn, G. D. (1993). 'Agricultural Pricing Policy in Eastern Africa', World Bank, Washington, D.C.

Gollin, D., Lagakos, D., and Waugh, M. (2014). 'The Agricultural Productivity Gap', *Quarterly Journal of Economics* 129(2): 939–93.

Government of Tanzania (2005). 'Agriculture Sector Development Strategy— Government Programme Document', Dar es Salaam, The United Republic of Tanzania.

Greeley, M. (2007). 'Formulating and Implementing Sector-Wide Approaches in Agriculture and Rural Development: The Agriculture Sector Development Programme (ASDP)—Tanzania', Part of the Study by Evans, A. et al. (2007), 'Formulating and

Implementing Sector-wide Approaches in Agriculture and Rural Development: A Synthesis Report', Donor Platform 2007, Bonn.

Lofchie, M. F. (1988). *Tanzania's Agricultural Decline*. In: Chazan, N. and Shaw, T. M. (eds), *Coping with Africa's Food Crisis*. Boulder, CO, and London: Lynne Rienner Publishers: 144–68.

Ministry of Industry, Trade and Marketing (2008). 'Agricultural Marketing Policy', Dar es Salaam, The United Republic of Tanzania.

National Bureau of Statistics, Ministry of Finance (2011). 'Tanzania in Figures 2010', Dar es Salaam, The United Republic of Tanzania.

Ndulu, B. J. and Mutalemwa, C. K. (2002). 'Tanzania at the Turn of the Century: Background Papers and Statistics', World Bank, Washington, D.C.

Neven, D. and Reardon, T. (2003). 'The Rapid Rise of Kenyan Supermarkets: Impact on the Fruits and Vegetables Supply System'. Paper prepared for the FAO technical workshop on 'Globalization of Food Systems: Impacts on Food Security and Nutrition', Food and Agriculture Organization, Rome.

Putterman, L. (1995). 'Economic Reform and Smallholder Agriculture in Tanzania: A Discussion of Recent Market Liberalization, Road Rehabilitation, and Technology Dissemination Efforts', *World Development* 23(2): 311–26.

Reardon, T. (2011). 'The Global Rise and Impact of Supermarkets: An International Perspective'. Paper prepared for presentation at the 'The Supermarket Revolution in Food: Good, Bad or Ugly for the World's Farmers, Consumers and Retailers?' conference conducted by the Crawford Fund for International Agricultural Research, Parliament House, Canberra, Australia, 14–16 August.

Reardon, T. (2015). 'The Hidden Middle: the Quiet Revolution in the Midstream of Agrifood Value Chains in Developing Countries', *Oxford Review of Economic Policy* 31(1): 45–63.

Reardon, T. and Timmer, C. P. (2014). 'Five Inter-Linked Transformations in the Asian Agrifood Economy: Food Security Implications', *Global Food Security* 3(2): 108–17.

Reardon, T., Timmer, C. P., Barrett, C. B., and Berdegue, J. (2003). 'The Rise of Supermarkets in Africa, Asia, and Latin America', *American Journal of Agricultural Economics* 85(5) (December): 1140–6.

Regmi, A., Gehlhar, M., Wainio, J., Vollrath, T., Johnston, P., and Kathuria, N. (2005). 'Market Access for High-Value Foods', Agricultural Economic Report No. AER-840, U.S. Department of Agriculture, Economic Research Service, Washington, D.C.

SFSA-SCBF (2014). 'Tanzania Agricultural Insurance Feasibility Study', Conducted by Syngenta Foundation for Sustainable Agriculture (SFSA) for the Swiss Capacity-Building Facility (SCBF).

Sutton, J. and Olomi, D. (2012). *An Enterprise Map of Tanzania*. London: The International Growth Centre.

Traill, W. B. (2006). 'The Rapid Rise of Supermarkets?' *Development Policy Review* 24(2): 163–74.

Wetengere, K. and Kihongo, V. (2012). 'Constraints in Accessing Credit Facilities for Rural Areas: the Case of Fish Farmers in Rural Morogoro, Tanzania', *Journal of Applied Aquaculture* 24(2) (April): 107–17.

Winter-Nelson, A. and Temu, A. (2005). 'Liquidity Constraints, Access to Credit and Pro-Poor Growth in Rural Tanzania.' *Journal of International Development* 17: 867–82.

7

Unlocking Tanzania's Manufacturing Potential

Margaret McMillan, John Page, and Samuel Wangwe

7.1 Introduction

Tanzania ranks among the stars of the 'African Growth Miracle'. Since the turn of the century, annual gross domestic product (GDP) growth has averaged around 6 per cent while growth in labour productivity has been 4.1 per cent per year. Much of this productivity growth is a result of structural change. Since about 2000 labour has been moving out of agriculture and into other more productive sectors of the economy. In other economies industry has been a key driver of such structural change, but industry has played a much smaller role in Tanzania's structural transformation. Manufacturing comprises less than 10 per cent of GDP and its share of the labour force is only about 3 per cent.

This is important because manufacturing has the potential to play a major role in Tanzania's economic future. Tanzania has a young and rapidly growing population. Approximately one million new workers enter the domestic labour market every year, but the economy is not creating that number of wage-paying jobs (World Bank, 2014a). Manufacturing is a high productivity sector with the ability to absorb large numbers of modestly skilled workers. In addition, recent evidence (Rodrik, 2012) suggests that modern manufacturing industries in low income countries converge to global best practice productivity levels regardless of geography, institutions, or policies. This implies that increasing the share of employment and output generated by the manufacturing sector could play a critical role in sustaining job growth and closing the income gap between Tanzania and advanced countries.

This chapter assesses the role that manufacturing has played in Tanzania and considers the role that it could play in its economic future. Section 7.2 examines the current pattern of structural change in Tanzania and estimates its 'manufacturing deficit' relative to lower-middle-income countries. Section 7.3 provides a snapshot of the formal manufacturing sector and suggests an 'investment climate plus' strategy to accelerate its growth. Section 7.4 presents new data on the size, structure, and productivity of micro, small and medium manufacturing. We find large numbers of firms in the right-hand tail of the micro, small, and medium enterprise (MSME) productivity distribution, with output per worker exceeding the economy-wide average for manufacturing. This 'in-between' sector (Lewis, 1979) offers the potential for growth and job creation, if policies are better targeted at firms with the potential to grow. Section 7.5 offers some conclusions.

7.2 Structural Change and Industrialization

The decade 2002–12 was one of unprecedented labour productivity growth in Tanzania. Based on Tanzania's most recent census (2012), labour productivity has grown at 4.1 per cent per year for the period 2002–12 (Table 7.1).[1] Three quarters of this labour productivity growth is a result of structural changes in the economy, as the share of total employment in agriculture—the sector with the lowest average productivity—fell from about 82 per cent to 66 per cent.

Unlike the economies of East Asia, however, economy-wide labour productivity growth in Tanzania has not been driven by a large expansion of manufacturing. Between 2002 and 2012, the share of manufacturing in GDP increased by only 1.4 per cent (Table 7.2). Instead, employment and output expanded rapidly in a wide range of services, some more productive than others. Employment in trade services and business services together accounts for more than half of the productivity growth attributable to structural change. Employment in personal services also expanded but average productivity in this sector is so low that this change did not contribute to overall productivity growth.

The goal of Tanzania's *Vision 2025* is to move from a least-developed country to middle-income status. In 2010 Tanzania had a per capita Gross National Income of about US$1,490 at purchasing power parity, placing it among the ranks of low income countries transitioning to lower middle income status. Table 7.3 compares Tanzania's employment structure with the distribution of employment of four 'benchmark' economies at increasing income levels, corresponding to the international classification of countries by per capita income.[2] The most striking feature of Table 7.3 is the 'manufacturing deficit'. Less than 3 per cent of Tanzanian workers were employed in manufacturing in 2010, compared with 12–14 per cent of workers in the low- and lower-middle-income benchmark economies.

Table 7.1. Labour productivity growth in Tanzania, 2002–12

	Labour productivity annual growth	Relative labour productivity		GDP share		EM share		Annual average growth rate		
		2002	2012	2002	2012	2002	2012	Within	Between	Total
Agriculture	3.8	0.4	0.4	34.2	27.0	81.7	65.8	1.3	−0.8	0.5
Mining	−9.0	4.9	1.3	2.4	3.3	0.5	2.6	−0.2	0.4	0.2
Manufacturing	0.4	4.3	3.0	8.2	9.6	1.8	3.2	0.0	0.5	0.5
Utilities	12.0	7.8	1.4	2.3	1.9	0.3	1.3	−0.3	0.3	0.0
Construction	−0.8	6.7	4.1	7.3	9.9	1.0	2.4	−0.1	0.6	0.6
Trade services	0.9	1.9	1.4	14.9	16.0	7.5	11.3	0.1	0.6	0.7
Transport services	−0.9	7.2	4.4	6.5	7.5	0.8	1.7	−0.1	0.4	0.4
Business services	−5.1	42.4	16.8	12.1	13.5	0.2	0.8	−0.4	1.2	0.8
Gov't services	1.7	3.8	3.0	11.2	10.7	4.1	3.5	0.3	−0.2	0.0
Personal services	−6.0	0.3	0.1	0.8	0.7	2.1	7.4	0.0	0.1	0.0
Total	4.1	1	1	100	100	100	100	0.7	3.1	3.8

Contribution to total economy's labour productivity growth

								Within	Between	Total
Agriculture								34.6	−20.4	14.2
Mining								−5.8	10.6	4.8
Manufacturing								0.7	12.2	13.0
Utilities								−7.5	8.6	1.1
Construction								−1.5	16.1	14.7
Trade services								3.5	16.3	19.8
Transport services								−1.4	11.8	10.4
Business services								−11.6	31.9	20.3
Gov't services								7.1	−6.4	0.7
Personal services								−0.9	1.8	0.9
Total								17.4	82.6	100.0

Notes: Source: Diao et al. (2016)
The agricultural employment share of 81.7 per cent in 2002 is higher than the rural population share of 76.9 per cent in the same year, which is quite unusual among developing countries. The change in agricultural employment in 2002–12 is primarily led by a significant decline in employment in forestry, fishery, livestock, and hunting, falling by 6.7 per cent annually, while farming employment actually grew modestly at 1 per cent per year in 2002–12. The reason for such a rapid decline in agricultural employment outside farming is not clear, and it is likely that there is inconsistency in the classification in some of economic activities between the two rounds of censuses.

Table 7.2. Structure and growth of Tanzania's economy (in constant prices)

	Structure of the economy (measured by the share of total economy's value-added, per cent)		Annual growth rate of sector GDP (per cent)	
	2002	2012	1988–2002	2002–12
Agriculture	34.2	27.0	4.1	4.2
Mining	2.4	3.3	16.0	10.0
Manufacturing	8.2	9.6	4.4	8.4
Utilities	2.3	1.9	3.1	4.4
Construction	7.3	9.9	3.1	9.9
Trade services	14.9	16.0	4.4	7.5
Transport services	6.5	7.5	3.8	8.2
Business services	12.1	13.5	3.9	7.8
Gov't services	11.2	10.7	2.8	6.2
Personal services	0.8	0.7	3.6	4.4
Total	100	100	4.0	6.7

Notes: Rebased national accounts are used for the period 2007–12.

Source: Diao et al. (2016), National account, NBS, Tanzania (various years)

Table 7.3. Benchmarking Tanzanian manufacturing

Country	Share of labour force			
	Agriculture	Manufacturing	Other industry	Services
Least Developed Country Benchmark (US$700)	70.0	9.0	3.0	18.0
Low Income Benchmark (US$1,100)	60.9	11.5	2.9	24.7
Lower Middle Income Benchmark (US$1,500)	57.9	13.7	3.0	25.4
Upper Middle Income Benchmark (US$4,200)	14.0	25.0	4.0	57.0
Africa Average 2010	49.8	8.3	5.1	36.8
Tanzania 2005	76.7	2.1	2.7	18.5
Tanzania 2010	73.4	2.7	3.3	20.6

Notes: Least developed country benchmark: BGD (1994), CAM (1996), CHN (1987), IND (1989), IDN (1982), VNM (1992)
Low income benchmark: BGD (2003), CAM (2002), CHN (1992), IND (1994), IDN (1986), THL (1980), VNM (1996)
Transitioning economies benchmark: CAM (2005), CHN (1995), IND (2000), IDN (1992), PHL (1982), THL (1985), VNM (2001)
Middle income benchmark: CHL (2003), KOR (1993), MYS (2004)

Source: Author's calculations based on World Development Indicators and de Vries, Timmer, and de Vries (2013).

Relative to international benchmarks Tanzania has too little manufacturing at its current level of per capita income. Perhaps more importantly, relative to Tanzania's ambitious plans to achieve middle-income status, the gap between the role of industry at middle-income levels and the current level of industrial activity is even greater. In Sections 7.3 and 7.4 we set out some policy initiatives to achieve more rapid industrial growth.

7.3 Growing Formal Manufacturing

Tanzania was among the first African countries to turn to industrialization after independence. The *Basic Industrial Strategy* (BIS) of 1975 emphasized structural change, self-reliance, and state-led industrialization, but the commitment to industry proved to be short-lived. Tanzania responded to the economic crisis of the early 1980s by adopting structural adjustment programmes under the Bretton Woods Institutions. Its Economic Recovery Program (ERP) pursued the twin objectives of restoring macroeconomic stability and accelerating market-based reforms. Trade liberalization was adopted to force enterprises to compete with imports, but contrary to what had been expected, industrial productivity did not improve. Most firms could not compete, and state-controlled industrialization gave way to privatization and industrial decline.

Industrialization faded from the development policy debate for nearly two decades. Although a twenty-five-year *Sustainable Industrial Development Policy for Tanzania* (SIDP 2020) was adopted in 1996 and in 1999 Tanzania's *Development Vision 2025* set the goal of achieving 'transformation from a weather and market dependent agricultural economy to a self-sustaining semi-industrialized economy', implementation of these long-term plans was put on hold. During the first decade after the launch of *Vision 2025* no five-year development plans, the principal instrument by which the *Vision* was to be implemented, were formulated. Instead, the government was occupied by the implementation of poverty reduction strategy papers (PRSPs), drafted at the request of the donors, to support debt relief. The first and second generations of PRSPs were predominantly focused on the social sectors with little attention to industry.

Today there are a relatively small number of formal manufacturing enterprises in Tanzania, around 1,000, but unlike many African economies industry is growing. Between 2000 and 2010, real manufacturing value-added more than doubled from US$894 million to US$1,992 million, and since 2010 growth of manufacturing has continued to outpace overall GDP growth (Table 7.2). Agroprocessing is the leading manufacturing sub-sector, accounting for 55 per cent of total output.[3] Manufacture of furniture, non-metallic mineral products, tobacco, and textiles round out the list of other major formal manufacturing activities.

Recently, industrialization has started to receive more policy attention. In June 2010 the *Integrated Industrial Development Strategy 2025* (IIDS) was adopted to provide concrete steps to implement SIDP 2020. The IIDS seeks to build industry by putting in place a competitive business environment, improving existing development corridors, removing infrastructure constraints and promoting agriculture-led industrialization. The IIDS has an ambitious growth target for manufacturing value-added of 15 per cent per year. The Tanzania Long-Term Perspective Plan (LTPP), 2011/12–2025/26, foresees manufacturing almost doubling its contribution to GDP to 18 per cent. That level of ambition has yet to be realized.

The policy stance embodied in both documents focuses on removing constraints to industrial development, through reform of the investment climate—the physical, institutional, and policy environment within which private firms operate. A number of investment climate reforms, mainly dealing with reform of the regulatory environment, have been included as performance criteria for donor budget support. In our view, an 'investment climate plus' approach is needed to boost formal manufacturing growth. This approach will need more selective public actions than investment climate reforms and will require a more active role for government. To illustrate the approach we focus here on two initiatives: creating an export push and linking industry to natural gas.

7.3.1 Creating an Export Push

Tanzania has had the most rapid growth in manufactured exports among its East African neighbours (UNIDO, 2012). Between 2000 and 2010 manufactured exports increased from US$129 million to US$1,904 million. The bulk of this increase took place in the second half of the decade when manufactured exports grew at 45 per cent per year and the number of new Tanzanian exporters grew by about 8 per cent per year (Cadot et al., 2012). Manufactured exports per capita increased from US$3 in 2000 to US$43 in 2010, exceeding the Africa-wide average (excluding South Africa) of US$40. Regional exports in East Africa and exports to Asia were the major sources of this export dynamism (Yoshino et al., 2013).

Tanzanian policy makers have recognized that the export market holds the key to more rapid industrial growth. The *Tanzania Mini-Tiger Plan 2020*, introduced in 2005, was an effort to replicate the East Asian model of export-led industrialization. Yet, despite some success, Tanzania's formal manufacturing sector has failed to achieve the levels of export dynamism seen in such recent East Asian success stories as Cambodia and Vietnam. Sustained and rapid export growth of the type envisaged in the *Mini-Tiger Plan 2020* and the *IIDS 2010* will need an 'export push'—a coordinated set of public investments, policy reforms, and institutional changes focused on increasing the share of industrial exports in GDP.

The policy actions needed to achieve an export push range from maintaining a competitive real exchange rate to public investments in trade-related infrastructure to institutional and regulatory reforms.[4] A full discussion would require a chapter in itself. Here, we focus on only two key areas—special economic zones (SEZs) and trade logistics. Both are cases of policy and institutional innovations that have been implemented in other newly industrializing countries, but which seem to perform less well in Tanzania. Both represent serious constraints to more rapid export growth. Thus, they are good places to begin.

7.3.1.1 STRENGTHENING SPECIAL ECONOMIC ZONES

Tanzania has been a relative latecomer to the use of SEZs. The government established the Export Processing Zones Authority (EPZA) only in 2006. In the same year, the *Mini-Tiger Plan 2020* emphasized cluster development, supported by SEZs. The Plan envisaged a wide range of SEZ modalities: EPZs, free ports, free trade zones, specialized industrial clusters, agricultural free zones, industrial parks for SMEs, microenterprise manufacturing parks, and information and communication technology parks. Faced with two competing programmes, the government enacted the Economic Zones Law of 2011, which unified the EPZ and SEZ programmes by making EPZs a subset of the SEZ programme and gave oversight authority for both programmes to the EPZA.

Not surprisingly, the long delays in clarifying the institutional and regulatory regime have resulted in a slow start for SEZs. The government has allocated thirteen sites for SEZs, but only seven have been licensed, and only one of these seven, the Benjamin William Mkapa Special Economic Zone in Dar es Salaam, is operated as an SEZ. There are also twenty stand-alone plant-level EPZs. In total, Tanzania's SEZs contain about forty firms, employing around 10,000 people. By way of comparison, SEZs in the Dominican Republic contain more than 550 firms and those in Vietnam hold 3,500. Firms in Tanzania's EPZs have the lowest export orientation among a sample of African countries studied by the World Bank, and production is spread across a variety of sectors (mainly in 'other manufacturing') with little evidence of clustering (Farole, 2011).

A number of reforms to the SEZ programme can be undertaken to improve its attractiveness to export-oriented investors. The most critical is to raise the infrastructure and institutional standards of SEZs to the levels needed to attract regional and global investors.[5] For example, the World Bank survey of SEZs found that firms in Tanzanian SEZs had an average downtime from electricity outages of fifty hours per month. Although this compares favourably with an average downtime of ninety-five hours per month outside the SEZs, it is not even in the top half of SEZs in Africa. Down times in such popular locations as the Dominican Republic, Bangladesh, and Vietnam average less than four hours. Customs clearance times in Tanzanian zones are about double that of their African counterparts. Only 20 per cent of SEZ firms have access to on-site customs clearance, and clearance times for imports into SEZs (including the stand-alone plants) averaged nineteen days, compared with fourteen days for the economy as a whole (Farole, 2011). To help encourage the formation of clusters of closely related firms, new zones should be located close to suppliers and customers.

Management of the SEZ programme is another factor critical to its success. The role and responsibilities of the EPZA need to be clarified and its ability to 'get things done' strengthened. The current position of the EPZA within government makes it difficult for it to play the coordinating role needed to achieve a 'whole of government' approach to zone development. To attract investment into the zones the EPZA needs to be able to streamline government services (including licensing, registration, utility connections, dispute settlement, and fee setting) and resolve disputes. Where zone authorities have played this role effectively they, together with the Investment Promotion Agency, have most often been placed under the Office of the President or of the Prime Minister.

7.3.1.2 IMPROVING TRADE LOGISTICS

In a world of task-trade, manufactured export success cannot be separated from the efficiency of trade logistics. Because new entrants to task-based production tend to specialize in the final stages of the value chain, poor trade logistics impact exporters through both the time and cost of export transactions and, perhaps more importantly, through the timeliness and cost of imported intermediates. 'Trade friction costs' resulting from inefficiencies at the port, in domestic transport, and in customs and handling can have a significant impact on the cost of imported intermediate inputs, and therefore on a country's attractiveness as a location for export-oriented investment.

The World Bank has developed a comparative measure of performance in trade logistics, the Logistics Performance Index (LPI). It provides qualitative and quantitative data on the logistics environment in each country, such as information on time and costs in a typical supply chain (World Bank, 2014b). There has been little improvement in the LPI for Tanzania since the survey began in 2007. In an effort to reduce the variability of year-to-year changes in the ranking, the World Bank (2014b) provides a long-run weighted score using the four waves of LPIs from 2007 through 2014. Except for Burundi, Tanzania underperforms other EAC countries in the LPI. It is ranked at 125 while Uganda is 69, Kenya is 89, and Rwanda is 119. Tanzania is well behind the leading Asian countries such as China, India, Indonesia, Malaysia, and Thailand.

The Port of Dar es Salaam is the most acute problem. The main symptoms of the port's inefficiency are long delays at anchorage and in the series of operations needed to remove merchandise from the port, the 'dwell time'. In addition, port tariffs are much higher than in Mombasa, Dar es Salaam's main East African rival. Customs clearance times are high by East African standards and even higher when compared to those of newly industrializing countries elsewhere (Yoshino et al., 2013). The total cost of extra delays and additional monetary payments compared to Mombasa has been estimated to be equivalent to a tariff of 22 per cent on a container of imports and of about 5 per cent on bulk imports.

There are currently some promising port reform initiatives underway. The proposed reforms have been known for a relatively long time and consist mainly of 'hardware' issues having to do with the infrastructure and layout of the port itself. The Government's recent 'Big Results Now' initiative on transportation has put improvements to the port at the top of the policy agenda. There is a broad consensus among public and private stakeholders about what reforms are needed, but they have been implemented slowly due to 'software' issues associated with the political economy of the port (Morisset et al., 2012). Accelerating the pace of reform will require measures to reduce the bargaining power of those who currently benefit from the status quo.

7.3.2 Linking Industry and Natural Gas

Natural gas has the potential to change Tanzania's industrialization prospects through three main channels: providing energy for industrial development, developing downstream industries, and developing the capacity to supply goods to the natural gas industry itself. Natural gas would be a cheaper source of energy for use directly in some types of manufacturing industries and would permit more cost-effective generation of electricity for industrial use. Energy-intensive industries such as cement manufacturers are already finding the utilization of gas directly in their production processes to be cost effective. In the Mnazi Bay gas field an 18MW power plant has been installed to supply electricity to the Mtwara and Lindi Regions. This has made the supply of electricity in the two regions not only reliable but attractive for use by industrial enterprises of all sizes. The government has come up with the Mtwara–Dar es Salaam pipeline project in anticipation of the substantial and growing national demand for natural gas. While these initiatives are encouraging, there is a critical issue of correctly pricing natural gas supplied to domestic users, whether directly or through power generation.

The development of downstream industries has the potential to make Tanzania a major player in the global gas industry through investments in the development of resource-based industries such as methanol, urea, and ethanol production. Tanzania may also have a comparative advantage in a range of petro-chemical industries and fertilizer manufacturing. The large scale of such investments implies that domestic demand will have to be supplemented by exporting to the region and globally. Linkages to agriculture can be strengthened by developing a fertilizer plant for domestic consumption and exports. Liquefied petroleum gas (LPG) and compressed natural gas

(CNG), products derived from processing natural gas, are significant to the national energy mix, especially for reducing reliance on alternative fuels that damage the environment and on hydroelectric power, which is becoming less reliable as the effects of climate change are increasingly felt. Here, the appropriate pricing of gas feedstock is again critical, and careful cost–benefit studies of proposed investments will need to be undertaken.

Development of natural gas also brings with it opportunities for supplying the various demands generated by the activities of the oil and gas industry. The local content policy aims to address the challenges of participation of Tanzanians in the sector, including procurement and use of locally produced goods and services, and local fabrication and manufacturing. Exploiting this potential requires implementing proactive policies that can overcome existing lack of local manufacturing capabilities and encourage capacity building and technology transfer. The demand side (such as procurement policies) needs to be favourable to local industrial development, while the supply side must address the capacities needed to supply the industry competitively.

Priority should be given to the capacity to foster the transfer of technology and knowledge, invest in research and development, and ensure close links between research and development and local industry. It is critical that policies, strategies, and action plans to help local manufacturing to meet demands of the gas industry are informed by continuous consultation with all industry stakeholders in the natural gas value chain, including MSMEs. Strengthening the capacity of institutions such as Local Government Authorities and community-based organizations in natural gas development areas is essential.

7.4 Manufacturing and the 'In-Between Sector'

Two-thirds of the increase in manufacturing employment in Tanzania between 2002 and 2012 took place in the informal sector (Diao et al., 2016). While employment in the formal manufacturing sector grew at 5.5 per cent per year, employment in informal manufacturing grew at 11 per cent. To understand the nature of these firms, we used Tanzania's first nationally representative survey of MSMEs, conducted by the Financial Sector Deepening Trust in 2010. While this survey is not without its limitations, it is the only comprehensive data we have for assessing the role of small (and particularly informal) firms in Tanzanian manufacturing.[6] The survey covers about 3 million formal and the informal businesses with around 5 million employees. These firms accounted for almost 30 per cent of national private non-agricultural GDP in 2010.

Manufacturing MSMEs contributed roughly 30 per cent of total manufacturing value-added in 2010. These smaller firms were concentrated in six manufacturing subsectors: beverages, food processing, textiles, wood processing, furniture, and building materials. In some of these six, such as food processing and building materials, small informal firms play a dominant role, and their total value-added is actually higher than that for their counterpart formal firms (Diao et al., 2016).

7.4.1 *Productivity and the In-Between Sector*

The literature on firm-level productivity commonly argues that firms in the MSME sector are unproductive (see for example La Porta and Shleifer, 2014). This literature misses the fact that there is actually an enormous amount of heterogeneity among firms in the MSME sector. We show this heterogeneity in Tanzania in Figure 7.1, which plots the distribution of the log of monthly value-added-per-worker for all firms in the MSME sector in 2010. The vertical lines in Figure 7.1 represent economy-wide average productivity in agriculture, trade services, and manufacturing.

Figure 7.1 shows that the majority of MSME firms have average productivity levels higher than average productivity in agriculture. This is consistent with evidence presented in McMillan and Rodrik (2011) and McMillan et al. (2014) that structural change out of agriculture in Tanzania has been growth enhancing since about 2000. A large share of these firms have productivity levels

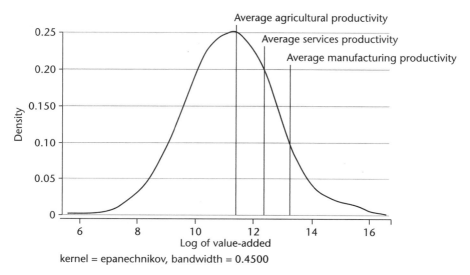

Figure 7.1. Productive heterogeneity of small firms
Source: Authors' calculations based on Diao et al. (2016).

higher than economy-wide trade services productivity and a smaller but still sizeable chunk of firms have productivity greater than economy-wide manufacturing productivity. This is important because it means that a good number of MSMEs contribute to raising labour productivity (and growth) in Tanzania's economy. In the process, they provide jobs for a large number of Tanzanians, especially the young.

Arthur Lewis (1979) was among the first to identify the subset of firms we find in Figure 7.1 as:

> units of production of all sizes, and in particular a great number of one-to five-man undertakings in manufacturing, transport and a wide range of services—often nowadays called the informal sector. Some of this activity belongs in the modern sector as we have defined it; i.e., it will expand with economic development; the rest—e.g., some of the handicrafts and some of the services—belong to the traditional sector in that they will contract.

He called these small- to medium-scale firms with the potential to grow the 'in between sector'—neither completely formal and modern nor traditional. Following Lewis, we label the MSMEs with relatively high productivity and the potential to grow 'in-between sector' enterprises.

In this chapter, we define firms in the in-between sector as those that have value-added-per-worker greater than economy-wide value-added-per-worker in manufacturing.[7] The reasoning behind this choice is that the exceptional performance of these firms is a strong indicator that, as the economy grows, the owners of these businesses have the skills required to stay in business and the potential to grow with it. This is consistent with recent writing on the importance of 'managerial capital' in economic development (Bruhn et al., 2011), a concept closely linked to that of 'firm capabilities' (Sutton, 2012). These are the subset of high capability firms in the MSME sector.

We report output per worker and the number of firms by sector in Table 7.4. The leading in-between sectors are in trade services, but manufacturing accounts for about 15 per cent of total in-between sector employment. Among the manufacturing firms in the in-between sector, firms in the building materials, furniture, and textiles sectors are more productive than the in-between firms in almost any other sector. In addition, firms in the building materials sector stand out as being large relative to other firms in the in-between sector with the average number of more than seven employees per firm. This is important since firms in the building materials sector have been targeted by the government in its attempt to link MSMEs to investments by large foreign firms in Tanzania's natural gas industry. The fact that these firms are relatively large and productive bodes well for their ability to benefit from investment in Tanzania's natural gas sector.

Table 7.4. Firms in the in-between sector by line of business

Sector	Monthly VA per worker	Number of firms	Total employment	Prody relative to average	Mean employees per firm
Retail Shop Foodstuffs	983,723	3,762	4692	1.96	1.25
Mfg.: Building Materials	859,682	5,288	42,130	1.72	7.97
Mfg.: Furniture	851,342	7,014	21,016	1.70	3.00
Mfg.: Textiles	697,944	10,214	13,837	1.39	1.35
Wholesale	686,069	20,303	46,460	1.37	2.29
Retail Shop Textiles	639,257	9,572	12,926	1.28	1.35
Repair Services	585,116	4,214	5879	1.17	1.40
Retail Shop General	561,051	70,524	122,520	1.12	1.74
Retail Street Vendor	536,882	20,090	31,315	1.07	1.56
Retail Stall Other	514,157	12,333	38,606	1.03	3.13
Food Services	467,149	60,386	154,888	0.93	2.56
Beverage Services	453,610	26,460	55,925	0.91	2.11
Retail Stall Food	450,036	70,240	139,478	0.90	1.99
Personal Services	450,017	4,989	16,733	0.90	3.35
Transport	442,272	1,127	2527	0.88	2.24
Retail Stall Textiles	396,044	26,723	50,322	0.79	1.88
Mfg.: Grain Milling	377,765	6,471	44,647	0.75	6.90
Mfg.: Wood Products	362,042	2,254	11,528	0.72	5.11
Retail Shop Household Items	337,604	19,729	96,015	0.67	4.87
Mfg.: Liquor	328,138	6,446	10,113	0.65	1.57
Business Services	323,566	6,219	20,105	0.65	3.23
Retail Fuel	140,746	685	1333	0.28	1.95
Retail Shop OMG	135,759	3,848	15,962	0.27	4.15
Extraction	49,327	974	3200	0.10	3.29
Total	501,220	399,865	962,157		
Total US$	351				

Note: Mfg.: manufacturing; OMG: Other Manufactured Goods
Source: Authors' calculations based on Diao et al. (2016)

7.4.2 MSME Policies

Tanzania implemented its first national MSME sector policy in 2003, when the Ministry of Industry and Trade published the *Small and Medium Enterprise Development Policy* (SMEDP). The SMEDP is one of several programmes designed to help achieve Tanzania's *Vision 2025*, an important part of which is focused on facilitating productivity growth in agriculture, manufacturing, and MSMEs. The policy commits the government to support SME development by addressing the constraints specific to SMEs. Two other policy initiatives of the early 2000s also address the development of MSMEs. The *National Microfinance Policy* of 2001 aimed to achieve widespread access to finance by MSMEs in urban and rural areas. The *Economic Empowerment Policy* of 2004 sought to empower Tanzanians to participate actively in the economy by creating a favourable business environment, improving the legal and regulatory framework and facilitating access to finance, skills, technology, premises, and information.

A wide range of MSME programmes are in place in Tanzania and are executed by an equally wide range of government institutions, donors, and NGOs. The rationale for most of these programmes is to contribute to job creation and growth, but assistance to the MSME sector by government, donors, and NGOs has been fairly ad hoc and certainly not targeted at firms with growth potential. A UNIDO (2012) report evaluating Tanzania's MSME policies found that inadequate coordination, weak synergies among stakeholders, insufficient resources to implement programmes, a lack of prioritization, and inconsistencies in legislation hampered Tanzania's efforts to foster productivity growth in MSMEs.

7.4.3 Targeting the In-Between Sector

One clear implication of our work is that not every owner of a micro or small firm is an entrepreneur. As illustrated in Figure 7.1, more than half of the MSMEs have extremely low productivity. These businesses help families to survive and so are important. But unlike the owners of the businesses in the in-between sector, many of these business owners report that they would prefer to have a wage-paying job. In other words, they are what Banerjee et al. (2010) have dubbed 'reluctant entrepreneurs'.

We have found a surprisingly large number of firms in the in-between sector. There is a significant right-hand tail of firms in the MSME manufacturing sector that have productivity levels equal to or greater than formal manufacturing. The total number of employees operating in the in-between sector in all activities falls slightly short of 1 million and average monthly value-added-per-worker for these firms is US$351. These are the firms that are most likely to have the capabilities to grow into a medium-scale manufacturing enterprise.

Sutton and Olomi (2011) provide a 'map' of Tanzania's firm capabilities in manufacturing. One of their conclusions is that in Tanzania, as in several other African economies where they had carried out enterprise mapping exercises, there was an absence of business owners capable of managing a well-functioning medium-sized firm. The scarce resource they argue is 'organizational capital' (Sutton and Olomi, 2011). This suggests that public policies aimed at growth and job creation should be attempting to identify and assist those micro and small firms that are in the right-hand tail of the productivity distribution, those with organizational capital.

A logical place to begin is by talking to the owners of these small businesses. There is no substitute for serious dialogue between business owners and government officials, but such structured engagements between the public sector and private firms, especially small enterprises, are rare in Tanzania.[8] An important lesson that the government of Tanzania can learn from China is that Chinese officials had and still have regular meetings with ordinary business owners. As a result of these meetings, officials often take concrete steps to remove constraints to profits and growth. An example is provided by Zhang and Hu (2014), who recount the story of one province's journey to becoming the largest potato grower in China and eventually an exporter of potato crisps.

The survey that we have been using to identify firms in the in-between sector asks MSME business owners to identify the three most important things that the government (or other partners) could do to improve small business in Tanzania. The results were as follows: 45 per cent of the firms in the in-between sector reported that providing access to finance was the most important way in which the government could facilitate business. The second and third most important requests were to provide information about market opportunities and to ease the regulations controlling business. It is telling that access to credit was repeatedly singled out as a severe obstacle, since the ratio of domestic credit to GDP in Tanzania is one of the lowest in the world.

The survey findings are consistent with the evolving literature on microfinance. The assumption that breaking financing constraints will boost business startups or allow micro and small business owners to scale up their operations and grow into larger firms appears to be true only when business owners have the skill and resources to profit from the investment (Banerjee et al., 2010; Bauchet et al., 2011). In Nigeria, for example, a business plan competition was used to identify 'high potential' entrepreneurs. Winners of the competition were given a substantial amount of money—on average US$50,000—to implement their business plans. Three years after the implementation a follow-up survey of these businesses showed that the programme had been successful at helping winning firms to purchase more capital and hire more labour (McKenzie, 2015). In India, Banerjee et al. (2015) found that while microfinance *on average* had no effects on firm performance, it did have a significant positive impact on firms with high growth potential. MSME finance programmes in Tanzania, on the other hand, make no attempt to screen firms for their growth potential.

Many programmes implemented in Tanzania focus on MSME training. Recent research from other countries suggests that microenterprise training initiatives have been largely ineffective (McKenzie and Woodruff, 2012). Impact evaluations of training programmes found that a combination of small changes in business practices and low statistical power meant that few studies found any significant impacts of training on sales or profitability. Although it is not clear from the existing evidence whether the training was ineffective because the trainers themselves were ineffective or because training is not what the business owners required, it is relevant that none of the programmes evaluated addressed market information, the second most important constraint identified by in-between sector business owners. Significantly, none of the MSME owners in the 2010 survey reported the need for training.

To support growth of in-between sector firms the government needs to develop more targeted interventions designed to identify small firms with the potential for growth and address the constraints they face. For example, rather than providing subsidized loans or training to an untargeted range of micro and small firms determined mainly by the availability of resources, the government might consider running a business plan competition similar to the one in Nigeria in which winners get a substantial sum money to expand their businesses. In the case of Nigeria, this competition was open to owners of existing businesses as well as startups.

Alternatively, the government might consider giving a small grant at startup to all new firms below a certain size. The grant, which would not be conditional on a credit appraisal, is intended to provide working capital for the startup phase of the firm. The implementing agency would refrain from further interventions designed to improve the 'creditworthiness' or profitability of the enterprise and observe over a period of two to three years which firms survived. It would then use information gathered from the surviving firms to provide support tailored to their needs. Such interventions are amenable to randomized experiments, and it should, therefore, be possible to conduct rigorous impact evaluations.

7.5 Conclusions

While Tanzania ranks among the leading stars of the 'African Growth Miracle', its industrial development has not been equal to its recent growth or its national aspirations. There are signs that things may be changing. In contrast with a number of the other African economies, industry is increasing as a share of output and employment in Tanzania. This new industrial dynamism appears to come from two sources. First, growth in formal manufacturing has been above the average rate of economic growth, although not as rapid as for some services. Second, a large number of micro- and small enterprises have entered manufacturing since 2005. These are firms that are not household enterprises but are not 'formal' either. They are quite heterogeneous and some have productivity levels that are equal to medium- and large-scale firms. This is the 'in-between' sector.

Since the mid-2000s industrialization has received more attention in the national development discussion than at any point since the post-independence era, but the results in terms of industrial development have failed to keep pace with the rhetoric. In part this is the consequence of the government's focus on the investment climate. A more selective and activist 'investment climate plus' strategy for industrial development in the formal sector is needed—one that in the first instance focuses on an export push and linking industry to natural gas. In mounting an export push priority should be given to making Tanzania's SEZs perform to a world class standard, and to improving the efficiency of trade logistics. In its efforts to link industrialization to natural gas, government will need to exercise great care in the pricing of gas for domestic industrial use and in designing the institutional framework governing participation by domestic firms in the gas sector.

Existing micro- and small enterprise programmes are misdirected, both in terms of the target and the instruments, and should be reformed. In order to be consistent with the growth and job creation objectives of *Vision 2025*, MSME interventions will need to be considerably more selective. Not every owner of a micro- or small firm is an entrepreneur. Most of the MSME programmes implemented in Tanzania focus on training and access to credit. Our research suggests that these initiatives are likely to be ineffective, except when business owners have the skill and resources to profit from the investment or training. The first priority for effective policymaking is, therefore, to identify firms in the in-between sector and to develop tailor-made programmes to relieve the constraints to their growth.

Notes

1. In contrast, annual labour productivity growth for the period 1961–2010 averaged only 1.5 per cent and was actually negative between 1975 and 1990 (de Vries, Timmer, and de Vries, 2013).

2. The benchmarks show the structural characteristics of economies—mainly in Asia—that have made or are making the transition to middle-income status. The labour share values for the benchmarks are the simple averages of the labour shares of the relevant countries at the time their per capita incomes were first equal to the income classification in Table 7.3.

3. The Annual Survey of Industrial Production (ASIP) collects detailed information on all registered industrial establishments with at least ten employees in mining, manufacturing, electricity, and water. It contains 729 firms of which 59.2 per cent are small-, 14.5 per cent are medium-, and 26.3 per cent are large-scale enterprises.

4. See Page (2012).

5. Farole (2011) finds that among the African countries surveyed, the top three factors determining investors' decisions to locate in an SEZ were: cost and quality of utilities, access to efficient transport, and the business regulatory environment.

6. The survey is not without its limitations. The sampling frame for this survey is households and the selection of households is based on the 2002 census. This poses at least two problems. First, because the survey is household based, it is representative of households and not businesses. Thus, since Tanzania is still a very poor country, we are likely to be missing some of the more productive businesses. Indeed, an analysis of the data reveals that mid-sized firms are under-represented in this dataset (Diao et al., 2016). Second, because the sampling framework is 2002 it oversamples rural households. This is because there was a significant reduction in rural activity between 2002 and 2012 (Diao et al., 2016). Therefore, readers should keep in mind that our analysis is likely to understate the contribution of small businesses to economy wide productivity and employment and also to understate the importance of small businesses in urban areas.

7. See Diao et al. (2016) for a more comprehensive analysis using different definitions of the in-between sector.

8. The Tanzania National Business Council (TNBC) is the umbrella organization that acts as Tanzania's forum for public private dialogue. Its membership consists of representatives drawn equally from the business community and the public sector, under the chairmanship of the President. The TNBC has attempted to represent the interests of small firms, but it has a strong large-firm bias in its membership, and it meets infrequently.

References

Banerjee, A., Breza, E., Duflo, E., and Kinnan, C. (2015). *Do Credit Constraints Limit Entrepreneurship? Heterogeneity in the Returns to Microfinance*. Cambridge, MA: MIT.

Banerjee, A., Duflo, E., Glennerster, R., and Kinnan, C. (2010). *The Miracle of Microfinance? Evidence from a Randomized Evaluation*. Cambridge, MA: MIT.

Bauchet, J., Marshall, C., Starita, L., Thomas, J., and Yalouris, A. (2011). 'Latest Findings from Randomized Evaluations of Microfinance', Consultative Group to Assist the Poor, Washington, D.C.

Bruhn, M., Karlan, D., and Schoar, A. (2011). *What Capital is Missing in Developing Countries?* Cambridge, MA: MIT.

Cadot, O., Régolo, J., and Yoshino, Y. (2012). 'Firm-Level Patterns of Export Expansion: Evidence from Tanzania', World Bank, Washington, D.C.

de Vries, G. J., Timmer, M. P., and de Vries, K. (2013). 'Structural Transformation in Africa: Static Gains, Dynamic Losses'. GGDC Research Memorandum 136 (University of Groningen). Africa sector database, available at: <http://www.rug.nl/research/ggdc/data/africa-sector-database> (accessed 16 August 2016).

Diao, X., Kweka, J., McMillan, M., and Qureshi, Z. (2016). 'Economic Transformation from the Bottom Up: Evidence from Tanzania'. IFPRI Discussion Paper (forthcoming). The International Food Policy Research Institute.

Farole, T. (2011). 'Special Economic Zones in Africa: Comparing Performance and Learning from Experience', World Bank, Washington, D.C.

La Porta, R. and Shleifer, A. (2014). 'The Unofficial Economy in Africa'. In: Edwards, S., Johnson, S., and Weil, D. N. (eds), *African Successes: Government and Institutions*. Chicago: University of Chicago Press.

Lewis, W. A. (1979). 'The Dual Economy Revisited', *The Manchester School* 47(3): 211–99.

McKenzie, D. (2015). 'Identifying and Spurring High-Growth Entrepreneurship: Experimental Evidence from a Business Plan Competition', World Bank Policy Research Working Paper 7391, World Bank, Washington D.C.

McKenzie, D. and Woodruff, C. (2012). 'What Are We Learning from Business Training and Entrepreneurship Evaluations around the Developing World?', Policy Research Working Paper 6202, World Bank, Washington, D.C.

McMillan, M. S. and Rodrik, D. (2011). 'Globalization, Structural Change and Productivity Growth'. No. w17143. National Bureau of Economic Research.

McMillan, M., Rodrik, D., and Verduzco-Gallo, I. (2014). 'Globalization, Structural Change, and Productivity Growth, with an Update on Africa', *World Development* 63(1): 11–32.

Morisset, J., Moret, C., and Regolo, J. (2012). 'How to Push Efficiency Enhancing Reforms in the Port of Dar es Salaam?' The World Bank Africa Regional Poverty Reduction and Economic Management, World Bank, Washington, D.C.

Page, J. (2012). 'Can Africa Industrialize?' *Journal of African Economies* 21(suppl. 2): ii86–ii124.

Rodrik, D. (2012). 'Unconditional Convergence in Manufacturing', *Quarterly Journal of Economics* 128(1): 165–204.

Sutton, J. (2012). *Competing in Capabilities: The Globalization Process*. (Clarendon Lectures in Economics). Oxford: Oxford University Press.

Sutton, J. and Olomi, D. (2011). *An Enterprise Map of Tanzania*. London: International Growth Centre.

UNIDO (2012). Tanzania Industrial Competitiveness Report 2012, UNIDO, Vienna.

World Bank (2014a). 'Productive Jobs Wanted: Tanzania Country Economic Memorandum', World Bank, Washington, D.C.

World Bank (2014b). 'Connecting to Compete', World Bank, Washington, D.C.

Yoshino, Y. with Cadot, O., Ratsimbazafy, F., and Regolo, J. (2013). 'Uncovering Drivers for Growth and Diversification of Tanzania's Exports and Exporters', World Bank, Washington, D.C.

Zhang, X., and Hu, D. (2014). 'Overcoming Successive Bottlenecks: the Evolution of a Potato Cluster in China', *World Development* 63: 102–12.

8

Building a Skills Agenda towards Productive Employment

Mahjabeen Haji and Jacques Morisset

8.1 Introduction

It is well known that productive jobs pave the way out of poverty, and history shows that economies that have been able to combine gross domestic product (GDP) growth with employment growth have been successful in reducing poverty. However, in spite of a stable and high GDP growth rate over the past decade, Tanzania has failed to create enough productive jobs. Indeed, the number of working-age Tanzanians has been growing faster than the number of jobs. With rapid population growth (2.7 per cent per year) and a youthful population (about half of the population below the age of seventeen), the country has almost 1 million new entrants into the domestic labour market every year. Notably, at US$1,700 per year, earnings per worker in Tanzania are still amongst the lowest in the world, and the slow decline in poverty does not match the rate of growth of the labour force.[1]

The gap in economic opportunity for Tanzania's youth arises from the largely young and rapidly growing population combined with a critical dearth in the pool of skills demanded by employers. This supply side problem is exacerbated by the quality of education received prior to entering the labour force. There have been several efforts to address education reform, but any far reaching benefits will take at least a generation to manifest in more productive livelihoods. Tanzania has no shortage of pilot programmes and small-scale employment and training programmes that have attempted to target unemployment or under-employment. These range from national programmes to well-meaning donor interventions. But with little evidence or measure on effectiveness, as well as a lack of scale and coordination between programmes, we still lack a robust understanding of the labour market in Tanzania and the prospects of employment growth.

The challenge to create jobs also needs to be qualified: as in most developing countries, the official unemployment rate in Tanzania is very low—less than 4 per cent and declining over time.[2] Most households cannot afford not to work. The true challenge is therefore not to find jobs but to find more productive jobs that generate sufficient income and help to propel the economy towards more equitable growth. Low-paid jobs, informal jobs, and vulnerable jobs do not have the same development impact as well-paid and formal jobs.

Realizing this vision will require a better understanding of how to best harness youth potential, accounting for about 18 per cent of the total population, and 28 per cent of the labour force.[3] At this time, when much of the world's population is ageing rapidly, it is true that Tanzanian youth represent vibrant resources that can be harnessed for the country's growth. In the short-term however, Tanzania is faced with a very young population and the prospect of a rapid increase in new labour market entrants in the next few years. This makes youth employment perhaps the most challenging challenge for overall economic development in Tanzania. For this reason, much of the discussion in this chapter identifies policies that can increase the productivity of overall employment, with a special focus on transition into the labour market for the youth population.

Using available data and concrete economic analysis, we explore how Tanzania can meet its vision for greater and more productive jobs for its population, with a focus on youth. Tanzania's sub-standard performance in productive job creation is related to challenges in both labour demand and labour supply. This chapter focuses on how to make human capital more productive, while other chapters complement this analysis with a greater focus on demand-side challenges of the labour market.[4] It looks at both the issue of how to upgrade the productivity of the existing stock of human capital and how to ensure that new workers will be ready to contribute to the dynamics of the overall economy. Section 8.2 describes the structure of the labour market in Tanzania, and provides a deeper understanding of the magnitude and complexity of the issues surrounding the youth labour market. Section 8.3 employs available microeconomic evidence to profile the levels of education and skills amongst the working population in Tanzania, and discusses the vital role of garnering basic education and skills in order to maximize the potential of human capital in Tanzania. The chapter concludes with forward-looking recommendations on how current findings can be used as a foundation to increase opportunities for youth in the labour market.

8.2 Growth, Jobs, and Patterns of Employment in Tanzania

Tanzania has been growing fast but poverty remains widespread. Annual GDP growth has been around 7–8 per cent per annum in the last few years, which is close to its ten-year average, and significantly higher than the rate of growth achieved by neighbouring Uganda and Kenya. However, growth has only marginally and recently contributed to poverty reduction. While poverty declined by approximately 25 percentage points between 2007 and 2014, about 43 per cent of the population continues to live below $1.25/day.[5] The low responsiveness of poverty to economic growth has been due to several factors, including the fact that the sectors driving this growth have not created better and more inclusive jobs. This is one of the critical pathways out of poverty, particularly for the youth population in the country.

While close to three-quarters of the working population is employed in agriculture, economic growth has been driven by a few (urban) selected sectors, particularly communications, financial services, construction, transportation, and trade. These sectors are also relatively capital intensive and/or reliant on skilled labour, creating a limited number of employment opportunities for low skilled workers, except through construction and trade activities. In contrast, the growth rate of the labour-intensive agricultural sector, which employs 75 per cent of the workforce and contributes to approximately 25 per cent of GDP, remained lower than that of the overall economy.

Looking forward, the recent discovery of natural gas reserves in the south of Tanzania has the potential to create a number of new jobs, principally through linkages with the local economy during the contruction phase and joint infrastructure.[6] Approximately US$35–40 billion is anticipated in investment by International Oil Companies in the coming years in upstream activities and studies indicate that this could translate to large economy-wide impacts, with the potential to contribute up to 7 per cent of the country's GDP by 2027.[7] However, this impact will still take some years to materialize (the final investment decision of mutinaltionls is expected in about 2022) even if it remains important to put in place the adequate legal and instutional foundations required to optimize the impact of gas exploitation on the local economic and national employment.[8]

Today, Tanzania has both high rates of employment and underemployment. The labour force is about 24 million in size, with a participation rate of close to 90 per cent over the last decade. As Figure 8.1 shows, the overall unemployment rate is quite low at 3–4 per cent for the labour force.[9] However, it is clear that these employment statistics hide a high degree of underemployment, with people stuck in unproductive activity and informality. For example, about 90 per cent of the employed population is self-employed— most of which are in the informal sector—with less than a tenth of the

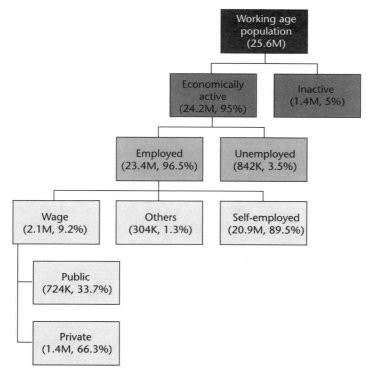

Figure 8.1. Tanzania employment categories

Note: 'Others' category includes unpaid or family work.

Source: World Bank (2014b), World Development Indicators, KILM indicators (ILO, 2014), and Tanzania National Bureau of Statistics, Employment & Earnings Survey Report (2012 & 2013).

population in wage work. The youth unemployment rate is not much higher than that of the general population; it decreased from 8.9 per cent in 2000 to 7.7 per cent in 2006, and was only 6.5 per cent in 2013.[10]

Approximately two out of three youths in Tanzania were active in the labour market in 2010/11, which is comparable to that of neighbouring countries such as Uganda. Employed youth typically hold informal and low-skilled jobs in the agricultural sector, which accounts for 60 per cent of employment in the general population, and approximately 75 per cent of employment amongst the youth. Other than agriculture, young women are more likely to be found in the trade and accommodation sector (including hospitality and food services), while young men are disproportionately represented in sectors such as construction and transportation, which also happen to be amongst the fastest growing sectors in Tanzania.[11] Youth are also disproportionately represented in the informal sector, accounting for almost

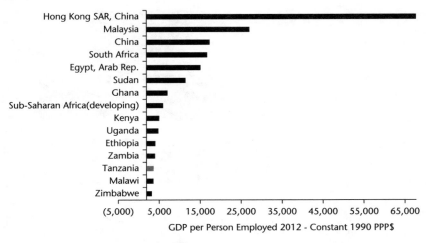

Figure 8.2. Cross-country comparison of earnings per worker (2012)
Source: World Bank (2014b), World Development Indicators.

a third of the informal sector population, and thus, highlighting their vulnerable state in the labour market.[12]

Tanzania's failure to generate a sufficient number of employment opportunities in productive sectors is clearly reflected by the country's average wages, which are still amongst the lowest in the world (see Figure 8.2). Only about 15 per cent of the working population is engaged in emerging sectors, including professional services, ICT, construction, transport and storage, hotels and restaurants, and other services. The other 85 per cent are concentrated in traditional sectors such as agriculture, mining, and trade. However, earnings per worker in traditional sectors, at US$700 per year, are about six times lower than in emerging sectors. The low average wages are reflected by the still relatively high levels of poverty, particularly in rural areas (close to 35 per cent in 2012).[13] The correlation between poverty and average per worker earnings is not surprising, given that the most direct way for a household to escape poverty is to generate a sufficient, long-term income from labour.

The overall domestic labour force is projected to grow to 45 million by 2030, and agriculture will only absorb a relatively small part of this growth. A significant share of this influx will come from the growth of the youth population. Approximately 900,000 youth entered the labour force in 2010/11, and Tanzania's youth population is expected to swell to 11 million by 2020, and 15 million by 2030. In absolute numbers, the size of Tanzania's youth population almost doubled from 4.4 million in 1990 to 8.1 million in 2010.[14] Hence, a movement of labour to more productive jobs is critical for driving job-generating growth and to absorb the current and the incoming labour force.

But the structure of employment is changing, showing that structural transformation is well underway in Tanzania. In recent years, non-farm household enterprises have been the fastest growing segment of the labour market, growing by approximately 10–15 per cent per year. This is fuelled by rapid urbanization, as well as a lack of other employment options for a majority of Tanzanian workers. As a result, the share of non-farm businesses has increased from 39.8 per cent to 45.5 per cent during this period. At this rate of structural change, more than 40 per cent of the labour force will be employed outside the agricultural sector by 2030, as compared to only 25 per cent today.[15]

The process of rapid urbanization is also evident in any of the country's cities. The 2012 population survey shows that approximately 15 million Tanzanians (or 27 per cent of the population) now live in urban areas, compared with 1990, when the urban population was only 4.5 million, or 18 per cent of the total population. In particular, Dar es Salaam is set to attain 'mega city' status with an estimated number of 10 million inhabitants by 2027 at its current annual growth rate of 5.8 per cent.[16] Cities in sub-Saharan Africa with growth patterns like Dar es Salaam are also referred to as 'consumption cities', which provide economies of scale in consumption but are not necessarily the front for productivity growth, as structural transformation does not necessarily follow urbanization, and most people work in non-tradable services.[17]

The increasing concentration of the population in urban areas is caused by the widespread expectation that economic conditions are better in these areas, and it is not surprising that migration to large cities (particularly to Dar es Salaam) is largely driven by those younger than the age of thirty, in search of productive economic opportunities. However, high barriers to entry into formal jobs and a large informal economy lead to self-employment as the only—or most viable option—for most Tanzanians. The youth employment landscape is also characterized by high levels of informality and vulnerability in self-employment, particularly in urban areas. The vast majority of businesses are owned by 'reluctant entrepreneurs'[18] who are confined in very small operations (generally self-employment) with little specialization, and operate a few hours per day or week in the margins of the economy. They have no choice—as wage employment is not an option—and have to operate their own businesses to survive. Approximately two-thirds of Tanzanian firms operate in the areas of general trade and non-farm-based agriculture, with almost 90 per cent of them confined to self-employment (see Figure 8.3).[19]

The entry point into the labour market is a critical moment for young Tanzanians, as it often correlates with how well they are likely to fare in the labour market. However, as the informal sector has low barriers to entry, most youth enter self-employment to make a living. This route offers few options for transition to other forms of employment such as wage-work. For example,

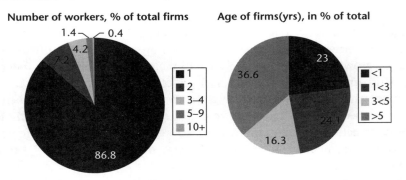

Figure 8.3. The predominance of self-employment and young firms
Source: World Bank, Tanzania Country Economic Memorandum (2014a).

Table 8.1. Movement between employment sectors in Tanzania

	Final State				
	Unemployed	Family Worker	Self-Employed	Wage Employed	Total
Entry as Unemployed	29	–	42	12	83
(%)	35%	–	50.6%	14.5%	100%
Entry as Family Worker	5	13	90	14	122
(%)	4%	10.7%	74%	11.5%	100%
Entry as Self-Employed	3	–	116	4	123
(%)	2.4%	–	94%	3.3%	100%
Entry as Wage Employed	3	1	22	58	84
(%)	4%	1%	26%	69%	100%
Total	40	14	270	88	412
(%)	10%	3%	66%	21%	100%

Note: Sample includes employment histories collected from 412 urban youth aged 20–35 from the 2004, 2005, and 2006 waves of Tanzania Household Urban Panel Survey. More details on sampling can be found in Bridges et al. (2013).
Source: Bridges et al. (2013).

labour histories of individuals aged 20–35 in Tanzania indicate that those that enter the labour market as self-employed or wage employed are much more likely to stay in that mode of employment (see Table 8.1). Interestingly, the minority of those from wealthier backgrounds and with higher education levels tend to stay unemployed for longer, and can afford to wait an average of 5.5 years for wage employment without a significant earnings penalty.[20] In fact, those that are wage employed spend more time searching for work, and find their first job a bit later than their self-employed counterparts. Most prefer wage employment over self-employment, and a majority of self-employed youth cited a lack of success in finding salaried work as the main reason for self-employment.[21]

Given the magnitude and complexity of the employment challenge, Tanzania cannot afford to neglect the constraints faced by its young and growing population. Population shifts from rural to urban areas have only added to this pressure. Generating new jobs and more productive ones will be critical to driving growth and absorbing the growing labour force. In parallel, providing the youth population with the tools needed to access these jobs will be paramount to ensure productive livelihoods, and hence, to enhance Tanzania's overall economic development. Today, many of the fastest growing sectors—communications, financial services, and transportation, for example—depend on skilled labour. Yet the labour force is dominated by unskilled or low skilled workers. Currently, less than 4 per cent of youth work in roles that require higher skill sets, and education and skills training will be essential to equip Tanzanian youth to benefit from transitions underway in the economy. Section 8.3 further details the various constraints and challenges related to entering the Tanzanian labour market, particularly with regards to education and skills.

8.3 Harnessing Human Capital: The Fundamental Role of Basic Education and Skills

To understand the challenges that constrain the productivity and opportunities for youth in the labour market, and to direct the way in which policy can be shaped, this section focuses on human capital and the role of basic education and skills in boosting favourable prospects for employment.

8.3.1 *The Disconnect between Formal Education and Learning*

Today, the Tanzanian labour force is characterized by a dominant proportion of unskilled or low skilled workers, a majority of which is composed of the youth. Despite the near-universal enrolment in primary schools, the proportion of the labour force with middle- and high-level skills remains very low, with less than 12 per cent of the total population having completed lower secondary education. While formal education is not the only way to acquire skills for a particular type of job, the acquisition of basic numeracy and literacy skills is imperative for a country that hopes to reap the demographic dividend of a largely young population.

Educational attainment tends to shape employment opportunities, and education policies in developing countries have typically focused on universal enrolment in primary education with the assumption that the returns are greatest at this level. However, school attendance does not guarantee learning, and in Tanzania, returns to education remain low at foundational levels of

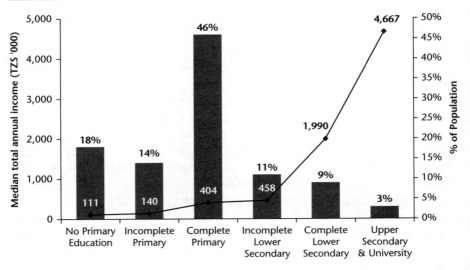

Figure 8.4. Returns to education are low at lower levels (2010/11)

Source: Tanzania National Bureau of Statistics, National Panel Survey (2010/11).

formal education.[22] For example, a worker with post-secondary or university level education earns approximately forty times more than a worker without education and about ten times more than a worker that has completed primary school. Additionally, almost half the population manages to attain primary level education; however, this segment of the population earns only about four times more than someone with no education (Figure 8.4). Schooling seems to pay off at secondary school level and beyond, but the surprisingly high returns to higher level education are also driven by the structural excess demand on the labour market, as the number of graduates is less than three per cent of the total population.

A deeply flawed formal education system in Tanzania also means that the effect of schooling on productivity is far from reaching its potential. National learning assessments conducted by Uwezo in Tanzania since 2010 have revealed that those currently enrolled in the education system do not seem to be learning. In particular, learning in primary school is often minimal: for example, by the time they enter the third year of primary school, about 70 per cent of children cannot read basic Swahili even though it is the national language, and widely spoken across the country. About 90 per cent of children cannot read basic English, and 80 per cent cannot do basic mathematics.[23]

Even students that complete primary school have low levels of basic skills: about 43 per cent of Tanzanian children are at or below 'basic numeracy' level, and cannot do what they should have mastered five years earlier in the second year of primary school.[24] For those that do make it to secondary school, empirical evidence indicates that an additional year of study in secondary education will not significantly modify the potential earnings of students on the job market. The implications of this lack of basic foundation learning are far reaching—if students cannot master basic literacy and numeracy skills after a few years of education, it is likely that the foundation to build upon for further specialized skills is fragile and an additional year of education will not make much of a difference for returns to productivity.

It is clear that schooling does not necessarily translate into learning. However, addressing this lack of learning is not a simple task. Service delivery is still a persistent problem in the education system. For example, in Tanzania, one out of every five teachers is absent from school on any given day. Even when teachers are present, primary school students experience less than three hours of learning per day on average.[25] Having said that, the government has paid special attention in recent years towards improving service delivery in the education sector through the 'Big Results Now' initiative,[26] and education sector spending as a share of GDP remains relatively high for a developing country at 5.9 per cent.[27] However, about half of the basic education budget is spent on students who are repeating classes and/or fail to graduate. This is due to high rates of repetition in the early grades of primary education and low examination pass rates at the end of the primary and lower secondary cycles. Such inefficiencies in the execution of public funds and the lack of a clear framework of accountability in service delivery point to the complex nature of challenges in the Tanzanian education system.

Improvements in the level of basic education are necessary to improve the chances of productive youth employment opportunities. However, beyond the cognitive skills typically acquired through formal education, many youth also lack the behavioural or 'soft' skills such as communicating effectively and getting along with others, that are also required in the workplace. Behavioural skills rank almost as high as numeracy among the most highly sought skills by employers (Figure 8.5). A majority of enterprises also report preferences for hiring individuals above the age of twenty-nine for professional jobs, and workers aged between fifteen and twenty-nine for elementary occupations.[28] When asked to specifically assess the skills of young employees, employers ranked young employees as less likely to be educated, and to exhibit poor technical and computer skills. The emphasis placed on level of education, age, and work experience place the youth population at an obvious disadvantage for attaining professional jobs.

While skills development takes place largely outside of the formal education system, there are opportunities to facilitate the acquisition of key skills at an early age by the inclusion of entrepreneurial and vocational training in the education system. The target would be relatively educated youth, building on their basic knowledge to improve specific skills. This curriculum can be

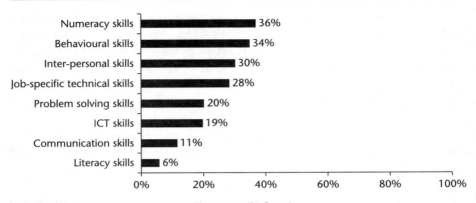

Figure 8.5. Skills that are scarce in Tanzania (% firms)
Source: World Bank, Tanzania Country Economic Memorandum (2014a).

designed with a practical component to supplement theoretical learning, and hence be more relevant for the job market. This idea has already been successfully implemented in other countries such as Singapore, where students receive one year of mandatory entrepreneurship education within the primary school system. In Mexico, students learn basic economics and business skills before high school and can progress towards creating and managing their own businesses by the time they are eighteen years old. The education system in Mauritius also provides entrepreneurship classes at the primary level. These programmes emphasize group learning, hands-on experience, critical thinking, and decisionmaking skills. Such best practices can be emulated to increase entrepreneurial education in Tanzania.[29]

8.3.2 *Alternative Options for Skills Development*

Despite the unambiguous positive impact of better skills and education on income and employment opportunities, the level of skills has remained low in Tanzania. However, weak labour market institutions combined with the low quality of the formal education system further perpetuate the disadvantages faced by entrants into the labour market. There are also significant information gaps, which lead to a mismatch between the supply and demand for skills. This is due to poor communication and lack of coordination between employers and the labour market. For example, it is telling that only 2.7 per cent of firms have contact with education institutions for hiring purposes.[30] The information gap also contributes to the high barriers to entry into formal jobs, but the presence of a large informal economy means that many youth enter the labour market as self-employed in low-skilled occupations.

Outside of the education system, training programmes—albeit imperfect—are regarded as a panacea to ensure that young workers have the necessary skills to undertake available jobs and perform effectively. These training programmes are most commonly provided by the government and international donors, and typically focus on the provision of technical training in a specific sector, business skills or financial literacy, behavioural and life skills, or a combination of these. In Tanzania, there are multiple organizations and partnerships that have worked towards promoting skills acquisition (both general and by sector), linking vocational training programmes with private sector needs, training entrepreneurs, and working with universities to increase access to information about job opportunities. But with little evidence or measure on effectiveness, as well as lack of scale and coordination between programs, there is still little understanding of the labour market in Tanzania and the prospects of employment growth.

Apprenticeships and on-the-job training are common in Tanzania, and often present the best source of training when provided by the private sector. Employers are more likely to provide training in sectors such as construction, manufacturing, and real estate, but less so in sectors such as wholesale and retail trade, and hotel and restaurants, which account for approximately two-thirds of informal sector workers.[31] The type of training in the informal sector varies by industry, where informal apprenticeships are the most common form of training (see Figure 8.6). And while employers seem reluctant to invest in training due to cost constraints and the mandatory skills development levy of 5 per cent paid to the government, about 44 per cent of employers offer some form of training to employees, including enterprise training, apprenticeships, and vocational training.[32]

Notably, vocational training is the least common type of training to be adopted. This is not surprising, as there is little evidence of the effectiveness of VETA (the Vocational Education and Training Authority) and NACTE (National Council for Technical Education) in Tanzania, where this type of training is considered to be an inferior choice and a 'last-resort' option for job seekers. Additionally, the training is often too theoretical and largely disconnected from private sector needs. The fact that there are two structures to target skill building (VETA and NACTE) also results in service duplication and wastage, and the post-technical training employment rate is reported to be only 14 per cent.[33] Tanzania's dismal experience with government-provided vocational training suggests that governments need not attempt to deliver training directly, but rather to play the role of coordinating programmes, disseminating information, and providing quality assurance on training and skills garnering opportunities in the marketplace.

Where reform is possible, a unification of these training bodies would increase efficiencies, where VETA becomes exclusively responsible for skill

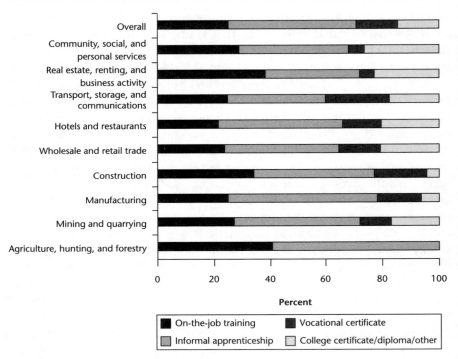

Figure 8.6. Distribution of training modes in the informal economy by sector

Note: Data based on: Tanzania National Bureau of Statistics, Integrated Labor Force Survey (2006).
Source: Adams, Johansson de Silva, and Razmara (2013).

delivery and NACTE for accrediting and regulating training. This can be done in coordination with the private providers, with potential employers in the private sector to ensure quality and match skills. But for such programmes to be successful, it is necessary to include mentorship and networking programmes where, for example, the private sector can partner with universities to provide support to budding entrepreneurs. Companies in the private sector could also be incentivized to participate in these skill-building programmes through subsidies and tax advantages. Additionally, other resources such as internet-based training in entrepreneurial management can be leveraged as a scalable and low-cost complementary intervention.

In addition to vocational training, the promotion of on-the-job training must be further encouraged in Tanzania. So far, only large firms with sufficient human and financial resources can afford to provide such training to their employees, and for small and growing companies, the costs of providing such services might be prohibitive. The government's role remains important to fill two gaps that are likely to emerge if the initiative were left to private firms alone: (i) small and medium sized enterprises (SMEs) and informal companies are often excluded since they lack sufficient resources to fund such programmes; and (ii) a company can decide to under-invest in training in order to prevent the poaching of trained workers by competitors.

Improving the level of skills and education is a long-term investment, and requires a combination of multiple initiatives. In the short and medium terms, the government can take concrete steps, in close collaboration with the private sector, to address some specific gaps around workforce skill acquisition and deployment. This includes addressing problems of coordination by linking vocational training programmes with private sector needs, and providing information to better match the demand for labour to the supply available. Currently, most Tanzanians rely on informal networks—most commonly family and friends—to find jobs, and only one in ten register at employment centres. This suggests a vital gap in the transmission of labour market information for jobseekers, which can be addressed through a central body of coordination and information dissemination. Additionally, for training initiatives already in place, the government could encourage the systematic use of careful evaluations, and require the tracking and reporting of outcomes to a central body. Programmes aimed at youth that integrate training with internship placements have also shown promise, but will require the creation of solid public–private partnerships for scale and effectiveness.[34] These reforms are not trivial, but if Tanzania can rise to the challenge, then the benefits will extend beyond the creation of productive jobs towards better and inclusive growth for the population.

8.4 Laying the Foundations of an Effective Employment Policy

The challenge of employment in Tanzania is complex and multifaceted, and reflects Tanzania's own challenges as well as its opportunities in today's globalized world. Weak labour market institutions combined with the low quality of the education system call for policy solutions that go beyond the effort to keep young people in school. The root causes of low productivity, and therefore lower earnings must be addressed, but simple solutions do not exist. Instead, a comprehensive approach that involves all stakeholders— including the government, private sector, the non-government sector and the workers themselves—must be considered in order to address the employment challenge in all its dimensions. This will propel the country towards paving a pathway for better and more productive opportunities for its young population.

A multifaceted approach to maximize Tanzania's human capital involves reform from both the supply and demand side. At the core of the issue is the fact that education and skills do matter. And attempts to improve human capital by providing opportunities for youth to garner the skills needed for productive work opportunities is important, but only represent a starting point. Better and more productive jobs for youth will also depend on policies that address the economic and business environment. Specifically, training and skilling programmes will not make as much of an impact if the business environment remains difficult for the private sector to operate, grow, and thrive. The skills agenda must be complemented by policies aimed at stimulating the creation and expansion of firms, including small firms, which hold potential for growth in a more enabling business environment. However, in an economy like Tanzania, where the majority of employment consists of the self-employed, supply and demand factors are closely interconnected, where a focus on skills can stimulate both the creation of firms, and the labour force employed within these firms. It is equally important to pay attention to improving the formal education system, even though returns will only be witnessed in the medium to long term. Improvements in basic education will serve as a foundation towards building other skills and improving outcomes for youth employment, as well as improving the process of transition from school into the labour force.

To improve the quality of human capital in Tanzania, a double strategy is needed. The first should focus on making the flow of new workers emerging into the labour market more productive and more adapted to the demand of private enterprises. This can be achieved through the combination of short-term and longer-term actions. There is little doubt that overall reform of the education system is needed. While this will take some time to impact on the labour market, Tanzania should focus on secondary and vocational/technical education. Specifically, public policy can facilitate access to information about existing training opportunities, which can start in school and target the poorest households, women, and those situated in rural areas.

Voucher programmes are an example of how government can successfully intervene in the post-school training market. For example, the Technical and Vocational Vouchers Program in Kenya encouraged enrolment in private and government training programmes for young people through the provision of subsidized vouchers that covered 90 per cent of the cost of training. This programme allowed for a choice of training providers, and not only increased the use of training programmes (placement rates were about 70–80 per cent), but it also produced a positive supply response to the number of programmes available.[35]

In Tanzania, the Buni technology hub works with university students in a specialized school-to-work transition programme where promising students are enrolled in an internship programme focusing on innovation training for technology products. The internship programme requires the creation of a product, for which the hub then provides support for in the going-to-market stage through the Mentorship programme. The hub has mentored several startup brands in Tanzania including Soka App, Agrinfo, and Time-Tickets.[36] While this is a specialized initiative, it serves as an example of a programme that could be combined with a voucher programme to increase access to specialized training services in Tanzania.

There is also encouraging evidence that managerial and technical skills can be taught and fostered among small entrepreneurs by combining both training and financing programmes. The Harambee programme in South Africa is an example of a successful vocational initiative. This government sponsored programme works closely with employers to equip unemployed youth with specific soft and hard skills for pre-identified jobs. These programmes run for six months to one year on average, and in 2011, the programme managed to place approximately 90 per cent of its participants.[37] These examples can be emulated for the development of skills in Tanzania, but requires better coordination with the private sector for an enabling environment for public–private partnerships.

The second strategy is to improve the existing stock of workers (about 24 million). If some can go back to school, the solution for others has to involve the participation of the private sector. There is a need to enhance training on the job through the development of incentives and attractive regulation. In the current business environment, over-regulation, over-taxation of labour, and the lack of mobility among workers all serve to increase the business cost of training and employing workers. Policy makers need to reduce the burden associated with excessive administrative procedures and reconsider the purpose of the 5 per cent levy for vocational education and training. Concurrently, special attention should be given to streamlining the taxation of small businesses, which are currently subject to presumptive income tax for earnings less than TZS 20 million. Lastly, an effort should be made to reduce the number of (central and local) agencies that collect their revenue through fees and inspections.[38] Constraints in the business environment are further elaborated upon in Gollin and Goyal (Chapter 6, this volume) and McMillan, Page, and Wangwe (Chapter 7, this volume) but easing these constraints would go a long way towards incentivizing the participation of the private sector in training programmes.

Despite these constraints, there have been programmes that have shown some success in encouraging the development of skills, particularly in the agricultural sector. One such scheme is contract farming, which links small-holder farmers with large farmers and/or processing companies. Small farmers can obtain cheaper inputs, improved access to modern technologies, and the use of transportation and marketing channels previously only available to large farmers. This scheme is prevalent amongst a number of traditional cash crops, such as sugar, tobacco, tea, coffee, and cotton, and is increasingly being promoted for selected other high-value crops. In the sugar industry, this scheme has shown to generate higher incomes for smallholder farmers.[39] Here, the government's role can be to facilitate the formation of farmers' communities or associations for more effective interaction with large investors.

For non-farm businesses, it will be important to increase virtual and physical connectivity between small and large firms through the approach of clustered development. The creation of special economic zones (SEZs), for example, should help the development of specific clusters. The proximity of firms to suppliers and/or customer markets should help to reduce transport costs and improve access to affordable and reliable energy as well as promote a skilled labour force.[40]

Lastly, the government should reconsider its role as a direct provider of technical and vocational skills training for the youth. Not only is the government best placed as a provider of public goods in training programmes such as quality assurance and information, but the public sector alone will not have the financial and human resources to provide the actions necessary to ensure better productivity and more employment for the vast majority of Tanzanian workers. In a coordinating role, government can act as a central point of information dissemination about training programmes. Where government can encourage the evaluation of programmes, information about the returns to training options can help to align youth expectations with the realities of the labour market. Government can also support public–private partnerships for the delivery of programmes, allowing programmes to be more cost-effective, and better targeted towards private sector needs.

There is no doubt that Tanzania has a tremendous amount of work to do going forward, but addressing the youth employment challenge is essentially addressing the fundamental factors for growth and economic development. As Tanzania identifies and implements policies to improve workforce productivity, the country must also harness the synergies that will come from a combination of reforms to address both the shortage of skills in the labour market, and the business environment constraints that hinder labour productivity. Done well, these changes will serve as the catalyst for Tanzania to begin to reap its demographic dividend.

Notes

1. Tanzania National Bureau of Statistics (statistics presented for 2013).
2. World Bank, World Development Indicators.
3. In this case, 'youth' refers to the share of the population aged between 15 and 24 years following the general ILO definition of 'youth unemployment' as the share of

the labour force aged 15–24 without work but available for and seeking employment (Morisset, Isis, and Waly, 2013).

4. See Chapters 4, 6, and 7, this volume.
5. World Bank, Tanzania Mainland Poverty Assessment (2015).
6. As of 2013, natural gas reserves have been estimated at 43tn cubic ft (35 offshore).
7. World Bank, EU, and DFID (June 2014).
8. An analysis of the natural gas value chain by the World Bank in Tanzania suggests that that while there are limited opportunities for local content in the upstream phase of development, there is higher potential for local content development in the midstream and downstream phases through the early development of linkages with the private sector. Experiences of countries such as Egypt, Malaysia, and Nigeria were considered in the analysis.
9. World Bank (2014b), WDI Indicators.
10. World Bank (2014b), WDI Indicators.
11. Morisset, Cunningham, and Haji (2015).
12. Tanzania National Bureau of Statistics, Integrated Labor Force Survey, 2014—Provisional Tables (2014). In this case, 'youth' refers to the share of the population aged between 15 and 24 years following the general ILO definition.
13. Tanzania National Bureau of Statistics, National Panel Survey (2010/11), World Bank Tanzania Mainland Poverty Assessment (2015).
14. Morisset, Cunningham, and Haji (2014).
15. World Bank, Tanzania Country Economic Memorandum (2014).
16. Morisset, Cunningham, and Haji (2014).
17. Gollin, Remi, and Dietrich (2013).
18. Banerjee and Duflo (2011).
19. Tanzania National Bureau of Statistics, National Panel Survey (2010/11).
20. Filmer and Fox (2014).
21. Bridges et al. (2013).
22. UWEZO Annual Learning Report (Uwezo Tanzania, 2010).
23. UWEZO Annual Learning Report (Uwezo Tanzania, 2010).
24. UWEZO Annual Learning Report (Uwezo Tanzania, 2010).
25. UWEZO Annual Learning Report (Uwezo Tanzania, 2010).
26. Tanzania Ministry of Education website, available at: <http://www.moe.go.tz>.
27. World Bank, Tanzania Rapid Budget Analysis (2013).
28. Shamchiyeva, Kizu, and Godius (2014).
29. Omidyar Network (2012).
30. World Bank, Tanzania Country Economic Memorandum (World Bank, 2014a).
31. Tanzania NBS, Integrated Labor Force Survey (2006).
32. World Bank, Tanzania Country Economic Memorandum (World Bank, 2014a).
33. See Adams et al. (2013) for a detailed discussion on the challenges of the vocational education and training system in Tanzania.
34. Berge, Bjorvatn, and Tungodden (2011).
35. Adams, Johansson de Silva, and Razmara (2013).
36. Buni Hub website, available at: <http://buni.or.tz/>.
37. Berge, Bjorvatn, and Tungodden (2011).

38. For a detailed discussion on demand-side constraints to employment, please refer to World Bank Tanzania Country Economic Memorandum (World Bank, 2014a).
39. World Bank, Tanzania Country Economic Memorandum (World Bank, 2014a).
40. For a detailed discussion of Tanzania's experience with clustered development, please refer to World Bank Tanzania Country Economic Memorandum (World Bank, 2014a).

References

Adams, A. V., Johansson de Silva, S., and Razmara, S. (2013). *Improving Skills Development in the Informal Sector: Strategies for Sub-Saharan Africa* (Directions in Development—Human Development series monograph). World Bank, Washington, D.C.

Banerjee, A. V. and Duflo, E. (2011). *Poor Economics: A Radical Rethinking of the Way to Fight Global Poverty*. New York: Public Affairs.

Berge, L., Bjorvatn, K., and Tungodden, B. (2011). 'Human and Financial Capital for Microenterprise Development: Evidence from a Field and Lab Experiment', Norwegian School of Economics Dept. of Economics Discussion Paper No. 1/2011. Available at: <http://ssrn.com/abstract=1750026> or: <http://dx.doi.org/10.2139/ssrn.1750026> (accessed 9 June 2016).

Bridges, S., Louise, F., Alessio, G., and Trudy, O. (2013). 'Labour Market Entry and Earnings: Evidence from Tanzania Retrospective Data', CREDIT Research Paper No. 13/05, University of Nottingham, Nottingham.

Filmer, D. and Fox, L. (2014). 'Youth Employment in Sub-Saharan Africa', Agence Française de Développement and World Bank, Washington, D.C.

Gollin, D., Remi, J., and Dietrich, V. (2013). 'Urbanization With and Without Industrialization', Working Papers 2013-290-26, Department of Economics, University of Houston.

ILO (International Labour Organization) (2014). *Key Indicators of the Labour Market (KILM)*, 8th ed. Geneva: ILO.

Morisset, J., Cunningham, V., and Haji, M. (2014). Tanzania Fifth Economic Update: Who Wants a Job? The Magnetic Power of Cities', World Bank, Dar es Salaam.

Morisset, J., Cunningham, V., and Haji, M. (2015). 'Tanzania Seventh Economic Update: Why Should Tanzanians Pay Taxes? The Unavoidable Need to Finance Economic Development', World Bank, Dar es Salaam.

Morisset, J., Isis, G., and Waly, W. (2013). 'Youth in Tanzania: A Growing Uneducated Labor Force'. Available at: <http://blogs.worldbank.org/africacan/youth-in-tanzania-a-growing-uneducated-labor-force> (last accessed 9 June 2016).

Omidyar Network (2012). 'Accelerating Entrepreneurship in Africa: Understanding Africa's Challenges to Creating Opportunity-Driven Entrepreneurship', Omidyar Network and the Monitor Group.

Shamchiyeva, L., Kizu, T., and Godius, K. (2014). 'Labour Market Transitions of Young Women and Men in the United Republic of Tanzania', International Labour Organization, Youth Employment Programme, Employment Policy Department, Geneva: ILO.

Tanzania National Bureau of Statistics (2006). 'Integrated Labor Force Survey', Government of Tanzania, Dar es Salaam.

Tanzania National Bureau of Statistics (2008/9, 2010/11 and 2012/13). 'National Panel Surveys', Government of Tanzania, Dar es Salaam.

Tanzania National Bureau of Statistics (2012 and 2013). 'Employment and Earnings Report', Government of Tanzania, Dar es Salaam.

Tanzania National Bureau of Statistics (2014). 'Integrated Labor Force Survey–2014 Provisional Tables', Government of Tanzania, Dar es Salaam.

Uwezo Tanzania (2010). 'Are Our Children Learning?', Annual Learning Assessment Report, Uwezo Tanzania, Dar es Salaam.

World Bank (2013). Rapid Budget Analysis 2013, Synoptic Note, World Bank Tanzania.

World Bank (2014a). 'Tanzania: Productive Jobs Wanted', Tanzania Country Economic Memorandum, Dar-es-Salaam.

World Bank (2014b). '2014 World Development Indicators', World Bank, Washington, D.C.

World Bank, EU (European Union), and DFID (Department for International Development) (2014). 'Tanzanian LNG Industry Demand and Local Supply Analysis: Phase I Findings Report'.

World Bank (2015). 'Tanzania Mainland Poverty Assessment', World Bank, Dar es Salaam.

9

Growth and Poverty

A Pragmatic Assessment and Future Prospects

Channing Arndt, Vincent Leyaro, Kristin Mahrt, and Finn Tarp

9.1 Introduction

This chapter considers the evolution of welfare of the Tanzanian population using two approaches. First, we employ a multidimensional measure of welfare that is well suited for the analysis of publicly provided services. Government expenditure has for many years been an important area of emphasis in Tanzania with much of this expenditure targeted at key public services in areas such as health, education, water, and sanitation. We use a series of four Demographic and Health Surveys (DHS) undertaken between 1992 and 2010 to consider the effectiveness of these investments using a relatively novel first order dominance (FOD) approach to non-monetary poverty measurement. Second, we employ a detailed economy-wide model of the Tanzanian economy to explore growth and poverty reduction scenarios from 2007 to 2015 with a focus on monetary poverty outcomes. The model attempts to track the basic observed facts between the 2007 and 2012 household budget surveys,[1] including an estimated six percentage point decline in the national monetary consumption poverty rate, and then projects an additional three years. It permits a rigorous assessment of the coherence of observed trends and provides, in our view, the best available projection of consumption poverty outcomes to 2015 and beyond.

With respect to publicly provided services, we find that, even by the very stringent FOD criteria applied for evaluating multidimensional non-monetary poverty, real gains have been achieved for these welfare indicators. Whether even more rapid improvements should have been expected remains an open question. More rapid gains than those registered in Tanzania over short time frames (four to six years) have been attained in other countries (Arndt et al., 2012a) indicating, at a minimum, room for improvement. Nevertheless, over longer time frames, it is clear that the investments made have yielded broad based socioeconomic welfare returns. With respect to monetary poverty, we find that the estimated six percentage point decline in the national consumption poverty rate between 2007 and 2012 is actually somewhat greater than what we generate using our economy-wide modelling framework. The principal driver for the six percentage point poverty decline identified by the recent (World Bank, 2015) assessment, much stronger consumption growth amongst poorer households than amongst better off households, is difficult to reconcile with a plausible growth story. Our analysis generates broad-based growth across the income distribution, which we regard as more plausible for reasons discussed in Section 9.4.5.

While puzzles certainly remain with respect to growth, poverty, and the distribution of income/wealth, we conclude that, given what is known about the patterns and rates of economic growth and given international price conditions, the recent estimated reductions in monetary poverty from 2007 to 2012 are in the plausible to favourable domain. From 2012 through 2015, we project that the observed declines in global commodity prices, particularly fuels, probably permit an increased rate of poverty reduction, with the poverty rate falling by nearly an additional six percentage points in this three-year period.

The remainder of this chapter is structured as follows. Section 9.2 briefly provides background on the growth and poverty debate, which has tended to focus on the monetary consumption poverty dimension. We then shift, in Section 9.3, to multidimensional measures of non-monetary poverty. Section 9.4 returns to the consideration of monetary poverty. Section 9.5 summarizes and concludes.

9.2 Background

Following the publication of results from the 2007 household budget survey (National Bureau of Statistics, 2009), Tanzania presented a notable conundrum for those following growth and development in Africa. On the one hand, gross domestic product (GDP) growth was reasonably rapid, at least according to Tanzanian national accounts; and available data and analyses pointed to a fairly steady level of inequality as measured by, for example, the Gini coefficient. In addition, a number of important non-monetary welfare indicators exhibited positive long-term trends. These indicators included, but were not limited to, infant mortality, life expectancy, asset ownership, school attendance, and availability of public health services (National Bureau of

Statistics, 2009). Importantly, Tanzania also exhibited, and continues to exhibit, a fairly high degree of political maturity and stability. On the other hand, despite conditions apparently conducive to increases in consumption across a broad swathe of the population, consumption poverty rates declined only slowly.

This apparent contradiction—solid per capita GDP growth, constant inequality, and yet less consumption poverty reduction than desired—generated considerable debate. This debate was further fuelled by a series of very difficult or impossible to reconcile measures of important statistics across alternative sources. Differentials between rates of inflation across alternative sources are one prominent example. Specifically, the official consumer price index (CPI) and GDP deflators indicated a much lower rate of growth of prices than unit values (price estimates) derived from the 2001 and 2007 household budget surveys, leading to speculation that real GDP growth may be substantially overstated (Atkinson and Lugo, 2010; Hoogeveen and Ruhinduka, 2009). Adam et al. (2012) illustrate that it is likely that the CPI and GDP deflators were downward biased; however, it is not clear that real GDP was substantially upward biased as a consequence. Arndt et al. (2013) illustrate that only mild reductions in GDP growth are required to reconcile the macroeconomic growth–poverty–inequality story due to shifts in terms of trade and direction of resources towards government spending as opposed to household consumption.[2]

As hinted at in Section 9.1, debate persists despite the recent publication of a new poverty assessment based on data from a 2012 household budget survey (World Bank, 2015). Section 9.3 takes on the question of the returns to the major government social spending investments undertaken over the past two and a half decades. Section 9.4 concerns itself with the consumption poverty debate with emphasis on the 2007–15 period.

9.3 Multidimensional Measures of Non-Monetary Poverty

We employ the FOD approach developed by Arndt et al. (2012a). The FOD approach is suitable for making welfare comparisons between populations when ordinal information is available at the micro level. In particular, it allows comparison of populations using multidimensional (discrete) well-being indicators, without arbitrary weighting schemes and other subjective judgements, or ad hoc simplifying assumptions about the social welfare function. The FOD criteria simply assert that it is better to be non-deprived than deprived in any given dimension. No assumptions are made about the strength of preference for each dimension, or about the relative desirability of changes between levels within or between dimensions or the complementarity/substitutability between the dimensions. The FOD results allow for comparisons over time and across space.

We apply this approach to data from the Tanzanian Demographic and Health Surveys (DHS) for the years 1991/92, 1996, 2004/05, and 2010. In this chapter, we focus on five binary indicators of well-being at the household level.[3] The following subsections (i) provide an intuitive review of the multi-dimensional first-order dominance methodology; (ii) describe the choice of binary welfare indicators employed to measure and compare welfare; and (iii) present results.

9.3.1 *An Intuitive Review of FOD*

FOD analysis in the context of multiple discrete welfare indicators draws upon a well-established literature of distributional dominance where the criteria for one distribution to be deemed better than another is referred to as first-order dominance or usual (stochastic) dominance (see for example Müller and Stoyan, 2002, or Shaked and Shanthikumar, 2007). FOD can be characterized by a set of mathematical conditions in both the single and multidimensional context (see Lehmann, 1955).

In order to intuitively present the FOD criteria, first consider two individuals, A and B, about whom information is available for a set of five binary well-being indicators. There are $2^5 = 32$ possible combinations of outcomes for each individual. Not deprived in an indicator is expressed as 1 and deprived as 0. It is clear that the welfare of individual A dominates B's welfare (meaning A is unambiguously better off) if A is not deprived in any indicator (1,1,1,1,1) and B is deprived in all indicators (0,0,0,0,0). Furthermore, a combination of indicators such as (0,1,0,1,0) dominates (0,1,0,0,0) because the first case is equal to or better than every outcome in the second case. However, we cannot determine domination in comparing a combination of indicators such as (1,1,0,0,0) to (0,1,1,0,0) without further assumptions because we cannot determine if it is better to be not deprived in the first indicator or the third indicator. Even in more extreme cases such as (1,1,1,1,0) compared to (0,0,0,0,1), dominance cannot be determined without additional information or assumptions because we don't know if being not deprived in the first four indicators is better or worse than being not deprived only in the last.

Next, let us expand from two individuals to two populations, again A and B, where the shares of individuals (or households) are calculated for each of the thirty-two possible outcomes (e.g., Y per cent is not deprived in any dimension, X per cent is deprived in all dimensions and, with all thirty remaining possibilities accounted for, the sum of the thirty-two shares is one). Is population A better off than population B? We say that population A first order dominates population B if one can generate distribution B by transferring probability mass from better to worse outcomes within A where better and worse are defined as in the preceding paragraph. Note that moving probability mass amounts to moving individuals (or households) from better to worse outcomes. Suppose we have 1,000 households each in population A and B. Population A and B have identical welfare distributions except population A has 31 individuals in (0,1,1,1,0) and 29 in (0,1,1,0,0) while population B has 30 individuals in each of these two particular welfare combinations. The distribution of population B can be created from A by making one individual strictly worse off, that is by moving one individual in population A from (0,1,1,1,0) to (0,1,1,0,0). Therefore, population A first order dominates population B (i.e., is better off).

While FOD analysis allows for comparison across populations without imposing subjective restrictions, this generality comes at a cost. The FOD criteria are strict leading to fairly frequent indeterminate outcomes. FOD is also binary providing no sense of the extent of domination. Arndt et al. (2012a) describe how these costs can be mitigated (but not eliminated) by conducting FOD analysis on repeated bootstrap samples drawn from each population.[4] The subsequent FOD results can be interpreted as empirical probabilities of domination providing significantly more information than FOD in the static case.

When spatial zones are compared to one another, the bootstrap approach generates a large number of comparisons. As discussed in Arndt et al. (2014), these multiple comparisons can be used to rank regions in a manner similar to ranking teams in a soccer league. Formally, we employ an approach suggested by Copeland (1951) whereby, for a given region, an outcome of dominance yields a score of one, an indeterminate outcome yields a score of zero, and an outcome of being dominated yields a score of minus one. A linear transformation can be applied to the results of this scoring system to yield a net dominance score in the interval $[-1,1]$. Regions with higher scores are ranked more highly (just as soccer teams with more points are ranked more highly in their league tables).

9.3.2 Data Sources and Choice of Welfare Indicators

As noted, the Tanzania Demographic and Health Surveys (TDHS) for the years 1991/92, 1996, 2004/05, and 2010 are the main data source used for this exercise. The samples for all TDHSs were drawn in a three-stage design and were designed to provide estimates for the whole country, for urban and rural areas in the country, and regions (which can then be aggregated into the zones of Tanzania). Sample sizes were, in chronological order of the survey: 8,327; 7,969; 10,312; and 10,300 households. We identify water, sanitation, shelter, education, and information as the five welfare indictors. A household is *water* deprived if the main source of drinking water is not

Table 9.1. Households not deprived by welfare indicator (per cent)

	Water		Sanitation		Housing		Education		Information	
	1992	2010	1992	2010	1992	2010	1992	2010	1992	2010
Nation	64.5	71.2	2.9	11.7	18.6	30.5	31.8	56.2	36.7	64.3
Rural	56.3	67.0	1.3	3.1	9.0	16.6	27.1	49.4	29.6	59.5
Urban	92.3	85.3	8.2	40.3	51.6	76.7	47.7	78.5	60.8	80.4
Western	56.6	77.1	3.2	6.5	9.6	15.0	23.4	45.6	30.5	64.5
Northern	57.8	62.8	3.9	11.0	26.3	36.8	38.3	62.5	48.0	64.2
Central	73.5	63.3	2.5	4.9	12.3	13.0	29.4	51.4	27.9	50.9
S. Highlands	60.0	66.5	1.2	9.8	13.9	32.0	33.2	59.4	32.5	65.7
Lake	51.2	70.7	2.7	12.7	12.0	25.7	30.4	51.1	32.9	64.1
Eastern	84.9	79.0	4.5	23.8	38.9	59.1	40.3	69.0	50.4	77.3
Southern	72.4	69.2	1.0	6.7	12.5	19.1	25.2	58.8	24.6	52.1
Zanzibar	90.3	98.4	3.3	27.6	34.0	66.5	33.3	50.1	55.1	75.5

Source: Authors' compilation based on TDHS 1992 and 2010.

Table 9.2. Households by number of deprivations in welfare indicators (per cent)

Welfare Deprivations	National			Urban			Rural		
	1992	2010	Change	1992	2010	Change	1992	2010	Change
5	20.14	6.88	−13.26	3.42	1.35	−2.07	25.03	8.54	−16.49
4	36.60	22.50	−14.10	21.33	6.67	−14.66	41.06	27.26	−13.81
3	22.16	29.04	6.88	20.52	11.79	−8.73	22.64	34.22	11.58
2	12.32	20.59	8.27	25.90	18.15	−7.76	8.35	21.32	12.97
1	7.37	13.43	6.06	23.65	33.68	10.04	2.61	7.34	4.73
0	1.40	7.56	6.16	5.18	28.35	23.17	0.30	1.32	1.02

Source: Authors' compilation based on TDHS 1992 and 2010.

from a pipe, tap, or well. For *sanitation*, the household is deprived if it has no flush toilet or ventilated improved pit toilet. A household is *shelter* deprived if the main floor material is dirt, sand, dung, or planks. A household is *education* deprived if the household head has not completed at least primary school. The household is *information* deprived if it does not have a functioning radio or television.

Table 9.1 simply presents the percentage of households not deprived in each dimension, over time and across space. Significant heterogeneity exists when comparing urban to rural areas or across zones and regions. With the exception of water, all welfare indicators experienced improvements between 1992 and 2010 at all levels of disaggregation.[5]

Table 9.2 presents the share of households deprived in a given number of welfare indicators. The first row of the table shows the share of households with deprivations in all dimensions, the second row those deprived in four of the five indicators, and so forth to the sixth row which shows the probability that households are not-deprived in any dimension. There have been substantial reductions in severely deprived households from 20 per cent in 1992 to 7 per cent in 2010 (13 percentage points). This was largely driven by a 16 percentage point reduction in rural areas from 25 to 9 per cent. At the same time, there has been a 6 percentage point gain to households not deprived in any dimension from 1 per cent in 1992 to 7 per cent in 2010.

Unlike severely deprived households where rural areas drove the improvements, the gain for households not deprived in any single dimension was derived from urban areas with a 23 percentage point improvement from 5 per cent in 1992 to 28 per cent in 2010. In contrast, rural areas improved slightly from 0.3 per cent in 1992 to 1.3 per cent in 2010. To summarize, based on these simple averages, most welfare indicators for all areas have shown significant improvement between 1992 and 2010.

9.3.3 FOD Results and Discussion

We start by discussing the temporal FOD results between 1992 and 2010 in Table 9.3. The table shows temporal net domination, which is the temporal equivalent of the spatial net domination measure discussed in Section 9.3.1 and can be interpreted as the probability that one year dominates another year minus the probability it is dominated by the other year. For example, the national results row indicates that, when comparing the selected indicators between 1996 and 1992, the surveys themselves point to an indeterminate outcome (nothing in the static column). However, when one hundred synthetic

Table 9.3. Temporal net FOD comparisons, households (probabilities)

	1996 FOD 1992		2004 FOD 1992		2010 FOD 1992		2004 FOD 1996		2010 FOD 1996		2010 FOD 2004	
	Static	Boot	Static	Boot	Static	Boot	Static	Boot	Static	Boot	Static	Boot
National	1	0.30	1	0.99	1	0.96	1	0.95	1	0.98		0.10
Rural	1	0.28	1	0.71	1	1.00		0.45	1	0.82		0.13
Urban	1	0.22		0.11		0.07		0.03		0.04		0.11
Western	1	0.27		0.23	1	0.66		0.12	1	0.44		0.22
Northern		−0.03	1	0.68	1	0.68	1	0.85	1	0.85		
Central		0.14		0.14		0.12		0.13		0.07		0.04
S. Highlands		0.12	1	0.67	1	0.74	1	0.46	1	0.59		0.11
Lake			1	0.62	1	0.99		0.17	1	0.85		0.16
Eastern	1	0.35		0.42		0.22		0.18		0.11		0.14
Southern		0.06	1	0.55		0.30	1	0.69	1	0.75		0.01
Zanzibar	1	0.22	1	0.99	1	0.99	1	0.86	1	0.79		

Notes: A '1' in the static case indicates that the most recent year net FODs the earlier year's welfare level, while an empty cell indicates no domination. In the bootstrap case a '1' indicates that all 100 bootstrap replications resulted in the net domination. A negative value in the 'Boot' column indicates positive probability of regress through time.

Source: Authors' compilations based on TDHS 1992, 1996, 2004, and 2010.

samples are created via the bootstrap, the 1996 indicators dominate 1992 thirty times, yielding an approximate 30 per cent chance of improvement, as measured by FOD.

Overall, FOD comparisons support the conclusion of reduction in deprivation and improvement in welfare over time and across space throughout Tanzania. For most areas, FOD comparisons provide evidence of advancement in welfare with both net domination in the static case (i.e., FOD comparisons conducted on the full set of data without bootstrapping) and significant probability of net domination in the bootstrap. Advancement in welfare between 1992 and 2004 or 2010 is registered at the national level, in rural areas, and in more than half of the zones (Northern, Southern, Southern Highlands, Lake, Zanzibar, and Western). Over shorter time frames, such as the 1992–96 and 2004–10 intervals, there is much less evidence of advancement with generally weak probabilities of domination in the bootstrap. Compared with Vietnam, these results point to relatively slow progression through time with a possible slow-down in the rate of improvement in the most recent six-year period (Arndt et al., 2012a). There is essentially no probability of regression through time in any of these areas.

Considering space, Table 9.4 shows spatial comparisons across zones for 2010. In the table, the row and column averages are provided. The row (column) average provides a measure of the probability that an area dominates (is dominated by) other areas. Thus, using these metrics, relatively well-off areas should have relatively large row averages while relatively poor areas should have relatively large column averages. Urban areas and the Eastern zone (which includes the Dar es Salaam region) are shown to be relatively well-off, and, to a lesser extent, Zanzibar. On the other hand, the rural areas and Central zone are shown to be relatively poor, and, to a lesser extent, Lake, Southern, and Western zones.

Table 9.4. 2010 Bootstrap spatial FOD comparisons, households (probabilities)

Area	National	Rural	Urban	W	N	C	SH	L	E	S	Z	Avg
National		1				0.82	0.04	0.04		0.18		0.21
Rural						0.01						0.00
Urban	1	1		0.96	1	1	1	1	0.75	0.99		0.87
Western		0.01				0.03						0.00
Northern		0.05				0.30	0.08	0.01		0.05		0.05
Central												0.00
S. Highlands	0.05	0.39		0.01	0.11	0.51		0.02		0.18		0.13
Lake		0.56		0.01		0.34	0.01			0.01		0.09
Eastern	0.93	0.99		0.61	0.87	0.97	0.89	0.86		0.84		0.70
Southern						0.25						0.03
Zanzibar	0.01	0.59		0.83		0.31	0.02	0.28				0.20
Average	0.20	0.46	0.00	0.24	0.20	0.45	0.20	0.22	0.08	0.23	0.00	0.21

Source: Authors' compilation based on TDHS 2010.

Table 9.5. Spatial FOD ranking and probability of net domination by region and year at household level

	1992		1996		2004		2010		
	Domination	Rank	Domination	Rank	Domination	Rank	Domination	Rank	Change
Zanzibar	0.65	2	0.73	2	0.83	1	0.71	1	−1
Dar es Salaam	0.77	1	0.86	1	0.64	2	0.66	2	1
Kilimanjaro	0.17	3	0.15	4	0.24	3	0.25	3	0
Coast	−0.02	9	0.08	5	0.00	9	0.08	4	−5
Unguja	0.09	4	0.36	3	0.08	4	0.08	5	1
Morogoro	−0.06	13	−0.11	15	0.05	5	0.05	6	−7
Mbeya	−0.03	11	−0.02	7	−0.06	12	0.05	7	−4
Ruvuma	−0.11	17	−0.02	6	0.04	6	0.02	8	−9
Pemba	−0.02	8	−0.10	13	0.01	8	0.02	9	1
Mwanza	−0.07	14	−0.09	11	0.00	11	−0.03	10	−4
Iringa	−0.26	22	−0.26	22	−0.12	18	−0.04	11	−11
Mara	−0.18	21	−0.14	17	−0.09	14	−0.06	12	−9
Tabora	−0.03	10	−0.09	10	−0.11	16	−0.07	13	3
Shinyanga	−0.15	20	−0.15	20	−0.09	13	−0.08	14	−6
Arusha and Manyara	0.04	5	−0.15	19	0.00	10	−0.11	15	10
Rukwa	−0.01	6	−0.14	18	−0.18	19	−0.11	16	10
Tanga	−0.01	7	−0.11	16	−0.10	15	−0.13	17	10
Singida	−0.05	12	−0.07	8	−0.39	23	−0.16	18	6
Kagera	−0.14	18	−0.15	21	−0.24	22	−0.17	19	1
Kgoma	−0.14	19	−0.10	12	−0.21	21	−0.20	20	1
Lindi	−0.07	15	−0.10	14	0.02	7	−0.20	21	6
Mtwara	−0.28	23	−0.32	23	−0.21	20	−0.25	22	−1
Dodoma	−0.11	16	−0.08	9	−0.11	17	−0.32	23	7

Source: Authors' compilations based on TDHS 1992, 1996, 2004, and 2010.

Finally, Table 9.5 examines spatial inequality by the twenty-three regions of Tanzania. Specifically, the spatial net domination measure is used to rank regions by welfare level. Regions are listed from best to worst off in 2010. The final column of the table shows the changes in ranking between 1992 and 2010 and gives a sense of how households in each zone or region have performed over time relative to other zones or regions. A negative change reflects a movement to a higher rank and therefore a relative improvement in well-being compared with other regions. Welfare rankings of Tanzania, divided into twenty-three regions and based on the indicators selected, are shown to be relatively stable. In 2010, Zanzibar, closely followed by Dar es Salaam, is ranked at the top. The poorest region in 2010 is Dodoma. Strong performers since 1992 are Mara, Ruvuma, and Iringa, whose ranking rose from second to last (twenty-second) to eleventh by 2010. Relatively poor performers include Rukwa, Tanga, and the combined Arusha and Manyara region.[6]

The FOD approach can also provide insight into spatial distinctness or hierarchy. To get an intuitive sense, a return to the example of a soccer league may be helpful. If every soccer game in a league always ended in a tie, then nothing would distinguish the teams in the league on the basis of wins, ties, and losses. The polar opposite situation, in a soccer league, would be a situation of maximal distinctness, whereby the highest ranked team won every game, the lowest rank team lost every game, the second from top team won every game except the ones against the best team, the second worst team lost every game except the ones against the worst team, which they won, and so forth. In soccer, this would be a rigidly hierarchical (and rather boring) league.

The first situation (all ties) corresponds, in FOD perspective, to no region dominating the other. Just as the records of the teams in our hypothetical soccer league fail to distinguish the teams, the FOD criteria as applied generate no distinction between regions. The second situation corresponds to a maximal distinctness across teams, in soccer, or across regions, in FOD. Turning to spatial comparisons across zones in Tanzania and using this metric, there is no definitive trend towards greater hierarchy. FOD 'matches' between regions yield a determinate outcome (A dominates B or B dominates A) 21.3, 20.5, 21.9, and 20.7 per cent of the time in 1992, 1996, 2004, and 2010 respectively. On this metric, Tanzania is becoming neither more nor less regionally distinct.

Overall, Tanzania has experienced noticeable but not spectacular improvements over time for the selected welfare indicators (water, sanitation, shelter, education, and information) over the period 1992–2010. The FOD analysis points to broad based improvements across these five indicators and throughout the welfare distribution. Notably, regional inequities are easily apparent and fairly persistent, though a subset of regions has moved sensibly within the rankings.

9.4 Growth and Monetary Poverty

In this section, we simulate growth and poverty reduction using an economy-wide model of the Tanzanian economy. The approach is similar to that applied by Arndt et al. (2012b) for the analysis of growth and poverty in Mozambique. These authors illustrated that the stagnation in poverty rates observed in Mozambique between 2002/03 and 2008/09 could be mainly attributed to a combination of rising world fuel and food prices, and disappointing rates of technical advance in agriculture. This work forms part of an emerging literature that employs detailed structural models to help explain observed phenomena. Other examples from this literature include Horridge et al. (2005); Dyer and Taylor (2011); and Arndt et al. (2016).

Section 9.4.1 provides a brief description of the economy-wide model employed. Section 9.4.2 focuses on external conditions and world prices.

These are important because the 2007–15 period contains numerous brusque movements in world price levels for key traded commodities for Tanzania as well as substantial investment from abroad as a consequence of natural resource finds. Sections 9.4.1 and 9.4.2 present in turn the model simulations and results.

9.4.1 *Description of the Economy-Wide Model*

Economy-wide models, also called computable general equilibrium (CGE) models, are often used to examine the impact of external shocks and policies in low-income countries. Their strength is their ability to measure linkages between producers, households, and the government, while also accounting for resource constraints and their role in determining product and factor prices. These models are, however, limited by their underlying assumptions and the quality of the data used to calibrate them. Tanzania's initial economic structure, discussed in Section 9.4.3, will strongly influence model results.

In the model, economic decisionmaking is the outcome of decentralized optimization by producers and consumers within a coherent economy-wide framework.[7] The model identifies fifty-eight sectors (i.e., twenty-six in agriculture, twenty-two industries, and ten services) with 2007 as the base year. Based on the 2000/01 Household Budget Survey (HBS) (National Bureau of Statistics, 2002), labour markets are segmented across four skill groups: (i) workers with less than primary education; (ii) workers with complete primary and possibly some secondary schooling; (iii) workers with complete secondary schooling; (iv) workers with some tertiary schooling or better. Agricultural land is divided across small- and large-scale farms using the 2002/03 Agricultural Sample Survey (Ministry of Agriculture, Food Security, and Cooperatives, 2004).

Substitution possibilities exist between production for domestic and foreign markets. Profit maximization drives producers to sell in markets where they achieve the highest returns based on domestic and export prices. Further substitution possibilities exist between imported and domestic goods. Households, firms, and government minimize costs in sourcing goods from domestic and foreign markets while accounting for potential differences in the characteristics of domestic and foreign commodities. Under the small-country assumption, world demand and supply is perfectly elastic at fixed world prices, with the final ratio of traded to domestic goods determined by the endogenous interaction of relative prices. Production and trade elasticities that govern these substitution possibilities are drawn from Dimaranan (2006).

The model distinguishes between fifteen representative households (rural farm, rural non-farm, and urban non-farm groups by per capita expenditure quintiles). Households receive income in payment for producers' use of their factors of production, and then pay direct taxes, save, and make foreign transfers (all at fixed rates). Households use their remaining disposable income to consume commodities with the allocations sensitive to movements in prices and income. In order to estimate poverty rates, the CGE model is linked to a micro-simulation module. In particular, each of the more than 22,000 respondents in the 2000/01 HBS is linked to their corresponding representative household in the CGE model. Changes in commodity prices and households' consumption spending are passed down from the CGE model to the survey, where total per capita consumption and poverty measures are recalculated.

The government receives revenues from direct and indirect taxes, and makes transfers to households and the rest of the world. The government purchases consumption goods and services, and remaining revenues are saved (budget deficits are negative savings). All private, public, and foreign savings are collected in a savings pool from which investment is financed.

The model includes three macroeconomic accounts: government, current account, and savings-investment. To balance these macro-accounts, it is necessary to specify a set of 'macro-closure' rules that provide a mechanism through which macroeconomic balance is maintained. A savings-driven closure is assumed in order to balance the savings-investment account. This means that households' marginal propensities to save are fixed, and investment adjusts to income changes to ensure that the level of investment and savings are equal in equilibrium. For the current account, it is assumed that a flexible exchange rate adjusts in order to maintain an exogenous level of foreign savings (e.g., the levels of aid and net private capital inflows are fixed outside of the model). For the government account, direct tax rates are fixed and the fiscal deficit adjusts to equate total revenues and expenditures. Finally, the producer price index is chosen as the model's numéraire, and so all product and factor price movements are relative to this fixed price index.

The aforementioned description of the model ignores the time dimension. The model is static in that it adjusts to shocks by restoring equilibrium in all markets subject to macroeconomic accounting identities and the macro-closure rules applied. The model is rendered dynamic by solving a series of static equilibriums. Unlike full inter-temporal models, which include forward-looking expectations, the recursive dynamic model used in this chapter adopts a simpler set of adaptive rules. Under this specification, the investment levels of the previous year are used to augment sectoral capital stocks, net of depreciation. The model adopts a 'putty-clay' formulation, whereby each new investment can be directed to any sector in response to differential rates of return to capital, while installed equipment must remain in the same sector. Unlike capital, growth in labour and land supply is determined exogenously. In addition, labour and land can be reallocated across sectors in response to changing economic conditions. Sectoral productivity growth is also exogenous, yet may vary by factor. While the level of foreign savings is also exogenous, it varies through time in accordance with the best estimate of capital inflows.

Using these simple relationships to update key variables, we can generate a series of growth paths. We can also examine and decompose exogenous events with implications for the Tanzanian economy, such as the major shifts in world prices that occurred within the period of reference.

9.4.2 *World Price Changes*

9.4.2.1 FUELS

Figure 9.1 illustrates trends in real crude oil prices since 1986 using the United States consumer price index as a deflator. The prices are presented in real 2012 US$. Oil prices are characterized by a period of stability up to the 2003. Prices then rose rapidly to about US$80 per barrel in 2006. Since 2006, the market has been characterized by substantial volatility with a peak of US $140 per barrel in 2008 and two lows near US$40 per barrel. As will be discussed, the oil price is highly relevant for Tanzania as it constitutes both a major import item and a key intermediate input in production (Adam et al., 2015).

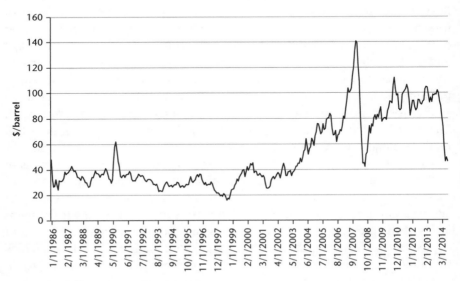

Figure 9.1. Real crude oil prices

Source: US Energy Information Administration (deflated by the US CPI obtained from the Federal Reserve Bank of St. Louis).

9.4.2.2 GLOBAL AGRICULTURAL MARKETS

Agricultural commodity prices are also important to Tanzania both in terms of imports and exports. With the exception of occasional price spikes, the prices for agricultural commodities received by farmers and paid by consumers declined broadly from the initiation of the industrial revolution to nearly the end of the twentieth century. Figure 9.2 depicts an index of prices received by farmers for forty-eight commodities in the United States divided by the general level of prices as measured by the United States consumer price index in order to account for inflation beginning in 1954.[8] During the latter half of the twentieth century, prices received by farmers declined nearly continuously in real terms. This general decline in prices was interrupted in the early 1970s when prices received by farmers briefly rose above the levels of 1954, the first year for the depicted price series. Nevertheless, this rise was short-lived. By the end of twentieth century, prices had declined by about 60 per cent from the levels observed in mid-century.

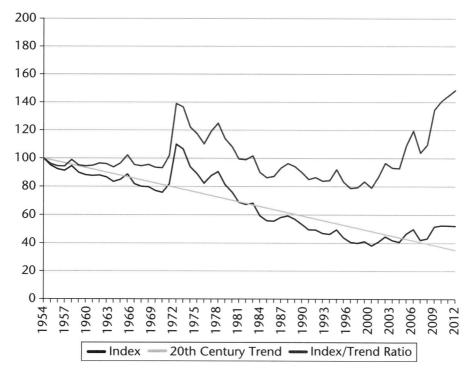

Figure 9.2. Index of real prices received by farmers in the United States

Source: United States Department of Agriculture (National Agricultural Statistics Service) (US CPI from the Federal Reserve Bank of St. Louis).

Since about 1995, this decline has ceased and been replaced by a flatter trend with some volatility. Rapid visual inspection of the level of the index makes the price increases observed since the mid-1990s appear to be rather small. However, in proportional terms—the more economically relevant measure—they are considerable. Real agricultural prices in 2014 were more than 35 per cent above the trough registered in 2003. Relative to the twentieth-century trend, the recent increases in prices are even more pronounced. By this index, prices relative to the twentieth-century trend were, in 2014, proportionally higher than at any time in the past fifty plus years. The relative firmness in agricultural commodity prices observed over the past twenty years represents a substantial change from the twentieth century that may persist. This firmer, though still volatile, international agricultural price environment presents opportunities for economies such as Tanzania where agriculture represents a large share of economic activity and looms even larger in terms of employment and welfare for the bulk of the population.

9.4.3 *Structure of the Tanzanian Economy*

Table 9.6 shows the structure of the Tanzanian economy in 2007, which is the base year for our analysis using the economy-wide model. Note that this year is convenient in that it allows us to consider the implications of the considerable world price movements that occurred over the period 2007–15 from the most recent possible base. It also allows us to consider recently observed behaviour of the macroeconomy and compare model produced poverty rates with rates from the latest household survey.

Agriculture accounts for nearly one third of GDP and more than four-fifths of employment. Within agriculture, most farmers are smallholders with average landholdings of 1.6 hectares. They produce most of the country's food, which dominates the agricultural and downstream manufacturing sectors. Tanzania also imports foods (mainly cereals), which account for about 5 per cent of total imports. This dependence on food imports stems in part from smallholders' low crop yields and a reliance on traditional rain-fed farming technologies. Larger-scale commercial farmers are more engaged in non-food export crops, such as coffee, tobacco, and tea, which together account for nearly a third of total merchandise exports.

Commodities strongly influenced by the world price for crude oil, including liquid fuels, fertilizer, rubber, and other chemicals, together account for 26 per cent of total imports. Of these four, liquid fuels represent the single largest import share at nearly 17 per cent of imports.[9] Unlike agriculture, these commodities account for very small shares of value added and exports. Hence, increases in the prices of fuels and derived products represent almost purely a terms of trade loss.

Table 9.6. Structure of the Tanzanian economy in 2007

	Shares					Ratios	
	Value Added	Production	Employment	Exports	Imports	Exports/ Output	Imports/ Demand
GDP	100.0	100.0	100.0	100.0	100.0	11.5	24.4
Agriculture	32.0	23.0	82.3	31.8	5.3	18.3	9.2
Food crops	19.2	13.2	40.1	2.2	5.1	2.1	13.4
Cereals	8.4	6.3	15.0	0.0	4.8	0.0	20.6
Export crops	3.2	2.8	12.1	18.6	0.2	67.5	7.4
Livestock	5.7	4.1	13.3	1.4	0.0	4.2	0.0
Other agriculture	3.9	2.9	16.9	9.7	0.0	43.5	0.0
Industry	23.3	31.3	2.7	32.5	93.4	11.7	48.6
Mining	3.8	3.0	0.2	21.5	3.7	74.7	59.2
Manufactures	9.0	14.9	1.5	11.0	89.7	9.1	66.0
Other chemicals	0.1	0.1	0.0	0.0	6.5	0.0	94.3
Fertilizers	0.0	0.0	0.0	0.0	1.6	0.0	95.0
Petroleum	0.1	0.1	0.0	0.0	16.8	0.0	98.1
Rubber	0.2	0.3	0.0	0.2	1.2	6.6	52.7
Other industry	10.6	13.3	1.0	0.0	0.0	0.0	0.0
Services	44.7	45.7	15.0	35.6	1.3	8.7	0.7
Private Services	31.9	32.4	13.5	35.6	1.3	12.4	1.0
Government Services	12.8	13.3	1.5	0.0	0.0	0.0	0.0

	Shares					Ratios	
	Value Added	Production	Employment	Exports	Imports	Exports/ Output	Imports/ Demand
Maize	4.5	3.1	7.2	0.0	0.7	0.0	7.4
Sorghum	0.7	0.5	0.9	0.0	0.0	0.0	0.0
Millet	0.2	0.2	0.3	0.0	0.0	0.0	0.0
Rice	2.9	2.3	6.1	0.0	0.0	0.0	0.0
Wheat and barley	0.2	0.2	0.5	0.0	4.1	0.0	87.3
Cassava	2.4	1.5	1.9	0.0	0.0	0.0	0.0
Other roots	0.9	0.6	1.7	0.0	0.0	0.0	0.0
Pulses	1.7	1.2	5.2	0.0	0.0	0.0	0.0
Coconuts	0.4	0.3	1.3	0.8	0.0	27.9	0.0
Oilseeds	0.6	0.4	1.9	0.4	0.0	8.4	0.0
Plantains	1.4	0.9	3.8	0.0	0.0	0.0	0.0
Fruits	0.8	0.5	1.9	0.0	0.0	0.0	0.0
Vegetables	3.0	1.9	8.5	1.8	0.3	14.9	6.8
Coffee	0.4	0.4	1.6	2.3	0.0	58.9	0.0
Cashew nuts	0.7	0.5	2.9	3.3	0.0	95.2	0.0
Cotton	0.4	0.5	1.8	4.9	0.1	80.9	21.6
Sisal	0.1	0.1	0.3	0.5	0.0	58.1	0.0
Sugarcane	0.4	0.4	1.8	0.9	0.0	29.2	0.0
Tea	0.1	0.1	0.5	1.2	0.0	74.0	0.0
Tobacco	0.3	0.3	1.2	2.9	0.1	73.3	33.5
Other cash crops	0.3	0.2	0.7	1.8	0.0	100.0	0.0
Cattle	3.5	2.5	8.0	0.7	0.0	3.2	0.0
Poultry	1.6	1.1	3.9	0.0	0.0	0.0	0.0
Other livestock	0.6	0.4	1.4	0.7	0.0	22.5	0.0
Fisheries	1.5	1.2	6.6	8.1	0.0	69.3	0.0
Forestry	2.4	1.7	10.2	1.6	0.0	15.3	0.0
Mining	3.8	3.0	0.2	21.5	3.7	74.7	59.2

(continued)

205

Table 9.6. Continued

	Shares					Ratios	
	Value Added	Production	Employment	Exports	Imports	Exports/ Output	Imports/ Demand
Meat and fish processing	1.9	2.0	0.6	0.0	0.0	0.0	0.0
Maize milling	0.3	2.0	0.1	0.0	0.0	0.0	0.0
Rice milling	0.1	0.9	0.0	0.0	1.8	0.0	44.7
Other milling	0.1	0.4	0.0	0.9	0.4	34.2	35.6
Other food processing	1.7	2.6	0.2	0.0	4.9	0.0	41.3
Sugar refining	0.2	0.2	0.0	0.6	1.0	29.8	65.3
Tobacco processing	0.3	0.4	0.1	0.3	0.0	7.4	0.0
Beverages	1.1	1.7	0.1	0.0	0.4	0.0	6.4
Textiles and clothing	0.7	0.8	0.1	3.1	7.2	39.4	81.3
Wood and paper products	0.3	0.4	0.0	0.7	4.6	18.0	78.4
Basic chemicals	0.1	0.1	0.0	0.0	6.5	0.0	94.3
Fertilizer	0.0	0.0	0.0	0.0	1.6	0.0	95.0
Petroleum products	0.1	0.1	0.0	0.0	16.8	0.0	98.1
Rubber and plastics	0.2	0.3	0.0	0.2	1.2	6.6	52.7
Non-metallic minerals	0.6	1.1	0.1	1.0	1.4	10.3	30.0
Metal products	0.4	0.8	0.0	1.7	7.2	21.9	74.8
Machinery and equipment	0.5	0.8	0.0	1.8	31.9	25.2	93.2
Other manufacturing	0.3	0.4	0.0	0.8	2.7	21.4	72.1
Electricity and gas	2.3	2.0	0.1	0.0	0.0	0.0	0.0
Water supply	0.6	0.5	0.0	0.0	0.0	0.0	0.0
Construction	7.7	10.8	0.9	0.0	0.0	0.0	0.0
Trade services	13.1	10.2	7.2	0.0	0.0	0.0	0.0
Hotels and catering	2.6	3.5	1.3	6.4	1.0	20.2	7.2
Transport	4.2	5.6	0.6	23.2	0.0	46.3	0.0
Communications	1.0	1.3	0.2	0.0	0.0	0.0	0.0
Financial services	0.7	0.7	0.1	6.0	0.3	100.0	100.0
Business and real estate	9.7	10.7	3.8	0.0	0.0	0.0	0.0
Public administration	9.3	9.5	1.1	0.0	0.0	0.0	0.0
Education	1.7	1.8	0.2	0.0	0.0	0.0	0.0
Health	1.9	2.0	0.2	0.0	0.0	0.0	0.0
Other services	0.4	0.5	0.2	0.0	0.0	0.0	0.0
Total	100.0	100.0	100.0	100.0	100.0	11.5	24.4

Source: Authors' compilations based on 2007 Tanzania SAM.

Table 9.7. Indices of real-world prices (2007=100)

	2008	2009	2010	2011	2012	2013	2014	2015[*]
Sugar	122.7	177.6	201.6	248.3	198.8	162.3	154.7	127.5
Tea	124.7	144.3	143.7	153.9	152.4	114.6	101.0	123.3
Wheat	125.4	85.3	84.2	116.8	113.6	111.6	100.4	84.0
Rice	206.6	172.8	150.6	156.3	161.6	142.5	115.4	109.8
Maize	134.2	98.8	109.5	168.4	169.2	144.8	106.3	95.8
Forestry	101.3	96.2	94.9	115.3	107.6	101.6	99.2	92.0
Cotton	110.7	96.6	157.2	230.5	130.6	130.3	118.2	97.6
Coffee	118.1	85.1	91.6	123.8	116.0	103.9	107.6	103.1
Veg. Oil	138.1	82.5	96.1	127.3	113.4	97.5	80.4	67.0
Fish	96.0	103.2	141.1	120.8	126.8	131.7	145.8	153.8
Rubber	112.0	81.7	153.3	198.3	136.6	111.4	76.9	67.9
Fertilizer	156.2	78.5	89.7	128.2	121.3	100.3	91.9	85.0
Crude Oil	134.6	88.0	109.8	146.1	147.5	140.7	127.2	68.9

Note: [*] The figures for 2015 represent only the first quarter.

Source: International Monetary Fund commodity price data combined with the US GDP deflator.

9.4.4 Simulations

We run the model forward through time attempting to track basic elements of Tanzanian macroeconomic performance. In the Baseline scenario, population growth is set at 3.0 per cent per year during 2007–15. Total labour supply grows at 2.1 per cent per year, reflecting a tendency for children to remain in school for longer periods of time. In addition, the work force becomes progressively more skilled with annual growth rates in the stock increasing by 7, 4, 1, and 1.5 per cent per annum running from highest to lowest skill categories. We assume full employment (perfectly inelastic labour supply) in all categories. Agricultural land expands at 1 per cent each year, capturing rising population density, especially in rural areas. Livestock capital is assumed to increase exogenously at 3 per cent per year.

Total factor productivity (TFP) growth is set at about 2 per cent per annum in agriculture and a bit more than 3 per cent per annum in non-agriculture. These assumptions combine to generate a smooth 6.5 per cent per annum GDP growth rate over the period 2007–15, which is reasonably consistent with experience. The simulation applies world price shocks as observed between 2007 and 2015 for each year of the analysis. These real-world price shocks are illustrated in Table 9.7.

Before proceeding to results, it is important to highlight the limitations of this approach. It is far from perfect. While considerable efforts are made to construct a model that looks and behaves like the Tanzanian economy, the model is, inevitably, a considerable simplification of reality. In addition, the shocks applied to this simplified reality are not known with certainty and are incomplete. For example, where credible international price data are not

Table 9.8. Comparison of macroeconomic indicators for model and reported data

	2007–12		2007–15
	Reported	Model	Model
GDP	6.6%	6.2%	6.4%
Household Consumption	8.0%	5.0%	6.1%
Investment[1]	14.0%	3.0%	2.4%
Government	12.0%	12.0%	12.0%
Exports	19.0%	6.1%	5.0%
Imports	20.2%	4.9%	6.0%
Agriculture	3.9%	4.0%	4.1%
Industry	7.5%	5.6%	5.4%
Services	8.1%	8.3%	8.5%
Terms of Trade (100 in 2007)		90.2	100.8
Reduction in national poverty rate	6.2%	3.5%	9.4%
Reduction in rural poverty rate	6.0%	3.9%	10.1%
Reduction in urban poverty rate	3.7%	1.5%	6.1%

Note: Figures are annual per cent growth rates for national accounts statistics, levels for terms of trade, and total percentage point reductions for poverty rates.

Source: Reported data are derived from the World Development Indicators.

available, no shocks are applied. There is no attempt to track other salient events, such as droughts or particularly good agricultural seasons, which may impact welfare and poverty rates over the period. Finally, data weaknesses are apparent, even at the macroeconomic level. Instead, the scenario attempts to apply plausible growth values and available world price data to generate a coherent series of growth-poverty outcomes. We then attempt to draw some insight from the growth process in Tanzania.

9.4.5 Results

The results from the modelling exercise are reported in Table 9.8, which also provides a comparison with the World Development Indicators (WDI). Both consistencies and inconsistencies are notable. Reasonable consistency is found in overall GDP growth. The components of growth in value added are also reasonably consistent between 2007 and 2012. The model essentially matches growth in agriculture and in services. The somewhat slower rate of growth recorded by the model is concentrated in industry where the rate of growth is about two percentage points lower. Consistent in direction with the household survey evidence, the model reports a much lower rate of growth in personal consumption expenditure than is recorded by national accounts.

The model exactly matches growth in government expenditure. While not shown in the table, this rapid growth in government is financed principally via an expansion in the government budget deficit. Neither volumes of aid nor tax revenue as a share of GDP rises in the model and in the reported data. This brings us to some inconsistencies. In particular, investment is reported to have grown very rapidly; however, in the model, investment is crowded out by the expanding government deficit. This large difference is explained by very considerable private capital flows over the period not captured in the model.

These flows also strongly influence the trade accounts. For example, in 2011, investment is reported to increase by 31 per cent relative to 2010. Imports increase by 48 per cent in the same year. In 2012 and 2013, these elevated import and investment levels are basically maintained. These numbers reflect, almost surely, major investments in natural resource extraction. However, this investment does not appear to come into production by 2013, which is the final year of data available. This is reflected in very stable rates of reported GDP and export growth in 2012 and 2013, both around 6.9 per cent in each year. Therefore, one suspects that the investment and trade figures are being strongly influenced by large capital inflows to support, for example, natural gas extraction. However, at least by about 2013, these investments had not yet begun to substantially influence exports or GDP, much less the welfare of the Tanzanian population.

To cope with these flows, we assume that the major private capital flows that have been occurring since 2011 are mainly directed towards resource extraction and that these investments have yet to exert a noticeable influence on the living standards of most Tanzanians. Because resource extraction is heavily capital intensive with much of the investment capital (and technical knowhow) sourced from abroad, the principal linkage providing benefits to the economy is frequently government revenue. As noted, the WDI data do not point to a substantial increase in revenue as a share of GDP. Hence, while these flows are very material for the investment and trade accounts, they likely mattered little for living standards over the period in focus.[10]

Turning to poverty reduction, the model employed here points to a 3.5 percentage point reduction in the national consumption poverty rate. This is less than the 6.2 per cent reduction reported for the period 2007–12. In both the model and in the reported figures, poverty reduction is substantially more pronounced in rural than in urban areas.

While certainly not exactly the same, these figures cohere to at least some degree. It is notable that the poverty reduction results derived from survey analysis are driven heavily by improvements in income distribution over the period 2007–12 rather than by growth in per capita consumption. As discussed in Arndt et al. (2015a), it is possible, yet not easy to generate plausible economic scenarios that would generate consumption growth amongst poorer households and not among those with somewhat higher incomes. This is particularly true if one focuses uniquely on rural areas, where most poverty reduction occurred. One alternative explanation is that the methodological shifts incorporated into the 2011/12 household survey succeeded in better capturing total consumption amongst lower-income households resulting in an overstatement of reductions in poverty.

It also appears likely that the latest poverty assessment underestimates inequality. From Table 9.7, we note that world commodity prices in 2012 were at very high levels. This includes basic foods such as maize and rice. As shown by Arndt et al. (2015b), changes in relative prices have differential implications across the income distribution and can have strong implications for measured inequality. As poor people tend to consume a much higher proportion of basic foods than wealthier people, changes in the relative price of basic foods and non-foods have differential impacts. If the recent poverty assessment had accounted for these changes in prices across the income distribution (as is done in the model), the gains in real consumption would likely be more evenly distributed across the income distribution (as opposed to skewed towards lower income households). Overall, while not definitive, the modelling results obtained thus far support a somewhat slower rate of poverty reduction over the 2007–12 period, as well as a more balanced incidence of growth across the income distribution than reported in the recent assessment.

Finally, it should be highlighted that poverty reduction proceeds at a more rapid pace between 2012 and 2015, according to the model. This is partly due to slightly more rapid rates of growth in GDP, including more rapid growth in agriculture. The larger part is due to improved terms of trade (based on 2007 trade shares) driven strongly by the decline in fuel prices experienced at the end of 2014. These improved terms of trade expand consumption possibilities, including consumption possibilities for the poor.

9.5 Conclusions

A reasonably coherent narrative may be emerging for the socioeconomic performance of Tanzania with two major elements. The first element involves large investments in social expenditures. Based on detailed analysis of four Demographic and Health Surveys, we find strong evidence for broad based improvements in key non-monetary welfare indicators when considering long periods of time. The growth and monetary poverty story, the second element, also falls within explainable ranges over the period 2007–15. Focusing on Tanzanian national income (and therefore essentially ignoring resource extraction investments and outputs) for the period since 2007, our model is able to broadly reproduce key macroeconomic features of the past eight years. We find that estimated consumption poverty rates for 2007–12 for Tanzania fall within a reasonable to optimistic range.

Our simulations continue to 2015. We find that the reductions in world prices for fossil fuels observed recently are favourable to growth and poverty reduction given Tanzania's current production structure. As Tanzania is in the process of shifting this structure by becoming a substantial producer/exporter of natural gas, low fossil fuel prices will no longer be as automatically favourable to welfare outcomes as they have been over the past several decades.

Notes

1. See World Bank (2007, 2015).
2. Other papers examining this incoherence include Kessy et al. (2013); Mashindano et al. (2011); Mkenda et al. (2010); Osberg and Bandara (2012); World Bank (2007, 2013); and Arndt et al. (2015a).
3. Elsewhere, Arndt et al. (2014) define three additional population categories (children aged 7–17, children under 5, and young women aged 18–30).
4. In a bootstrap, synthetic samples are generated by drawing from a parent sample with replacement. For example, the 10,300 households in the 2010 DHS survey (the parent) would be effectively placed in an urn. We then create synthetic samples of the same size (10,300 households) by drawing households from that urn (using the stratified approaches employed for the DHS) with replacement. In one synthetic sample of size 10,300, a single household from the parent sample may appear zero, one, two, three or more times. This approach is a highly effective way of estimating sample variation and is used to consider the robustness of FOD results to sample variation.
5. Smaller gains in the water dimension are observed if one restricts the set of households not deprived in the water dimension to those with access to a clean well within thirty minutes by foot from their residence.
6. The net domination score presented in Table 9.5 gives an idea of the robustness of the ranking. In 2010, Dodoma is fairly robustly the poorest region in Tanzania with a score of −0.32, meaning that, across all regions and bootstrap repetitions, Dodoma is dominated about one-third of the time. The second poorest region in 2010 registers a score of −0.25. Regions with very similar net domination scores, such as Kgoma and Lindi, which have the same score rounded to two decimal points, are not robustly ranked one above the other.
7. The model's mathematical specification is discussed in Diao and Thurlow (2012).
8. Data are from the National Agricultural Statistics Service of the United States Department of Agriculture. The United States is chosen because it offers a long price time series. The United States is also a major agricultural producer, importer, and exporter making it a reasonable global price bellwether. The application of a US price index to Tanzania is limited by substantial differences in the commodity composition of output and the influence of US price policies. Nevertheless, the US index is adequate for the general purposes considered here.
9. Data from UN Comtrade point to even higher import levels for fuels in 2007.

10. In addition, the WDI reports increases in real exports in 2010 and 2011 of 30 and 27 per cent respectively. These big leaps in volumes are difficult to reconcile with UN Comtrade data. These two big leaps are the major source of difference between the growth rate of real exports as reported by WDI, and as generated by the model.

References

Adam, C., Bevan, D., and Gollin, D. (2015). 'Rural–Urban Linkages, Public Investment and Transport Costs: The Case of Tanzania', unpublished manuscript.

Adam, C., Kwimbere, D., Mbowe, W., and O'Connell, S. (2012). 'Food Prices and Inflation in Tanzania', International Growth Centre Working Paper, London/Oxford, July.

Arndt, C., Azhar Hussain, M., Leyaro, V., Jones, E., and Tarp F. (2013). 'Poverty and Growth in Tanzania', paper presented at the Conference on 'Inclusive Growth in Africa: Measurement, Causes and Consequences', 20–21 September 2013, Helsinki, Finland (draft dated August 2013).

Arndt, C., Distante, R., Osterdal, L. P., Huong, P. L., and Ibraimo, M. (2012a). 'Ordinal Welfare Comparisons with Multiple Discrete Indicators: A First Order Dominance Approach and Applications to Child Poverty', *World Development* 40(11): 2290–301.

Arndt, C., Hussain, M. A., Jones, E. S., Nhate, V., Tarp, F., and Thurlow, J. (2012b). 'Explaining the Evolution of Poverty: The Case of Mozambique', *American Journal of Agricultural Economics* 94(4): 854–72.

Arndt, C., Leyaro, V., and Mahrt, K. (2014). 'Multi-Dimensional Poverty Analysis for Tanzania: First Order Dominance Approach with Discrete Indicators', UNU-WIDER Working Paper WP/2014/146, Helsinki.

Arndt, C., Demery, L., McKay, A., and Tarp F. (2015a). 'Growth and Poverty Reduction in Tanzania', UNU-WIDER Working Paper 2015/051.

Arndt, C., Jones, S., and Salvucci, V. (2015b). 'When Do Relative Prices Matter for Measuring Income Inequality? The Case of Food Prices in Mozambique', *Journal of Economic Inequality* 13: 449–64.

Arndt, C., Pauw, K., and Thurlow, J. (2016). 'The Economy-Wide Impacts and Risks of Malawi's Farm Input Subsidy Program', *American Journal of Agricultural Economics* 98(3): 962–80.

Atkinson, A. B. and Lugo, M. A. (2010). 'Growth, Poverty and Distribution in Tanzania', International Growth Centre Working Paper 10/0831, London/Oxford, November.

Copeland, A. H. (1951). 'A "Reasonable" Social Welfare Function', paper presented at the University of Michigan Seminar on 'Applications of Mathematics to the Social Sciences'.

Diao, X. and Thurlow, J. (2012). 'A Recursive Dynamic Computable General Equilibrium Model'. In: Diao, X., Thurlow, J., Benin, S., and Fan, S. (eds), *Strategies and Priorities for African Agriculture: Economywide Perspectives from Country Studies*. Washington, D.C.: International Food Policy Research Institute (IFPRI).

Dimaranan, B. V. (ed.) (2006). 'Global Trade, Assistance, and Production: The GTAP 6 Data Base', Center for Global Trade Analysis, Purdue University.

Dyer, G. A. and Taylor, J. E. (2011). 'The Corn Price Surge: Impacts on Rural Mexico', *World Development* 39(10): 1878–87.

Hoogeveen, J. and Ruhinduka, R. (2009). 'Poverty Reduction in Tanzania since 2001: Good Intentions, Few Results', paper prepared for the Research and Analysis Working Group.

Horridge, M., Maddan, J., and Wittwer, G. (2005). 'The Impact of the 2002–2003 Drought on Australia', *Journal of Policy Modeling* 27: 285–308.

Kessy, F., Mashindano, O., Shepherd, A., and Scott, L. (eds) (2013). 'Translating Growth into Poverty Reduction: Beyond the Numbers', Mkuki na Nyota, Dar es Salaam.

Lehmann, E. L. (1955). 'Ordered Families of Distributions', *The Annals of Mathematical Statistics* 26(3): 399–419.

Mashindano, O., Kayunze, K., da Corta, L., and Maro, F. (2011). 'Agriculture Growth and Poverty Reduction in Tanzania 2000–2010: Where Has Agriculture Worked for the Poor and What Can We Learn from This?' Chronic Poverty Research Centre Working Paper No. 208, June.

Ministry of Agriculture, Food Security, and Cooperatives (2004). 'National Samples Census of Agriculture, 2002/03', Dar es Salaam.

Mkenda, A., Luvanda, E., and Ruhinduka, R. (2010). 'Growth and Distribution in Tanzania: Recent Experience and Lessons', Interim Report to REPOA.

Müller, A. and Stoyan, D. (2002). *Comparison Methods for Stochastic Models and Risks.* Chichester: John Wiley and Sons.

National Bureau of Statistics (2002). 'Household Budget Survey 2000/01', Government of Tanzania.

National Bureau of Statistics (2009). 'Household Budget Survey 2007—Tanzania Mainland', Government of Tanzania.

Osberg, L. and Bandara, A. (2012). 'Why Poverty Remains High in Tanzania: and What to Do About It?' Special Paper 12/3, Dar es Salaam, REPOA.

Shaked, M. and Shanthikumar, J. G. (2007). *Stochastic Orders.* New York: Springer.

World Bank (2007). 'Tanzania: Sustaining and Sharing Economic Growth (CEM and Poverty Assessment)', World Bank, Washington, D.C.

World Bank (2013). 'Tanzania Economic Update: Raising the Game', PREM Issue 4, World Bank, Washington, D.C.

World Bank (2015). 'Tanzania Poverty Assessment', World Bank, Washington, D.C.

10

Public Investment and Fiscal Reforms

Christopher S. Adam, Jehovaness Aikaeli, and Anne Laski

10.1 Introduction

The success of any growth strategy in Tanzania over the coming decades will necessarily be underpinned by a coherent fiscal framework, one that defines, regulates, and resources the economic domain of the state. How wide its boundaries should be and how the economic role of the state should be financed are the fundamental fiscal questions facing all societies: once the 'night-watchman' role—the protection of citizens and their property from predation and from internal and external aggression—is secured, the fiscal policy debate then turns to what goods and services the state should and should not provide, how these should be financed through taxation and debt, and how, through its regulatory capacity, the state should seek to regulate private markets.[1] In Tanzania, perhaps more than elsewhere in sub-Saharan Africa, the debate over where these boundaries should be drawn has been an active one since independence (see Chapter 2, this volume, and also Coulson, 2013). Towards the end of President Nyerere's term in office in 1985, however, the cumulative effect of the desperately poor economic performance over the previous decade, which had exposed the limits of the government's capacity, set the stage for fiscal policy to take a supporting role within an economy that is now increasingly governed by private rather than public sector economic activity.

This transition is not yet complete but the system that is emerging sees fiscal policy operating along three principal axes. The first is the use of the tax system and the direct provision of public services and transfers to address distributional considerations, between groups in society, and between current and future generations, where distributional objectives may reflect a desire to ensure access to basic economic opportunities, to redress historical or structural disadvantage, or to provide a counterweight to market outcomes. The second is the indirect pursuit of the same objectives through the provision of public infrastructure, in the form of both physical and human capital that complements and enhances the productive capacity of the private sector. And the third function—which historically has not been a central feature of the fiscal policy debate in low-income countries—is the use of fiscal policy instruments in support of macro-economic stabilization objectives.

In the past, and certainly during the two decades from the mid-1970s, the debate on fiscal policy, both in the country itself and in particular with the IMF and other external partners, was embedded in a diagnosis that identified weak fiscal control as the principal cause of economic under-performance. The sequence of adjustment programmes throughout this period sought to limit discretion in the conduct of fiscal (and monetary) policy. The legacy of this period can still be seen in the authorities' money-targeting approach to stabilization that is anchored on controlling the growth in domestic credit to government (see Chapter 11, this volume). But in contemporary Tanzania, where the risks of severe fiscal dominance have been substantially if not wholly contained, it must surely be appropriate to start to think of fiscal policy as part of the solution rather than part of the problem. Whether this can be achieved depends crucially on state capacity. Critical is the extent to which the state can finance the provision of goods and services—through taxation and borrowing—in a manner that is both efficient, in the sense that the mobilization of resources for the public sector is achieved at the lowest possible cost in terms of the burden it places on the private sector, and also equitable, in the sense that financing choices between taxation and debt-financing not only ensure long-run debt sustainability but strike a balance between current and future generations.

In recent years, there has been an enormous literature concerned with the growth in fiscal capacity and the emerging fiscal challenges facing Tanzania. Much of this literature is from the external institutions—see, for example, Bevan (2010 and 2012) for the IGC and Nord et al. (2009) for the International Monetary Fund (IMF), and World Bank (2015)—but some comes from the Ministry of Finance's own public expenditure review group. A key refrain in this literature is that the fiscal system is now much more transparent and efficient than before. Some of this reflects reforms dating back to the mid-1990s when government introduced a cash-budgeting system of expenditure control. Built around the Single Treasury Account at the central bank and the Integrated Financial Management System, this played a decisive role in eliminating, or at least containing, pressures for money-financing of the deficit. On the revenue mobilization side, the establishment of the quasi-autonomous Tanzania Revenue Authority has brought increased transparency and efficiency in revenue mobilization, while the introduction of a value-added tax (VAT) has helped improve Tanzania's historically poor revenue mobilization rate. In parallel, multiple rounds of reform in public financial management have improved auditing at various levels of government, put in place better financial controls in government ministries and have improved the quality of public expenditure planning and execution.

This is not to say that all in the fiscal garden is rosy. As we note in Section 10.3, Tanzania still struggles relative to its peer group to raise public revenue in an equitable and efficient manner, while problems of expenditure budgeting and control, especially over the accumulation of arrears, remain major challenges to the fiscal authorities.

These issues lie at the heart of fiscal policy discussions, within government and between government and the IMF and other external players. In this chapter, however, we approach the issue of fiscal reforms and revenue mobilization from a slightly different angle, one that pays particular attention to the interplay between certain types of expenditure reforms on the one hand and revenue mobilization on the other. Specifically, we focus on the provision and financing of public goods, and in particular public infrastructure. It is a strongly-held tenet of the public policy debate in Tanzania, as elsewhere in Africa, that a key constraint on growth and employment remains the shortage of high-quality economic and social infrastructure, which in turn has encouraged a push for increased public investment in transport and communications, in power networks and distribution (although less so in generation), and in social infrastructure, such as in the health and education sectors.

Moreover, although Tanzania (among other countries) currently faces difficult external conditions, the environment for public investment in recent years has been very favourable, and these conditions are expected to persist, at least over the medium term. Given the shortage and degraded quality of much of the existing public infrastructure, the *ex ante* expected social returns to new investment in public capital are assumed to be high. Evidence from the World Bank's *Doing Business* surveys and regular country growth diagnoses, such as those carried out by the US and Department for International Development (DFID), all point to the belief that the continent as a whole, and Tanzania in particular, faces an 'infrastructure gap', a situation in which poor-quality and high-cost infrastructure hold back private investment and market integration. There is clearly a perceived need for more public capital.

At the same time, real investment costs and the world cost of capital are at historically low levels, at least on global markets. Even allowing for the much-anticipated increase in US policy rates by the US Federal Reserve in 2016/17, interest rates are likely to remain low over the medium run (see, for example, Larry Summers' remarks on 'secular stagnation' at the IMF Annual Research Conference in 2013 (IMF, 2013) and Thwaites (2015)). Moreover, as African countries' macroeconomic conditions and capacities have improved, long-run country risk premia have fallen. While the financial environment since late 2015 has proven difficult, it is likely country risk premia will return to relatively low levels over the medium term, particularly if the expectation of future natural resource revenues are factored in.

But even as pressures mount to identify new infrastructure investment projects and priorities, the existing stock of public capital is often degrading more rapidly than it should and contributing less to economic growth than *ex ante* assessments of returns to investment would suggest. This is entirely consistent with evidence that purposive public investment programmes often show positive strong short-run impacts on growth (most likely as a result of demand-side effects), but the longer-run growth effects of public investment appear to be rather muted and certainly weaker than initially expected (Warner, 2014). Since what matters for growth is not the capital stock per se but the sustained flow of productive capital services the public infrastructure provides to private factors of production, closing the 'infrastructure gap' entails more than simply increasing new public investment: the public capital stock needs to be efficiently operated and maintained.

Maintaining operations and maintenance (O&M) expenditures at an efficient level is, however, expensive, and actual expenditures commonly fall well below what is optimal or even just sufficient. For example, the recent World Bank's Africa Infrastructure Country Diagnostic (2010) programme found that 'on average, about 30% of the infrastructure assets of a typical African country need rehabilitation . . . [reflecting] . . . a legacy of underfunding of maintenance'.[2] Public investment in new infrastructure therefore needs to be accompanied by actions to address the problem of deficient O&M expenditures. This 'recurrent cost problem', which is far from new,[3] is rooted in two key features of public finance both of which are very much present in Tanzania. The first is that O&M expenditures often enjoy very limited 'protection' in the government budget. These are not glamorous expenditures and rarely do powerful coalitions form to protect them in the face generalized spending pressures. This vulnerability is acute when public budgeting systems are weak and when pressures from interest groups raise the political costs of trimming back other components of the budget. Cutting back on O&M is invariably a more appealing means of achieving short-term fiscal adjustment than is capping the public sector wage bill or reducing subsidies and entitlements, not least because the costs of doing so tend to be diffuse and the adverse effects of such actions only come home to roost at some point in the future. These political economy factors also tend to favour new capital formation over the maintenance, rehabilitation, and operation of the existing capital stock, particularly in systems of weak public financial management, where rents are larger and more readily extracted from new capital projects than from routine operations and maintenance.

The second characteristic of the recurrent cost problem is the interaction between the incomplete appropriability of the returns from public investment and the distortionary nature of the tax system. The appropriability issue here describes the difficulty of recouping returns to public infrastructure investment by public authorities, even when the potential to raise productivity among private factors of production is high. This may be due to the intrinsic public good characteristics of public investment (where the returns are diffuse, accrue to those not directly using the capital, or are otherwise difficult to monetize directly) or may reflect political economy considerations that, for example, limit the ability to fully recoup costs through tariffs or other fees. Clearly, some forms of public investment are relatively easy to recoup (power generation and distribution being the most obvious example), but arguably these are precisely the areas where private finance may be more appropriate and more willing to go.

The point remains: typically only a fraction of the ongoing recurrent expenditure requirements to operate and maintain the capital (in addition to the costs of meeting the 'normal' depreciation and debt financing costs associated with the investment) can be collected directly from the users of public capital, so that at the margin, fiscal balance is satisfied by some mixture of non-concessional external borrowing, domestic borrowing, and adjustment to taxes. It should be noted here that debt financing of investment does not remove the burden on taxation but merely changes the time profile of taxation. Debt financing, whether domestic or external, keeps current tax rates low, but unless and until borrowing is repaid, future tax rates must rise to cover higher debt service costs, *ceteris paribus*. So regardless of the mix, the burden ultimately falls on the domestic tax system. The essential point is that domestic taxation is distortionary; thus raising a dollar of government revenue imposes more than a dollar of cost on the private sector.

Factoring in these three features—high O&M costs, limited appropriability of returns, and distortionary taxation—has important implications for debates on public investment and fiscal policy. Whilst the issue is fundamentally one of the microeconomic and political economy of public expenditure, failure to address the recurrent cost problem has powerful macroeconomic consequences for the sustainability of growth.

In this chapter we bring an analysis of this fundamental public finance problem to the Tanzanian context. Anticipating the analysis to follow, we make three major policy points. The first is that the return to fiscal reforms that protect operations and maintenance expenditure and that help to reduce the distortionary character of the tax system may have as large an impact on growth as new public investment. Second, given the stakes, public investment decisions need to be evaluated in a full general equilibrium framework that factors in the public finance impact of public investment. Finally, fiscal adjustment that seeks to address short-term fiscal crises by economizing on operations and maintenance expenditures may be the worst sort of false economy.

The rest of the chapter is as follows. Section 10.2 provides a brief review of the recent evolution of the fiscal structure in Tanzania and a discussion of the perceived 'infrastructure gap'. Section 10.3 examines patterns of revenue mobilization, in Tanzania and regionally, and the associated evidence on the marginal cost of government funds which helps clarify the paradox of coexisting high marginal tax rates and low revenue mobilization. This section then concludes with a discussion of current reforms and anticipated changes in the revenue potential over the coming decades. These two sections set the scene for the formal analysis of the chapter which is based around a numerical simulation model designed to highlight the interaction between these characteristics of public finance on the one hand and public investment and growth on the other. The model is described in Section 10.4 and results presented in Section 10.5. Section 10.6 concludes with a discussion of the policy implications of this analysis for Tanzania.

10.2 The Public Balance Sheet: Public Debt, Fiscal Balance, and the 'Infrastructure Gap'

We start by looking at aspects of the public balance sheet for Tanzania. From a macroeconomic perspective, fiscal performance in Tanzania in the last decade has been reasonably good. In part, this reflects strong economic growth and favourable external conditions, which together have imparted a very positive impulse to public debt dynamics, but the favourable outturn also reflects good fiscal management and purposive reforms that have kept the fiscal deficit at a low and sustainable value.

A useful way to organize this discussion is through the simple dynamics of the public debt-to-GDP ratio which can be written as a function of four variables. Equation (10.1) describes the period-to-period growth of public debt (expressed as a share of gross domestic product (GDP)), denoted $\dot{d}_t$,

$$\dot{d}_t = (r_t - g_t)d_t + b_t \qquad (10.1)$$

where d_t is the public debt-to-GDP ratio, r_t and g_t are the effective real interest rate on public debt and the rate of growth of GDP respectively, and b_t is the fiscal deficit net of grants.[4] It follows from (10.1) that high and sustained growth, relative to the cost of servicing public debt, will lower the debt-to-GDP ratio over time, other things equal. Stated differently, the stronger is growth relative to the real interest rate, the larger is the fiscal deficit the authorities can run without jeopardizing debt sustainability. It also follows

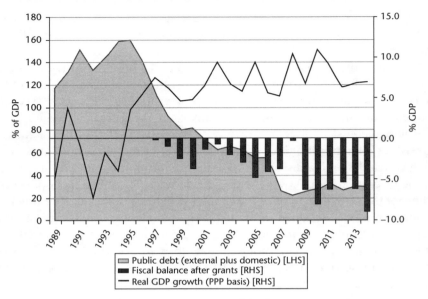

Figure 10.1. Tanzania debt dynamics

rather trivially that debt relief (represented as a one-off reduction in d_t) has a permanent positive effect on debt dynamics, other things equal.

Since the mid-1990s, all four elements on the right hand side of equation (10.1) have combined to initially reduce and then stabilize public debt (see Figure 10.1), even during the global financial crisis of 2008/09. This stabilization has been primarily driven by steady and strong output growth, averaging over 7 per cent per annum from 1999/2000 to 2013/14 at a time of low real interest rates (reflecting the combination of low global interest rates, the high share of concessional borrowing by Tanzania, and the steady reduction in the country-risk premium on non-concessional borrowing).[5] The successful HIPC/MDRI debt relief also had a large effect, following Tanzania's qualification in 2001 and subsequent US$3.5bn of debt-relief in 2005/06, ultimately reducing Tanzania's debt by approximately 54 per cent in net present value terms, and entailing an ongoing reduction in external debt service of between 0.5 and 1 per cent of GDP.[6] But over the same period aggregate fiscal discipline—supported to a substantial degree by ODA grants—kept the fiscal deficit after grants to a moderate level, especially up to and beyond the onset of the global financial crisis in 2008/09. As Ndulu and Mwase (Chapter 2, this volume) and Nord et al. (2009), amongst many, have noted, control over the aggregate fiscal balance has been one of the major achievements of the Tanzanian government over the last two decades.

The public debt ratio has increased gradually since around 2011, and since the end of 2014 debt dynamics have become much less favourable as the external environment has worsened and the domestic fiscal stance has weakened markedly. Global economic growth has slowed and with it external aggregate demand for Tanzania's exports, particularly from China. At the same time, the demand for imports has remained firm—primarily because of the capital good imports linked with strong public investment—so that the current account remains in deficit around 10 per cent of GDP. This weakening of the current account has been compounded by a worsening capital account position, where the prospective increase in US interest rates (as of late 2016), combined with investors' reassessment of the region and Tanzania's perceived riskiness, has seen bond spreads increase sharply and stifled somewhat the appetite of foreign investors to hold Tanzanian assets (IMF (2015) notes that spreads on Tanzanian sovereign debt have increased by 300 basis points between October 2014 and October 2015).[7] Consequently, net capital inflows have slowed, and with net international reserves close to their minimum prudential level, this has put pressure on the nominal and real exchange rate (see IMF, 2015). The pressure on the external balance has been exacerbated by a weakening domestic fiscal position as the strong revenue performance of the last decade appears to be levelling off (see Section 10.3).

Taken together, public debt is currently forecast to rise by around 5 percentage points over the short run, from around 35 per cent to over 40 per cent of GDP (IMF, 2015). This level does not present substantial risk of debt distress but does highlight the need to consolidate the fiscal position so that the modest upwards drift in public debt does not become unsustainable. In terms of equation (10.1), this means targeting a fiscal balance after grants consistent with stabilized debt (i.e., $\dot{d}_t = 0$), given the expected real growth of the economy and the cost of debt over the medium term. An important element of this calculation is the likely evolution of the real exchange rate; the more the real exchange rate depreciates, the higher the effective cost of carrying external debt.[8] It is reasonable to assume that the equilibrium real exchange rate will appreciate over the longer term as offshore natural gas fields are developed. But this is at least a decade off (see Chapter 3, this volume), and in the interim the economy faces an extended period of necessary investment in anticipation of resource development, during which pressures on the real exchange are likely to be from the other direction. The critical issue for the fiscal authorities is how this consolidation is to be achieved, how the balance between revenue mobilization and expenditure control is struck. This is what the remainder of this chapter is concerned with, but before we turn to the core analysis we briefly examine the asset side of the public balance sheet.

The quality of public infrastructure in Tanzania, as in many countries in sub-Saharan Africa, is relatively poor. With the exception of relatively new sectors such as mobile phone telephony, the 'reach' of key elements of the infrastructural network tend to lag significantly behind that of other low income countries, including some of Tanzania's regional neighbours, and falls far short of the median levels of infrastructure capital enjoyed in the group of middle-income countries that Tanzania aspires to join. This is the case in the physical infrastructure networks—the road and railway networks and the port of Dar es Salaam (see Chapter 5, this volume); in power provision for the household, industrial, and commercial sectors; and in water and sanitation provision, especially in rural areas. For example, the World Bank's *Africa Infrastructure Country Diagnostic* (AICD), carried out in the late 2000s, estimated the paved road density in Tanzania to be about half that of low-income countries on average and only one tenth of that enjoyed by middle-income countries, while the proportion of the rural population living within 2 km of an all-season road was only 24 per cent (compared to 60 per cent for people in middle-income countries).[9] The AICD report paints a similar picture in the power sector where low installed capacity—and therefore low consumption, frequent power outages, and low levels of access, even in urban areas—result in low-quality, high-cost power being frequently cited as the single major constraint on firms' economic performance. A similar picture emerges in other areas of the public infrastructure such as schools, hospitals, and health facilities. Aggregating across all sectors suggests a very substantial infrastructure gap relative to the lower-middle-income benchmark to which the authorities aspire. The AICD (2010) estimates it would take more than a doubling of the public investment rate, sustained for over a decade, to close this gap.

The challenge of how the authorities can do so without jeopardizing macro-economic stability is discussed in Section 10.4. Before we turn to this we briefly discuss revenue mobilization.

10.3 Revenue Mobilization, Tax Reforms, and the Marginal Cost of Funds

Revenue mobilization has shown impressive growth since the big macro-economic reforms of the mid-1990s (see Chapter 2, this volume).[10] Comparable data—over time and across countries—are only available on the basis of 'old' GDP data. However, what is clear from Figure 10.2 is that Tanzania's tax to GDP rate, which had been pretty stagnant since the early 1980s, started to rise steadily throughout the early 2000s, from the extremely low levels of less than 10 per cent of GDP to around 15 per cent of GDP by 2008 and around 17.5 per cent by around 2013. Given that GDP itself was growing at 7 per cent per annum over the same period, this represents a very substantial increase in

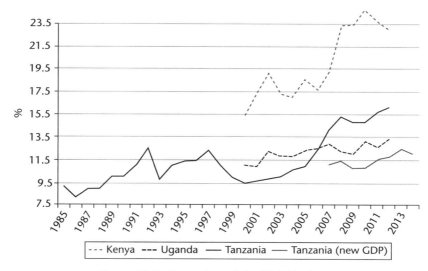

Figure 10.2. Tanzania and the EAC big three

revenue mobilization (see IMF (2011), which described Tanzania as a 'strong performer'). This improvement very much complemented developments in the East African Community (EAC), which was concurrently increasing mobilization from an unweighted average (excluding Burundi) of 11.25 per cent of GDP to over 16 per cent of GDP (note that the rapid growth rates were in Kenya, from 17.5 per cent in 2006 to over 23 per cent in 2010, and Tanzania, from 10.9 per cent in 2005 and 15.2 per cent in 2009).

This rise in revenue mobilization was initially not accompanied by a similar rise in total expenditure so that, as seen in Figure 10.1, the fiscal deficit before grants contracted from over 10 per cent of GDP to closer to 5 per cent between 2005 and 2008 which, with grants to the budget remaining around 3 per cent to 5 per cent per annum, meant the deficit after grants (what matters for debt dynamics), was contained to very low single digits. Thus, pressures of debt accumulation, from both external and domestic sources remained modest.

From around 2010, progress in revenue mobilization began to slow so that Tanzania's revenue mobilization continues to underperform relative to its peer group, including key countries in the EAC—despite the fact that its marginal tax rates, for trade taxes, VAT, and for income taxes, are more or less in line with or exceed those in similar countries. So, for example, even with a tax rate of 20 per cent, revenue from VAT is only around 3 per cent of GDP, about two-thirds the VAT performance in the rest of the EAC and less than half that of the median lower-middle-income country (LMIC).[11] In part, this reflects Tanzania's still large informal economy and the fact that basic foodstuffs, which still account for a large share of average household consumption, are exempt from VAT. The exemption of basic foods is conventional around the world, but the biggest impairment to Tanzania's VAT mobilization is the associated host of exemptions, special reliefs, zero-rating, and VAT deferments, which together provide enormous opportunities for tax evasion and avoidance. Because zero-rating allows producers to claim back taxes paid on inputs, it removes all VAT from the process and thereby avoids the cascading of tax through multi-stage production. In contrast, VAT exemptions relieve only final stage VAT but not the tax levied on intermediate inputs, in this case rendering the VAT more like a conventional final sales tax that incorporates the cascading of taxation of intermediate inputs. While this means that a zero-rating approach to tax relief preserves the desirable tax-efficiency properties of the VAT, it does so at the cost of lower revenue mobilization.[12] This revenue effect may be particularly large if the production of zero-rated goods involves high levels of taxable inputs.[13] Conventionally, in any destination-based tax regime, exports are zero-rated, as are medical and phytosanitary supplies, and agricultural and fishery inputs. Exemptions cover a wide range of goods and services, including books, education supplies, and the main staple food, crop, and livestock supplies. But they also cover a range of transport and financial services, tourist services, and even computing services. Special relief is provided to a range of taxpayers, including investors registered with the Tanzania Investment Centre (TIC); firms operating in the many export processing zones; non-governmental organizations (NGOs) and charities; firms in the offshore exploration sector; and other designated private entities, often granted on a one-off basis. Crucially, however, special relief is treated equivalently to zero-rating, so that the supplier selling to the exempt taxpayer reclaims all input VAT and does not levy output VAT. Exemptions, zero-rating, and especially special relief, severely undermine revenue mobilization and create enormous opportunities for tax arbitrage.

This theme of relatively high marginal rates, low revenue mobilization, and widespread exemptions is repeated broadly across the tax regime. A number of recent studies on tax effort and tax potential confirm the view that there may be substantial scope to improve tax effort. The standard analysis in this literature employs a two-step approach. The first step is to use cross country or panel data to estimate a notional tax potential as a function of a range of structural characteristics, such as income per capita, the composition of production, degree of urbanization, openness to trade, demographic structure, and various measures of institutional capacity. Using stochastic frontier analysis methods, the second step is then to measure how far inside the frontier a specific country lies. A country operating on the frontier is said to be working at full tax effort, and the gap measures the potential for increased tax effort.

10.3.1 *Revenue Effort and the Marginal Cost of Funds*

The foregoing analysis begs the question of how much more revenue the Tanzanian authorities could extract in the future. There are two key elements to this. The first is the 'positive' notion of tax potential: given the underlying structure of the economy, how much more revenue could be extracted in principle. The second is an issue of welfare: namely, determining the cost to the private sector in terms of the distortions imposed by the tax structure. We discuss each in turn.

Recent work by Langford and Ohlenburg (2015) using a newly-published ICTD Government Revenue Dataset (see Prichard et al., 2014) suggest that, given their underlying economic structures, the EAC big three (Kenya, Uganda, and Tanzania) are all operating at between 50 per cent and 70 per cent of their tax potential. Based on data for Uganda and Tanzania for 2010, this means that, compared to the current level of around 15 per cent, a potential revenue to GDP rate (the old GDP series) of slightly over 20 per cent of GDP is feasible, given prevailing levels of income and the structure of the economy. Kenya's estimated potential is rather closer to 30 per cent, reflecting the greater buoyancy of the revenue base.

Separate work by IMF (2015) arrives at a broadly similar estimate of the EAC tax gap of around 4.5 per cent of GDP (based on the new GDP series). It is important to note, however, that these estimates of tax effort are crude: the estimated gap is simply a residual, so will include both administrative inefficiencies and losses in the literal sense of the word, including losses due to corruption. It also captures the revenue losses due to specific policy choices, in particular widespread exemptions and special reliefs provided by the tax regime. Recent estimates (Ministry of Finance, Government of Tanzania, 2013) suggest that over the last decade exemptions accounted for around 2 per cent of GDP, although this fell slightly in 2014/15.[14]

Concerns about the sprawl of exemptions and special relief measures that have invaded the tax regime in Tanzania, and the enormous scope this presents for tax evasion and avoidance, have increased in recent years. With the new VAT (2015) Act, the 2015 Budget sought to eliminate excessive exemptions while addressing concerns about equity. Thus the Budget provided for a significant curtailment of the scope of the Minister for Finance to grant discretionary tax exemptions and at the same time eliminated the special relief and zero-rated schedules to the Act, but at the same time exempted 'essential' goods such as agricultural implements, fishing equipment, medical supplies, and all capital goods from VAT, and retained the provision for granting strategic tax exemptions for so-called 'strategic super-investors', essentially large (usually foreign) investors generating significant employment.

There is a widespread belief that revenue mobilization may be enhanced, and possibly substantially, if and when off-shore hydrocarbon resources are developed. It is important, however, to calibrate these expectations. With the final investment decision still some way off and considerable uncertainty about the prospects for gas prices over the coming decades, the scale of revenues are necessarily difficult to forecast. Henstridge and Rweyemamu (Chapter 3, this volume) suggest that revenues from production sharing may plateau at 'a modest number of single digits of GDP...material but not transformative'. Put differently, while the contribution of revenues from natural resources to total revenue mobilization will be important, the contribution might realistically be of a similar order of magnitude to the gains that could accrue to the elimination of tax exemptions and other leakages from the current revenue regime.

10.3.2 *The Marginal Cost of Funds*

While addressing the problem of excess leakages is clearly important, a narrow focus on revenue mobilization can divert attention from the second key feature of the tax system, namely the distortionary effect it has on the efficient allocation of resources in the economy.[15] From a social welfare perspective, the distorting effect of taxes means that a dollar of tax collected by the government imposes a greater than one dollar burden on the private sector. Different taxes impose different distortions—hence different marginal costs of funds (MCF)—but the three main margins affected by taxation are: (i) between classes of goods produced under different technologies (for example, taxing formal sector goods creates an incentive to consume goods produced in the informal sector, typically produced at lower efficiency); (ii) between labour and leisure (or labour supplied to the informal sector); and, critically, (iii) between saving and investment and consumption.[16]

The quantitative importance of these distortions remains an open question. The earliest work, from Browning's pioneering study (1976) estimated the MCF in the US to be between US$1.09 and US$1.16 per dollar of revenue raised, across a range of taxes. Work on developing countries, most famously by Ahmad and Stern (1984) on India, produced much higher estimates of the MCF of US$1.50 to US$2.50 per dollar of revenue transferred to government; this much greater distortion reflected a range of factors, particularly the presence of a substantial untaxed informal sector in India. And, critically, as Emran and Stiglitz (2005) have shown, this formal/informal margin can impart potentially large distortions into otherwise benign consumption or value-added tax regimes. More recently, model-based analysis by Auriol and Warlters (2012) generate MCF estimates for thirty-eight sub-Saharan African countries that are somewhat closer to Browning's estimates than to those of Ahmad and

Stern, albeit with a substantial range. Their estimates for Tanzania suggest the MCF for the least distortionary taxes (the VAT) is around US$1.20 per dollar of revenue, rising to close to US$1.80 for the most distortionary taxes (taxes on capital).

Finally, it is important to note that these estimates are computed for small movements in tax rates away from their prevailing levels. It is well known, however, that since the distortionary effect of tax changes tends to rise more than proportionally to the increase in the tax rate, large and rapid changes in tax structures become increasingly more damaging to the economy.[17] Two key implications follow from this observation. The first is that attempts to raise more revenue, even in order to finance higher public investment, simply by ratcheting up rates in a tax system with relatively high distortions may be counter-productive in that the gains from higher investment may be more than offset by the countervailing drag of a highly distorted tax system. Second, the corollary to this is that the payoffs to tax reforms that are focused on removing distortions in the system may be particularly high. We explore these policy implications in Section 10.4.

10.4 Public Investment and Public Finance

In this section we draw heavily on recent work by Adam and Bevan (2014) to examine the recurrent cost problem using a dynamic general equilibrium macroeconomic model of a representative low-income country. To explore the interactions between O&M expenditures, a distortionary tax regime, and alternative fiscal reforms, they use the model to examine the effects of a public investment surge under alternative fiscal finance rules, ranging from fiscal reforms—both tax and budgetary reforms—to alternative debt-financing strategies. This analysis is conducted on a version of the Adam and Bevan (2014) model that is calibrated to the broad structural characteristics of Tanzania. The analysis demonstrates clearly the potentially large social returns on fiscal reforms and the institutional arrangements for budgeting and implementing operations and maintenance expenditures.

10.4.1 *The Model*

The model is of a small open economy characterized by two sectors, tradables and non-tradables.[18] The model is 'real' in the sense that the monetary side of the economy is not considered, so for example, it does not examine inflation or nominal exchange rate dynamics.[19] Production in each sector is a function of public and private capital and of labour, and is carried out by competitive, price-taking firms. There are no intermediate goods so that gross output is equal to value added. There are constant returns to the private factors and increasing returns to all three factors taken together. There is steady trend growth in productivity, uniform across sectors. Public debt may be domestic, external concessional, or external non-concessional. The external cost of capital is subject to an exogenous world interest rate, compounded by a country risk premium that rises with the government's external indebtedness. Domestic interest rates are determined in local bond markets. On the household side, the model distinguishes between 'rationed' and 'unrationed' households. The former own none of the physical capital in the economy and thus cannot access financial markets; with no capacity to save or borrow are constrained to consume their current income, which consists of their net-of-tax labour income, remittances from overseas, and any transfers from government. In terms of fiscal policy, government actions impact on these households through three channels: first and most directly via decisions on transfers; second, through changes in taxes on labour and consumption; and third, through the investment and maintenance of public capital. This third channel is critical: increased public capital raises the productivity of private capital and labour. With an inelastic supply of labour this drives up real wages.

By contrast, the 'unrationed' households own physical capital and have access to financial markets. These households therefore allocate income between investment in physical capital, bonds, and consumption in order to maximize an additive intertemporal utility function. In the version used in this chapter, we assume full employment of labour. This is a simplification, and one that has implications for how we think of fiscal distortions (see Section 10.5) but does not affect the principal messages of the analysis.[20]

We adopt a stylized representation of the aforementioned tax system. Taxes are the fundamental fiscal instrument in the model and are used to make transfers to citizens, to service debt, and to finance public investment. In principle, the model can accommodate a rich menu of taxation with differentiated taxes across the main tax bases—that is, on consumption (a VAT), trade (tariffs and duties), labour (pay-as-you-earn tax (PAYE)), and capital (corporate income taxes and withholding taxes on interest income). To focus on the core question concerning the degree of distortion in the tax system (and hence the payoff to tax reforms that reduce distortions), we opt for a stylized representation of the system by reducing it to a two-tax structure. Essentially, revenue can be raised from: (i) a uniform consumption tax, which features a very low degree of distortion (in the sense that it carries a low deadweight loss and functions essentially as a lump-sum tax that does not distort production and investment decisions); (ii) a more distortionary tax on incomes; or (iii) both. The second policy option is again uniform across capital and labour, which in this simple value-added model means it is equivalent to an output tax. Essentially, the model implies that an output tax is distortionary across steady states. An output tax drives a wedge between the net-of-tax marginal product of capital and the cost of capital. This results in lower private capital and hence lower output, real wages, and consumption.

A second feature of the tax regime is that not all of the revenue that a given tax rate would raise, given the tax base, actually accrues to government as spendable resources. This leakage may reflect a range of issues, including the costs of tax administration, the existence of tax exemptions, tax avoidance and tax evasion, and indeed some degree of corruption. Including leakages of this sort allow us to reflect accurately the 'paradox' of the Tanzanian tax system in which relatively low revenue mobilization rates coexist with high marginal tax rates facing firms and households.[21] This paradox leverages up the pre-existing distortions in the tax regime but, at the same time, allows us to explore tax reforms addressing both the structure of taxation and tax administration.

The model is focused on public investment and the related operations and maintenance expenditures. As a result, other public expenditures are not modelled other than as a transfer to private consumers. Critically, the costs of public investment are not restricted to the upfront capital cost and associated financing; they also include ongoing recurrent costs for operations and maintenance, and since—even when adequately maintained—capital depreciates, costs include the cost of future replacement. The scale of recurrent costs per dollar of investment varies very significantly with the type of investment, tending to be much higher for social than for economic infrastructure (Heller, 1991). In addition, for reasons ranging from the technical to the political, government is typically unable or unwilling to fully recover these recurrent costs through user charges. As a consequence, public investment creates fiscal burdens necessitating finance and its potential sources.

Moreover, the public investment programme may be inefficient, both in the quality of public investment and in the sense that an additional dollar of public investment may not lead to an additional dollar of public capital being installed. As with the 'recurrent cost problem' described above, there is always a risk that these inefficiencies may all worsen during a phase of accelerated investment, whether this is occasioned by an ambitious investment programme or the need to replace destroyed assets. There may also be adjustment costs during this phase, associated with capacity limitations in the private and public sectors, which raise the unit cost of investment.

10.4.2 *Firms and Technology*

Firms produce output using a Cobb–Douglas technology to convert labour, private capital, and *effective* infrastructure capital (a non-excludable public good) into output. There are constant returns to private factors but increasing returns when private factors combine with public capital. Both public and private capital is built by combining imported machines and a non-traded input (e.g., construction) in fixed proportions. Competitive profit-maximizing firms equate the (private) marginal value product of each input to its factor price. Labour is inter-sectorally mobile, so wage rates are equalized across sectors. Capital is sector-specific, but at equilibrium, the allocation across sectors ensures net-of-tax rentals are equalized. Critically, taxes on factors drive wedges between private and social values. In the presence of a tax on labour, the real wage is reduced below the marginal product of labour.

10.4.3 *The Government and Operations and Management Expenditures*

Government provides public infrastructure and makes transfers to both kinds of households. To finance these activities, it raises taxes on domestic economic activity, borrows from domestic and external creditors, and receives concessional aid and grants from development partners. Government may also levy user charges on households for the use of public capital.

Operations and maintenance expenditures affect public capital through two channels in the model. On the one hand, deficient maintenance expenditure leads to an increase in the rate at which the public capital stock depreciates through time. On the other hand, deficient operations expenditure reduces the flow of output produced by the current stock of public capital, implying reduced depreciation. Both effects can be temporary so that a return to 'full' maintenance and operations expenditures restores the (technical minimum) depreciation rate and the full flow of output, respectively.[22] Estimates of the scale of 'efficient' O&M costs are extremely sparse. We calibrate this to values that are broadly consistent with Heller's (1991) 'r-coefficient' estimates. These are estimates of the required annual recurrent expenditure in dollars per dollar of installed capital and vary widely depending on the type of public capital involved. Roughly speaking, required O&M expenditures are lower per dollar of installed physical infrastructure such as roads which require maintenance but little by way of operations, and higher on social infrastructure such as rural schools and health centres which are simple (and cheap) to build but require sustained operations expenditures, on teachers, nurses, school books, drug supplies, electricity, and so forth, to be effective. The key point emerging from this analysis is that 'fully efficient' O&M expenditures are typically of the same order of magnitude as the level of gross public investment: in other words, every dollar of public investment the government undertakes needs to be matched by a dollar of recurrent expenditure to efficiently operate and maintain this capital. For the model, this means efficient O&M costs account for approximately 5 per cent of GDP.

There is no empirical evidence on the scale of the losses inflicted by inadequate O&M, so the assumptions made here are necessarily speculative.

However, we believe that these are probably quite conservative: in the simulations reported in Section 10.5, the measure of excess depreciation is set so that if maintenance expenditures are at only 80 per cent of the efficient level, the depreciation rate rises to 6 per cent per annum. Even if maintenance were abandoned entirely, the depreciation rate would only double, for example from 5 per cent to 10 per cent. As regards operational expenditures, we make a proportionality assumption, which again seems on the conservative side.[23]

The problem may of course be temporarily worsened during an investment surge if that leads to fiscal difficulties, but on the other hand, a programme of reforms to public financial management may yield a sustained improvement in the relationship. We note but do not explore these specific variations, although the model is capable of so doing.

10.4.4 *Public Sector Budget Constraint*

Combining these elements we derive the government's budget constraint. The government spends on debt service, infrastructure investment, associated operations and maintenance, and transfers to the private sector. It collects tax revenue from consumption taxes and from taxes on capital and labour, net of 'leakages' to the private sector in all cases. Additional revenue accrues from grants from development partners and from user fees for infrastructure services. When revenues fall short of expenditures, the resulting deficit is financed through domestic borrowing, external concessional borrowing, external commercial borrowing, or by drawing down net international reserves. Given the exogenously determined paths for public infrastructure investment (that is, concessional and non-concessional sovereign external borrowing), the residual fiscal adjustment falls on domestic taxes and domestic debt. Debt sustainability necessarily requires that domestic debt is bounded (for example, we may assume that the domestic debt is constrained to converge to a constant share of trend GDP) which means that taxes eventually adjust to cover the entire gap, conditional on the long-run domestic debt ratio. Finally, we assume that taxes cannot adjust instantaneously to their new target levels so that over the adjustment path domestic debt may overshoot its steady-state level.

10.5 Simulation Results

To focus on the core questions of the interaction of fiscal reforms and public investment, the analysis is built around a central policy experiment in which public investment is raised by 50 per cent—from 6 per cent to 9 per cent of initial GDP—and kept at this level. Initially, this increased public investment is financed through domestic taxation; later the gross (additional) public investment profile is matched by non-concessional external borrowing. In the former case, tax reform is modelled as a transition from a highly distortionary output tax to a low-distortion consumption tax, although in principle any blended tax structure could be examined.

Table 10.1 describes the key features of the model in the context of a tax-financed public investment surge, comparing a baseline case in which the tax structure is, in effect, non-distortionary with the case where the tax system is represented by a distortionary output tax set at an initial rate of 17 per cent, to reflect a typical tax revenue to GDP ratio in low-income countries. Given the parameterization of the original model, a consumption tax at a rate of 20 per cent generates broadly similar revenue. The financing of the investment surge is executed entirely via changes in the relevant tax rate. Efficient operations expenditures and efficient maintenance expenditures are both equal to 2.5 cents per dollar of installed public capital, so that O&M outgoings are 5 cents per dollar. No cost recovery takes place.

Column [1] describes the effect of the investment surge in the 'undistorted' case. The increase in public investment (3 percentage points of GDP) crowds

Table 10.1. Public investment, O&M and distortionary taxation
Public infrastructure investment increased by 3% of initial GDP Steady-state comparisons

	O&M	Consumption Tax Baseline [a]		Output Tax Deficient [b]	
		[1]	[2]	[3]	[4]
	Notes				
Initial GDP	[c]	100.00	80.81	80.81	80.81
Increase in effective public capital	[d]	50.0%	50.0%	37.8%	14.8%
Crowding-in	[e]	2.53	1.5	1.34	−0.89
GDP growth	[f]	14.6%	13.0%	9.6%	1.9%
Consumption growth	[f]	10.7%	9.2%	6.2%	−1.6%
Real product wage					
Initial		1.00	0.66	0.66	0.66
Final		1.14	0.73	0.71	0.64
Final tax rate	[g]				
Consumption		22.6%	–	–	–
Output		–	18.6%	18.8%	20.1%
O&M costs as % GDP					
Initial		2.0%	2.0%	2.0%	2.0%
Final		2.5%	2.6%	2.3%	2.3%

Notes: [a] baseline O&M set to 80% of fully technical efficient levels; [b] deficient O&M sees maintenance expenditures (column [3]) and both operations and maintenance expenditures (column [4]) held at baseline levels despite increased public investment. Evaluated over the total capital stock, O&M rates are 67% of fully efficient levels; [c] Per capita GDP. With fixed labour supply, differences in initial GDP reflect impact of tax rate on optimal steady-state private investment rate; [d] increase in effective capital; with O&M at baseline levels, effective capital increases by 50% (reflecting increase in investment rate). Deficient O&M expenditures lower stock of effective public capital; [e] increase in private capital formation per dollar of net public investment; [f] percentage change per capita between steady-states; [g] initial consumption tax rate = 20% and initial output tax rate = 17%

in private investment, which rises by US$2.53 for each US$1 of public investment. Per capita GDP increases by 14.6 per cent between steady states in a broadly balanced fashion. (Although not reported in the table, the real exchange rate appreciates by just over 2 per cent between steady states in this case.) Real product wages increase by 14 per cent, which, combined with the higher level of public capital, causes the budgetary cost of O&M to rise from 2.0 per cent to 2.5 per cent of (the now larger) current GDP, which in turn requires the consumption tax rate to increase by around 2.6 percentage points of GDP.

Column [2] shows the direct comparison between the non-distortionary consumption tax and the distortionary output tax. The first point to note is that initial GDP is more than 19 per cent lower when the economy operates under an output tax regime, even with efficient O&M expenditures. The reason is simply that a distortionary tax regime lowers the private sector's net return to capital, thereby lowering the economy wide equilibrium capital–labour ratio and, by the same mechanism, the real product wage. The tax distortion also results in lower growth in GDP and consumption in response to the investment surge, again due to the lower rate of private capital accumulation. (Private capital is crowded-in by the infrastructure investment, but the effect is only about 60 per cent as strong as that achieved under the consumption tax.) The direct costs of financing the investment surge, plus the additional fiscal burden of O&M expenditures, raise the output tax rate by around 1.6 percentage points, while the *ex post* cost of O&M is slightly higher than in column [1], since the dollar expenditures are spread over a smaller GDP base.

Columns [3] and [4] show the effect of the public investment surge when unaccompanied by a commensurate increase in O&M expenditures. For simplicity, the comparison is with the distortionary tax case shown in column [2]. In this case, public investment is again increased by 3 per cent of initial GDP, but now neither maintenance expenditures alone (column [3]) nor operations and maintenance expenditures together (column [4]) rise in line with the additional installed public capital. When maintenance expenditures are deficient, the public capital stock is allowed to depreciate more rapidly than its technical maximum rate; when operations expenditures do not keep pace, the flow of public capital services (i.e., the effectiveness of the public capital stock) deteriorates correspondingly.[24]

Failing to maintain O&M is extremely costly. 'Economizing' on maintenance expenditures (column 3) is directly equivalent to lowering the effective investment rate per dollar of investment expenditure, but since the investment expenditure itself plus the ongoing maintenance have still to be financed, the policy adds further pressure on public finances. Economizing on both operations and maintenance is even more damaging. For the model calibration presented in Table 10.1, deficient O&M means the increase in effective capital *for the same gross investment surge* is greatly reduced which, combined with the now much higher distortionary tax rate (which rises by 3 percentage points of GDP), results in a crowding out of private capital, a decline in real wages and in consumption, and only a very marginal increase in output, reflecting the demand-side effects of the (relatively ineffective) public investment surge (as suggested by Warner, 2014). This is as clear an illustration of the false economy of the recurrent cost problem as one could see.

Building on this evidence, Table 10.2 examines the implications of a set of fiscal reforms, starting with measures that reverse latent inefficiencies in the level of operations or maintenance expenditures, then considering a reform of the tax regime, and finally incorporating both. The tax reform experiment is a radical one and consists of the complete replacement of the distortionary output tax with a non-distortionary consumption tax. Clearly this is a carica-ture of any actual tax reform package, but it is consistent with elements of the tax reforms across many low-income countries in the 1990s and early 2000s that saw highly distortionary elements of tax regimes eliminated and replaced by valued-added taxes (see Kloeden, 2011; Keen, 2012). The present treatment can be thought of as providing an upper bound on the gains from reform. Likewise the reforms are characterized as stroke-of-the-pen changes to budget-ary processes that ensure O&M expenditures are pegged to their efficient levels. A useful reference case for this table is column [2] of Table 10.1, in which both operations and maintenance are at only 80 per cent efficiency and the economy operates under an output tax. That column illustrates the growth effects of a public investment surge. The key difference here is there is *no new investment*. The macroeconomic and growth effects are driven entirely by fiscal reforms. Column [1] of Table 10.2 reports the effect of comprehensive O&M reforms without adjustment to the initial tax regime; column [2] the effect of the tax reform (with no O&M reforms); and column [3] the combined effect.

Table 10.2. Fiscal reforms
No public investment surge steady-state comparisons

	Notes	Budget reform [1]	Tax reform [2]	Combined [3]
Crowding-in	[a]	2.64	–	17.21
GDP growth	[b]	14.6%	29.2%	46.1%
Consumption growth	[b]	14.4%	23.9%	40.2%
Product wage growth		18.2%	83.6%	109.1%
Final output tax rate	[c]	15.5%		
Final consumption tax rate	[c]		16.5%	15.4%
Final O&M costs as % GDP	[d]	2.5%	1.48%	1.9%

Notes: See Table 10.1. [a] Crowding in coefficient cannot be computed in column [2] because public capital stock does not increase; [b] percentage change per capita between steady-states; [c] initial consumption tax rate = 20% and initial output tax rate = 17%; [d] initial O&M costs 2.0% of initial GDP

From an initial position, where both operations and maintenance are 20 per cent below their efficient level and the economy operates under an output tax, reforms that restore efficient levels of O&M spending generate increases of around 15 per cent in both real output and consumption between steady states (column [1]). Recall that there is no increase in the net public investment rate here, so the entire growth effect comes from the increase in effectiveness of the existing public capital stock, which in turn raises the productivity of private factors of production, thus increasing private investment and driving up real wages. But crucially, although the budget must bear higher O&M costs absolutely and as a proportion of GDP (since the budgetary reforms are now committing government to meet their fully efficient expenditures), the efficiency gains resulting from efficient operations and maintenance for public capital stock crowds-in private investment and allows these higher budgetary costs to be financed at a lower rate of output tax, which falls from 17 per cent to 15.5 per cent of GDP.

When accompanied by a wholesale tax reform, the output and welfare gains are even more substantial. A deficit neutral tax reform results in aggregate consumption rising by almost 24 per cent across steady states, and by 40 per cent if accompanied by reforms to O&M spending that operate on the intensive margin of public capital. The removal of tax on output induces a very substantial increase in private investment across steady states, which provides the mechanism for output growth. For example, where tax reform is accompanied by O&M reforms, the capital stock in the exportable sector rises by 132 per cent between steady states and by 106 per cent in the non-tradable sector. The corresponding surge in absorption sharply drives up real product wages, measured in terms of the tradable goods (by over 100 per cent in the comprehensive reform case shown in column [3]), although the effect on real consumption wages is somewhat dampened by the sharp appreciation of the real exchange rate, which in this instance is approximately 12 per cent above its initial steady-state value (not shown in Table 10.2).

The fiscal consequences of reform are highly attractive. As noted, the restoration of efficient O&M allows for a modest decline in the steady-state output tax rates, from 17 per cent to 15.5 per cent, while in the case of a tax reform, the growth effects are sufficiently powerful to ensure both that the O&M cost share in GDP falls and that the consumption tax rate required to balance the budget settles at around 15.4 per cent. In other words, the economy can achieve a lower rate of tax on a narrower tax base.

10.5.1 *Debt Financing*

The analysis to this point has focused on public investment that is entirely tax-financed. In terms of the core fiscal analysis, the insights from

Tables 10.1 and 10.2 go through for the case of debt-financed public investment. The key role of public debt here is to allow the borrower (i.e., government) to break the concurrent link between expenditure and taxation, so as to allow for a different—usually smoother—inter-temporal path of taxation and, hence, consumption. Borrowing thus permits low tax rates early on, even though the logic of the inter-temporal budget constraint means they have to rise in the future to service the debt. However, to the extent that the growth- and welfare-reducing effects of distortionary taxation is usually thought to rise in the square of the change in the tax rate, a smoother path for taxation may confer substantial welfare gains even if the long-run tax rate is permanently higher.[25] But if the government's revenue position is confidently expected to improve over time as a consequence of improved tax administration (and other fiscal reforms), the case for borrowing may be strengthened, although this line of thinking, of course, assumes away risk and incentive effects.

Clearly, if the government is able to fund the public investment surge through concessional financing, the steady-state and dynamic outcomes look rather different. Concessional external finance allows the economy to enjoy a consistently and permanently higher level of consumption than under either tax or non-concessional debt financing, as well as a lower increase in the required tax rate. Moreover, since the required tax rate is also lower at all points on the dynamic path, the policy maker is no longer required to trade lower current taxes off against higher future taxes: here the concessional financing path unambiguously dominates both the tax-only and non-concessional financing outcomes. It follows that this dominance will also hold when the investment pulse is financed by a portfolio of external concessional and non-concessional financing, so long as the share of concessional financing is high enough.

10.6 Conclusions and Looking Forward

The preceding analysis has adopted a stylized approach to two staples of public finance theory, that taxation inflicts deadweight costs and that public investment imposes ongoing budgetary costs for O&M. The analysis demonstrates that these public finance considerations have material consequences for the public investment, debt sustainability, and growth. But it also highlights a set of highly practical fiscal policy challenges that need to be addressed if the substantial fiscal reforms of recent years are to be converted into sustained growth, both in the context of an increased level of public investor or on their own. The first challenge is the need to address the 'recurrent cost' problem to ensure that the investment in public infrastructure that is widely seen as integral to any future growth strategy is accompanied by sufficient and predictable resources allocated to the operations and maintenance of the capital stock. This requires both improved systems of planning and budgeting—many of which are already in place—but also a greater political and organizational commitment to resisting the easy and short-term expedient of paring back O&M expenditures when fiscal pressures arise. Except for the most myopic political regimes this is, as the analysis clearly shows, a false economy. The second challenge is the recognition that the gains to effective tax reforms, both to the structure of taxation itself and its administration may be substantial. Critically, however, reforms should be seen not simply as a means of improving current fiscal aggregates but more importantly as laying the foundations for enhancing the complementarity between public investment on the one hand, and private sector investment and growth on the other.

Acknowledgements

This chapter draws heavily on joint work by Christopher Adam and David Bevan (see Adam and Bevan, 2014). We acknowledge David's substantial contribution but absolve him of any errors of omission or commission that may remain in this chapter.

Notes

1. What constitutes legitimate minimal protections, and hence the legitimate reach of taxation, is contested and depends on context. For example, do these include protection against ignorance, ill-health, environmental degradation? This debate is beyond the scope of this chapter.
2. Foster and Briceno-Garmendia (2010).
3. See, for example, Rioja (2003), who builds on earlier work by Heller (1974); Gray and Martens (1983); and Howell (1985), among others.
4. There are, of course, many subtleties in this simple presentation. The fiscal balance should strictly be net of income from seigniorage, while we have also abstracted from exchange rate effects, revaluation effects, and other complexities associated with a complex, multi-currency debt portfolio. These effects are subsumed in the cost of capital term, r_t.
5. GDP growth data from Penn World Tables (version 8.0).
6. See Nord et al. (2009).
7. 'IMF Regional Economic Outlook', October 2015.
8. The relevant measure is the real exchange rate since what matters for debt dynamics is the resource cost, measured in units of real GDP, of servicing the external component of sovereign debt.
9. See Shkaratan (2010: table 5).

10. Understanding the evolution of the fiscal picture is complicated slightly by the major revision in GDP published in 2014. This long-awaited fifth revision of Tanzania's GDP data, which re-based GDP to 2007, led to an upward revision in nominal GDP at market prices of 27.8 per cent. Relative to earlier analyses (including recent reports published by the Ministry of Finance and some regional measures published by the East African Community) this adjustment to the denominator reduces the scale of government operations relative to GDP; it makes the fiscal deficit and public debt figures look much better but it also high-lights the relatively low level of revenue mobilization (and the more modest scale of public infrastructure investment). Because the new GDP series was not back-casted before 2005, the fiscal aggregates presented in this chapter are scaled by the 'old' GDP data, unless explicitly stated.

11. Clearly, with no exemptions or zero-rating, so that all of value added is indeed taxed so that the average and marginal rates coincide, a VAT rate of 20 per cent would raise 20 per cent of GDP in revenue. In all tax regimes, VAT exemptions, including for investment, and zero-rating, lowers revenue prod-uctivity relative to this benchmark, but even so Tanzania's collection rate is particularly low.

12. For goods that are VAT-exempt, either because the goods are exempted from VAT in their own right, or because the supplier operates below the VAT threshold, no tax is chargeable on the final sale, but equally no VAT is recoverable on inputs. For zero-rated goods, on the other hand, a tax of 0 per cent is levied on the sale of goods but payment of VAT on inputs can be reclaimed.

13. The classic example is in the mining industry in Zambia where zero-rated copper exports are produced using enormous quantities of taxable inputs, most notably electricity, which results in VAT refunds to the mining industry, representing a large share of VAT receipts gathered in from other sectors of the economy.

14. National Budget, 2015.

15. The exception, of course, in a well-designed tax regime, is where the distortionary effect of the tax is exactly why it is employed to correct an externality. In this case the distortionary taxation leads to greater efficiency.

16. It is not always the case that the marginal cost of funds exceeds unity; in a poorly designed tax system, raising a less distortionary tax to allow for the reduction in a more distortionary tax elsewhere will lead to an MCF of less than unity.

17. This observation comes from the simple partial equilibrium analyses of the dead-weight loss arising from taxation. Conventionally, the deadweight loss of a tax is given by the 'Harberger triangle', the height of which is given by the tax rate and the base is proportional to the height. It follows that the area defining the welfare loss is $\frac{1}{2}t^*bt=(b/2)t^2$ which rises in the square of the tax rate.

18. A full description of the model can be found in Adam and Bevan (2014).

19. In other words, there are no nominal rigidities or money illusion in the economy so that resource allocation is fully described by movements in relative prices (real exchange rates, real wages, real interest rates).

20. At a technical level allowing for an elastic household labour supply is a simple modification; doing so means that, in contrast to the currently model, by altering

labour supplies, the consumption tax is distortionary across steady states as well as on the transitional path.

21. Firms and households always face the *nominal* tax rates when making choices over factor allocations and consumption decisions: tax revenues that are 'retained' rather than remitted to government are treated as if they were lump-sum transfers from government. What this means is that in the face of leakages, a given government revenue requirement entails a structure of nominal tax rates that is higher and thus more distortionary that in the absence of any leakages.

22. This is a simplifying assumption: in practice, the capital stock may be so degraded as a result of deficient maintenance expenditures that it cannot be restored to 'full' efficiency without rebuilding afresh.

23. See the discussion in Adam and Bevan (2014) on the strengths and limitations of this assumption of linearity.

24. In the Adam and Bevan (2014) model the effective O&M coverage is simply the total O&M spend spread over the installed capital stock. To the extent that the O&M does not keep pace with the rising public capital stock, the average declines so that both the marginal and infra marginal capital stock depreciates more rapidly and delivers lower per unit capital services to private factors.

25. The exact nature of this trade-off depends crucially on how quickly the debt is financed, both absolutely and relative to the productivity of the investment it was acquired to finance.

References

Adam, C. and Bevan, D. (2014). 'Public Investment, Public Finance and Growth: the Impact of Distortionary Taxation, Recurrent Costs and Incomplete Appropriability', IMF Working Paper WP14/73.

Ahmad, E. and Stern, N. (1984). 'The Theory of Reform and Indian Indirect Taxes', *Journal of Public Economics* 25(3): 259–98.

Auriol, E. and Warlters, M. (2012). 'The Marginal Cost of Public Funds and Tax Reform in Africa', *Journal of Development Economics* 97(1): 58–72.

Bevan, D. (2010). 'Fiscal Policy Issues for Tanzania', IGC Working Paper 10:01.

Bevan, D. (2012). 'Fiscal Challenges Facing Tanzania', IGC Working Paper.

Browning, E. (1976). 'The Marginal Cost of Public Funds', *Journal of Political Economy* 84(2): 283–98.

Coulson, A. (2013). *Tanzania: A Political Economy*. Oxford: Oxford University Press.

Emran, M. and Stiglitz, J. (2005). 'On Selective Indirect Tax Reform in Developing Countries', *Journal of Public Economics* 89(4): 599–623.

Foster, V. and Briceno-Garmendia, C. (2010). 'Africa's Infrastructure: A Time for Transition', World Bank, Washington D.C.

Gray, C. and Martens, A. (1983). 'The Political Economy of the "Recurrent Cost Problem" in the West African Sahel', *World Development* 11(2): 101–17.

Heller, P. S. (1974). 'Public Investment in LDCs with Recurrent Cost Constraint: the Kenyan Case', *Quarterly Journal of Economics* 88(May): 251–77.

Heller, P. S. (1991). 'Operations and maintenance'. In: *IMF Public Expenditure Handbook*. Washington, D.C.: IMF.

Howell, J. (1985). 'Recurrent Costs and Agricultural Development', Overseas Development Institute, London.

IMF (International Monetary Fund) (2011). 'Revenue Mobilization in Developing Countries', Fiscal Affairs Department, IMF, Washington, D.C.

IMF (2013). 'Crises Yesterday and Today', presented at the IMF Annual Research Conference, 8 November 2013. Available at: <http://www.imf.org/external/np/res/seminars/2013/arc/> (last accessed 10 June 2016).

IMF (2015). 'African Regional Economic Outlook', October 2015, IMF, Washington D.C.

Keen, M. (2012). 'Taxation and Development; Again'. IMF Working Paper 12/220.

Kloeden, D. (2011). 'Tax Policy and Administration Technical Assistance'. IMF Fiscal Affairs Department Revenue Mobilization and Development Conference, IMF Washington, D.C., April.

Langford, B. and Ohlenburg, T. (2015). 'Tax Revenue Potential and Effort: An Empirical Investigation', IGC Working Paper.

Ministry of Finance, Government of Tanzania (2013). 'Public Expenditure Review, Tax Exemption Study'.

Nord, R., Sobolev, Y., Dunn, D., Hajdenberg, A., Hobdari, N., Maziad, S., and Roudet, S. (2009). 'Tanzania: The Story of an African Transition', IMF, Washington D.C.

Prichard, W., Cobham, A., and Goodall, A. (2014). 'The ICTD Government Revenue Dataset', International Centre of Tax and Development Working Paper 19.

Rioja, F. K. (2003). 'Filling Potholes: Macroeconomic Effects of Maintenance versus New Investments in Public Infrastructure', *Journal of Public Economics* 87: 2281–304.

Shkaratan, M. (2010). 'Tanzania's Infrastructure: A Continental Perspective', AICD Country Report, World Bank, Washington, D.C.

Thwaites, G. (2015). 'Why Are Real Interest Rates So Low? Secular Stagnation and the Relative Price of Investment Goods', Mimeo, LSE and Bank of England.

Warner, A. M. (2014). 'Public Investment as an Engine of Growth', IMF Working Paper WP/14/148.

World Bank (2015). 'Tanzania Economic Update: Why Should Tanzanians Pay Taxes? The Unavoidable Need to Finance Economic Development', World Bank Working Paper 97720.

11

Monetary Policy in Tanzania

Accomplishments and the Road Ahead

Pantaleo J. Kessy, Johnson Nyella, and Stephen A. O'Connell

The reserve-money programming framework that has successfully guided monetary policy in Tanzania over the past two decades is on the cusp of what is arguably its first major change—a transition from monetary aggregates to interest rates as the operational target of policy, in the context of taking on many of the core elements of inflation targeting. We focus in this chapter on the road ahead and the issues the Bank of Tanzania (BoT) will confront as it makes this transition. Our focus throughout will be on the conduct of national monetary policy, noting that the BoT's direction of travel is fully consistent with the convergence process towards East African Monetary Union.

Our central argument is that the BoT is continuing to evolve towards a modern system of what Bernanke and Mishkin (1997) called constrained discretion, in which monetary policy provides a strong anchor for inflation expectations while also performing a role in stabilizing the real economy. We will argue that a clearer focus on interest rates can improve the transparency of policy and strengthen the BoT's leverage over inflation—and also that it can enhance the development of the financial sector, a key secondary objective of monetary policy in Tanzania. We begin, however, with the origins of the current system and the sources of its success to date.

11.1 The Monetary/Fiscal Accord of the Mid-1990s

The current framework for monetary policy dates from the fiscal and legislative reforms of the mid-1990s. By the early 1990s, a decade of market-based reforms had restored the role of market prices throughout the economy, including the exchange rate and interest rates (Chapter 2, this volume). Exchange controls had been eliminated for current account transactions, privatization of the banking sector was underway, and the government bond market was being developed. A situation of *fiscal dominance* nonetheless persisted, in which the banking system and the central bank were obliged to finance any public-sector spending not covered by tax revenues or foreign grants. Domestic financing therefore ballooned when the government's commitment to revenue mobilization and expenditure control slackened in the early 1990s and conflict with external donors emerged (Mpango, 2002).

The Bank of Tanzania was operating at that time under the 1978 Amendments to the Bank of Tanzania Act, which obliged the Bank to support the development priorities of the government (Appendix Table 11A.1 shows the relevant provisions). Market-based reforms and privatization of the banking system had allowed the BoT to retreat from the wide range of quasi-fiscal roles it had assumed in the long wake of the Arusha Declaration,[1] but the BoT arguably had neither the mandate nor the political independence in the early 1990s to contain inflation in the face of large fiscal deficits. To do so would have required holding back overall money growth, which would have required a sharp and costly contraction in bank lending to the private sector. What was needed to bring down inflation at a tolerable cost to the economy— and to open the space for a monetary policy capable of delivering price stability on an ongoing basis—was an accord that would lock in fiscal discipline in the near term while placing the BoT at arm's length from future demands for excessive monetary finance.

The key elements of the accord that emerged in Tanzania in the mid-1990s were an explicit acknowledgment, at the highest levels of government, that inflation was being driven by the monetary finance of fiscal deficits; an International Monetary Fund (IMF)-supported agreement that directly prevented monetary finance by imposing a monthly cash budget on the spending ministries; and a new Bank of Tanzania Act (1995) that bolstered the institutional independence of the BoT.[2]

Section 5.3 of the BoT Act of 1995 elevated price stability to unambiguous status as the chief objective of monetary policy in Tanzania. The increased clarity that this conferred may have made little difference at first to the disinflation that got underway in 1995/96; and on paper, the BoT's capability to pursue its mandate appeared to be undermined by a passage in the 1995 Act— never activated, and eliminated in the Bank of Tanzania Act of 2006—that authorized the Minister of Finance to conduct monetary policy unilaterally for a period of up to a year in the event of 'irreconcilable disagreement' with the Board of the Central Bank (see Appendix Table 11A.1). But the cost of that disinflation to the aggregate real economy—looking at Figure 11.1—appears to have been extremely mild. By comparison with the growth that was taking

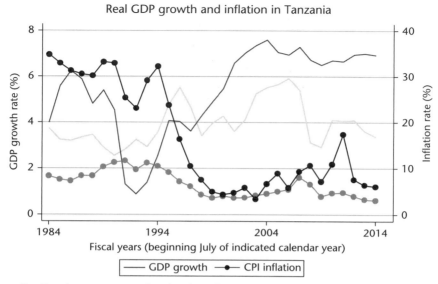

Real GDP growth and inflation in Tanzania

Grey lines show average growth and median inflation for 114 emerging/developing countries.

Figure 11.1. Inflation and growth in Tanzania, 1984/85–2014/15
Source: BoT and IMF October 2015 World Economic Outlook database online.

place in other developing countries, Tanzania's cost was centred in 1996/97, when growth was unchanged in Tanzania while it rose in other countries, and completely absent by 1997/98, when Tanzania's GDP growth rate did fall by a small amount, but by less than that in the rest of the developing world.

The buoyancy of Tanzania's real economy in the face of a concerted money-based disinflation is at odds with the typical experience in emerging-market economies, where stabilizations accomplished through tight monetary policy have been associated with a demand-driven recession as high interest rates take a toll on aggregate demand (Calvo and Vegh, 1999). Tanzania's milder experience may reflect the prevalence of flexible prices in Tanzania's large agricultural and urban informal sectors, along with the impact of direct government controls over some influential prices (e.g., for public utilities) and wages (e.g., in the public sector)—these factors may have facilitated rapid disinflation without requiring a major contraction in aggregate demand. Structural reforms helped to reduce inflationary pressures from the supply side (Chapter 2, this volume), and donor inflows softened the underlying fiscal adjustment. But the low aggregate cost of Tanzania's disinflation is also consistent with a favourable credibility effect. In this interpretation, participants in the economy interpreted the multifaceted accord as a durable change in the fiscal and monetary policy regime, and adjusted their inflationary expectations accordingly. This adjustment in expectations allowed inflation to fall without requiring a sharp economic contraction (Sargent, 1982).

11.2 Reserve-Money Programming since 1995

The operational legacy of the mid-90s accord, in terms of BoT practice, was the reserve-money-targeting framework that has governed the conduct of monetary policy over the two subsequent decades. The hallmark of this framework is a set of monthly ceilings for the growth in reserve money that are derived from the inflation and growth targets in the government's annual budget.

Three main considerations favored the choice of reserve-money targeting in Tanzania, both during the disinflation episode and after inflation had fallen into the 5 per cent range by the late 1990s (Figure 11.1).[3] The first was that any framework for price stability needs a nominal anchor, and restoring the fixed-exchange rate system for this purpose was out of the question. The government was committed to a market-determined exchange rate, having laboured over much of the previous decade to dismantle the highly distorting exchange-control regime that had emerged from the balance-of-payments crises of the 1970s. So the system would need a different nominal anchor.

Inflation itself had emerged as a possible nominal anchor in the formal inflation-targeting (IT) system introduced by the Reserve Bank of New Zealand in 1989. The Reserve Bank's framework combined an explicit numerical range for inflation with new standards of communication, transparency, and independence in central bank practice. But as of the mid-1990s, IT was regarded as an option limited to countries with well-developed financial markets and high-quality data, and with established traditions of fiscal discipline. The main alternative to the exchange rate among developing countries—and the natural choice for the BoT—was the path of a broad monetary aggregate like M2.[4]

Given a monetary aggregate as nominal anchor, a second decisive feature favoring reserve-money targeting was the rudimentary condition of Tanzanian financial markets. In a well-developed financial market, a central bank can pursue a broad monetary aggregate using either a short-term interest rate or some variant of reserve money as its operating target.[5] But interbank and short-term government bond markets were in their infancy in Tanzania in the 1990s, and large parts of the rural economy continued to operate mainly on currency. The interest-rate option was therefore unrealistic. It is only recently that the option of setting a target for a short-term interest rate, and relying on financial markets to translate the BoT's target into economy-wide lending conditions and the exchange rate and other key asset prices, has become potentially viable.

A final and non-trivial consideration in favour of reserve-money targeting grew out of its distinctive role in accomplishing the disinflation. The central focus of reforms and IMF conditionality was ending the monetary finance of fiscal deficits. The BoT had been providing this finance through its accumulation of government securities, other advances to government, and loans to commercial banks that could be on-lent to public entities. A sequence of explicit ceilings on the BoT's net domestic assets, implemented with high transparency via the cash budget and specified as IMF programme conditions, therefore played a key role in the disinflation strategy. In the context of a flexible exchange rate and a sequence of separate targets for the BoT's international reserves (the main component of the BoT's net foreign assets), these ceilings implied a target path for the *sum* of the BoT's net domestic assets and net foreign assets—in effect, for the size of the BoT's overall balance sheet. By the balance-sheet identity, this in turn meant a target path for the BoT's main liability, reserve money. Targets for reserve money therefore played a key role during the disinflation episode, simultaneously providing a nominal anchor for inflation and supporting an accord that very clearly and publicly distanced the BoT from fiscal pressures.

By the late 1990s, the success of the disinflation was clear and the question of an appropriate monetary framework could in principle have been posed anew. But the conditions emphasized in this section remained relevant, including the commitment to exchange-rate flexibility, the thinness of domestic financial markets, and the familiarity of the framework within the context of an ongoing policy dialogue with the IMF. Added to these was the basic suitability of the IMF's financial programming model to the data-poor environment of the BoT.[6] Reserve-money programming was therefore a natural choice for Tanzania even outside of a stabilization context, as it was starting in the 1990s for many low-income countries transitioning away from fixed exchange rates and developing the capacity to conduct an independent monetary policy (Berg et al., 2015).

Tanzania's system has been remarkably successful, as illustrated in Figures 11.2a and 11.2b. The BoT's primary legislative mandate, dating from the BoT Act of 1995, is to maintain 'price stability conducive to a balanced and sustainable growth of the national economy of Tanzania'.[7] This objective reflects the twofold principle that the ultimate aim of monetary policy is to provide an environment conducive to favourable performance of the real economy, and that the single most important contribution the central bank can make to this goal is to achieve price stability, defined in practice as a reasonably low and stable rate of inflation.[8] The BoT's mandate includes the crucial secondary objective, also grounded in the ultimate aim of balanced and sustainable growth, of supporting the development and stability of the financial sector (see Appendix Table 11A.1).

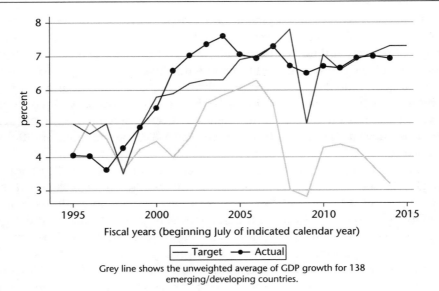

Figure 11.2a. Targeted and actual real GDP growth in Tanzania, 1995/96–2014/15
Source: BoT and IMF, April 2015 World Economic Outlook database online.

Figures 11.2a and 11.2b compare the performance of gross domestic product (GDP) growth and consumer price index (CPI) inflation to the government's annual fiscal-year targets for these variables. With the exception of 2008/09—the inaugural year of the global financial crisis—the real economy has met or out-performed the government's growth targets despite their rapid increase from 4 per cent at the outset of the disinflation to roughly 7 per cent per year by the late 1990s. By comparison with 138 other developing countries, Tanzanian GDP growth has proven remarkably robust to the global shocks of the post-2006 period, including the global food price shocks of 2006 and 2007, the global financial crisis, and the collapse of global commodity prices (particularly energy) starting in 2011. Energy prices have a special status—their recent collapse has helped the Tanzanian economy while simultaneously dampening the future prospects of the natural gas sector and serving as an early warning of the volatility to which Tanzania will be exposed if it becomes a major energy exporter.

The real-side accomplishments in Figure 11.2a provide indirect testimony to the success of monetary policy since the mid-1990s—at the very least it has apparently done little harm, unless substantially more ambitious growth targets were appropriate for the period. A similarly favourable—but somewhat more complex—story emerges in Figure 11.2b, which shows CPI inflation. Following its rapid decline during the second half of the 1990s, headline

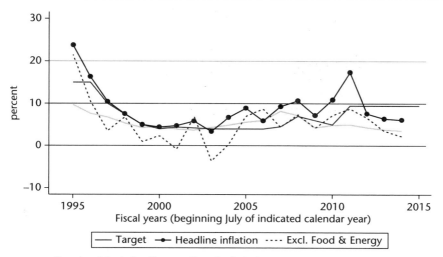

Target pertains to headline; see discussion in text.
Grey line shows median CPI inflation rate for 138 emerging/developing countries.

Figure 11.2b. Targeted and actual real CPI inflation in Tanzania, 1995/96–2014/15

Note: From FY2011/2012 to FY2015/16 the Government's inflation target has been stated as 'CPI inflation in single digits.' In the Figure we use 9.5% to denote this target. The BoT continues to maintain an internal medium-term target of 5%.

Source: BoT and IMF, April 2015 World Economic Outlook databaset online.

inflation has remained below 10 per cent in most years and within 5 points of the median for 138 developing and emerging-market countries with the exception of 2010 and 2011. Core inflation, which excludes food and energy prices, has been even lower, remaining below 10 per cent since FY1996/97.[9] Headline inflation has nonetheless remained above the BoT's 'medium-term target' of 5 per cent since FY2004/05, and some dissonance has emerged between this aspirational goal and the government's annual fiscal-year target, which has been stated since 2011 as the less demanding 'inflation in single digits'. As of 2014/15, however, inflation was once again under firm control, approaching 5 per cent on a headline basis and well below that for core.

11.2.1 *Implementing the Framework*

Figure 11.3 provides a sense of reserve-money targeting in action. Annual targets for the growth in reserve money are derived within the framework directly from the government's growth and inflation targets shown in Figures 11.2a and 11.2b. To show how, we need a bit of notation: we will use P to denote the CPI, y to denote real GDP, M to denote the monetary aggregate

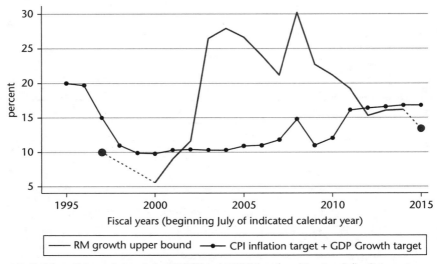

Dotted lines: RM growth targets for 1997/98 and 2015/16 are from Monetary Policy Statements. All other RM growth rates are calculated using end-yr targets and end-previous-yr actual levels.

Figure 11.3. Fiscal-year reserve-money growth targets in Tanzania
Source: Bank of Tanzania.

that serves as the BoT's intermediate target (M2 or M3), and H to denote reserve money, defined as the sum of currency in circulation and the deposits of commercial banks at the BoT. The links between the targets are then defined by two key empirical relationships within the monetary block of the IMF's financial programming model. These are $M \cdot v = P \cdot y$, where v is the velocity of the BoT's intermediate target; and $M = \mu \cdot H$, where μ is the money multiplier. Taken together, these relationships imply $P \cdot y = v \cdot \mu \cdot H$ or, using the notation $g(\cdot)$ to denote a growth rate from one year to the next,

$$\pi + g \cong g(H) + [g(v) + g(\mu)], \tag{11.1}$$

where we have used $\pi \equiv g(P)$ to denote the CPI inflation rate and $g \equiv g(y)$ to denote the growth rate of real GDP.

Equation (11.1) provides a consistency framework that relates the growth rate of reserve money to the growth rates of nominal income, velocity, and the money multiplier. The fiscal-year budget adopted by Parliament includes the inflation and real GDP growth targets for the year, which tie down $\pi + g$. The BoT then forecasts the growth rates of velocity and the money multiplier using a combination of econometric modeling and expert judgement. This leaves $g(H)$ as the growth rate of reserve money that is consistent with the government's targets.

Holding the growth rates of velocity and the money multiplier constant at their forecasted values—more on this in Sections 11.2.2 and 11.3.1—the

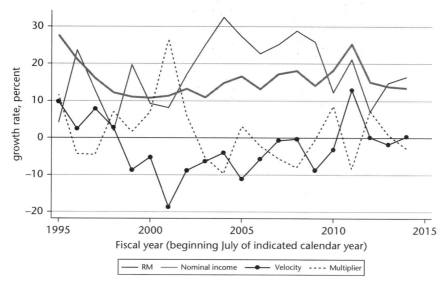

Figure 11.4. Relation of reserve money growth to nominal income growth
Source: Bank of Tanzania.

reserve-money-targeting (RMT) framework incorporates a simple account of what monetary economists call the *transmission mechanism* of monetary policy, defined as the link between the operational targets directly under the central bank's control and the ultimate economic outcomes the central bank is seeking to influence. For given values of $g(v)$ and $g(\mu)$, faster growth in reserve money drives the growth of nominal income above the government's implied target, with the split between higher π and higher g determined by the slope of the economy's short-run aggregate supply curve. To anchor inflation at the targeted level, therefore, the growth of reserve money should not exceed the value in equation (11.1).

Figure 11.3 plots the BoT's fiscal-year target for reserve-money growth against the government's target for nominal income growth. Given the relative stability of targeted nominal income growth, the wide amplitude of fluctuations in programmed reserve-money growth was driven by large and variable trends in velocity and the money multiplier (Adam and Kessy, 2011; Adam et al., 2012). While the BoT was reasonably successful at extrapolating ongoing trends over this period—Figure 11.4 shows the actual evolution of the components of equation (11.1)—some portion of the large cumulative decrease in velocity starting in the late 1990s was unanticipated, and led to a combination of programme overshoots (see Figure 11.5) and interest-rate volatility.

11.2.2 *Evidence of Flexibility in the Application of Reserve-Money Targeting*

We emphasized in the previous subsection the broad success of the reserve-money-targeting framework—first, at achieving disinflation, and subsequently at providing an anchor for inflation expectations that was consistent with rapid and stable growth of the real economy. Some portion of the latter success may be due to an ongoing policy dialogue with the IMF that allowed greater flexibility in the conduct of monetary policy than the rigid sequence of target-setting exercises and programme reviews would appear to have allowed. Table 11.1 provides some direct evidence on this point. We consider the dynamic relationship between the monthly reserve-money ceilings that were derived from semi-annual programme targets and the monthly actual performance of reserve money. For each of the two variables—the logs of target and actual reserve money—we estimate an error-correction model that shows how the variable responded to the previous month's gap between reserve money and the target. We include lags of both variables to control for other features of the dynamics, and we estimate two versions of the model, one in which the gap is simply defined by the difference between the logs of reserve money and the target, and one in which we define an adjusted gap that has a mean of zero over the full sample but has separate nonzero means before and after July 2007.[10]

Two suggestive findings stand out from this exercise.[11] First, it is clear that the framework operated to constrain monetary policy, as it was intended to do. Gaps between reserve money and the ceiling generated policy adjustments that altered reserve-money growth in a direction that would reduce the gap. This is apparent in the negative and statistically significant coefficient on the gap in columns 1 and 5. These adjustments are consistent with an interpretation of the gap as a slippage in policy that required—and produced—a corrective adjustment in policy.

Second, however, the targets themselves also appear to have responded to the lagged gap. This is not apparent in columns 2 and 6 where the gap enters symmetrically, but Granger causality runs in both directions between these variables, and when we allow for asymmetric responses—allowing targets to adjust differently depending on whether reserve money is above or below the ceiling—we find that adjustments in the target did play a systematic role in responding to observed gaps (columns 4 and 8).[12] Strikingly, these adjustments took place when the gap was positive. Their impact was therefore to partially accommodate the 'excessive' reserve money growth that had taken place.[13]

This evidence of accommodation has at least two possible interpretations, with different implications for the ability of the system to anchor inflation expectations. The first is that deviations from target were interpreted with some regularity as appropriate responses by the BoT to new information about

Table 11.1. Responses to deviations from the reserve-money ceiling

Variable	Regressions with unadjusted gap				Regressions with adjusted gap			
	log(RM)	log(Ceiling)	Log(RM)	Log(Ceiling)	log(RM)	log(Ceiling)	Log(RM)	Log(Ceiling)
Gap (t-1)	**-0.301*** -3.53 p=0.001	**0.053** 0.84 p=0.401			**-0.489*** -4.67 p=0.00	**0.081** 1.03 p=0.31		
Gap > 0 (t-1)			**-0.134** -1.01 p=0.316	**0.234**** 2.40 p=0.018			**-0.353**** -2.16 p=0.03	**0.298**** 2.44 p=0.02
Gap < 0 (t-1)			**-0.514*** -3.28 p=0.001	**-0.179** -1.56 p=0.120			**-0.607*** -4.00 p=0.00	**-0.108** -0.95 p=0.34
Month=Jul 07	**-0.025** -0.68 p=0.497	**-0.018** -0.65 p=0.519			**-0.027** -0.73 p=0.468	**-0.021** -0.76 p=0.451		
Lags	2	2	2	2	2	2	2	2
N	184	184	184	184	184	184	184	184
r2_a	0.251	0.193	0.258	0.215	0.285	0.192	0.285	0.212

Notes: * $p<0.05$; ** $p<0.01$; *** $p<0.001$. t values are below the coefficient estimates.
The unadjusted gap is the difference between the log of reserve money and the log of the reserve-money ceiling. The adjusted gap is the residual from a regression of the unadjusted gap on a constant and a dummy variable that equals 1 starting in July 2007 and zero otherwise. Monthly data are from the Bank of Tanzania.

the state of the economy—in other words, as appropriate monetary policy decisions that should not be reversed in the absence of even newer information. For example, reserve money growth might have exceeded targets because the BoT observed that money demand was rising faster, and therefore velocity falling faster, than was predicted when the targets for reserve-money growth were set. Allowing reserve money to exceed the targets was perfectly appropriate in such a situation, and would have been non-inflationary; in fact, a policy of forcing reserve-money growth back to pre-existing programme targets would have created an unnecessary contraction in credit conditions and the real economy.

The other interpretation is that the system was unwilling to absorb the political costs of correcting episodes of over-expansionary policy, and was therefore subject to a degree of inflation bias despite the presence of the IMF as an external monitor. Headline inflation does appear to be less well anchored after 2005 than before (Figure 11.5 shows the gap between headline inflation and the BoT's own medium-term target of 5 per cent). But some portion of this is driven by adverse supply shocks originating in Tanzania's large food-production sector and world energy markets. Figure 11.2b shows core inflation, which excludes food and energy prices and is often viewed as a more accurate proxy for expected inflation than headline inflation. Core inflation remains below headline over most of the period since 2005. This is

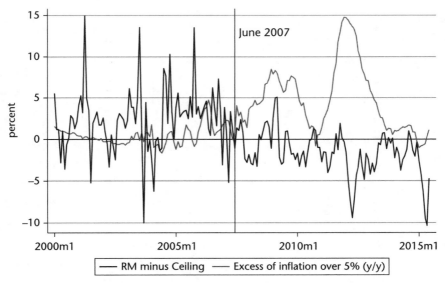

Figure 11.5. Reserve-money targeting in Tanzania
Source: Bank of Tanzania.

consistent with a policy that allowed headline inflation to reflect the first-round effects of supply shocks, while seeking to limit the transmission of these shocks into expectations and core inflation.[14] Figure 11.5 also shows the BoT's tendency to run reserve-money growth below targets after 2007, suggesting a real-time response to inflation developments that suggested faster-than-anticipated growth in velocity (equation (11.1)). Our own interpretation of Table 11.1 therefore leans more heavily on the first explanation—the argument that reserve-money targeting, as actually practiced in Tanzania, reflected a collaborative dialogue with the IMF that allowed an otherwise relatively rigid framework to achieve some desirable degree of flexibility in practice. Elements of both explanations may of course be present.

11.3 Practical Challenges: Portfolio Shocks, Policy Transmission, and Financial Development

Bernanke and Mishkin (1997) use the term *constrained discretion* to describe a monetary policy that provides a strong anchor for inflation while also acting to stabilize the real economy. To anchor inflation successfully, the monetary authority must be genuinely constrained by its price stability mandate, in the sense of being willing to take corrective policy action to bring inflation into line even when doing so is costly. Its commitment to doing so must be communicated to the public and demonstrated in action, because actual inflation depends on expectations of inflation. But if inflation expectations are anchored in this sense, then the monetary authority also has scope to improve the performance of the real economy by counteracting costly fluctuations in aggregate demand over the business cycle.

We have argued that the success of RMT in Tanzania reflects elements of both constraint and discretion. Despite its success, however, RMT has three emerging limitations at this stage in Tanzania's development. The first is its vulnerability to shocks to velocity and the money multiplier. This vulnerability is a familiar property of systems that target monetary aggregates, and when other considerations favour a flexible exchange rate as in Tanzania, it is generally thought to favour a *policy rate* system, where inflation serves as the intermediate target and a short-term interest rate serves as the operational target. Much of modern monetary economics is built around the analysis of such systems. The second limitation of RMT is its relative lack of transparency, a potentially serious weakness when monetary policy is largely about the management of private-sector expectations.

The third limitation of RMT is more speculative, and relates to the two-way relationship between the BoT's policy framework and financial development in Tanzania. We will argue that even in the absence of fiscal dominance, monetary policy in low-income countries may be subject to a subtle but challenging trap, where in the short run poorly-developed financial markets favor a policy framework that relies for its effectiveness on quantity targets and direct interventions—but where these interventions then create a barrier to the long-run development of a financial sector that is competitive and inclusive enough to support strong transmission of the central bank's policy rate throughout the economy.

A policy rate system has advantages in dealing with each of these challenges. Other combinations of operational and intermediate targets are possible—for example, targeting inflation but using reserve money as the operating target (as the Bank of Mexico has done for extended periods) or targeting broad money but using a short-term interest rate as the operating target (as the US Fed did during episodes in the 1970s). And Tanzania's RMT framework is itself under constant internal review to improve its operating characteristics.[15] In our view, however, the appropriate direction of travel is clear: towards a policy rate system in which the role of monetary aggregates is de-emphasized and a short-term interest rate is used to target inflation and communicate the stance of policy.

11.3.1 *Accommodating Portfolio Shocks*

The most obvious shortcoming of RMT is its tendency to produce interest-rate volatility in the presence of unforeseen shocks to velocity or the money multiplier. Figure 11.6 illustrates this point analytically, focusing on the interbank market for liquidity in the form of deposits at the BoT.[16] The Figure illustrates the market for overnight interbank loans, where banks that are short of liquidity can borrow at the interbank call money rate i_{IBCM} from banks with liquidity to spare.

The downward-sloping line in Figure 11.6 shows the net demand for liquidity by all banks taken together. The position of this curve reflects all of the determinants of bank demand, including the public's preference for currency versus demand deposits, the stringency of legal reserve requirements, and the eagerness of banks to lend. But it also depends on the overall supply of commercial bank deposits at the BoT. The BoT directly controls this supply by purchasing securities or foreign exchange from the banks when it wants to expand reserve money and selling securities or foreign exchange when it wants to contract reserve money. Net purchases inject liquidity, shifting the curve to the left; net sales withdraw liquidity, shifting it to the right. Because the interbank market clears at a net inter-bank trade of zero, the resulting interbank interest rate is given by the intersection of the demand curve with the vertical axis. Net injections reduce the interbank rate, other things equal, while net withdrawals (often referred to as 'mopping up') increase it.

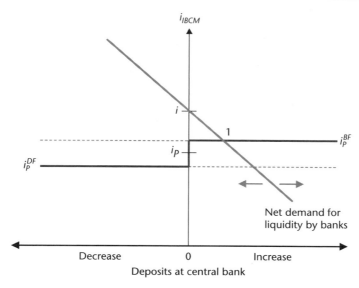

Figure 11.6. An interbank market with and without standing facilities

Note: Given the position of the demand curve for liquidity, the equilibrium is at *i* in a system without standing facilities and at point 1 when standing facilities are in operation.

What this implies is that a system that prioritizes a sequence of reserve-money targets must accept the resulting path of short-term interest rates. This may in fact be one of the main virtues of reserve-money targeting in a situation where the monetary authority wants to adopt a very tight stance—for example, in a disinflation where the key objective is to achieve a shift in inflation expectations. The quantity target provides the central bank with political cover for a policy that will create very high interest rates, with attendant costs to borrowers and potentially severe impacts on aggregate demand. But when expectations are reasonably anchored, a system that forces overall bank liquidity onto a predetermined path can create damaging volatility in short-term interest rates. This volatility emerges when shifts in portfolio preferences or bank behaviour create unanticipated movements in the net demand for liquidity by banks (in equation (11.1), these shifts produce forecast errors in the growth rates of velocity and/or the money multiplier). The key feature of RMT is that does not accommodate such shifts until after the fact, and possibly after an extended period of debate and inaction during which the stance of monetary policy is unintendedly loose or tight.[17]

A *policy-rate system*, by contrast—one in which the BoT determines (and communicates) the stance of monetary policy as a target level of some key short-term interest rate—automatically accommodates shocks to velocity and the money multiplier. Figure 11.6 illustrates the role of open-market operations and the potential role of standing facilities in such a system. To keep the interbank rate near the policy rate i_p, the BoT would have to forecast the total demand for interbank liquidity at this rate, and use open-market operations to nudge that demand close to zero. In Figure 11.6 this would require a net injection of liquidity, to shift the demand curve to the left and bring the interbank rate down towards the target. These operations could be complemented by the use of standing facilities—a deposit facility that allowed banks to deposit any amount at the BoT, and receive an interest rate below the policy rate, and a borrowing facility that allowed banks to borrow overnight from the BoT, at a rate above the policy rate. If conditions in the interbank market were as shown in Figure 11.6 (net of the BoT's open-market operations),[18] the interbank market would clear at a rate very close to i_p^{BF}, with banks satisfying their excess demand at the standing borrowing facility.

In the process of steering short-term interest rates, the BoT would lose control over the supply of bank reserves, which would respond endogenously to the demand for reserves via the BoT's open-market operations and any transactions at the standing facilities. Monetary aggregates could of course serve as information variables, with unusual behaviour of reserve money or broader aggregates leading to possible revisions in the policy rate.

11.3.2 *Improving Transparency*

Because wage- and price-setting is a forward-looking process, the management of inflation expectations is a central task of monetary policy (Woodford, 2003). The disadvantages of monetary aggregates from this perspective have become clearer as central banks have increased their focus on price stability and placed greater emphasis on communication with the public. By contrast with a broad monetary aggregate, inflation is a widely understood concept that is readily observable as an intermediate target and (by definition) directly related to the objective of price stability. A similar point applies to the choice of operational target. Few people understand and follow reserve money, and despite the simplicity of equation (11.1) the empirical links between reserve money and inflation are complex. Short-term interest rates, by contrast, are easily observed and interpreted, and their relevance to the private spending decisions of firms and households are widely understood.

11.3.3 *Strengthening Policy Transmission and Fostering Financial Development*

In well-developed financial markets, the impact of interest-rate volatility operates through aggregate demand, as in the classic analysis by Poole (1970). But when financial markets are less developed, a set of new considerations become important. First, the transmission of short-term interest rates into longer-term rates and aggregate demand tends to be weak (Mishra et al., 2014), suggesting that conventional concerns about the demand-side effects of interest-rate volatility may be overstated. Second and by the same token, the absence of a reliable transmission mechanism from monetary policy to aggregate demand may appear to limit the scope for virtually *any* discretionary demand management by the central bank—while in reality its main impact may be to encourage the continued use of direct, quantity-based interventions that impose high costs on the banking system. Finally, the impact of interest rate volatility and direct interventions on banking-sector development gives rise to a link between the monetary framework and long-run growth that is largely absent in advanced economies.

Taken together, these arguments suggest that the RMT framework may be less well adapted to an environment of rapid financial-sector innovation and economic transformation than it has been to the conquest of fiscal dominance and the establishment of a credible monetary-policy anchor for inflation.

The common thread in these concerns is apparent in Figure 11.7—which shows the high volatility of short-term interest rates in Tanzania and their limited pass-through into bank deposit and lending rates[19]—and Figure 11.8, which uses a rough measure of pass-through to compare Tanzania with other countries in sub-Saharan Africa (SSA). Figure 11.8 shows the year-by-year ratios of the standard deviation of monthly bank loan rates to the standard deviation of monthly short-term T-bill rates. Higher values of this index are

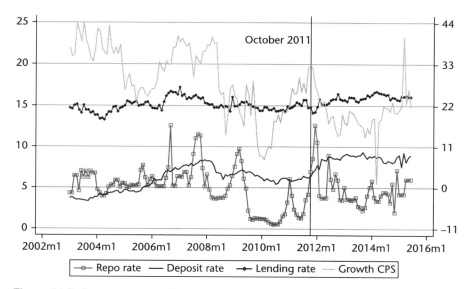

Figure 11.7. Interest rates and monetary transmission in Tanzania
Source: Bank of Tanzania.

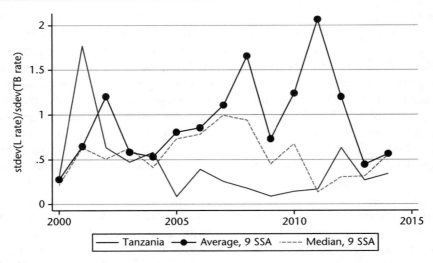

Figure 11.8. Volatility of monthly interest rates: Tanzania vs. nine other SSA

Note: this figure includes all countries with in SSA with available data (Cape Verde, Kenya, Malawi, Nigeria, Seychelles, Sierra Leone, South Africa, Tanzania, Uganda, Zambia), except the CFA countries and non-South African members of the Rand Monetary Area.

Source: IMF, International Financial Statistics online.

associated with stronger pass-through of short-term to long-term interest rates. Tanzania's ratio is consistently below the median for twelve comparator countries with available data, and far below the average for these countries.[20]

The weak pass-through in Figures 11.7 and 11.8 is consistent with broader difficulties empirical researchers have encountered in uncovering evidence of strong and systematic transmission from monetary policy actions to desired impacts on the Tanzanian economy (Davoodi et al., 2013; Montiel et al., 2012). In substantial part, these difficulties reflect the limitations of conventional methods in a data-poor environment subject to ongoing financial innovation and frequent supply shocks (Li et al., 2016). But even by comparison with Kenya and Uganda, where policy makers have operated within broadly similar RMT-style frameworks, evidence of conventional transmission from short-term interest rates to inflation and GDP growth appears to be more difficult to detect in Tanzania using standard macroeconomic models and econometric approaches (Goncalves, 2015).

Figure 11.7 suggests that despite the challenges of discovering the transmission mechanism from the data, the BoT can exert a powerful influence on economic conditions when it implements a clear change in its policy stance. Drawing on Berg et al. (2013), the figure shows the impact of the concerted monetary tightening by the central banks of Kenya, Tanzania, and Uganda in October of 2011. Short-run rates rise sharply in Tanzania, and there is a modest but perceptible pass-through to deposit rates. Lending rates hardly budge, consistent with the apparent absence of conventional transmission through the term structure of interest rates. But consistent with bank-level evidence in Tanzania (Mbowe, 2012), lending *volumes* respond strongly to the tightening. Berg et al. (2013) also document a turn-around in exchange-rate depreciation—the main focus of the intervention—and inflation, the reversal of which is evident in Figure 11.5 in this chapter.

Monetary policy can therefore exert strong leverage over inflation in Tanzania, and the BoT's willingness to do so when necessary has helped to establish an effective monetary-policy anchor for private-sector expectations—an outcome made possible by the relative absence of fiscal dominance since the mid-1990s, but by no means guaranteed. Financial-sector development—a key secondary objective of the BoT—has proceeded rapidly in key respects, including declines in interest-rate spreads and increases in the ratio of claims on the private sector to overall deposits (Figure 11.9).[21] But the policy environment remains one of high interest-rate volatility, limited transparency, and occasional recourse—particular at moments of clear policy action—to direct interventions. The behaviour of banks will of course reflect the environment

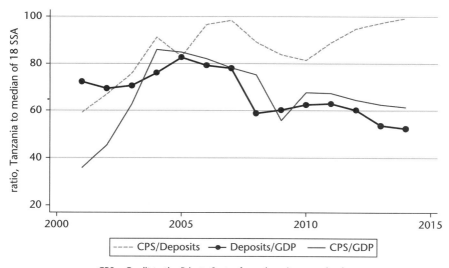

CPS = Credit to the Private Sector from deposit money banks.

Figure 11.9. Financial deepening: Tanzania vs. Other SSA

Note: this figure excludes the CFA countries and non-South African members of the Rand Monetary Area, but includes all other countries in SSA with available data (Angola, Botswana, Burundi, Cabo Verde, Comoros, Democratic Republic of Congo, The Gambia, Ghana, Kenya, Mauritius, Mozambique, Nigeria, São Tomé and Principe, Seychelles, Sierra Leone, South Africa, Tanzania, Uganda, and Zambia).

Source: IMF, International Financial Statistics online.

within which they operate, including any systematic features of the BoT's policy framework. If volatile overnight rates are a consequence of RMT, bank behaviour will adjust to this volatility. Large excess reserves, for example, have been a feature of Tanzania's banking sector throughout the RMT era, and have been associated in cross-country work with a weakening of the transmission mechanism of monetary policy (Saxegaard, 2006). These reserves may in part reflect self-protection against episodes of very high interbank rates. Volatility of short-term rates can also weaken the transmission of short-term interest rates into the longer-term rates that matter more directly for lending and aggregate demand (Woodford, 2003).

We emphasized in Section 11.2 that one of the continuing rationales for RMT has been the rudimentary nature of the financial sector. Figure 11.9 suggests that after an initial decade of very rapid expansion in the wake of banking-sector privatization and the mid-1990s accord, the pace of financial deepening has slowed considerably over the past decade in Tanzania, relative to that among comparator countries in SSA. In our view, this constitutes a final—and admittedly speculative—argument in favour of transition towards a policy-rate system. Particularly in an environment of ongoing financial-sector innovation and rapidly increasing financial inclusion, a system that stabilizes interest rates is likely to provide stronger encouragement for development of the banking sector, while simultaneously preserving and even strengthening the BoT's ability to conduct discretionary policy.

11.4 Emerging Issues in Tanzanian Monetary Policy

We close by briefly addressing a set of emerging issues that will shape both the BoT's policy framework and the conduct of policy within that framework. We focus in turn on achieving East African Monetary Union (EAMU) convergence, retaining policy independence, and accommodating the natural gas sector.

11.4.1 *Achieving EAMU Convergence*

The convergence process towards East African Monetary Union—with full convergence by 2023 at the earliest—both confirms and accelerates the direction of travel laid out in this chapter. In contrast to the Eurozone, East Africa's convergence process is unlikely to involve exchange-rate commitments except perhaps over a final period of a few months before union, when members may elect to adopt a fixed grid of internal rates. A union-wide central bank, in turn, is virtually certain to reflect the practices of its largest members by adopting a version of inflation targeting and operationalizing it using a policy rate system. The developments discussed so far therefore place

Tanzania's framework on a course of convergence towards the eventual union-wide framework.

In the meantime, an EAMU-driven process of financial-sector harmonization is already altering the BoT's operating environment by shaping the set of relevant policy instruments and altering the BoT's exposure to portfolio shocks. The harmonization of reserve requirements, for example, narrows the set of policy instruments by limiting the BoT's recourse to (already very intermittent) changes in reserve requirements—appropriately, as we argued earlier. The opening of Tanzania's capital account is likely to increase the mobility of short-term capital, a development that will heighten the disadvantages of RMT by transmitting interest-rate volatility more strongly into exchange rates. These considerations add further impetus to Tanzania's shift towards a policy rate system.

11.4.2 *Retaining Policy Independence*

We have emphasized the crucial importance of the mid-1990s accord in overcoming fiscal dominance and thereby allowing the establishment of a monetary-policy anchor for inflation. Two concerns will have to be navigated if the BoT is to retain the appropriate degree of independence from the fiscal authorities. One is that a policy-rate system forces the monetary authority to take transparent responsibility for the level of short-term interest rates. Even in the absence of direct pressures for monetary finance, a period of fiscal indiscipline can put the central bank into the difficult political position of having to set a very high policy rate in order to avoid inflationary finance of the deficit. To be able to do so effectively requires a political consensus that supports the continued pursuit of an inflation target—and places the burden of adjustment on the fiscal authorities—even when high interest rates are doing clear short-term damage to both private and public borrowers.

The fundamental point is that debt sustainability is a fiscal responsibility. Monetary policy cannot be expected to keep interest rates low in real terms, and attempting to do so when the fiscal accounts are out of control leads to the loss of the inflation anchor. Even formal commitments to inflation targeting are no rescue in such a situation, as illustrated forcefully by Ghana's experience since 2011. Such commitments must be backed by a fiscal policy that can be sustained without excessive monetary finance. Retaining policy independence therefore requires continued recognition that the fiscal/monetary accord achieved in the mid-1990s was crucial to the two subsequent decades of macroeconomic stability.

The second concern is more subtle and relates to the BoT's capacity to handle the budgetary costs of managing monetary policy. Central banks have a monopoly on the currency issue, and more broadly on the issuance of reserve money. The BoT must absorb the costs of producing currency, but neither currency nor (at present) bank reserves pay interest. The BoT is therefore typically in the position of earning net profits, because the interest on its assets—foreign-exchange reserves, and government securities—is more than enough to cover salaries and other operating costs. These profits are transferred to the government's budget after due provision for maintaining the BoT's capital and other financial buffers.

Central banks cannot go bankrupt, but profits can become negative when balance-sheet trends sharply reduce net interest earnings. In such a situation, the BoT's financial health may become the subject of public concerns, and the BoT itself may be subject to scrutiny regarding its financial management. Despite the explicit provision for recapitalization in the BoT Act of 2006, the danger is that concerns about profitability will exert an undue influence on the BoT's monetary policy stance. A looming example relates to the BoT's agreements under EAMU and the Southern Africa Development Community (SADC), which require convergence to much higher levels of gross official reserves—4.5 months of imports in the case of EAMU and 6 months of imports for SADC. Reconciling a substantial build-up of foreign-exchange reserves with low inflation is likely to require a shift in the composition of the BoT's balance sheet, with the additional reserves financed through costly domestic liabilities rather than reserve money. The resulting budgetary pressures call for a well-defined framework of liquidity-management cost sharing with the government.

11.4.3 Accommodating the Natural Gas Sector

Tanzania may soon be receiving large foreign direct investment inflows to support the development of offshore deep-water natural gas. The projects under consideration involve both upstream (extraction) and downstream (pipeline and processing and liquefaction) components, and will generate well over twenty-five years of natural gas production for domestic consumption and exports. Government revenues will increase substantially once exports are underway, in the form of income taxes, royalties, production-sharing, and government equity participation (see Chapter 3, this volume). Changes in world energy prices will generate volatility in export revenues, with implications for foreign exchange markets both directly and via potential linkages to foreign creditworthiness and capital flows.

The main macroeconomic issues associated with the gas economy are fiscal rather than monetary: the Government must convert a large and persistent increase in its spending power into a sustainable increase in the well-being of the private sector. The most important responsibility of monetary policy is in fact to be clear that it is fiscal policy that matters most of all. This includes underscoring the need for sustainable debt accumulation and emphasizing the dangers of a pro-cyclical spending response to fluctuations in natural gas prices. As a centre of high-quality economic research, the central bank is in a unique position to contribute to debates on best practices and to monitor the implications of ongoing fiscal management.

Two monetary policy issues, however, will occupy the BoT as the gas economy expands. The first is responding (or not) to the wealth effect of the resource discovery. Even in the face of a prudent public spending response, a substantial increase in the economy's net external wealth means higher sustainable consumption spending. This is likely to produce a modest and long-lasting real appreciation relative to what would have occurred without the resource discovery. Attempts to peg the real exchange rate at its pre-discovery level are unlikely to be successful; a policy of resisting nominal appreciation, for example, would tend to generate either domestic inflation or—holding fast to inflation targets—a contractionary bias in monetary policy (Calvo, Reinhart, and Vegh, 1995).

To the degree that spending is front-loaded and has a high domestic component, the short-run appreciation that would occur under a passive exchange rate policy during the development and early production phases is likely to be considerably larger than the real appreciation that is ultimately required to absorb the economy's increased spending power. Managing this potential overshooting requires an empirical assessment of the appropriate long-run appreciation—as a benchmark—and a judgement regarding the costs of a large and ultimately temporary real appreciation relative to this benchmark.

The major challenges for monetary policy, however, will emerge once exports are underway, and have to do with managing the volatility in global energy prices. The macroeconomic management of commodity-price volatility has been the subject of a voluminous literature—see Frankel (2012) and IMF (2012). For a given *ex ante* exposure to shocks, a distinction can be made between policies that improve risk-sharing with external partners (e.g., denomination of debt contracts in gas), fiscal rules designed to smooth spending and ensure debt sustainability in the face of shocks, and monetary policy rules that target an appropriate balance of volatility in inflation and real GDP. We focus here on the response of monetary policy to volatility in export revenues.

The literature on managing external shocks has focused largely on the merits of alternative degrees of exchange rate flexibility. A time-honoured result states that when domestic prices are sticky, floating exchange rates allow for efficient macroeconomic adjustment to shocks that call for a change in the real exchange rate. An example is a shock to commodity export prices: a favourable shock increases the spending power of a commodity-exporting economy, and calls for a real appreciation to induce the appropriate production shift towards non-traded goods. A floating nominal exchange rate accomplishes this more quickly and at lower macroeconomic cost than a peg.

Inflation-targeting frameworks tend to incorporate a substantial degree of exchange-rate flexibility, because the nominal anchor in the system is inflation rather than the exchange rate. The appropriate measure of inflation may differ, however, for a country subject to large swings in export prices. The reason is that an inflation-targeting central bank will tend to react indirectly—and possibly inappropriately—to commodity prices, via their impact on the nominal exchange rate. Thus a boom in export prices generates nominal appreciation, which tends (other things equal) to reduce inflation. A strict inflation targeter pushes back, by lowering interest rates in order to expand aggregate demand. But the boom has already expanded aggregate demand, to a degree that combines the fiscal response with any increase in the commodity sector's demand for domestically produced inputs. If spending on domestic output is already procyclical with the export price, a procyclical monetary easing may create excessive volatility in the real economy (Lama and Medina, 2012; Ferrero and Seneca, 2015). A good fiscal rule can soften this conflict very considerably, by generating a more neutral spending response. But an inflation-targeting rule that uses domestic price inflation rather than the CPI inflation may also have a favourable impact, by down-weighting the nominal exchange rate and avoiding excessive real-side volatility in the face of commodity price fluctuations.

Appendix

Table 11A.1. Aspects of the legislative mandate of the Bank of Tanzania

Bank of Tanzania Act	Objectives of Monetary Policy	Provisions on Non-Financial Relationship to Fiscal Authorities
1965	5.–(1) The principal functions of the Bank shall be to exercise the functions of a central bank, and, without prejudice to the generality of the foregoing, to issue currency, to regulate banking and credit, to manage the gold and foreign exchange reserves of Tanzania, and to perform any function conferred upon it (or to act as the agent of the Government in respect of any function conferred on the Government) by or under any international agreement to which Tanzania is a party. 5.–(2) Within the context of the economic policy of the Government, the activities of the Bank shall be directed to the promotion of credit and exchange conditions conducive to the rapid growth of the national economy of Tanzania, due regard being had to the desirability of fostering monetary stability.	61.–(1) The Bank may advise the Government on any matter relating to its functions, powers and duties under this or any other law and shall advise the Government when, in the Bank's opinion, any such matter is likely to affect the achievement of the principal objectives of the Bank as set forth in section 5. 61.–(2) The Government may require the Bank to give its advice on any matter relating to the functions, powers and duties of the Bank and credit conditions in Tanzania or any proposals, measures or transactions relating thereto, and the Bank shall give its advice accordingly.
1978 Amendment	5.–(2) [. . .] due regard being had to the desirability of fostering domestic and external monetary stability. 5.–(3) Subject to sections (1) and (2) of this document, the Bank shall engage in the promotion of rural development, industrial and agricultural production and the development of such other sectors of the economy of Tanzania as the Bank may deem appropriate. The Bank shall carry out its functions under this subsection through, amongst other ways— (a) the provision of financial facilities, under such terms and conditions as the Bank may determine, to banks and designated financial institutions engaged in the financing of the economic sectors referred to in this subsection; (b) the guaranteeing, through funds created under Section 46B, of loans, investments or advances made available by banks and other designated financial institutions engaged in the financing of the economic sectors referred to in this subsection; (c) the provision of training facilities or opportunities designed to promote the development of a system of sound financial management in Tanzania;	

(continued)

Table 11A.1. Continued

Bank of Tanzania Act	Objectives of Monetary Policy	Provisions on Non-Financial Relationship to Fiscal Authorities
	(d) the supervision and inspection of the activities of banks and specified financial institutions.	
1995	5.–(1) The principal functions of the Bank shall be to exercise the functions of a central bank and, without prejudice to the generality of the foregoing, to formulate, implement and be responsible for monetary policy, to issue currency, to regulate and supervise banks and financial institutions and to manage gold and foreign exchange reserves of Tanzania. 5.–(2) The Bank shall promote sound monetary, credit and banking conditions conducive to the development of the economy of Tanzania. 5.–(3) The primary objective of the Bank shall be to formulate and implement monetary policy directed to the economic objective of maintaining price stability conducive to a balanced and sustainable growth of the national economy of Tanzania. 5.–(4) Without prejudice to its primary objective as stated above, the Bank shall support the general economic policy of the Governments.	7.–(1) There shall be regularly held consultations between the Governments and the Governor on monetary policy. 7.–(2) In the event of fundamental and irreconcilable differences between the Minister and the Governor over monetary policy, the Minister shall by Order published in the Gazette direct the Governor to formulate and implement monetary policy along the position of the Minister for a period not exceeding twelve months or any other period as shall be specified in the Order. 7.–(3) Except as provided herein above nothing in this section shall be construed as to limit or affect the obligation of the Bank to carry out its primary objective.
2006	7.–(1) The primary objective of the Bank shall be to formulate, define and implement monetary policy directed to the economic objective of maintaining domestic price stability conducive to a balanced and sustainable growth of the national economy. 7.–(2) Without prejudice to subsection (1), the Bank shall ensure the integrity of the financial system and support the general economic policy of the Government and promote sound monetary, credit and banking conditions conducive to the development of the national economy.	7.–(3) The Minister and the Governor shall, where circumstances require, consult each other with a view to exchanging information and seeking coordination on economic and financial matters. There is no counterpart in the BoT Act of 2006 to Section 7.–(2) of the BoT Act of 1995.

Sources: Government of Tanzania, BoT Acts of 1965, 1995, and 2006, and 1978 Amendment to the BoT Act of 1965.

Notes

1. See Kaufmann and O'Connell (1997) on the quasi-fiscal implications of the exchange-control system in Tanzania, and Collier and Gunning (1991) on the quasi-fiscal implications of financial repression in Tanzania's socialist banking system.

2. See Mpango (2002) on Tanzania's experience with the cash budget. Cash budgets also played an important role in Uganda (Kasekende and Hussain, 2000) and Zambia (Adam and Bevan, 2000) during the 1990s.

3. The US Fed famously adopted a variant of reserve-money targeting (focused on what the Fed defined as non-borrowed reserves) at the outset of the Volcker disinflation in 1979.

4. The BoT has recently begun to take on many elements of IT, and we will focus on this ongoing transition in Section 11.3.

5. The former approach implies allowing elements of its balance sheet to adjust as may be required to keep the interest rate close to its target; the latter allows short-term interest rates to adjust. The US Fed used a short-term interest rate target to pursue broad monetary aggregates during episodes in the 1970s and 1980s.

6. The financial programming model was designed to guide monetary and fiscal policy when balance-sheet data were available from the banking sector but a dearth of real-time information about the state of the economy limited the scope for fine-tuning the government's efforts to achieve economic stabilization (Polak, 1957).

7. This language is from the BoT Act of 2006 but is virtually identical with section 5.3 of the BoT Act of 1995, which represented a major departure from the 1978 Amendment to the BoT Act of 1965.

8. In contemporary monetary policy analysis, price stability is usually interpreted as a low and stable rate of *expected* inflation—a situation in which expectations are anchored in the sense that wage- and price-setters view shocks to inflation as temporary. Inflation itself may be variable, but around a constant and low medium-term average.

9. The differences between headline and core inflation are striking in Figure 11.2b: there are only two years out of twenty in which core exceeds headline, suggesting that food and energy prices (taken together) have been rising in real terms over the entire twenty-year period.

10. The adjusted gap allows for a distinction between the programme ceiling and the implicit target of BoT behaviour and policy dialogue between the BoT and the IMF. In July 2007 reserve-money programme targets were redefined as applying to average reserve money in the final month of each quarter, rather than to reserve money on the final day; and rather than a single ceiling, a narrow target range was specified. The targets used in the regressions are the actual programme targets before July 2007, and the upper bound of the target range starting in July 2007. In Figure 11.5, these changes coincide with an apparent change both in the volatility of the gap—which the move to a monthly average was intended to reduce—and the average level of the gap.

11. The logs of these two variables are non-stationary, but they share a common random walk component or stochastic trend. We cannot reject the hypothesis

that the gap between the two variables is stationary, and we can only marginally reject the hypothesis that the cointegrating vector relating the two variables is [1 -1]. Given the theoretical appeal of this restriction and the short data sample, we impose this restriction on the data and therefore estimate the error-correction equations using the gap as the lagged equilibrium error.

12. The statement that Granger causality runs in both directions means that each of these variables helps to predict the other, conditional on the other variable's lagged values.

13. There is weaker evidence of asymmetry on the reserve-money side, but columns 3 and 7 suggest that adjustment was faster when reserves were below the ceiling than when they were above.

14. Portillo et al. (2016) note that food prices are considerably more flexible than non-food prices. They show that in a low-income economy with a large food-production sector that is subject to droughts and other supply shocks, the optimal inflation objective may be to stabilize non-food rather than headline inflation. The reason for this is that stabilizing headline inflation creates excessive volatility in inflation and output in the non-food sector.

15. Examples include the July 2007 adjustment in how reserve-money targets were calculated, the accommodation of quarterly real GDP data since 2010, and current discussions of improving policy responsiveness by elevating the informational role of free reserves (bank deposits at the BoT in excess of the statutory minimum) in the BoT's internal deliberations.

16. The classic analysis is Poole (1970), who focused on the markets for broad monetary aggregates and government securities. In a well-functioning financial market, the short-term rates determined in the interbank market feed through to the longer-term rates emphasized by Poole—an issue we address further in Section 11.3.3.

17. The BoT is of course alert to this concern, and pays attention to movements in exchange rates and market interest rates when deciding on monthly reserve-money targets. It also stands ready to alter liquidity conditions through direct interventions that include changes in reserve requirements or foreign exchange cover requirements.

18. The demand for liquidity by banks will depend on the BoT's operating procedures and on the presence or absence of standing facilities. There is therefore no presumption that the position of the demand curve in Figure 11.6 is independent of the policy framework.

19. Interbank interest rates are not shown in Figure 11.7 but are even more volatile than the repo rate (on short-maturity repurchase agreements by the BoT).

20. The financial-sector comparisons in this section are based on publicly available IMF data and use all countries in sub-Saharan Africa with available data, with the exception of countries in the CFA franc zone and non-South African members of the Rand Monetary Area. We exclude these countries because they are on fixed exchange rate systems.

21. The average monthly interest-rate spread in Tanzania (overall lending rate minus overall deposit rate) fell from 12.8 percentage points in 2000–04 to 6.9 in 2010–14,

and is now below the median for eighteen comparator countries in sub-Saharan Africa (this group excludes the CFA zone and non-South African members of the Rand Monetary Area). The median spread among the comparator countries fell from 11.1 to 8.8 percentage points for the same periods.

References

Adam, C. S. and Bevan, D. (2000). 'The Cash Budget as a Restraint: The Experience of Zambia'. In: Collier, P. and Pattillo, C. (eds), *Investment and Risk in Africa*. London: Palgrave Macmillan: 185–215.

Adam, C. S. and Kessy, P. (2011). 'Assessing the Stability and Predictability of the Money Multiplier in the EAC: The Case of Tanzania', International Growth Centre Working Paper, May.

Adam, C. S., Kessy, P. J., Nyella, J. J., and O'Connell, S. A. (2012). 'The Demand for Money in Tanzania', *Tanzanian Economic Review* 2(1): 21–38.

Bank of Tanzania (various years). *Monetary Policy Statements, Monthly Economic Reviews*, and *Quarterly Economic Bulletins* (http://www.bot.go.tz/Publications/publications-AndStatistics.asp).

Berg, A., O'Connell, S., Pattillo, C., Portillo, R., and Unsal, F. (2015). 'Monetary Policy Issues in Sub-Saharan Africa'. In: Monga, C. and Lin, J. Y. (eds), *The Oxford Handbook of Africa and Economics, Volume II: Policies and Practices*. Oxford: Oxford University Press: 62–87.

Berg, A., Charry, L., Portillo, R., and Vlcek, J. (2013). 'The Monetary Transmission Mechanism in the Tropics: A Narrative Approach', IMF Working Paper WP/13/197.

Bernanke, B. S. and Mishkin, F. (1997). 'Inflation Targeting: A New Framework for Monetary Policy?', *Journal of Economic Perspectives* 11(2)(Spring): 97–116.

Calvo, G. A., Reinhart, C., and Vegh, C. (1995). 'Targeting the Real Exchange Rate: Theory and Evidence', *Journal of Development Economics* 47: 97–113.

Calvo, G. A. and Vegh, C. A. (1999). 'Inflation Stabilization and BOP Crises in Developing Countries'. In: Taylor, J. and Woodford, M. (eds), *Handbook of Macroeconomics*, vol. C. Amsterdam: North-Holland: 1531–614.

Collier, P. and Gunning, J. W. (1991). 'Money Creation and Financial Liberalization in a Socialist Banking System: Tanzania 1983–88', *World Development* 19(5): 553–38.

Davoodi, H., Dixit, S. and Pinter, G. (2013). 'Monetary Transmission Mechanisms in the East African Community: An Empirical Investigation', IMF Working Paper WP/13/39, February.

Ferrero, A. and Seneca, M. (2015). 'Notes on the Underground: Monetary Policy in Resource-Rich Economies', Norges Bank Working Paper 15/02.

Frankel, J. (2012). 'The Natural Resource Curse: A Survey of Diagnoses and Some Prescriptions'. In: Arezki, R., Patillo, C., Quintyn, M., and Zhu, M. (eds), *Commodity Price Volatility and Inclusive Growth in Low-Income Countries*. Washington, D.C.: International Monetary Fund.

Goncalves, C. E. (2015). 'Taylor Visits Africa', IMF Working Paper WP/15/258.

Higgins, B. (1980). 'Free Reserves and Monetary Policy', *Federal Reserve Bank of Kansas City Economic Review* July/August: 15–29.

IMF (International Monetary Fund) (2012). 'Macroeconomic Policy Frameworks for Resource-Rich Developing Countries', IMF, Washington, D.C.

Kasekende, L. and Hussain, I. (2000). 'The Central Bank as a Restraint: The Experience of Uganda', In: Collier, P. and Pattillo, C. (eds), *Investment and Risk in Africa*. London: Palgrave Macmillan: 169–81.

Kaufmann, D. and O'Connell, S. A. (1997). 'Fiscal and Monetary Effects of the Parallel Premium: Theory and the Tanzanian Case'. In: Kiguel, M. Lizondo, J. S., and O'Connell, S. A. (eds), *Parallel Exchange Rates in Developing Countries*. London: Macmillan: 247–90.

Lama, R. and Medina, J. P. (2012). 'Is Exchange Rate Stabilization an Appropriate Cure for the Dutch Disease?', *International Journal of Central Banking* 8(1)(March): 5–46.

Li, B. G., O'Connell, S., Adam, C., Berg, A., and Montiel, P. (2016). 'VAR Meets DSGE: Uncovering the Monetary Transmission Mechanism in Low-Income Countries', IMF Working Paper 16/90.

Mbowe, W. (2012). 'The Bank Lending Channel of Monetary Policy Transmission: Dynamic Bank-Level Panel Data Analysis on Tanzania'. Research Department, Bank of Tanzania.

Mishra, P., Montiel, P., Pedroni, P., and Spilimbergo, A. (2014). 'Monetary Policy and Bank Lending Rates in Low-Income Countries: Heterogeneous Panel Estimates', *Journal of Development Economics* 111: 117–31.

Mpango, P. A. (2002). 'Review of Recent Macroeconomic Performance'. In: Ndulu, B. J. and Mutalemwa, C. K. (eds), *Tanzania at the Turn of the Century: Background Papers and Statistics*. Washington, D.C.: The World Bank): 10–46.

Montiel, P., Adam, C., Mbowe, W., and O'Connell, S. (2012). 'Financial Architecture and the Monetary Transmission Mechanism in Tanzania', International Growth Centre Working Paper 12/0343, May.

Polak, J. (1957). 'Monetary Analysis of Income Formation and Payments Problems', *IMF Staff Papers* 6(1): 1–50.

Poole, W. (1970). 'Optimal Choice of Monetary Policy Instrument in a Simple Stochastic Macro Model', *Quarterly Journal of Economics* 84(2): 197–216.

Portillo, R., Zanna, L.-F., O'Connell, S., and Peck, R. (2016). 'Implications of Food Subsistence for Monetary Policy and Inflation', *Oxford Economic Papers* 68(3)(July): 782–810.

Sargent, T. (1982). 'The Ends of Four Big Inflations'. In: Hall, R. E. (ed.), *Inflation: Causes and Effects*. Chicago: University of Chicago Press: 41–97.

Saxegaard, M. (2006). 'Excess Liquidity and the Effectiveness of Monetary Policy: Evidence from Sub-Saharan Africa', IMF Working Paper 06/115.

Woodford, M. (2003). *Interest and Prices: Foundations of a Theory of Monetary Policy*. Princeton, NJ: Princeton University Press.

12

Financial Sector Development and Financial Inclusion

Natu Mwamba, Nangi Massawe, and Kennedy Komba

12.1 Introduction

This chapter traces developments in the financial sector in Tanzania, from the advent of financial sector reforms to current progress and concludes by outlining key policy and regulatory challenges facing the sector over the coming decades. Current reforms in the financial sector in Tanzania are enabling an environment for economic growth by financing economic activities, although the low level of financial inclusion continues to create inequalities and may slow economic growth and hamper the prospects of becoming a middle-income country by the end of the first quarter of the twenty-first century. Recognizing this risk, concerted efforts across the sector are being undertaken to address the structural constraints to financial inclusion and financial deepening. In terms of financial inclusion, the government and the Bank of Tanzania (BoT) have made inclusive finance an important agenda in the development plans, evidenced through several government policies that aim to enhance inclusivity and by implementing a National Financial Inclusion Framework through public–private partnership initiatives. In addition, financial deepening is being addressed by policy and regulatory reforms in the financial sector to encourage supply-side provision of financial services. Overall, the development of the financial sector has indicated that different policy and regulatory approaches are required to usher more progress in this area, including engaging the private sector in policy development and embracing innovation and technology. This approach has shown a positive impact in increasing the levels of financial inclusion, improved financial stability and optimistic trends in financial deepening. These positive trends are expected to continue through the next decade, although several challenges that need to be addressed through proactive policy and regulatory responses remain. These challenges lie in three broad areas: firstly, innovation and technology, in particular the digitization of financial services; secondly, financial deepening through non-bank service providers; and thirdly, regional integration.

12.2 Overview of Tanzanian Financial Sector Development

The Tanzanian financial sector has been evolving over the past two decades, traversing through different phases of economic policies, from a state command economy starting a few years after independence to the late 1980s, and thereafter to a market-based economy. During the first phase, the Tanzanian financial sector, as observed by Ndulu and Mutalemwa (2002), was fragmented and relatively shallow, with a weak competitive base and structural challenges characterized by state ownership of financial institutions, that is, banks, insurance corporations, and pension funds. There was no capital or money market during this phase. The central bank did not have direct supervisory or regulatory powers over the financial institutions. The existing banks were each created by statutes that granted the bank powers to operate as state-owned parastatals. This led to direct lending to state-owned parastatals and cooperatives under a controlled interest rates regime, ultimately resulting in huge non-performing assets which affected the performance of the banking industry in general. The insurance and pension funds provided the only major collective investment schemes. The National Insurance Corporation, a state-owned corporation, was a monopoly that mainly covered life insurance products and served public sector clients (Ndulu and Mutalemwa, 2002). The pension funds were mainly focused on retirement schemes with no social security coverage.

As the country progressed towards a market-based economy in the mid-1980s, the Economic Recovery Plan (ERP) was initiated. This necessitated structural and legal reforms in the political and economic sector. It became evident that the effectiveness of the ERP was dependent on a well-functioning financial sector, thus calling for the prioritization of in the ailing financial sector. In 1988 the government established a Presidential Commission of Enquiry into Monetary and Banking System in Tanzania. The Nyirabu Commission was led by the former Governor of the BoT Ambassador Charles Nyirabu. The main task of the Nyirabu Commission was to propose strategic reforms to revamp the financial sector in order to address the challenges that were impeding economic growth. The Nyirabu Commission recommended reforms in the areas of regulatory process and institutional structure. The implementation of these recommendations is referred to as the 'first generation financial sector reforms' in Tanzania.[1]

The broad outcome of these reforms resulted in structural changes in the financial sector by enhancing private sector participation, increasing competition and improving the regulatory environment. This in turn led to supply-side provisions of a wide range of financial services. Roger Nord et al. (2009) observed that the outcome of the reforms resulted in an increase of commercial bank lending to the private sector which contributed to economic growth while the participation of the non-bank financial institutions (notably pension funds) made a significant impact on channeling savings into the domestic financial market and direct investment. Nord also observed that liberalization of interest rates encouraged domestic savings (Nord et al., 2009).

12.2.1 *Policy and Regulatory Reforms in the Banking Sector*

The recommendations of the Nyirabu Commission regarding the regulatory regime granted the BoT with regulatory and supervisory powers over the banking sector through the enactment of the Banking and Financial Institutions Act (BAFIA) in 1991. BAFIA empowered the BoT to license, supervise, and regulate banks, including foreign or joint venture banks. Internal structures in the BoT were also reviewed to accommodate the new banking supervision function that adopted international standards of banking supervision. The banking sector weathered a brief 'problem-bank' period from the mid-1990s to early 2000s where six banks faced distress. During this time four of these banks were taken over by others and two were liquidated, although depositors did not lose their funds.

The banking sector continued to grow in urban centres and had a heavy presence in Dar es Salaam as the commercial hub of the country, with branch networks in other major commercial cities. However, the private banks had a very small market share compared to the state-owned bank, the National Bank of Commerce (NBC). Cull and Spreng (2008) observe that collectively the private banks occupied merely a niche in the market, offering financial services almost exclusively in and around Dar es Salaam, and that the banking sector continued to be dominated by the original, state-owned NBC with over 80 per cent of the market share in deposits. NBC on the other hand was not performing effectively and hence had to undergo a restructuring process under the banking sector reforms.

The reforms in the banking sector were aimed at reducing the dominant role of the government in the financial sector. The government commenced privatization of the state owned banks in 1996 by privatizing the Cooperative and Rural Development Bank (CRDB), which had only 5 per cent market share in deposits. In 1997, the government decided to split NBC into two banks: NBC Limited as a commercial bank targeting commercial enterprises primarily in urban centres, and the National Microfinance Bank (NMB) with a mission to provide access to financial services to the rural areas and the urban poor.

Despite this progress, the first-generation financial sector reforms led to massive closures of loss-making branches that were mainly in rural areas, thereby negatively impacting rural access to financial services. Cull and Spreng (2008) found that in the Tanzanian market there were tensions between pursuing profitability and extending the outreach of a bank after its privatization, which might come at the expense of reduced access to financial services for some groups, especially the rural poor. At the same time, the existing microfinance institutions were not able to fully cover the demand for access to financial services to rural areas and urban poor for a number of reasons, including a lack of common standards and monitoring mechanisms for microfinance institutions, and weak financial controls of Savings and Credit Cooperative Societies (SACCOS).[2]

12.2.2 Policy and Regulatory Reforms in the Non-Bank Sector

Developments in the non-bank institutions (pensions, insurance, and capital markets) also commenced in the last two decades through recommendations from the Nyirabu Commission and the Financial Sector Assessment Program (FSAP) review mission conducted jointly by the International Monetary Fund (IMF) and the World Bank. The Bank of Tanzania Act 1995, and the Capital Markets and Securities Act of 1994, facilitated the establishment of a financial market primarily comprised of Treasury bills and bonds, repurchase agreements, interbank foreign exchange trading, and corporate bonds and equities. The money and capital markets enabled the BoT to conduct monetary policy and the government to borrow from the public as opposed to directly borrowing from the Central Bank which had been the case prior to the reform period. In August 1993, the BoT introduced Treasury Bills Auctions, as a tool for financing short-term government deficit, an instrument for liquidity management, and as a reference point for the determination of market interest rates. The Treasury bills market is dominated by commercial banks and participation is limited to East African Community (EAC) residents. The tenure of Treasury bills is 35, 91, 182, and 364 days, they are issued in the primary market fortnightly, and settlement is done on the next day. Secondary market trading is done over the counter.

The equity market commenced in Tanzania following the establishment of the Capital Markets and Securities Authority (CMSA) in 1994. CMSA was established under the Capital Markets and Securities Act, 1994, with a prime objective to promote and regulate securities business. To enable equity trading, the Dar es Salaam Stock Exchange was established in 1997.

The pension sector reforms commenced during the liberalization period of the 1990s with the assistance of the International Labour Organization (ILO). Reforms began with the establishment of the National Social Security Fund Act in 1997, which converted the National Provident Fund into a comprehensive social insurance scheme. In 2008, the Social Security Regulator Authority (SSRA) Act paved the way for a regulated pension sector in Tanzania.

12.2.3 Banking Sector Developments

The first-generation financial sector reforms were able to achieve the objective of creating an enabling regulatory environment for free market operations in the banking sector.

In the year 2013, the banking sector remained adequately capitalized with core capital and total capital adequacy ratios of 17.47 per cent and 18.06 per cent, compared with minimum regulatory requirements of 10 per cent and 12 per cent respectively. In addition, the sector recorded a significant growth of 14.95 per cent in total assets, which was slightly lower compared to 16.84 per cent recorded in 2012. Total deposits grew by 13.46 per cent from 2012 while total capital increased by 19.41 per cent. Lending to private sector to GDP was 21.86 per cent, which was above the 18.26 per cent achieved in 2012. The banking sector remained profitable as the sector registered an average return on assets of 2.55 per cent at the end of 2013. Total profit before tax of the banking sector grew by 13.19 per cent in 2013 compared to 18.63 per cent recorded in the previous year.[3] The banking sector expanded from only three commercial banks that were state owned in 1991 to fifty-three banking institutions by December 2014, consisting of thirty-four fully fledged commercial banks, twelve community banks, five financial institutions and two deposit-taking microfinance companies. The reforms also facilitated improvements of service delivery through automation of the banking process and use of innovation.

12.2.4 Development in Non-Bank Institutions

Development in the securities and capital markets sector has continued to follow a positive trend from their inception in the late 1990s. By February 2002, the BoT on behalf of the government launched a five-year Treasury bond with a fixed coupon rate of 7.5 per cent. The aim was to extend the maturity profile of government debt, lengthen the yield curve, and increase the number of tradable instruments in the market. In April 2002, the BoT changed the two-year Treasury bond auctions from uniform prices to multiple prices. In July 2002, a seven-year Treasury bond with a fixed coupon rate of 7.75 per cent was launched, and in August 2002, a ten-year

Treasury bond with a fixed coupon rate of 7.75 per cent was launched. In November 2013, the BoT on behalf of the government launched a fifteen-year Treasury bond with a fixed coupon rate of 13.5 per cent.

The Treasury bonds market has five maturities of two, five, seven, ten, and fifteen years that are issued in the primary market by the Bank on behalf of the government and are dominated by commercial banks. The auction is held twice every month and the bonds are listed on the Dar es Salaam Stock Exchange (DSE).

Technology has facilitated efficiency in issuing and trading of securities. Since 1999, amendments of and issuance of regulations under the Government Loans, Guarantees and Grants Act of 1974 have enabled the issuance of government securities and the establishment of the Bank of Tanzania Central Depository System (CSD) using a book entry system. The book entry system entails record keeping, transfer, and updating ownership of Treasury bills and bonds without having to issue physical certificates. The system also enables the division of securities into smaller lots, which promotes secondary market trading. In August 2012, the Government Securities System (GSS) was enhanced to accommodate on-line transactions and the introduction of Central Depository Participants as an agent to the BoT in government securities auctions.

The secondary transactions of the government bond market are steadily growing. During the quarter ending December 2014, the Bank offered Treasury bills worth TZS 810.0 billion in the Treasury bills market, compared with TZS 835.0 billion offered in the preceding quarter. The total amount tendered was TZS 942.9 billion compared with TZS 1,704.1 billion tendered in the preceding quarter, with the successful bids amounting to TZS 768.4 billion. Overall weighted average yield (WAY) increased by 77 basis points to an average of 14.20 per cent from 13.43 per cent recorded in the preceding quarter (Figure 12.1).

Listing on the DSE has grown steadily from two domestic listed companies in 1998 to fourteen domestic companies and seven cross-listed companies from the EAC Countries in 2014 with a market capitalization of TZS 22.3 trillion by the end of December 2014. The liquidity level market turnover during increased by 52 per cent to TZS 383 billion compared to TZS 252 billion in 2013 and an average annual turnover of TZS 50 billion prior to last year.[4]

Despite the steady progress, the financial market in Tanzania has a narrow investor base of few institution investors (banks and pension funds, few corporates and individuals). Secondary market trading of government bonds is not vibrant and there are few entities listed at the DSE. The trading instruments only comprise equity and government securities leaving room for more vibrant financial instruments that would attract different players and

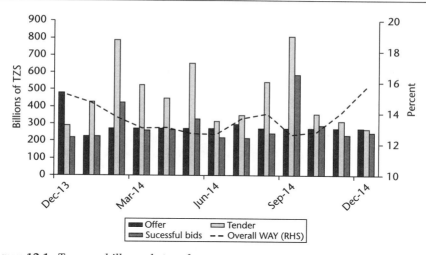

Figure 12.1. Treasury bills market performance

Source: Bank of Tanzania. Available at: <https://www.bot.go.tz/publications/QuarterlyEconomic Bulletins/QEB%20DEC%2014.pdf>.

segments of society, and the possible provision of investments options to investors by extending the instrument base.

The insurance sector reforms also commenced during the liberalization period, with the main objective of providing national underwriting capacity and contributing towards the mobilization of financial resources for the sustainable economic development of the country. Following enactment of the Insurance Act of 1996 that paved the way for private insurance companies, the insurance sector has gradually grown from one state-owned insurance company in 1996 to twenty-nine and one reinsurance company, in 2013. In 2009, the Tanzania Insurance Regulatory Authority (TIRA) was established by the Tanzania Insurance Act to regulate the insurance industry. The insurance industry grew at an average annual growth rate of 19.9 per cent from 2008 to 2013. In 2013, the insurance industry grew by 17.1 per cent to a total insurance premium of TZS 474.1 billion. The insurance industry contributed 0.9 per cent to the national GDP.[5] Despite promising trends, the insurance sector is still small with an insurance penetration of 1 per cent of the adult population compared with regional average of 10 per cent penetration. Efforts to address the challenges of reaching the underserved segment of the population has begun with the introduction of micro insurance products using mobile phone based financial services offering medical cover and accident insurance.

The pension sector has continued to show optimistic outcomes. There are four public contributory defined-benefit pension schemes and one provident fund. According to the SSRA's 2013 Annual Report, the membership size of these social security funds has increased from 1.7 million members in 2012 to 1.84 million in 2013. Contributions to the funds grew from TZS 1.4 trillion in 2012 to TZS 1.7 trillion in 2013 indicating a growth of 21 per cent. Likewise, benefits payments have shown an upward trend of 30 per cent growth from TZS 733 billion in 2011/12 to TZS 1.04 trillion in 2012/13. The number of pensioners grew by 20 per cent from 72,751 pensioners in 2011/12 to 86,995 pensioners in 2012/13. Investments portfolios for the years 2011/12 and 2012/13 were skewed towards fixed income assets (above 60 per cent) and relatively smaller amounts in equity and properties. Investment growth was 11 per cent from TZS 4,827 billion in 2011/12 to TZS 5,343 billion in 2012/13. The social security sector is still limited to the formally employed who account for 2 million adults. This is about 4 per cent of the labour force of 25 million Tanzanians, leaving 24 million people engaged in informal sector out of social security protection.

12.2.5 *Payment Systems Developments*

Reforming the payment and settlement systems that facilitate the flow of money in the economy was considered pivotal to support the overall financial sector reforms due to the fact that an efficient and safe payment system contributes to efficiency in the financial system transmission mechanisms. The payment systems reforms began with the liberalization of the financial sector, where banks adopted information technology to automate their payments operations and the BoT responded by embarking on a payment system modernisation programme. The payment and settlement systems have improved efficiency with the introduction of the Tanzania Interbank Settlement System (TISS), a real time settlement system that has made it possible to have real time payments for large value transactions. Linkages of the TISS and GSS has further enhanced the process for the government securities facilitating efficiency in monetary policy transmission. Government revenue collection has also significantly improved by requiring tax payments to be made through TISS and linkages with the Tanzania Revenue Authority tax collection systems. Improvements in electronic cheque systems have reduced the cheque clearing cycles of an average of four days to only one day. Table 12.1 highlights these interbank payment systems.

A digital revolution in retail payment systems, particularly in mobile phone financial services, has made making payments for the banked population more convenient, and also contributed to financial inclusion by providing access to the unbanked population. By December 2014 there were 216.79 million transactions valued at TZS 6,972.42 billion. After factoring in multiple accounts, there were 27,588,573 registered accounts, and 13,856,667 or 57 per cent of adult population (of approximately 24.5 million) active users. Tanzania

Table 12.1. The progress of selected financial market infrastructures in Tanzania

S/N	Financial market infrastructures	Participants	December 2014	
			Volume	Value
1	Tanzania Inter-bank Settlement System *(for large payments)*	• Commercial banks • Financial institutions • Tanzania Revenue Authority • Zanzibar Revenue Board • Ministry of Finance	97,067	TZS 10.44 (trillion)
2	Electronic Clearing House *(for cheques clearing)*	• Commercial banks • Financial institutions • Ministry of Finance	149,658.00	TZS 1.5 (trillion)
3	Electronic Funds Transfer *(for recurring bulk payments)*	• Commercial banks • Financial institutions • Ministry of Finance	355,498.00	TZS 206.7 (billion)

Source: Bank of Tanzania

is one of the fastest growing markets in advanced digital financial services in the world. It has a very competitive market of four mobile money operators who are providing this service. Peter Zetterli (2015) observes that the more competitive Tanzanian market delivers good value for customers and a steady stream of innovations. He further observes that Tanzania's innovative market has made the country the forerunner in the world in interoperability of mobile payments and distribution of interest to mobile wallets.

On the regulatory front, the government has enacted cyber laws to regulate, supervise and create certainty for electronic transactions and to enhance cyber security (the Cybercrime and Data Protection Act, 2015, and Electronic Transactions Act, 2015). In addition, an enabling regulatory environment has been created through enactment of a National Payment System Act, 2015.

12.3 Financial Sector Developments and Financial Inclusion in Tanzania

The reforms in the financial sector aimed, among other things, to enhance the outreach of financial services in the country, thus contributing to financial inclusion. The financial sector developments highlighted in the preceding paragraphs have had a significant impact on the levels of financial inclusion in the country. The trends of access to financial services from the Finscope surveys conducted in 2006, 2009, and 2013 are outlined in Figure 12.2.

Figure 12.2 shows that the use of banking services grew from 9 per cent in 2006 to 14 per cent in 2013, that is, a change of 5 per cent. Significant percentage increase is noted in the use of non-banks (which include microfinance institutions and mobile financial services): from 2 per cent in 2006 to

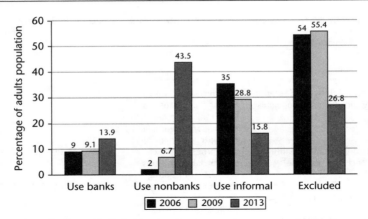

Figure 12.2. Access and usage of financial services in Tanzania, 2009–13
Source: Finscope Survey data. Available at: <http://www.fsdt.or.tz/finscope/>.

43.5 per cent in 2013. Exclusion levels were significantly reduced by 27 per cent, from 54 per cent in 2006 to 27 per cent in 2013.

The key driver in this growth is digital financial services, particularly the mobile phone financial services. The Finscope survey 2013 reveals that 49.9 per cent of adults used the mobile phone financial service, out of which 25.6 per cent stored or saved money on the mobile money wallets. It is worth noting that there was a reduction of 1 per cent on membership in the Microfinance Institutions (MFI) and Savings and Credit Cooperatives Societies (SACCOS) from 4.5 per cent in 2009 to 4.4 in 2013. Insurance uptake increased by 6.7 per cent from 6.3 per cent in 2009 to 13 per cent in 2013.

The BoT has played a significant role in championing initiatives for financial inclusion, through coordination and leadership. The Bank led the process for development of a national financial inclusion framework in 2013 that provided a clear vision of financial inclusion in Tanzania and articulated a roadmap for implementation of activities by a wide range of stakeholders from the public and private sector. These efforts have received global recognition. A survey conducted by the Economist (Economist Intelligence Unit, 2014) ranks Tanzania first in sub-Saharan Africa and ninth worldwide for a conducive environment for financial inclusion.[6]

Despite the positive trends, there are still challenges concerning financial inclusion that range from financial capabilities (literacy) to structural barriers such as stringent identification conditions in an environment of inadequate identification documentations, and the costs of maintaining and opening a bank account including distance from the bank. Deepa Narayan (1997) noted that the principal barriers to the use of savings accounts held in banks by rural village households consisted of high opening costs and minimum account

Table 12.2. Status of microfinance institutions in the country as of December 2014

S/N	Type of institution	Number of institutions
1	Commercial banks with microfinance window	5
2	Regional and rural banks	12
3	Microfinance banks	3
4	Savings and credit cooperative societies	3,790
5	Governments programmes (Women/Youth Development Funds, SELF, SIDO, NEDF,TASAF)	166
6	Informal groups (VICOBA, VSLAs, Money lenders)	Numerous

Source: Bank of Tanzania

balances; travel time and transport costs involved in making deposits and withdrawals at the bank branch (in town or market centre); and a lack of familiarity with bank branch operations and procedures. Inroads are being made towards addressing these barriers, which from 2013 include the implementation of an agent banking model. Other efforts include formulating Islamic banking processes aimed at including a segment of the society that would prefer to use Sharia compliant financial instruments. Nine banking institutions by the end of December 2014 were engaged in agent banking. The total number of bank agents was 1,652 with total deposits of TZS 306,192.17 million and cash withdrawals of TZS 46,220.25 million. Islamic banking is offered by six banks, one bank offering fully fledged services with the others formulating and finalizing their processes.

Microfinance sector developments have also been considered a key component in inclusive finance through their ability to address the challenges of expanding outreach of financial services. The government is in the final stage of issuing a revised National Microfinance Policy[7] following reviews of the policy issued in 2000. The overarching objective of the new microfinance policy is to enhance an efficient and effective financial system that will be able to provide effective regulation, while spurring growth in the microfinance sector, consisting of commercial banks, regional and rural unit banks, savings and credit cooperative societies, and several non-governmental organizations (NGOs). Table 12.2 provides the status of microfinance institutions in the country at December 2014.

The microfinance sector, despite considered as a key contributor in enhancing outreach of financial services to the low-income segment of the society it has not fully achieved its objective, this is shown by the recent survey by the FinMark Trust (2014) that there has been a reduction of 1 per cent on membership in the MFI/SACCOS from 4.5 per cent of adult population in 2009 to 4.4 per cent in 2013.

12.4 Mortgage Market Developments

The developments in the mortgage market in Tanzania faced a number of challenges during the pre-liberalization period resulting from non-preforming assets of the state-owned banks. Following the reforms, in 2008 the government enacted the Mortgage Finance Act, 2008, and made other reforms in the Land Act to enhance foreclosure of mortgage and established a Housing Finance Project (HFP) in 2010 sponsored by the World Bank that will run until 2018. The HFP facilitated establishment of the Tanzania Mortgage Refinancing Company (TMRC), which is playing a key role in developing the mortgage market by providing long-term funding both in the forms of refinancing and pre-financing. The refinancing and pre-financing mortgages advanced by TMRC to banking institutions are equivalent to 14 per cent of the total outstanding mortgage debt. These efforts in the mortgage market are yielding positive results although the country's mortgage market is still low compared to its East African neighbours. The mortgage debt outstanding as a proportion of Tanzanian gross domestic product (GDP) was equivalent to around 0.46 per cent at the end of 2014, while that of Kenya was about 3.4 per cent and Rwanda 3.6 per cent. Overall, the mortgage market has continued to grow steadily, recording an annual growth rate of 59 per cent (with a growth rate of 23 per cent recorded only in the last quarter of 2014). Nineteen lenders are now offering mortgage products with more due to enter the market. Outstanding mortgage debt stood at TZS 248 billion. Average mortgage debt size was TZS 69 million equivalent to around US$41,000. Mortgage debt advanced by top four lenders accounts for 67 per cent of the total outstanding mortgage debt.

Demand for housing and housing loans remains high but is constrained by inadequate supply of affordable housing and high interest rates. The housing deficit in Tanzania is estimated at three million housing units with a 200,000 unit annual demand.[8] Most lenders offer loans for home purchase and equity release while a few offer loans for self-construction, which is expensive beyond the reach of the average Tanzanian. High interest rates are another factor that impedes the growth of the mortgage market. The 182 days T-Bill rate ranged from 13 per cent to 15 per cent during 2014, whereas interest rates offered by mortgage lenders continued to vary between18 per cent to 21 per cent. The decline in the 182 days T-Bill rate as low as 8.99 per cent towards the end of March 2015 is, however, promising a positive impact on all forms of long-term debt, including mortgages.

The continuing projects by National Housing Corporation (NHC) being carried out from the company's 2010–15 strategic plan focusing on high-, medium-, and low-income earners are expected to have a positive impact on the mortgage market. Likewise, the Public Servants Housing Scheme, which is being administered by Watumishi Housing Company (WHC), is specifically tasked to build 50,000 affordable housing units in five years' time (2015–20) in various phases and is expected to fill the affordable housing gap in the market as public servants will be able to buy the houses through affordable mortgages of between 10 and 13 per cent, repayable in twenty-five years' time.

Most pension funds are also actively engaged in advancing mortgage loans to their members. NSSF is also embarking on large housing developments that will bring to the market a supply of 7,460 housing units in three years' time (2015–18). Likewise, private developers are also actively engaged on the supply of housing activities with more than 5,000 housing units in three years' time (2015–18). Additionally, the Tanzania Buildings Agency is embarking constructing 10,000 affordable housing units under the initiative of the government. All these initiatives are expected to further boost the growth of the mortgage market.

12.5 Regional Integration and the Impact on Domestic Financial Sector Developments

Tanzania is a member of two Regional Economic Communities (RECs) that have had a positive impact on her domestic financial sector developments: the East Africa Community (EAC) and the Southern Africa Development Community (SADC). The EAC was re-established in 2001 by a Treaty, and consists of five countries.[9] SADC was established by the Windhoek declaration and Treaty in 1992 and consists of fifteen countries.[10] Both RECs have common objectives of widening and deepening cooperation among the partner states in economic, social, research, and technology, political, legal, and culture for the mutual benefit of the countries. Financial integration is part of the process.

In both RECs, the financial integration initiatives are driven through regional economic protocols that are implemented through institutionalized committees. In the case of SADC, Article 17 of the Protocol on Finance and Investment of 2006[11] establishes the Committee of Central Bank Governors (CCBG) with responsibilities for implementing aspects that are specifically allocated to it by the Committee of Ministers for Finance and Investment. It is also responsible for the following: macroeconomic convergence; cooperation and coordination of exchange control policies; harmonization of legal and operational frameworks; cooperation on payment, clearing, and settlement systems; and cooperation in the area of information and communications technology amongst central banks. Also, cooperation and coordination in the areas of banking regulatory and supervisory matters; cooperation in respect of development finance institutions, non-banking financial institutions and

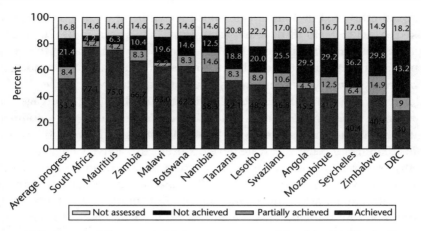

Figure 12.3. Status of finance and investment protocol implementation by country (using country-level commitments)

Source: SADC, GIZ, FinMark Trust. Available at: <http://www.finmark.org.za/wp-content/uploads/pubs/SADC-FIP-Baseline-Study-Regional-Summary-Report-Final-5-August-20113.pdf>.

services, and SADC stock exchanges. The Protocol's focus is on banking supervision, payment systems, exchange control policies, and stock exchanges.

The domestic financial sector development has been positively impacted by implementation of the initiatives under the SADC cooperation. A 2011 baseline study that was commissioned by SADC in partnership with FinMark Trust and Deutsche Gesellschaft für Internationale Zusammenarbeit (GIZ) on behalf of the German Federal Ministry for Economic Cooperation and Development (BMZ) on the implementation of the SADC Protocol on Finance and Investment,[12] revealed that Tanzania is among the countries that have implemented more than half of the country level commitments (Figure 12.3).[13]

In the context of Tanzania, domestication of some of the SADC Protocol on Finance and Investment has had an impact on aspects that relate to financial sector development. The country has enacted investment law that protects investors, allows repatriation of profits, and allows access to courts, and has maintained a low and stable inflation rate (less than 9 per cent). In addition, Tanzania has collected and publicized data on foreign exchange transactions, and payments systems have been implemented for large and low values. Some commercial banks have joined the Southern African Development Community Integrated Regional Settlement System (SIRESS). Tanzania has enacted a National Payments System Law and is a member of Eastern and South Africa Anti-Money Laundering Group (ESAAMLG), participating in mutual evaluations. Tanzania has also ratified regional agreements on the framework for Central Bank supervision.

Similar arrangements exist in the EAC. In 1997, the Monetary Affairs Committee (MAC) was formed with the mandate of enhancing monetary and financial cooperation in accordance with the approved macroeconomic policies, harmonization programmes, and the convergence framework of the Community. The MAC is composed of Central Bank Governors, with a broad objective of facilitating monetary and financial integration in the East African Community. The MAC has undertaken the following activities which impact on the domestic financial sector developments of member states: harmonization of monetary policy, legal and regulatory framework of banking supervision; development of capital markets and payment systems in the EAC Partner States; and achieving macroeconomic convergence in the EAC Partner States.

In Tanzania's context, implementation of MAC directives have had the following impact on financial sector development: liberalization of the capital (financial) account; clearing of foreign currency denominated cheques; adoption of quarterly publication requirements for banks; joint inspections conducted amongst the East African Central Banks; enactment of Anti-Money Laundering Legislation; issuance of 'Know Your Customer Guidelines' to supervised financial institutions; and the establishment of the Financial Intelligence Unit.

Directives also contributed to the establishment of a financial stability forum; adoption of risk-based supervision; establishment of credit reference systems (regulatory framework and credit reference bureaus). With regard to payment systems, EAC regional integration has contributed to the adoption of collateralization of central bank lending; enactment of national payment systems legislation; establishment of 'failure to settle' arrangements; development of harmonized payment system standards; adoption of Society for Worldwide Interbank Financial Telecommunication (SWIFT) standards; and implementation of a regional cross border payment system East African Payment System (EAPS) that become operational in 2013. Other initiatives include; integration of TISS with the Ministry of Finance and Tanzania Revenue Authority and the implementation of cheque capping.

12.6 Outlook for Financial Sector Developments

Prospects for the Tanzanian financial sector are encouraging. The preceding paragraphs shed light on the financial sector developments over the past two decades, starting from inadequacies in the banking and non-banking sectors to a promising financial sector today. The journey has been cautious and steady. Innovations in these sectors are encouraging, with the rapid adoption of technology in operations and delivery of financial services. Regional integration and increased globalization have had a positive impact in developing the financial sector, providing an optimistic outlook. Looking to the future, it is expected that the factors that are currently influencing positive development will continue, albeit with an increased necessity to manage risks that may arise in an advanced financial sector.

The following areas are likely to have a positive impact on the financial sector development in the coming decade, and policy intervention in these areas will be key to spur on and support sustainable growth.

12.6.1 *Digital Revolution and Financial Inclusion*

The future is promising in this area despite new challenges that come along with advanced digitization of financial services. The application of technology in the industry is a global phenomenon, and the financial sector is now heavily reliant on information technology in its operations and service delivery. The sector is engulfed by a myriad of digital technologies ranging from the rapidly growing use of mobile devices and cloud computing, to digital currency, big data, and social media. These technologies and more on the horizon have the potential to change the ecosystem of the sector by introducing new players in the market, disrupting the traditional players, and enhancing customer's experience. These changes in the operational landscape have consequences for policy responses. The BoT will face new challenges of addressing and creating a conducive environment for the growth and sustainability of the sector, stability, and consumer protection in application of and adoption of technology. Foreseeing these challenges, the Bank has established a consumer complaints helpdesk as a precursor to the establishment of a banking ombudsman in the future.

The use of a mobile financial service is expected to continue, increasing beyond the current usage levels of 57 per cent of the adult population. This will increase the avenues to provide customers with wide range of financial services using digital financial services. Customers' demand for more convenient and better service is also expected to increase, thus building pressure on financial services providers to respond to customer demands. The continued integration of technologies on mobile devices will empower customers to make choices, compare prices, manage their portfolios, and have a wide range of payment options from different financial services providers. These will lead to an increase in the number of new entrants expecting the provision of digital financial services, require new partnerships to enhance service delivery, and increase interdependencies of systems. It will also add to the potential of using client data for a wide array of analytics ranging from credit referencing and business intelligence to improvements in service delivery. All these will require the BoT not only to be proactive in creating an enabling environment for growth in the sector, but also to enhance risk mitigation regulatory frameworks to ensure a balance between financial stability and financial inclusion. Regulatory reviews will need to be considered in the following areas: non-bank service providers' scope and range of financial services; digital currency (cryptocurrencies and e-money); risk mitigation and the role of the central bank in the issuance of cryptocurrency; data protection, systems resilience and security; cybercrime; credit referencing; and better cooperation between regulators in the domestic and international markets.

12.6.2 *Non-Bank Financial Sector Outlook*

Developments in the non-bank sector (capital markets, insurance, and pensions) have continued their positive trend as the economy continues to grow, and as a result of adoption of regional and international best practices.

The capital market in Tanzania will continue to grow in the coming decade and its outlook is positive with opportunities for investments and trades in the capital market. The implementation of the strategic plan of the Capital Markets and Securities Authority (CMSA) has contributed to this positive outlook. The enactment of the Commodity Exchange Act, 2015, opens the market for commodity exchange in the country. There are seven cross-listed companies at the DSE and it is expected that the cross-listing of securities in the EAC will continue to increase. The CMSA is also planning to use digital technology to enhance secondary market outreach for securities. The aim is to reach wider population participation. With the capital account liberalization and the steady increase of secondary market trading, there are possibilities of development of derivatives, securitizations, and other structured products in the near future. For the regulator, this will entail enhanced regulation on the structured products and the digitization of the securities trading.

Insurance sector outlook is open for growth opportunities with the continued uptake of insurance products particularly resulting from the general growth in the assurance business and the positive growth of the economy. Opportunities are being created also by economic growth in the agriculture and mining sectors The government is working to develop a National Insurance Policy which is expected to spur growth. Partnerships with the banking sector is also leading to greater bank assurance relationships, entailing regulatory cooperation between the BoT and the TIRA.

12.6.3 *Regional Integration Outlook*

The positive influence of regional integration initiatives will continue to have an impact on the development of the financial sector in Tanzania. Implementation of regional finance, economic, and investment protocols will continue. For instance, the EAC roadmap for operationalising the East Africa Monetary Union (EAMU) Protocol has activities on the horizon for implementation by

2015.[14] This will have an impact on the following areas: growing collaboration in the capital markets sector with respective Capital Market Authorities to enhance the free movement of capital by ensuring full capital account liberalization; reviewing of legal frameworks to allow the BoT to broaden the list of eligible instruments for collateral management; enhancing the current Government Securities System (GSS) to allow for online bidding for non-competitive bidders; future adoption of Code of Conduct and Guidelines for Designated Market Makers of Government Securities, and integration of the DSE with partner states stock exchanges[15].

In the area of banking supervision it is expected that impact will continue. It will particularly affect the adoption of common principles and rules for the regulation and supervision of the financial system. With regard to payment systems, the impact will be on the domestic payment systems; promoting the use of EAPS; the implementation of a memorandum of understanding on currency convertibility and repatriation of EAC currencies; implementing Electronic Fund Transfer (EFT) for government departments and assuring the connectivity of other independent government agencies with a view to implementing cheque capping; and the continued efforts to enhance integration of regional payment systems.[16]

12.7 Conclusion

Although the Tanzania financial sector is not deep and wide, it nonetheless shows a promising future. The structural reforms that commenced two decades ago are steadily bearing fruit. The key lesson is that a free-market economy that creates an enabling environment for the private sector to operate efficiently and in a level playing field, lays the foundation for growth and the subsequent deepening of the financial sector. The overall health of the economy and the growth prospects from a country's comparative advantage resulting from either the potential of tapping a natural resource base or from its strategic geographic location, depend on a deep and efficient financial sector. The efforts that the government has made thus far need to be reinforced and consistently applied in order for Tanzania to ascend to middle-income status. In addition, we note that leadership in financial sector reforms is a key component: the role of financial sector regulators with the support of the government have led to enhanced confidence from the private sector and the supply of the financial services and products that have increased the level of financial inclusion and steadily improved financial deepening.

The future of Tanzania's financial sector is bright. However, in order to achieve positive outcomes, the country must steadfastly continue to implement policy and regulatory reforms that are proactive, to embrace an enabling environment for the private sector at the same time as enhancing financial stability to boost confidence in the sector overall. This will require changes in the bureaucratic culture of government institutions that support the financial sector, and a concerted effort to enhance capacity in regulating a dynamic industry.

Notes

1. Bank of Tanzania (2011).
2. Bikki and Joselito (2003).
3. Bank of Tanzania, Directorate of Banking Supervision Annual Report, 2013.
4. Dar es Salaam Stock Exchange (2014).
5. TIRA 2013 Annual Report.
6. The Economist Intelligence Unit conducts surveys for enabling regulatory environment for financial inclusion known as the 'Global Microscope: The Enabling Environment for Financial Inclusion'.
7. Ministry of Finance (2000) is finalizing issuance of a revised National Microfinance Policy.
8. NHC Strategic Plan 2010–15.
9. Tanzania, Burundi, Kenya, Uganda, and Rwanda.
10. Angola, Botswana, Democratic Republic of Congo (DRC), Lesotho, Madagascar, Malawi, Mauritius, Mozambique, Namibia, Seychelles, South Africa, Swaziland, United Republic of Tanzania, Zambia, and Zimbabwe.
11. SADC (South Africa Development Community) (2006) 'Protocol on Finance and Investment.
12. SADC, GIZ, and FinMark Trust (2011: 9).
13. We acknowledge FinMark Trust for permission to use this information; however, FinMark Trust is not liable for any analysis or interpretations that we have made in the use of the information from the 2011 Baseline Study.
14. Article 5 (a) of the EAMU Protocol requires Partner States to fully implement Common Market Protocol by 2015 as one of the pre-requisites for a Monetary Union.
15. The EAC provided a report on its 18th Ordinary Meeting of the Monetary Affairs Committee that highlighted the directives and status of implementation by member states.
16. The EAC provided a report highlighting achievements, challenges and way forward for the Monetary Affairs Committee.

References

Bank of Tanzania (2011). 'Tanzania Mainland's 50 Years of Independence: A Review of the Role and Functions of the Bank of Tanzania (1961—2011)', Bank of Tanzania, Dar es Salaam.

Bank of Tanzania (2014). *Quarterly Economic Bulletin*, December 2014.

Bikki, R. and Joselito, G. (2003). 'Microfinance Regulation in Tanzania: Implications for Development and Performance of the Industry Africa Region', Working Paper Series No. 51, June, World Bank, Washington, D.C.

DSE (Dar es Salaam Stock Exchange) (2014). *Quarterly Update*, Issue No.63, December, DSE, Dar es Salaam.

EAC (East African Community) (2009). 'Monetary Affairs Committee Achievements, Challenges and Way Forward (1998–2008)', EAC, Arusha.

EAC (2015). 'Report of the 18th Ordinary Meeting of the Monetary Affairs Committee'. EAC, Arusha.

Economist Intelligence Unit (2014). 'Global Microscope 2014: The Enabling Environment for Financial Inclusion', New York.

FinMark Trust, FSDT (2014). 'FinScope Survey, Tanzania'.

Lucky, Y. and Eno, I. (2013). 'Financial Sector Reforms in Bank Ownership and Its Impact on Service Quality Case of Commercial Banks in Tanzania', *Journal of Business Administration and Management Sciences Research* 2(12)(December): 335–51. Available at: <http://www.apexjournal.org> (accessed 12 June 2016).

Ministry of Finance (2000). 'National Microfinance Policy', Dar es Salaam.

Narayan, D. (1997). *Voices of the Poor: Poverty and Social Capital in Tanzania*, vol. 1. 'Environmentally and Socially Sustainable Development Studies and Monographs Series 20'. Washington, D.C.: The World Bank.

Ndulu, B. J. and Mutalemwa, C. K. (2002). 'Tanzania at the Turn of the Century', Background Papers and Statistics, World Bank, Washington, D.C.

Nord, R., Sobolev, Y.,Dunn, D., Hajdenberg, A.,Hobdari, N., Maziad, S., and Roudet, S. (2009). 'Tanzania: The Story of an African Transition', International Monetary Fund, Washington, D.C.

Robert, C. and Connor, P. S. (2008). 'Pursuing Efficiency While Maintaining Outreach: Bank Privatization in Tanzania', Policy Research Working Paper 4804, World Bank Washington, D.C.

SADC (South Africa Development Community) (2006). 'Protocol on Finance and Investment'. Available at: <http://www.sadc.int/files/4213/5332/6872/Protocol_on_Finance__Investment2006.pdf>.

SADC, GIZ (Gesellschaft für Internationale Zusammenarbeit), and FinMark Trust (2011). 'Striving for Regional Integration: Baseline Study on the Implementation of the SADC Protocol on Finance and Investment. Available at: <http://www.giz.de/en/downloads/giz2012-en-implementation-sadc-finance-investment.pdf> (last accessed 12 June 2016).

SSRA (Social Security Regulatory Authority) (2013). 'Annual Report, 2013', SSRA, Dar es Salaam.

TIRA (Tanzania Insurance Regulatory Authority) (2014). 'Annual Insurance Market Performance Report for Year Ended 31 December 2013', TIRA, Dar es Salaam.

Zetterli, P. (2015). 'Tanzania: Africa's Other Mobile Money Juggernaut', CGAP blog. Available at: <http://www.cgap.org/blog/tanzania-africa%E2%80%99s-other-mobile-money-juggernaut#comment-169021> (accessed 12 June 2016).

Index